ISRAELI COMMUNITY ACTION

PERSPECTIVES ON ISRAEL STUDIES

Perspectives on Israel Studies

S. Ilan Troen, Natan Aridan, Donna Divine, David Ellenson, and
Arieh Saposnik, *editors*

Sponsored by the Ben-Gurion Research Institute for the Study of Israel and
Zionism of the Ben-Gurion University of the Negev and
the Schusterman Center for Israel Studies of Brandeis University

ISRAELI COMMUNITY ACTION

Living through the War of Independence

Paula Kabalo

INDIANA UNIVERSITY PRESS

This book is a publication of

Indiana University Press
Office of Scholarly Publishing
Herman B Wells Library 350
1320 East 10th Street
Bloomington, Indiana 47405 USA

iupress.indiana.edu

© 2020 by Paula Kabalo

All rights reserved
No part of this book may be reproduced or utilized in any form or by any means, electronic or mechanical, including photocopying and recording, or by any information storage and retrieval system, without permission in writing from the publisher. The paper used in this publication meets the minimum requirements of the American National Standard for Information Sciences—Permanence of Paper for Printed Library Materials, ANSI Z39.48-1992.

Manufactured in the United States of America

Library of Congress Cataloging-in-Publication Data

Names: Kabalo, Paula, author.
Title: Israeli community action : living through the War of Independence ; civic associations and community resilience / Paula Kabalo.
Description: Bloomington : Indiana University Press, [2020] | Series: Perspectives on Israel Studies | Includes bibliographical references and index.
Identifiers: LCCN 2020018507 (print) | LCCN 2020018508 (ebook) | ISBN 9780253050755 (hardback) | ISBN 9780253050793 (paperback) | ISBN 9780253050762 (ebook)
Subjects: LCSH: Israel-Arab War, 1948-1949—Social aspects. | Associations, institutions, etc.—Israel—History. | Voluntarism—Israel—History. | Israel—Social conditions—20th century.
Classification: LCC DS126.9 .K33 2020 (print) | LCC DS126.9 (ebook) | DDC 956.04/21095694—dc23
LC record available at https://lccn.loc.gov/2020018507
LC ebook record available at https://lccn.loc.gov/2020018508

1 2 3 4 5   25 24 23 22 21 20

To my godparents,
Anita Sielecki
Isztar (Jose) Zawadski

We are but templates of our native landscapes.
Shaul Tchernichovsky

CONTENTS

Acknowledgments ix

Introduction: Association, Efficacy, Capabilities *1*

I. Civic Association and Self-Help in a Voluntary Community, November 1947–May 14, 1948

1 Multiple Paths to Community Resilience—Displacement as an Impetus to Association *23*

2 Economic War and War Economy—The Challenge to Business and Commercial Life *64*

3 "Literally Abandoned to Starvation"—The Bureaucratization of Relief and the Question of Responsibility for Soldiers' Families *110*

II. Association and Self-Help in a Sovereign Society, May 14, 1948–1949

4 The Displaced Communities Regroup *145*

5 Emergency Economy amid Emergency Normalcy— The Quest for Regularization, Improvement, and Influence *184*

6 Soldiers' Wives and a Nongovernmental Government Committee for Inductees' Families—The Question of Responsibility *213*

7 The War Veterans' Civilian Struggle—Discharged Soldiers and Disabled Veterans Confront the Policy Makers 250

Conclusion 290

Bibliography 301

List of Archives 311

Index 313

ACKNOWLEDGMENTS

Like many voyages of discovery, this one, which lasted a decade, began almost by chance. It started with a single telephone call.

On the line was Mordechai Bar-On, who told me about a new project that he and Meir Chazan had agreed to spearhead—writing the "civilian" (i.e., the nonmilitary) history of Israel's War of Independence.

"What have I got to do with the War of Independence?" I asked in puzzlement. Bar-On, known to friends and admirers as Moraleh, replied: "You're interested in voluntary civic associations in the Yishuv and Israel's earliest period, aren't you? So why not see whether this pattern existed during the war as well?" My answer was, "I'll look into it." Truth to tell, I was skeptical. I surmised, like many who preceded me, that this chapter of Israel's history was not one of "active citizenship among bottom-up interest groups" but an episode in the ideal of collectivism, a stage in which society had reached a peak of mobilization and self-mobilization. Therefore, I assumed that the voices of small grassroots associators, and even more institutionalized but essentially sectorial ones, would be less heard.

To my delight, I was wrong. Thus it happened that the phone call and Chazan and Bar-On's initiative became the first step on the decade-long voyage that yielded this book. Therefore, my gratitude goes first and foremost to them.

The Israel Galili Defense Force Research Association mobilized to co-fund the infrastructural part of the research by means of its research foundation, allowing me to glean the initial documentation on which this study rests. I thank the association for this support.

On this voyage, as on any voyage, the traveler encounters good people along the way. In this drama, which casts the historian as the hero, these good people are, of course, the staffs of various archives. Thus, I thank the staff of the municipal archives of Haifa, Jerusalem, and Tel Aviv; the Abba Khoushy Archives in Haifa; the Chamber of Commerce Archives in Tel Aviv; the Israel Defense Forces Archives; the Lavon Labor Archive; the Central Zionist Archives; the Israel State Archives; and, of course, those of my professional home—the Ben-Gurion Archive. In each of them I found a devoted staff that helped me perform the cerebral labor of my project and extracted from the depths of their facilities the containers and files that concealed the evidence of the range of civil-association activities in the Yishuv and Israel's society-in-formation.

At a certain stage, when the picture came into focus and showed that there was not only a story but a big story, I recruited students who worked with me to gather, catalogue, and sort the documentation. I thank Na'ama Smoliar, Paula Perpinial, Maya Reitan, and, in particular, Amit Hacham—my research student, an alumnus of the Woodman Scheller Israel Studies International Program (master's level), and a doctoral student at the Ben-Gurion Research Institute for Study of Israel and Zionism. Amit, in turn, marshaled his superb skills as a source hunter to track down the documents; indeed, he managed to find the treasures that lurked behind the scenes and in the shadows of history.

A decade is nearly half a generation; in academic terms, it's enough time for innumerable lectures and presentations at seminars and conferences and also—and mainly—talks in the corridor and social get-togethers where opportunities to present my research materialized. Here, a social network of Israel scholars came onto the scene—a close-knit circle of colleagues/friends that formed largely under the inspiration of Professor Yosef Gorny, our teacher and mentor: Orit Rozin, Meir Chazan, Avi Bareli, Ofer Shiff, and Gili Gofer. Each and every one of them heard, more times than I can count, about the anonymous associationists of 1948/1949—grocers, inductees' wives, committees of refugees and of amputees. And each and every one of them challenged me to reexamine my findings and my basic assumptions.

An important stimulus for my research was my two-year stay at the Elie Wiesel Center for Jewish Studies at Boston University, headed by Professor Steven Katz. During my stint there, I taught American students and used the university's lavishly appointed library to fill gaps in my research on the civil aspects of wars. My brief stay in Heidelberg, too, as a guest lecturer at the Hochschule für Jüdische Studien, gave me entrée to dozens of studies about the civilian aspects of World War I. Here is the place to thank the staffs of Boston University and the University of Heidelberg, as well as my hosts in Germany and the United States, Johannes Heil and Steven Katz, respectively. A special corner in my heart is reserved for the then-administrative assistant of the Elie Wiesel Center, the late Pagiel Czoka, who helped me find my way in a strange land as a mediator and a friend.

To probe another dimension of the topic, I was able to call on my friends, researchers of Israel's third sector, and in particular Michal Almog-Bar and Haggai Katz, for assistance. Michal introduced me to the world of cross-sector collaboration and helped me to understand the meaning of the multidirectional interaction that takes place between volunteer-sector activists and policy makers. Haggai and I coauthored an article that compared patterns of civil association in the War of Independence with voluntary self-organization initiatives in the Second Lebanon War. The comparison fine-tuned my findings from the 1948 war and enhanced the effectiveness of organizing concepts from the field of research on civilian self-organization for the examination of the phenomenon on the historical timeline.

The journey that gave birth to this book also spawned a university course: War in the Home Front: 1948 as a Case Study. Dozens of students in the Israel Studies program and the Woodman Scheller Israel Studies International Program at Ben-Gurion University of the Negev took the course in its various versions and served me as litmus paper for my thoughts and findings. Their questions called my attention to additional spheres, and their quizzical expressions forced me to revisit sources and make sure no mistakes crept into my assessments and conclusions. The adage *My best teachers are my students* indeed proved true here—and significantly so.

I was privileged not only with being a teacher in the various undergraduate and master's programs but with being a faculty member at the Ben-Gurion Research Institute for Study of Israel and Zionism. The institute is rich in academic staff, all experts in Israel studies, colleagues who provided me with an intensive study environment, intellectual partners with whom I shared professional challenges and, no less, the task of setting up an international program in Israel studies at the heart of the Negev and putting together The Azrieli Center for Israel Studies, hosting outstanding postdoctoral fellows and visiting scholars from all over the world. The historian's work is a one-person enterprise that's usually typified by loneliness and self-seclusion. This was not my experience—I have always found a source of support and a wellspring of ideas in the community of learners to which I belong.

The Ben-Gurion Research Institute for Study of Israel and Zionism also has a top-notch professional and administrative staff that coordinates the managerial aspects of its activity and maintains the units that support its research—a group of colleagues that created a quasi-family reality for itself. In the past seven years, I have been the director of the institute, meaning that my time is not my own. To complete the complex task of writing a book of this kind, I needed large-scale assistance from the institute's administrative team. Here I mobilized my associates to help by handling routine managerial tasks and giving me weeks off, largely during the summer months, that allowed me to finish the writing at long last. I thank Michel Mouyal, Adi

Portughies, Einav Melamed Donyetz, Lihi Turgman, Noa Gilboa, and Esther Ohayon. Special gratitude is owed to the institute's executive secretary of the director, Hagar Swissa, who sometimes had to serve as a buffer between me and the world so that I could wrest away the cherished moments that I needed to finish a chapter or correct a paragraph. This book owes its birth to this devoted team of midwives.

As for the writing itself, this is an English-language book by an author who thinks and writes in Hebrew. For years, Naftali Greenwood has stewarded me in crossing this divide by helping me to translate my writings from Hebrew into English. The Hebrew language is stingy in its supply of synonyms; English, in contrast, bursts with idioms, reverberations, and meanings. The rich inventory of lexemes and expressions in both languages combined would not suffice to express all the praise and gratitude that I owe Naftali for my innumerable drafts and for the rare combination of curiosity, meticulous attention, and openness that he brings to the craft of translation. I am privileged.

I presented the manuscript to the Israel Studies book series of Indiana University Press, a series published under the academic cosponsorship of Brandeis University and Ben-Gurion University, headed by academic editor Ilan Troen and editor-in-chief Dee Mortensen. Ilan Troen, a colleague and a long-time mentor, was rigid and uncompromising—for which I thank him. As expected, the manuscript received tough and uncompromising treatment. Anonymous reviewers ripped through it mercilessly and returned it to me for corrections and rearrangement. The demands for improvement related not only to the contents and structure of the book but also to the future readership, most of which is probably unfamiliar with the era and the topic discussed. In this respect I am especially grateful to my friend and colleague Debbie Bernstein, who gave me some tips that are worth their weight in gold. Pursuant to the reviewers' remarks, the manuscript underwent a face-lift or, to be precise, a "face-shrink" that left it tighter and sharper. In the final phase, I was lucky to have the most professional and meticulous Hadas Blum attend to the indexing. I thank the editors, the reviewers, and the academic editorial board of the series. Needless to say, responsibility for the final product is mine alone.

Finally, a person is but a mirror of the landscapes of his or her homeland. At the beginning of this project, I was still being helped by my mother, Perla Federman, in tracking down press clippings in English. She gleaned pieces of information from the margins of the daily press and provided further proof or evidence of the existence of some phenomenon that I had encountered in the archive research. Her contribution, however, far exceeds the temporary research assistant role that I imposed on her. In fact, I learned from my mother everything that I know about hard and steady work and gradual and patient progress toward a goal. Recently she passed away, and this book is merely a small element of the gratitude that I owe her for everything she gave me in life.

Alongside my late mother and my late father, who brought me into the world, two additional dear people strode at my side and gave me their backing as devotedly as shadows—so much that in recent years I have begun to call them my godparents. Jose Isztar Zawadzki and Anita Sielecki served me as role models, gave me intellectual inspiration, and, above all, have lent me their emotional support all my life. I held a great many conversations and consultations with them in the past few years, during which I took the voyage of writing this book—which I also dedicate to them gratefully and lovingly.

My closest circle is, of course, that of my children and husband. My children were indeed children when this journey began. Honi was a young adult doing his university studies, and Mush and Avigail were teens in secondary school. They may not even have understood that as they were growing up, I was raising another offspring, hidden from sight but nevertheless perceptible: this book. The person who knew this well and also undertook to be an extra parent is my husband Shlomo, whom we call Kabalo—a beloved partner, an ally, and an intimate friend. Kabalo not only provided parental backing during my absences for years of research and writing; for lack of choice, he also served as a shadow reader of each and every stage of the writing. He put in hundreds if not thousands of hours of "chatting" about the War of Independence and the role of civilians in coping with the crisis that a war of that type brought in train. His command of the minutest details of the book is total. He is familiar with the anonymous heroes whose stories unfold across the pages of the book. Also, it seems to me, he likes them—as I do. Had we, Kabalo and I, stumbled into the realities of 1948 in a script such as that of a popular television show, *The Stranger*, or time-tunnel technology, we surely would have felt at ease there because we indeed split our lives between "here" and "there" in the past decade.

I owe a final and special debt of gratitude to the desert—the expanses of the Negev or, to be more precise, those that surround my home at Midreshet Ben-Gurion, between the hut (Ben-Gurion's desert home) and the grave (also Ben-Gurion's). I thank the beloved landscapes that extend from the brink of the Zin Cliff toward Ḥod 'Aqev, Ma'ale Divshon, and Mount Tzaror. How grateful I am to have had the privilege of living in such a thought-provoking and inspiring place.

ISRAELI COMMUNITY ACTION

INTRODUCTION

Association, Efficacy, Capabilities

Mr. Ordentlich's apartment on Ben-Yehuda Street in Jerusalem was totally destroyed in an explosion in February 1948. His source of livelihood, a needlework shop, met the same fate. After efforts, Ordentlich found an alternative place to live but had to vacate it several months later. Mr. Rudnick's apartment in Haifa was also demolished, as were the furniture shop and the factory from which he had made a living. He found shelter for himself and his three children at a girls' school in town.

The Shabbati, Levi, Nissim, Berabi, and Rachimov families, along with many others in the Shapira quarter of Tel Aviv, were forced out of homes that had become stations on the firing line; for the next half year and more, they found shelter in stairwells and schools. After returning to their homes, they were ordered to pay taxes and rent for the term of their absence, during which they had had no income. Uri, Reuven, Michael, and Avraham were severely injured, each losing an arm or leg. They spent many days in a rehabilitation center without finding an employment situation that would allow them to return to independent life.

This is a random selection among the otherwise nameless Jewish inhabitants of Mandate Palestine and its successor, Israel, who sustained bodily and property damage, not to mention impairment of earning ability and livelihood, during the violent events that would come to be known as Israel's War of Independence. Their war experience and the coping mechanisms that they developed to deal with it are the focus of this book.

Few historians have seen fit to relate en bloc to the destruction of Mr. Ordentlich's business, Reuven's frustration, and the Rachimovs' and Levis' distress. These people's war experiences, if documented at all, are usually woven into the story of the war as it affected their socioeconomic group or as it concerns the steadfastness or downfall of their town or village. If history catalogues them at all, it does so by compartmentalizing them, just as their daily lives before and after the war placed them in separate circles.

This book gathers them under one roof. It does this by identifying the commonality that unites them all, a pattern of response and coping with the war crisis that befell them—the choice of availing themselves of a voluntary association that would represent their interests and speak on their behalf. Many such associations were established by those affected; others had already been active, uniting people on a professional, gender, or neighborhood basis. Many of them operated as membership organizations and refused to define themselves in partisan political terms; others adhered to a covert or overt ideological agenda. All, however, responded to their beleaguered members, striving to call attention to their stories and offer balm, however incomplete and minimal, for their anguish.

The casualties themselves participated in associative initiatives in diverse ways. Many played active roles in electing their representatives, setting their association's agenda, and promoting said agenda vis-à-vis governing authorities. They did so by writing letters, signing petitions, placing advertisements, and taking part in members' rallies, support assemblies, and demonstrations.

The war, lasting more than a year and engulfing the entire country, affected almost every Jewish household for the worse. Amid the turmoil, these voluntary representative associations bridged the divide between the affected individuals and the authorities. Representing casualties vis-à-vis local and national policy makers, they amassed data about the extent and types of damage, gathered information for casualties about their entitlements and possible sources of aid, and, above all, unfurled a psychological safety net by speaking out on behalf of ordinary people whose interests, however dire, were crowded out by the challenges of managing the protracted war and the attendant chronic shortages of means and resources.

The War of Independence, or, from an Arab point of view, the Palestinian Nakba, has been extensively researched: from its planning and goals to its démarches and its implications for the Jewish side, the Arab side, and, in particular, the Arab inhabitants of Palestine, many of whom had become refugees by the time it was over. The political dimension of the war, the decision-making processes, the struggles at the highest levels of Israel's defense leadership, and the global balance of forces in relation to regional doings during the war have also attracted much research attention. Recently one also encounters many studies on daily civilian life at that time. Some focus on the functioning of particular communities and, foremost, relations between community members and local leadership.[1] Others track economic policy-making processes and/or the establishment of the state's institutional infrastructure in mid war.[2]

Focal in much prior research is the assumption that Jewish society was *mobilized*—a term denoting an especially high level of civil obedience and responsiveness to the leadership and the policies that it handed down. The collectivist image of the Yishuv before and during the war and the tendency to focus on the dominance of its political center (the Zionist National Institutions) as a stable leadership core whose policies were usually accepted unquestioningly have overshadowed the coping mechanisms of other players within the Jewish community in Eretz Israel—players who were inseparable, if not central, in experiencing the war and, no less, in its outcomes.[3] It is these mechanisms and these players that this book proposes to illuminate.

Thus, the current work serves as an introduction of sorts to Orit Rozin, who identifies individualistic elements that were already common in Israeli society in the state's first years. However, while Rozin dates the inception of the individualistic ethos to the outset of statehood and interprets this individualization as a reaction to the demands of a centralistic collectivist establishment, the study that follows broadens her thesis and sets it back to the war era (if not earlier), thereby reinforcing the emphasis on average Israelis and ordinary citizens as agents of change.[4]

These ordinary citizens and their activity within voluntary associations stand at the center of this book. It thus follows that these people should be treated neither as supporting actors in this war nor as passive objects on history's chessboard, pawns who could be pushed forward or left standing, sacrificed, or captured.[5] Reality was in fact quite the opposite; it included a litany of actions taken by associating individuals who organized within the communities of Tel Aviv, Jerusalem, and Haifa in response to blows that they sustained, which allowed them to leave their imprint on events and, to some extent, determine their course. This array of organized entities became a force to be reckoned with—a player of its own right in the scenery of the war.

Borrowing concepts from research on civil society, the third sector, and the roles of community in disasters and crises, it is shown below that the various associative initiatives on which this study focuses provided advocacy and self-help services, produced social capital, and allowed coping mechanisms and efficacy to find expression. Ultimately, they animated capacity-building processes that—challenging the convention in research literature—were not directed top-down or from the outside but emanated from the inside as products of community action. Thus, they can be added to the growing literature on community resilience. It is within this conceptual and theoretical framework, then, that the study examines and analyzes the case of voluntary associations in Jewish society during the War of Independence.

The associations at issue are formal organizations (as opposed to one-off amalgamations for nonrecurrent action) that were usually recognized by some governmental authority. They were nongovernmental and not-for-profit. They had autonomous decision-making mechanisms and exhibited an element of voluntarism in their activity or their organizational structure.[6] Together, they constituted what today is customarily called the third or nonprofit sector. This conceptual framework draws no distinctions among contents of activity, the identity of those behind the associations, and the extent of the association's institutionalization.

In the research literature on voluntary associations and their place in a democratic regime, it is customary to use the term *association* without any modifier whatsoever. This book will do the same, invoking the generic *associations* to include corresponding terms such as *civic associations* and *voluntary associations*.[7] Importantly, the Jewish community in Eretz Israel had been quite familiar with this pattern of association since the Ottoman era and a fortiori under the British Mandate. Under the 1908 Ottoman Law of Associations, adopted by the Mandate government, thousands of associators—Jewish, Muslim, and Christian—registered themselves within the purview of the British government in order to promote a wide spectrum of matters from economic and professional interests to cultural and leisure activity.[8]

Members of the Jewish community stood out in particular among those registering associations during those years—numerically, in their diversity, and in the objectives they wished to pursue.[9] Therefore, it is no surprise that when intercommunal violence broke out in early December 1947 and escalated into a state of war in 1948 and up to the middle of 1949, the number of those associating steadily grew, as did their expectations of being included in the decision-making processes that would address their distress. This is the immediate background for the choice of this pattern of activity as the central theme of the current study. This choice, in the specific context of Israel's War of Independence, may also shed light on the internal dynamic that evolved in the Yishuv (soon to become Israeli society) during the war and the proposition that these organizations played a role that influenced the progression of the war, foremost by strengthening community resilience.

Natural or anthropogenic crises have been inseparable in the human condition since time immemorial. In recent years, a research field has developed that seeks to determine the roles that communities play in these events. Its intent is to examine the resources that community settings can pledge to coping with a disaster as it occurs and in the course of the revitalization that follows.[10] A UN interagency committee that looked into this focused on two parameters that it viewed as key to a community's ability to contend with disaster: local capacities and coping mechanisms (systematic methods of dealing with shocks such as military attacks, natural disasters, or economic collapse). Such mechanisms mitigate helplessness and attenuate the impact of the crisis.[11]

To explain what a community must have to cope with a crisis situation, various researchers refer to the concept of social capital. What they mean by this are norms and patterns of reciprocity and trust on the basis of which collective actions that amalgamate individuals, groups, and institutions take. Such devices broaden the range of possibilities, expand the resources available to the community, and abet the development of intra- and intercommunity cohesion.[12]

Under what conditions may a community remain resilient during a crisis and in its immediate aftermath? Research on the matter stresses the importance of social networks, social cohesion, social interaction, and solidarity as elements that create community social capital. When such elements exist, better preparedness and superior ability to respond to the disaster and its implications effectively are assured.[13]

The tactics that people use to adjust to a violent conflict and its attendant processes depend largely on the extent of trust and cooperation that exist among community members—which may resemble or differ from that preceding the conflict—and on the types of civic organizations that develop and change at the local level.[14]

Studies about recent disasters provide important support for the approaches that stress the roles of community organizations and social networks in community coping with catastrophes and crises.[15] Thus, knowledge accumulated in the aftermath of the August 2005 Hurricane Katrina disaster in the southeastern United States did much to answer questions that had surfaced after the genocide in Rwanda more than a decade earlier—questions about community sources of resilience and examination of community-based coping mechanisms on which local populations relied in coping with the crisis and that helped them to tackle the subsequent processes of recovery and revitalization.

There seems to be a broad consensus about the need to co-opt community organizations into disaster response and to create partnerships between communities and government agencies. The fundamental advantages that these organizations offer include their members' trust and the moral authority that they project, both of which allow them to demand teamwork. In addition, community organizations can assess needs and apportion goods and services efficiently and equitably. At the same time, such entities often suffer from the familiar syndrome of factionalism, sectarianism, and exclusion.[16]

My research on patterns of association during Israel's War of Independence yields an additional case study for these frames of discussion. The historicity of the war lends this study an advantage because it sheds light on a crisis event that has already ended, as opposed to one in progress.

All the associations examined in this book are set within a community framework of some kind. Sometimes the framework preexisted the period discussed due to a shared residency or a common profession; in other instances, it was formed ad hoc around a concrete experience. In all cases, the associative enterprise reflects a social fabric, exhibits some degree of trust among its members, and represents a general common goal that the members wish to promote by its means. In all cases, too, there is contact between the associations and additional players. Before the State of Israel was declared, most of these additional players had operated at the local level or were departments of the National Institutions; afterward, they were state agencies and governing systems, including ministries and army units.

Another dimension through which the advantages of voluntary associations in times of distress are reflected pertains to the question of how associations influence individuals' attitudes, skills, and behaviors. Intrinsic to this level of investigation is the assumption that associations have the potential of abetting the trickle down of civic values that include habits of cooperation, tolerance, respect for others and for law, willingness to take part in public life, self-confidence, and efficacy.[17]

The concept of efficacy was originally developed by psychologists and education researchers to explain differences in individuals' personal attainments.[18] Mark E. Warren, studying the democratic effects of associations, invokes it to deconstruct the way the associative experience influences people at the personal level, in what he calls "developmental effects." Efficacy, he says, is an important positive effect of civic-association action in that it addresses the extent of the individual's confidence in his or her ability to create change and influence collective action, along with self-confidence and the habit of responding to problems and proposing actions that aim to solve them. Efficacy relates not to the objective results of an action taken but to the recurrent effects of experiences that permeate people's biographies during their lives and manifest at the psychological level.[19]

Up to a certain limit, a sense of efficacy or inefficacy is a barometer of an individual's ability to bring about actual change on the basis of available resources and opportunities. A salient factor in the empowerment of personal efficacy is individuals' very success in creating change; as Warren explains, "Nothing succeeds like success." Success, however, is not always necessary. There are types of associations that specialize in nurturing feelings of efficacy as part of a more general strategy of developing and enhancing awareness.[20]

The concept of efficacy figures importantly in this study because it furthers our understanding of the empowerment processes that individuals may experience when they act within an associative framework.

An additional function that stands out for its centrality in the Israeli case is the role of the associations in advocacy. Studies that describe and model the functioning of community-based organizations in times of crisis customarily stress the organizations' role as service providers and, within this generality, their contributions to personal and community resilience. The actions underscored in these works include the creation of relief and rescue mechanisms and self-help networks.[21] Less attention is paid to the role of associations as mediators between individuals and authorities and as entities that make demands of the authorities, at times of crisis, for resource allocation and promulgation of rules that will take the represented group's needs into account.

Nevertheless, it only stands to reason that insofar as contemporary research continues to probe and elucidate relations between governmental and local organizations, the advocacy aspects of the latter organizations' activity will rise to the surface. Thus, the advocacy, claims, arguments, and criticisms that players in the field address to policy makers at the government level (municipal or national governing entities) will receive more thorough attention in scholarship than they have to date.[22]

This study aims to describe the advocacy functions of particular community-based civic associations in times of crisis, a dimension of activity that has attracted little attention thus far and has been sidelined by the attention devoted to the perceived focal question when a humanitarian crisis is being faced—the delivery of emergency services such as housing, food, and medical aid.

Phases and Characteristics of the War of Independence

The violent struggle between the Jewish inhabitants and the Arab inhabitants of Mandate Palestine began on November 29, 1947, when the United Nations General Assembly passed Resolution 181, recommending the partitioning of the country into Jewish and Arab states. The escalation started when armed Arab units began to attack Jewish vehicles on the roads and when, in Jerusalem, an enraged mob of Arab inhabitants torched the jointly tenanted Shama commercial center on the dividing line between the eastern and western sectors of the city. The ensuing events—the War of Independence from the Israeli perspective and the Nakba from the Palestinian-Arab one—officially ended only a year and a half later, in the middle of 1949. It was then that the last armistice accord, which sketched the frontiers of the State of Israel but neither ordained peace nor settled the Palestinian refugee problem, was signed.[23]

The discussion in this study is divided into two parts, reflecting the political and military changes that occurred during the war in the country's governing structure after Jewish sovereign statehood was attained (May 14, 1948). It adheres to the commonly found division of the treatment of the conflict into an early (pre-statehood) intercommunal war and subsequent (post-statehood) hostilities among regular armies. The intercommunal stage was characterized by guerrilla fighting on both the Arab and Jewish sides. At this stage, warfare engulfed all of Mandate Palestine, including the urban centers and connecting roads. Since regular armies were not included among the belligerents, combat was typified mainly by sniper fire, bombings in population centers, and armed ambushes along the roads. This, of course, degraded the personal security of all urban dwellers, Jewish and Arab alike, and set in motion a process of rapid physical separation of two populations that until then had maintained diverse points of contact, including mixed or adjacent neighborhoods and varied business and professional relations.

In the second phase of the war, the newly established Israeli army, the Israel Defense Forces (IDF), faced regular expeditionary forces of Arab states.[24] By then, Jewish forces had already taken control of two cities, Jaffa and Haifa, and Israel and the Hashemite Kingdom of Transjordan would complete the partitioning of Jerusalem within a few days. Although the urban centers—particularly Jerusalem and Tel Aviv—were still being shelled by heavy artillery and bombarded from the air, the center of the warfare had moved elsewhere. From July 1948 on, the IDF, some forty days old, launched an offensive that was meant to create Jewish territorial continuity and establish the borders of the State of Israel. Initially, the fighting was most intensive on the central front or, to be more precise, on the roads that connected Jerusalem and Tel Aviv, with focal efforts made to widen the country's narrow waist eastward. With the approach of autumn and winter, the locus of combat shifted to the Negev and Galilee. As the combat distanced itself from the urban centers, the daily agenda of the Jewish urban civilian population that remained there now shifted mainly to efforts to revitalize and to restore routine life.

The organizing fundamental of this study is the community axis in its broad sense: "a complex construct composed of many important dimensions [that] subsumes people, locality, place, organizations, and in some ways the forces that affect them all."[25] Accordingly, the following chapters are divided on the basis of associations that brought together individuals within "a spatial location"—Jerusalem, Tel Aviv, or Haifa—and involved "the character of networks ... organizational systems that allow a community to define problems, get work done and achieve coordination."[26] In each of these phases of the war, individual members of the Yishuv who chose to associate had to navigate a slightly different organizational and bureaucratic labyrinth. Until May 14, 1948, the British Mandate government was present, and the Jewish leadership functioned by means of recognized but non-sovereign National Institutions. Afterward, the newborn Jewish state gradually activated diverse executive authorities that wielded powers and held resources. This institutional change projected onto the fabric of life in all urban centers but found main expression in the three major cities on which this book focuses. To understand the space in which the civilian associations operated in Tel Aviv, Jerusalem, and Haifa, we now turn our gaze to the institutional and internal leadership structure that developed in each city and map the leading actors in coping with the humanitarian crisis that the state of war had brought on.

The Nature of "Authority" in Tel Aviv, Haifa, and Jerusalem

The study that follows focuses on the Jewish side of the 1948 war—looking at the interrelations that evolved between individuals who associated volitionally to answer a need that the state of war had exacerbated and representatives of the "authority." To understand the organizational and human space in which the associations operated, one must grasp the structure of authority at that time of transition from Yishuv to sovereignty. The concept of authority in this study includes the organs of the Zionist National Institutions (the "government" of the Yishuv) and those of early-statehood Israel (including those of the transitional government). It excludes those of the British Mandate government because the Jewish civilians who formed associations rarely turned directly to these authorities to obtain assistance or present claims and demands. Instead, they managed their regular interaction with official (de jure or de facto) Jewish entities, accepting them as their superordinates and perceiving them as the addresses for responses to their problems.

By mapping the organizational structure of the military and civilian authorities that operated in each of the urban centers that stand at the center stage of attention in this book, one discovers similarities and dissimilarities among the cities. These factors obviously affected the level of expectations, the avenues of access, and, above all, the ability of the authorities' representatives to offer or purport to offer a response, if only a partial one, to the crisis. The following overview sets the stage and the background for understanding the patterns of relations that are investigated in subsequent chapters. It is divided by geographic key and examines the military and civilian authorities in each town.

Tel Aviv

Fighting Forces on the Tel Aviv Front: Haganah and IDF

With the eruption of violence that followed the UN General Assembly's approval of Resolution 181 on November 29, 1947, Tel Aviv had a garrison force composed mostly of members of the Haganah (the mainline militia of the Yishuv, which functioned under the auspices of the Yishuv's political authority and therefore served as the armed force of the leadership) and mobilized for operations several times weekly on a volunteer basis. Alongside this force, the city had a company-strength unit of the Field Corps, specially trained to defend the outlying parts of town.²⁷ The Haganah devoted special attention to operations in neighborhoods where it had established cells that functioned under an operations commander.²⁸ The treatment of the neighborhoods took account of the political leaning of the residents, many of whom identified with other militias that had seceded from the Haganah and opposed the political coalition of which the official leadership of the Yishuv was composed.²⁹

A third entity tasked with the city's security was the Civil Guard, an urban militia made up of volunteer townspeople that operated under municipal management.³⁰ The Civil Guard was eventually partly integrated into the Tel Aviv section of the Haganah.³¹ The defense forces received logistical backing for their operations in Tel Aviv from the General Service (Ha-Sherut ha-Kelali), a unit of Haganah loyalists composed of diverse professionals who were well acquainted with the city and bridged the gap between the Haganah and the broad population of townspeople.³² They were volunteers who had passed military induction age or had been excused from mobilization for various reasons. Most had been recruited by economic trade associations, such as the Manufacturers Association, the Chamber of Commerce, and the Merchants Association, meaning that they interacted closely with groups of stakeholders and had relatively formal channels of information sharing and consultation. It was the General Service's task to maintain order and internal security in the city.³³

Shortly before the partition resolution, the Haganah city commander sought to strengthen the area in his purview both in human resources and by creating logistical support groups.³⁴ These forces, however, were so scantily deployed as to leave inhabitants who lived on the front without the permanent presence of security personnel.³⁵ Into this vacuum stepped members of the non-Haganah militias—those of the secessionist organizations: the IZL (Irgun Zvai Leumi, National Military Organization) and Lehi (Lohamei Herut Yisrael, Jewish Freedom Fighters, or Sternists). These entities were sympathetically regarded in those parts of the city that had been annexed to the municipal territory from Jaffa in recent years, for which reason they felt like the stepchildren of the city's formal leadership.³⁶

After the Israel Defense Forces were established, the army's Kiriati Brigade continued to operate in Tel Aviv on a militia format and using militia methods. The city, however, was required to hand over its best Field Corps units to a different brigade, Givati.³⁷ Tel Aviv itself became the target of Egyptian Air Force aerial attacks that lasted from mid-May to June 11, when a cease-fire went into effect. During that time, a wide range of military and civilian targets in Tel Aviv sustained daily assault.³⁸

The Municipal Authority

The Jewish municipality of Tel Aviv remained on a normal operational footing throughout the war.³⁹ With its roster of regular municipal departments, it facilitated the assignment of casualties of various kinds to the care of professionals. The Social Work Department, for example, treated civilians who had sustained property damage and families of persons who had been killed or wounded. Eventually, the department also helped families of internally displaced persons (IDPs).⁴⁰ The Sanitation Department provided medical aid and supervised sanitation in IDP concentrations.⁴¹ The municipality tasked the treatment of the IDP problem to a special office headed by Haim Alperin, a municipal inspector and erstwhile Civil Guard commander who cooperated with the other municipal departments in dealing with displacement problems and their attendant difficulties.⁴² The efficiency of the municipal structure allowed supplicants to understand more readily where they should turn for attention to their needs. Also, however, it exacerbated the state of alienation that prevailed between townspeople in need of aid and the municipal authority, which considered itself the sole address for such matters and sometimes frowned on the independent associative initiatives and supplicants' tendency to approach volunteer brokers for assistance.

Haifa

Fighting Forces

Haifa and its suburbs had a population of approximately 130,000, of whom half were Jewish and half Arab.⁴³ The Haganah treated Haifa as an autonomous urban district and divided it into two subdistricts—the city proper (*the city*) and its hinterland (*the subdistrict*). From early 1947 on, Haifa District was commanded by Moshe Zelicki (Carmel). The Haganah was firmly ensconced among the residents of Haifa, whom Yehuda Slutsky describes as "a lively public with a well-developed and effervescent public consciousness." The secessionist organizations had only the barest of toeholds in the town.⁴⁴

The Jewish garrison force in Haifa was organized in the Hadari subdistrict under Moshe Carmel, who believed that this unit should bear the brunt of the defense of Haifa and intended to release the Field Corps forces for combat outside the city.[45] The garrison force comprised several hundred men who had been trained mainly to defend positions within Jewish neighborhoods.[46] It also held frontier positions and maintained contact among the neighborhoods. The Field Corps, in turn, defended access roads to the city and initiated attacks of its own.[47] Temporarily assigned to it was a unit of the People's Guard (Mishmar ha-'Am), a "legal militia organization" that had been set up during World War II and was comprised of older members.[48]

The battle for Jewish control of the city was led by forces from the Carmeli Brigade command. By the time the IDF was established, the brigade was operating outside of town, and responsibility for security in Haifa District was transferred to Hadari forces that were composed of units of the People's Guard, Gadna (youth troops), and Haganah members in various service functions. Many members of the Hadari apparatus were incorporated into the new units, leaving the city proper to older people.[49]

The Municipal Authority

Until the violence broke out, Haifa had a joint Arab-Jewish municipality that confined itself to local affairs and made every effort to skirt state-level issues and disputes. The municipality ceased to function shortly after the hostilities began, and the void on the Jewish community side was filled by the Hebrew Community Council (Va'ad ha-Kehila), a body that represented the Jewish population of Haifa vis-à-vis outside players (i.e., departments of the National Institutions) as well.[50] During the war, the council interacted with additional leadership organs at the municipal and national levels—the Haifa Situation Committee, the Haganah command and that of its successors (the IDF authorities), and the political establishment, which was represented by a set of entities. Since members of the Community Council presidium served as de facto members of the Haifa Situation Committee, the boundaries between the two were blurred.[51]

Community councils (va'adei kehila) in Mandate Palestine dealt with education, health, religious needs, and welfare.[52] In 1947, at the behest of the National Institutions, a Situation Committee was reinstated to deal with problems occasioned by the peculiar situation that was brewing. At first, this panel had fifty-two members, elected by the public and by political-party key. They included Jewish delegates to the municipality and representatives of public and economic institutions in the city.⁵³ The Situation Committee was to focus strictly on emergency actions and was by definition subordinate to the Community Council. Just the same, it grew in status until it was considered the leading agency in the civilian sector of Haifa during the war.⁵⁴ Hard-hit civilians turned to the Community Council and the Situation Committee via various organizations of their own. Often they could not tell the entities apart, and, in any event, they regarded their local representatives as those most committed to solving their problems—if not the most capable of doing so. Several weeks after the conquest of the town by Haganah forces, civilian control there was handed to the Situation Committee. However, the blurring of boundaries among the authorities continued for much time, abetted among other things by David Ben-Gurion's displeasure with the members of the elected leadership and his appointment of Abba Khoushy, secretary of the Haifa Labor Council, as the official in charge of special affairs of national importance. Over the summer of 1948, many powers and assets of the Community Council were transferred to the municipality and to government ministries, leaving the Community Council to reassume its traditional prewar roles and confine itself to religious affairs.⁵⁵

Jerusalem

The Fighting Forces

Enlistment of young urbanites in the Haganah did not proceed smoothly in Jerusalem. Young people were scarcer there than elsewhere, and half of them belonged to impoverished or ultra-Orthodox strata that either ruled out the Zionist movement or were indifferent to its goals. The Haganah was not liked in various parts of town.⁵⁶ As a result, the availability of recruits varied widely in different parts of the city.⁵⁷

Haganah activity in Jerusalem took place under the command of the Etzioni Brigade. A garrison force guarded neighborhoods under partial mobilization, its members serving at night and working during the day. They created a defensive cordon around Jerusalem, manned checkpoints at neighborhood entrances, and demarcated front lines.⁵⁸ When the violence began, two Field Corps battalions were set up in Jerusalem; their members were called up provisionally, and some took time off from work or school to serve.⁵⁹

In September 1947, shortly before the war began, a People's Guard (Mishmar ha-'Am) was established—a legal organization that inducted older people or those who could not serve in regular Haganah units for various reasons. This organization, mobilized under the auspices of the Jerusalem Community Council, was tasked with maintaining public order in town and organizing the public around the Haganah.[60] Apart from being subordinate to the Haganah, the People's Guard also answered initially to the Community Council and later to the Institutions Committee, the Jerusalem Committee, and finally to the city's military governor.[61] The People's Guard amassed a membership of more than 3,000 Jewish volunteers from all public circles and intra-ethnic communities. In its duties, it functioned as a militia and a keeper of public order. It distributed water, food, and kerosene. Later on, it manned barricades and carried out fortification work. Female members provided medical aid and ran refugee centers. Eventually, some participants in the People's Guard joined the battalions of the garrison force. The People's Guard continued to play a role even after statehood was declared; it was disbanded only in May 1949, by which time Jerusalem had returned to full civilian rule.[62]

The Municipal Authority

Although the Zionist National Institutions were headquartered in Jerusalem, they moved their main activity to Tel Aviv in December 1947. Jerusalem also lacked a municipal leadership echelon because the mixed (Arab-Jewish) town council had ceased to function as soon as the violence began.[63] Thus, the only institution that operated in the first stages of the war as a Jewish local leadership was the Hebrew Community Council. Although the existence of this body was anchored in the Mandatory Communities Ordinance, its members operated on a voluntary basis and had little financial wherewithal.[64] In response to the state of emergency, this group set up a Situation Committee to deal with problems occasioned by the state of war. Its actions often clashed with those of the People's Guard.[65]

As demonstrated below, the council was an important address for civilians in distress, particularly those who had been displaced from their homes and those who had been rendered destitute. However, financial limitations and lack of authority made it very hard for the council to respond to the problems in any real way. Thus, it ended up serving mainly as a conduit for the forwarding of complaints and demands to the national authorities for a response, if only a partial one.[66]

Given the weakness of the municipal leadership structures, the importance of Jerusalem to all belligerents, the cruciality of the Jewish toehold in the city, and the internationalization of Jerusalem as envisaged in the UN partition plan, the National Institutions decided to establish a local committee that would act on their behalf there. Thus, the Committee of Institutions for Jerusalem Affairs, generally known as the Institutions Committee, came into being under the baton of Dov Yosef, the future military governor of the Jewish part of town.[67] The Institutions Committee was composed of representatives of the Jewish Agency, the National Committee, the Jerusalem Community Council, and (the ultra-Orthodox) Agudath Israel. It was empowered to manage and supervise all public services in Jerusalem, oversee order and safety of property, assure supplies of food, water, and medical services, and prevent profiteering. The People's Guard was tasked to the committee as a civil police force.[68]

The Institutions Committee operated for about four months, after which its status was changed. Convening ahead of the establishment of statehood, the Zionist General Council decided to form a "central emergency authority in Jerusalem." This entity, also known as the Jerusalem Committee, was chaired by Dov Yosef, who served as the de facto mayor until early August, when military rule was proclaimed in Jerusalem and he was named military governor. This form of governance lasted until February 1949.[69] As military governor, Yosef had a council that dealt, in practice, with civilian matters as opposed to military ones. Its purpose was to serve as a governing auspice for the transition period, during which the overall status of Jerusalem and western Jerusalem's link to the State of Israel would be resolved. Unlike Tel Aviv and Haifa, Jerusalem was a front outpost of sorts for the state authorities; therefore, the council became an important address for the city's volunteer associations.

Structure of This Study

The guiding principle in structuring this book is that the absence and formation of state authorities, as well as the nature of warfare before and after the invasion by Arab regular forces and the founding of the IDF, affected the modus operandi of the civilian associations. Specifically, the declaration of statehood weakened the pre-statehood leadership institutions and strengthened new ones that came into being under the new governing systems. Therefore, the study examines the patterns of interest group and subcommunity activity within a rough periodization that distinguishes between actions taken before sovereignty and those initiated under the nascent state. The associative actions themselves, however, are discussed in a parallel manner in parts I and II of the book, following a thematic principle that focuses above all on the types of crises that inspired the establishment of associations and powered their members' doings. This division of purposes illuminates four main motives for Jewish associative activity in the War of Independence: internal displacement, economic hardship, mobilization of head of household, and the challenges that inductees faced as they were demobilized.

The civilians who organized in these associations or were represented by them came from diverse socioeconomic strata and experienced the hardships of the war in different ways. They included members of the urban upper- and lower-middle classes, for whom the war struck a blow to livelihood; families that had been driven from their homes and left destitute; and women and mothers, many of whom belonged to the core of the Yishuv elite but needed economic/material support due to the mobilization of a family member. Others were disabled veterans who had become dependent on governmental assistance and demobilized soldiers who, during and after the war, felt excluded from the evolving national ethos.

Although highly diverse in terms of their members and their associative initiatives, all these associations were gifted with will, awareness, and the ability to unite around a common goal. All perceived associative endeavor as a legitimate tool for action—and all expected it to be effective.

Along these lines, this study demonstrates the existence of a civilian pattern of action that found expression in the middle of a crisis—a pattern of self-efficacy that brought the associative act to fruition and made the act itself into a civilian statement and an expression of civic engagement with the policy-making echelon in the middle of a war and the transition to statehood.

By illuminating patterns of community resilience and collective coping with crises from within, this study broadens the conventional boundaries in research on Israel and presents the Israeli case as a way to test the effectiveness of coping mechanisms that are familiar in the current research literature. Concurrently, it turns a powerful spotlight, based on the tools of historical research and analysis—reconstruction based on primary documentation—on dozens of cases studies that fill in the mosaic of the civil dimension of Israel's War of Independence. In this sense, this is a full-fledged piece of historical research that furnishes missing information that must be appreciated in order to understand the Israeli War of Independence as a total war that derived its outcomes from the functioning of the rear and not only from that of the front and the démarches of the military forces.

Notes

1. Moshe Naor, *On the Home Front: Tel Aviv and Mobilization of the Yishuv in the War of Independence* (Jerusalem: Yad Izhak Ben-Zvi, 2009); Moshe Ehrenwald, *Siege within Siege: The Jewish Quarter in the Old City of Jerusalem During the War of Independence* (Sede Boqer Campus: Ben-Gurion Research Institute, 2004); Nurit Cohen-Levinovsky, *Jewish Refugees in Israel's War of Independence* (in Hebrew) (Sede Boqer Campus and Tel Aviv: Am Oved, 2014). See also, for example, article collections published as part of a larger project on civilian aspects of the war: Mordechai Bar-On and Meir Chazan, eds., *Civilians at War: Studies on the Civilian Society during the Israeli War of Independence* (in Hebrew) (Jerusalem and Tel Aviv: Ben-Zvi Institute, 2006, 2010).

2. Shmaryahu Ben Pazi, "Not by Bread Alone: The Cereal Market During the Intercommunal War," in *Civilians at War* (2006), Bar-On and Chazan, eds.; Shmaryahu Ben Pazi; "The Citrus Harvest and its Impact on the Intercommunal War During the Winter and Spring of 1948," in *Civilians at War,* Bar-On and Chazan, eds. (2006); Itzhak Greenberg, "Military Recruitment of Manpower for Vital Services and Economic Enterprises," in *Civilians at War,* Bar-On and Chazan, eds. (2006); Jonathan Fine, "The Impact of the War on the Establishment of the Government System of Israel, 1947–1949," in *Civilians at War,* Bar-On and Meir Chazan, eds. (2006); see also Bar-On and Chazan, eds., *Politics in Wartime: Studies on the Civilian Society during the Israeli War of Independence,* Vol. C (Jerusalem: Ben-Zvi Institute, 2014). At the present writing, a fourth volume of this series is on its way; all articles will be dedicated to economic aspects of the war.

3. A term denoting the Jewish community in pre-independence Israel, first invoked in the late nineteenth century and developed on the basis of a shared national consciousness and established self-leadership institutions.

4. Orit Rozin, *The Rise of the Individual in 1950s Israel: A Challenge to Collectivism* (New England: Brandeis University Press, 2011), xxi.

5. Sebastian Haffner, *Defying Hitler: A Memoir (Geschichte eines Deutschen)*, Oliver Pretzel, trans. (New York: Picador, 2002).

6. Lester M. Salamon and Helmut K. Anheier, "In Search of the Nonprofit Sector II: The Question of Classification," *Voluntas* 3, no. 3 (1992): 267–309.

7. The use of this term without quotation marks is based on Mark E. Warren, *Democracy and Association* (Princeton and Oxford: Princeton University Press, 2001), and Archon Fung, "Associations and Democracy: Between Theories, Hopes and Realities," *Annual Reviews of Sociology* 29 (2003): 515–39.

8. Paula Kabalo, "The Historical Dimension: Jewish Associations in Palestine and Israel, 1880s–1950," *Journal of Civil Society* 5, no. 1 (2009): 1–20. For a list of Muslim and Christian associations, see Israel State Archives, Governor of Jerusalem District Division, 23/3939.

9. Paula Kabalo and Alon Lazar, "Jewish Social Entrepreneurship in Jerusalem and Jaffa 1880–1914," *Giving, Thematic Issues in Philanthropy and Social Innovation* 2 (2008): 151–68.

10. Sue Lautze and John Hammock, "Coping with Aid Capacity Building, Coping Mechanisms and Dependency, Linking Relief and Development," paper prepared for the UN Inter-Agency Standing Committee Sub-Working Group on Local Capacities and Coping Mechanisms and the Linkages between Relief and Development, Lessons Learned Unit Policy and Analysis Division, Department of Humanitarian Affairs, United Nations Organization (1996), 3; Daniel P. Aldrich, *Building Resilience: Social Capital in Post-Disaster Recovery* (Chicago: University of Chicago Press, 2012).

11. Lautze and Hammock, "Coping," chapter 2.
12. Robert Putnam, *Bowling Alone: The Collapse and Revival of American Community* (New York: Simon and Schuster, 2000); Golam M. Mathbor, "Enhancement of Community Preparedness for Natural Disasters: The Role of Social Work in Building Social Capital for Sustainable Disaster Relief and Management," *International Social Work* 50, no. 3 (2007): 357–69; Aldrich, *Building Resilience*, loc. 80 (Kindle edition).
13. Mathbor, "Enhancement of Community Preparedness," 357–69; Aldrich, *Building Resilience*, loc. 80.
14. Patricia Justino, *War and Poverty: IDS Working Paper* 391 (2012), 11–12, Institute of Development Studies, Conflict Violence and Development Research.
15. Olivia Patterson, Frederick Weil, and Kavita Patel, "The Role of Community in Disaster Response: Conceptual Models," *Population Research and Policy Review* 29 (2010): 129.
16. Ibid., 137.
17. Fung, "Associations and Democracy," 519–21.
18. See, for example, Albert Bandora, "Exercise of Personal and Collective Efficacy in Changing Societies," in *Self-Efficacy in Changing Societies,* Albert Bandora, ed. (Cambridge: Cambridge University Press, 1995), 1–45.
19. Mark E. Warren, *Democracy and Association* (Princeton and Oxford: Princeton University Press, 2001), 71.
20. Ibid.
21. See, for example, Marc Vincent and Birgitte Refslund Sørensen, eds., *Caught between Borders: Response Strategies of the Internally Displaced* (London: Pluto, 2001).
22. Aldrich, *Building Resilience*. See, for example, 130–47.
23. Benny Morris, *1948: A History of the First Arab-Israeli War* (New Haven, CT: Yale University Press, 2008).
24. Ibid.
25. Ram A. Cnaan, Carl Milofsky, and Albert Hunter, "Introduction: Creating a Frame for Understanding Local Organizations," in *Handbook of Community Movements and Local Organizations,* Cnaan, Milofsky, and Hunter, eds. (New York: Springer Science and Business Media, 2008), 5.
26. Ibid., 6.
27. Yehudah Slutsky, ed., *History of the Haganah, Vol. 3, Part II* (in Hebrew) (Tel Aviv: Am Oved, 1973), 1277–80; Nahum Ziv-Av, "Towards a Popular Organization," in *The Book of the Haganah in Tel Aviv* (in Hebrew) (Tel Aviv: Haganah Foundation, 1957), 140–3.
28. Kiriati (Michael Ben-Gal) to Nimrod, "Order for Operation in Frontier Neighborhoods," Israel Defense Forces Archives (hereinafter: IDFA), 1948-321-59.
29. Slutsky, *History of the Haganah*, 1281; Ziv-Av, "Towards a Popular Organization," 148.
30. Slutsky, *History of the Haganah*, 1276–7.
31. Ziv-Av, "Towards a Popular Organization," 144.
32. Slutsky, *History of the Haganah*, 1277; Ziv-Av, "Towards a Popular Organization," 148–9.
33. Report of the General Service, IDFA, 1949-8275-140, April 7, 1948.
34. Kiriati to Personnel Department, IDFA, 1948-321-9, November 11, 1947.
35. To Kiriati, IDFA, 1948-321-88, December 3, 1947.
36. Daily compilation of news, IDFA, 1949-8275-136, December 8, 1947.
37. Slutsky, *History of the Haganah*, 1284.
38. Naor, *On the Home Front*, 161–2.

39. Naor, *On the Home Front*, 5.
40. Ibid., 182–3.
41. Ibid., 184–5.
42. Ibid., 178.
43. Anat Kidron, "The Committee of the Jewish Community in Haifa and its Role in the Struggle to Shape Haifa's Civilian Character," in *Civilians at War*, Bar-On and Chazan, eds. (2010), 353.
44. Slutsky, *History of the Haganah*, 1289–90.
45. Tzadok Eshel, *The Haganah's Battle for Haifa* (in Hebrew) (Tel Aviv: Ministry of Defense, 1978, 1998), 303.
46. Slutsky, *History of the Haganah*, 1291.
47. Eshel, *The Haganah's Battle for Haifa*, 303.
48. Slutsky, *History of the Haganah*, 1291.
49. Ibid., 376.
50. Importantly, both representatives of the Jewish community to the mixed municipal council were chosen by the Community Council and were its delegates to the council.
51. Kidron, "The Committee of the Jewish Community in Haifa," 344, 349–50.
52. Ibid.
53. Ibid.
54. Ibid.
55. Ibid., 374, 378–9.
56. Slutsky, *History of the Haganah*, 1388.
57. Ibid., 1287.
58. Ibid., 1390.
59. Ibid., 1391.
60. Ibid., 1288.
61. Michal Yaron, "The Roles and Activities of Women in the People's Guard [Mishmar ha-'Am]," in *Anthology of the People's Guard [Mishmar ha-'Am] in Jerusalem, 1947–1949* (in Hebrew) (Jerusalem: Mishmar ha-'Am Activists and Organization of Haganah Members, 1965), 24.
62. Slutsky, *History of the Haganah*, 1399, 1401.
63. Itzhak Levy, *Jerusalem in the War of Independence* (in Hebrew) (Tel Aviv: Ministry of Defense, 1986), 380.
64. Arnon Golan, *Wartime Spatial Changes: Former Arab Territories within the State of Israel, 1948–1950* (in Hebrew) (Sede Boqer Campus: Ben-Gurion Research Center, 2001), 23.
65. Ibid.; Levy, *Jerusalem in the War of Independence*, 380.
66. Dov Yosef, *The Faithful City: The Siege of Jerusalem, 1948* (in Hebrew) (Tel Aviv: Schocken, 1960) and (in English) (Simon and Schuster, 1960), 33.
67. Yosef, *The Faithful City*, 33. Notwithstanding his military title, Yosef (Joseph) was the civilian governor of the Jewish sector of Jerusalem during the era of military rule.
68. Levy, *Jerusalem in the War of Independence*, 380.
69. Ibid.

I.
CIVIC ASSOCIATION AND SELF-HELP IN A VOLUNTARY COMMUNITY, NOVEMBER 1947–MAY 14, 1948

1

MULTIPLE PATHS TO COMMUNITY RESILIENCE

Displacement as an Impetus to Association

ONE OF THE EARLY MANIFESTATIONS OF THE STATE of war, felt among both the Jewish and Arab civilian populations, was imposed homelessness. The serpentine and sometimes blurred lines that separated Jews' and Arabs' residential quarters in the major cities created a mirror effect when the first sounds of gunfire were heard, with each population group fleeing from the danger zone to a relatively well-protected rear. While many Arab residents of Jaffa, Haifa, and western Jerusalem fled Mandate Palestine or retreated toward its eastern frontier, most of the Jews remained near their original homes, finding impromptu shelter in public buildings, yards, stairwells, and laundry rooms.[1] These were some of the first indications of the humanitarian crisis that the Jewish side would endure—one reflected foremost in the transformation of ordinary civilians into internally displaced persons (IDPs).

In this chapter, I shed light on the establishment of voluntary organizational structures by and for Jewish IDPs and by other members of the Yishuv community who felt harmed by the IDPs' "invasion" of their space (yards, businesses, and other places of encounter and worship). Amid these initiatives, the internal-displacement phenomenon projected onto the public order and created flash points between populations that had clashing interests.

To make these initiatives understandable, I begin by defining the phenomenon, presenting it in the context of the War of Independence and briefly summarizing the insights that surface from the historical and contemporary research literature about the challenges that internal displacement presented to the society in question and the possibility of responding to the crisis. I continue with a brief overview of the separation of the Jewish and Arab populations along the serpentine frontier and the mixed urban neighborhoods and the Jewish local authorities' initial response to it. Most of the chapter, as stated, maps the associative organizations and initiatives that reacted to, or tried to thwart, the internal-displacement predicament. Some of these initiatives were the products of "outsider" volunteers, specifically women, who sought to alleviate the steadily eventuating humanitarian crisis. Another reaction to the displacement was one of resentment by sectors of society that found their yards, businesses, and places of worship occupied by IDPs. Other associates represented frontier neighborhoods and their inhabitants; their actions were geared toward keeping the neighborhood population in place. Another level of association—a unique one—manifested in the IDP centers themselves for the purpose of presenting policy makers with the IDPs' needs and trying to stanch, or reverse however feebly, the steady deterioration of their living conditions.

The term *internally displaced persons* denotes people who are "forced or obliged to flee or to leave their homes or places of habitual residence . . . in order to avoid the effects of armed conflict, situations of generalized violence, violations of human rights or natural or human-made disasters, and who have not crossed an internationally recognized state border."[2] At the peak of the war, some 60,000 urban inhabitants—some 10 percent of the country's Jewish population—met this definition for many months.[3] IDP communities gathered in provisional shelters, their members reorganizing their lives in a physical space that was limited in many ways. No few of them rushed to form associations and elect representatives who would present their demands to the authorities.

Current works on Israel's War of Independence emphasize the socioeconomic stress that this humanitarian crisis generated.[4] Nurit Cohen-Levinovsky's investigation of the calamity flows from the premise that the urban fabric influenced the way refugees and other inhabitants experienced it; thus, it points to the implications of displacement for various levels of social relations.[5]

These findings are consistent with studies on internal displacement in World War I, which illuminate the social implications of such refugeeism. A conspicuous discovery in these studies is the ambivalence displayed toward IDPs, irrespective of their ethnic or national identity. This pattern of response is frequently characterized by a blend of rejection and compassion that often reflects prewar relations among the groups in question.[6]

Despite the typical ambivalence of host communities toward displaced persons, research reveals a set of relief strategies that are invoked by or for IDPs in extremis, including self-help and volunteer organizations and government intervention at international, national, and local levels.[7] The steadily growing roster of studies on present-day coping with internal refugeeism also investigates the strategies that IDPs themselves invoke in response to their plight.[8] These studies reveal the processes that IDP communities undergo as their members begin to realize that they must become self-reliant by means of grassroots organization, with emphasis on the advantage of trust in self-initiative and existing community structures. It is with precisely these aspects that this chapter deals.

Parting of Populations: A Problem Evolves

The events that would occur during the war on the seam between Jewish and Arab neighborhoods on the outskirts of Tel Aviv–Jaffa were portended in the summer of 1947, when a murder at the Gan-Hawaii café precipitated a series of arsons and clashes between Jews and Arabs and an outflow of Jewish inhabitants who lived near Tel Aviv's southern edge and in the Jewish neighborhoods of Jaffa.[9] Tel Aviv municipal officials were sent to the frontier neighborhoods to soothe jitters and discourage departure.[10] Many refugees in this early wave did return to their homes sometime later. The intercommunal violence in these frontier neighborhoods, however, resumed after the UN General Assembly resolved to partition the country, leaving those who lived along the twisting fourteen-kilometer zone that separated Tel Aviv and Jaffa—from the Mediterranean shore inland to the edge of the Hatikva quarter—on the front lines of a battlefield.[11] As the Jewish population abandoned the frontier neighborhoods in and around Jaffa, the Arab population began to do the same in the seam area in search of refuge in Jaffa and elsewhere.[12] As these quarters steadily depopulated, they quickly became firing positions, each abandoned building serving as a potential observation point into the enemy's territory.[13]

In Haifa, too, both communities retreated from the buffer zones. Press reports, referring to this as a "flow of refugees," noted the departure of Arab inhabitants from the Wadi Rushmiyya area to nearby caves.[14] The areas abandoned by Jews in Haifa were three: those along the line of engagement with Arab neighborhoods, the Arab neighborhoods themselves, and the Jewish enclave in the Lower City. Approximately 1,000 Haifa families, numbering some 6,000 people, were affected.[15]

In Jerusalem, internal displacement began as soon as the violence did, as residents of the Jewish neighborhoods near the Arab quarter of Sheikh Jarrah (Shimon ha-Tsaddik, Nahalat Yitzhak, and Batei Siebenburgen) left their homes, as did those living on the "first line" (Batei Ungarin, Shmuel ha-Navi Street, Beit Yisrael, and parts of the Bukharan quarter). The northern quarters of Jerusalem were home to roughly one-third of the city's Jewish population; most of these residents were members of *haredi* (ultra-Orthodox) communities. Many such groups maintained slack relations with the Yishuv's self-leadership institutions, instead relying largely on religious and neighborhood auspices of their own.[16]

The Jewish neighborhoods in southern Jerusalem—Mekor Hayyim, North Talpiot, Talpiot, and Arnona—became isolated enclaves when the intercommunal war broke out. The same fate befell the neighborhoods west of the Old City, Yemin Moshe and Mishkenot Sha'ananim, which were separated from the main Jewish population centers in western Jerusalem by a British security buffer zone. Notably, of course, the inhabitants of the Jewish Quarter in the Old City were the most isolated of all, surrounded by non-Jewish neighborhoods and encased by a wall that made ingress and egress even harder than they were elsewhere.[17] Jews in the engagement zone in northeastern Jerusalem and the core of the Jewish sector also began to leave. During these months, the emptying of the Jewish Quarter of the Old City was most salient among residents who lived on its fringes, adjacent to the Arab population.[18]

Establishing IDP Caregiving Authorities: The Institutional Response Pattern

The most serious problem that the residents of Tel Aviv faced in the early months of the violence concerned snipers who shut down traffic and thwarted work on streets near the city limits.[19] Some inhabitants fled in response to a focused attack on their neighborhood; others were evacuated by security forces from quarters that were considered strategically located.[20]

Most of the IDPs found shelter in improvised provisional venues—synagogues, schools, the district court building, and private premises such as stairwells, building entrances, shops, storerooms, and buildings under construction.[21] By mid-December, they congregated in twenty-seven centers, including eleven synagogues and five schools.[22] Others lived under the open sky, roving and availing themselves of random shelters. Their conspicuity began to attract press reportage that reflected discomfort about their situation: "How can the people of Tel Aviv sit quietly in their homes while . . . Jews languish in the corridors and stairwells of the Hebrew city? . . . How can anyone who sees families migrating from house to house with their belongings, seeking a place to spend the night, hold his silence?" In bewilderment, the writer asked whose fault it was before answering, "We are all responsible for the fate of our outcast brethren in Tel Aviv. Every inhabitant of this city, from the mayor to the simple citizen, ought to be ashamed."[23]

The Tel Aviv Municipality did appear to respond quickly and to take the magnitude of the problem very seriously. At the very beginning of the crisis, it set up a refugee care office under Haim Alperin, a municipal inspector and erstwhile commander of the Civil Guard, who tackled the IDP predicament in concert with other municipal departments.[24] The city's action plan included attention to arrangements for children, the establishment of a committee to look into housing possibilities, and a 10 percent surtax to pay for everything being done.[25] The city also set up a tent encampment at Kiryat Meir, accommodating some 1,000 refugees, and appointed a special confiscation officer to search for alternative places of refugee housing.[26] None of this, however, defused the crackling tension that had begun to build up in the organized and improvised refugee centers.[27] Furious outbursts against municipal workers, occasionally escalating into fisticuffs, erupted frequently.[28]

Although the government was mindful of the combustibility of the problem and designated a department and experienced high-ranking officials to tackle it, it was the IDPs themselves who determined the locations of their centers in Tel Aviv by breaking into them, irrespective of coordination with the property owners.[29]

By early January 1948, as the number of IDP asylums in Tel Aviv increased,[30] the bureaucratic mechanisms became increasingly efficient and began regularizing the IDPs' status by registering them and issuing them with refugee cards. The municipality issued instructions forbidding the migration of refugees from place to place without permission. IDPs were warned not to deposit money with housing profiteers. Families that had left homes in areas that were not recognized as danger zones were told that their dwellings would be confiscated for others' use.[31]

In Haifa, the IDPs found shelter in eleven locations, some swapping apartments with Arab acquaintances who lived in Jewish neighborhoods. The Haifa Hebrew Community Council (see the introduction) had already set up a subordinate entity that called itself the Emergency Housing Committee; its main responsibility was to make arrangements for housing and for children. More than a hundred school-age youngsters were gathered separately in Geula School; volunteer teachers were recruited to take care of them. Relevant professionals were mobilized to help the refugees alongside members of women's volunteer organizations (the Organization of Working Mothers [OWM] and WIZO [Women's International Zionist Organization]), community activists, and community officers.[32]

The Jewish community leaders in Haifa, however,[33] had failed to anticipate the intensity of the outflow from Arab and mixed neighborhoods and were unable to arrange as many housing places as were needed.[34] "The refugee question seems almost as important as the security question," warned a member of the city's Situation Committee in late December. Tension between IDPs and the authorities was already surging as frustrated, furious people burst into the Community Council offices and disrupted the work.[35] At the local level, there was a feeling that the problem exceeded the municipal leadership's authority and resources. Thus, eyes turned to the security forces, on the one hand, and to the national leadership on the other.[36] Until a lasting solution could be found, however, temporary housing arrangements were needed, and for this purpose the community leadership had to dun the non-displaced townspeople for the requisite sums and rely on their good will.[37]

Within a month, the Haifa Community Council institutionalized its treatment of the internal refugee problem by setting up two panels, one for IDP affairs and one for housing.[38] The two entities, investigating possibilities of provisional and permanent housing for refugees, proposed a series of solutions that included a tent encampment, shanties, and the construction of real dwellings.[39] The IDPs in Haifa, however, like their counterparts in Tel Aviv, did not wait for the authorities to arrange housing for them; instead, they invaded additional schools, causing local players to lose control and ask the security forces in Haifa to help restore discipline.[40, 41]

In Jerusalem, the care of IDPs was tasked to a housing panel that operated under the Situation Committee, an organ of the Community Council. By the time this entity came into being, the IDP problem was in full swing, and people who lacked basic shelter clogged the entrances of the

Community Council premises in search of solutions. At the initiative of the members of the council, several apartments were obtained on the basis of direct negotiations with Muslim and Christian Arabs who had left Jewish neighborhoods. There were also cases of apartment swapping between Jews and Arabs and rental of dwellings from the Mandate government.[42]

The Situation Committee maintained communication with the security forces and the People's Guard (Mishmar ha'Am—see the introduction) in the city. The power to approve the abandonment of frontier locations was vested in the former. Most residents of the northern neighborhoods near Sheikh Jarrah left their homes in late December and early January and became IDPs.[43] They were temporarily housed in classrooms at the schools in downtown Jerusalem. Others, not waiting for the Community Council's go-ahead, invaded schools and empty apartments.[44]

"The attempt to police the mass of refugees ended with only partial success," Cohen-Levinovsky notes, adding, however, that the authorities in all three cities displayed "an impressive degree of control of the supply of housing available to them and, more so, in tracking residents' comings and goings."[45] Importantly, too, even though a central authority for the care of the internally displaced had been designated in each of the three cities, associational initiatives in response to the IDP problem began to take shape in diverse circles: some by the internally displaced themselves, others against the background of the harm caused by the IDPs, and yet others locally, meant to thwart the flight of residents who would join the displaced population. In each of these circles, processes of response and evolution that reacted to the prolongation of the crisis and its stages may be detected.

Associational Moves in Response to the IDP Crisis Between the Authorities and Those Affected

Preventive Actions—Initiatives to Keep Residents in Their Homes

The authorities came under pressure in various ways (e.g., in attempts by residents of frontier areas to obtain "endangered area" status for their neighborhoods or in demands for better defense in order to discourage flight). In Tel Aviv, representatives of the Maccabi Barracks neighborhood approached the mayor, Israel Rokach, and described the plight of the residents of this quarter, many of whom were living under the open sky after having fled for their lives and now realizing that they had been gerrymandered out of the Jewish defense region. To return the inhabitants to their homes, the envoys argued, the neighborhood needed reinforcement and should be defined as a security zone. Alternatively, they continued, an orderly exodus of residents should be approved. The neighborhood delegates did not consider it enough to correspond with municipal decision makers; they also asked to meet with the acting mayor, Eliezer Perlson, in order to present him with their proposals on how to cope with the outflow. Perlson forwarded their request to the municipal secretary, Yehuda Nadivi, along with a handwritten note: "Please receive them promptly to hear what they have in mind."[46]

A leading member of the Hatikva quarter committee, Yehezkel Shoshani, faulted residents who had chosen to leave their homes despite having suffered no harm. Shoshani appealed to city hall on behalf of "the vestiges of the neighborhood" who wanted the municipality to repopulate the neighborhood with others in order to prevent looting.[47] The inhabitants of the Kerem Hatemanim (Karton) quarter, bordering Jaffa, held an assembly at which they demanded the annexation of their neighborhood to Tel Aviv. (De jure, the neighborhood was already part of Tel Aviv; the inhabitants spoke this way in the belief that this affiliation did not find practical expression.)[48] The Tel Amal neighborhood committee published a warning to residents who had left the area and had not turned their apartments over to others: those failing to return by a specified date would find their belongings removed from the dwelling and refugees resettled there.[49]

The socioeconomic and military background of the neighborhood inhabitants projected onto how the state of emergency was confronted at the local level. Thus, some Tel Aviv neighborhoods saw the formation of defense committees that maintained contact with various Civil Guard or municipal elements. In the Yad Eliyahu quarter, for example, a neighborhood of quondam British Army soldiers, representatives of the Haganah concluded an arrangement with the defense committee. According to the terms of the deal, neighborhood inhabitants, male and female alike, would be drafted into the Civil Guard and placed in charge of civil defense and "internal order" in the neighborhood.[50]

In Jerusalem, residents of the southern neighborhoods—Talpiot and North Talpiot, Arnona, Givat Eliyahu, Ramat Rahel, and Efrat—set up a situation committee that aimed to keep the deterioration of security from triggering abandonment. In the first few weeks of the intercommunal violence, transport from these neighborhoods to the center of Jerusalem had already come under attack, jolting the residents' sense of security and disrupting public transport in and out. The neighborhood committees countered by organizing to work out a consensual response. One of their decisions pertained to the construction of an alternative access road by repairing a ruined byway. To pay for the repairs, they imposed a levy on the inhabitants; to do the work itself, they established a coalition that they called the Talpiot Bloc Committee and even opened a special bank account for it.[51]

The neighborhood envoys gave themselves license to interfere in outright military considerations, asking the local Haganah people not to set out from North Talpiot for punitive actions against the Abu Tor neighborhood until their quarter was adequately defended. Unless transport, deliveries, and guarding were forthcoming, they warned, the residents would get up and leave. Concurrently, a water problem had come about: the neighborhood had not received water for four days. The regional commander, Shalom Dror took the united residents seriously; he ordered an inspection of water systems, had preparations made for the purchase of catchment tanks, and spoke about the added manpower that would be needed to staff the checkpoints at the neighborhood entrance.[52]

When Dror's efforts proved futile, the local association turned to Dov Yosef, who had just taken over as head of the National Institutions Committee for Jerusalem Affairs. The military and civilian authorities, aware of the gravity of the situation in the outlying neighborhoods, sent representatives there and met with the coalition of neighborhood committees.[53] Pursuant to the meeting and at Yosef's request, the neighborhood residents produced a written list of urgent problems and hurriedly (the next day) sent off the memorandum that the authorities had asked them to draw up.

The memorandum provides a glimpse into the dominant trend of thought in these isolated neighborhoods of southern Jerusalem. It also reflects the balance of forces among the stakeholders in that area, representatives of the military forces, and the local leadership. The inhabitants of the neighborhoods, it turns out, distrusted those responsible for their security. They described the military staff in the area as "clueless" and "lacking any comprehensive defense plan." Their critique, however, was not limited to the professional aspects of these entities' work; they also decried the exclusion of representatives of the frontier neighborhoods from the management of the crisis at large. "It's as though our high command . . . is oblivious to our existence," they protested.[54] Moving on to the issue itself, the representatives of the neighborhood situation committee demanded that armored buses be assigned to their area so that people could get to work and maintain their normal lives. When this request went unanswered, they perceived it as a breach of assurances "in a most shameful manner," due to which neighborhood inhabitants had to "waste five hours or more" waiting for armored vehicles that did not arrive or arrived too full to accommodate all prospective passengers, leaving some to sleep overnight elsewhere in town, away from their families.[55]

The problem of access to and from the neighborhoods became an important stimulus for residents' flight. The problem worsened after two inhabitants perished while traveling in unprotected vehicles. By the time the letter was written, the neighborhood situation committee had reported the flight of more than 70 percent of the population of Talpiot and Arnona, nearly all of whom worked in downtown Jerusalem and could not commute due to what the committee called "irresponsible conduct by those who control our armored vehicles."[56] Eight days later, the neighborhood delegates returned to Dov Yosef and expressed astonishment over his not having bothered to confirm receiving the letter. They also complained that the promises about introducing additional armored vehicles had been "totally dishonored." They gave examples of vehicles standing immobile at bus stops while crowds of would-be passengers waited for them at others. The situation committee kept track of such cases and reported them in minute detail, including exact dates and times, and drew a connection between the transport failure and the outflow of additional families from the neighborhood.[57]

However, while the residents' representatives complained about the area security officials' inadequacies and assumed that their plight traced to the military command's impotence, it turns out that area headquarters had been striving to solve the problem and were attempting to redirect neighborhood traffic to alternate routes.[58] In the estimation of a Haganah official, the state of transport was indeed "the main reason . . . for the departure of some residents from Arnona and Talpiot, and this has a definitive effect on the area residents' state of mind and, in turn, the state of security."[59]

"External" Service Providers in IDP Centers

As the neighborhood committees and municipal and security agencies attempted to cope with the flow of people to places of refuge and somehow maintain a semblance of regular life in neighborhoods not yet abandoned, humanitarian activity in the provisional refuges began.

Much of this activity rested on the shoulders of volunteers who operated under recognized organizational auspices that were linked in some way with a municipal authority, a community council, or local security forces.[60] In Tel Aviv, for example, the Culture Department's clubs were handed over for use as IDP children's shelters and clubs for school-age youngsters, with volunteers from women's organizations doing the work.[61] In Haifa, kindred organizations established schools for refugees, set up a clothing warehouse, and distributed free meals at the refugee centers.[62] In Jerusalem, a feeding committee and health centers run by the Hadassah women's organization helped to deliver food to the internally displaced.[63] Hashahar, an association active among adolescents in the southern neighborhoods of Tel Aviv, also responded swiftly to the new situation and opened an activity center at the makeshift refugee camp that had formed on the premises of Takhkemoni School.[64] In Haifa, doctors formed a committee and proposed various ways to improve sanitation in the refugee centers.[65] These are only a few examples among many. In fact, all the refugee centers based their operations on volunteers, usually women, who worked with the relevant municipal authorities.

The women's organizations mediated between the authorities that were officially in charge of maintaining order in the improvised centers and the inhabitants who were often alienated from them.[66] Even though many women activists in these organizations belonged to affluent and well-connected social circles that were far from the lower-income neighborhoods from which many of the IDPs came, their perspective welled from a deeper contemplation of the realities of life that had taken shape in the refugee centers. Women volunteers in Haifa warned against misjudging the displaced population, arguing that in many cases, despite the neglect and poverty, its social situation was not all that bad. They also alluded to the cultural aspect of what they termed "our first encounter with families from the Oriental communities."[67]

The Council of Women's Organizations (CWO)—a long-standing entity established against the background of the Arab uprising and now reactivated—amalgamated all registered women's organizations in the Yishuv as well as Zionist women's entities that operated abroad.[68] Among the leaders of this umbrella association were Beba Idelson, secretary of the Women's Labor Council, and Rachel Cohen-Kagan, head of WIZO and director of the Social Work Department for the National Committee, a post that she held in addition to managing social work for the Haifa Community

Council. Each of these women's organizations had financial resources, owned a set of educational and early-childhood institutions, and deployed a large and experienced team of volunteers countrywide. Tackling the Jewish IDP problem that was taking shape in the urban centers, they placed children at the front and center of their efforts. In their judgment, arranging reasonable living conditions for displaced children would allow their parents to continue making a living and, in turn, mitigate the mounting humanitarian crisis in the towns.[69] To set this sequence in motion, they made a strenuous initial effort to persuade families to take displaced children into their homes. In Tel Aviv, they implemented this initiative in full coordination with the municipal Social Work Department.[70] The Tel Aviv Municipality's makeshift camp posted volunteer counselors to supervise social educational activity. All efforts notwithstanding, however, many refugee children remained idle and continued to roam the streets.[71]

The children's institutions of the women's organizations, particularly the large ones, enrolled hundreds of youngsters and subsidized the cost of receiving more.[72] Existing buildings and institutions were converted into makeshift dormitories and day centers for displaced children.[73] The same was done in additional locations around the country.[74]

The emphasis on caregiving services for children in locations other than IDP centers assured adequate nutrition and reasonable hygienic conditions for the youngsters but did not necessarily help to strengthen relations between the volunteers and the population in need. Examining the patterns of these relations on the basis of the "capacity-building" element that Lautze and Hammock specify, one finds that this input was absent in the humanitarian intervention that the women's organizations offered.[75] Those in the IDP centers soon realized that they would have to speak out to make sure that their inadvertent humanitarian crisis would be treated to their satisfaction and in a way that would take their wishes and preferences into account.

Self-Organization by the Internally Displaced

IDPs in several provisional centers began to organize the moment they settled in. One presumes that local action committees were formed in many refugee centers but left few traces because they were ad hoc initiatives that rarely manifested outwardly.[76] Most associations that produced a documentary trail were the sort that had undergone institutionalization (e.g., local organizations that had been established in order to expand the basis of an internally displaced population's representation vis-à-vis the authorities).

A case in point was the General Council of Frontier Refugees, which declared its inauguration on January 13, 1948, at a conference of IDP committees in Tel Aviv.[77] The interesting thing about this entity, like its counterpart in Haifa, is its members' consciousness of being represented and their demand to be heard by policy makers. In the aftermath of the Tel Aviv initiative, IDP leaders were received for an interview with the acting mayor, Eliezer Perlson, who gave them an opportunity to present, directly, the gamut of problems that beset people who by this time had spent more than a month in provisional and improvised places of concentration. In their talk with Perlson, the delegates brought up issues in economics, education, and sanitation, as well as social needs and housing problems.[78] The General Council, chaired by Menahem Cohen,[79] was headquartered in the area between the frontier and the safe parts of town, on Yehuda Halevi Street in the Heichal Hatalmud Yeshiva building, itself an IDP center. The newly founded body earned recognition as the refugees' representative, and Haim Alperin, municipal inspector and superintendent of refugee care in Tel Aviv, was asked to meet with its officials and establish working relations with them.[80]

In Haifa, the first testimonies about IDPs organizing on their own date from mid-December 1947, only a few days after the violence erupted and at the very start of the humanitarian crisis. Those behind the associational initiative, via their representatives, turned directly to the top of the Yishuv pyramid, the chair of the National Committee, David Remez, introducing themselves as "representatives of the refugees" in this city. Remez forwarded their appeal to the Jewish Agency Political Department.[81] Concurrently, the IDPs' representatives turned to the Haifa Situation Committee and presented it with an assessment: children were roving in the streets, more and more families were living in one room, disgruntlement was rising, and things were about to explode.[82] About three months after being displaced, the IDPs in Haifa were functioning as a full-fledged interest group. They held assemblies, appointed representatives, and negotiated with the authorities to improve their living conditions. As often happens with such patterns of grassroots association, the identity of those authorized to speak on behalf of the interest group was not always clear. As a result, officials charged with handling their affairs found it difficult to maintain steady relations with them.[83]

From the standpoint of the Haifa Community Council, the refugees issued "exaggerated demands that cannot possibly be met under the conditions of our reality."[84] A member of the Situation Committee revealed the acute suspicion that pervaded relations between the sides: "It's our duty to state that covert and inflammatory players are organizing the refugees and steering them toward a dangerous course of action. The Refugees Committee won't even share the names of its members."[85]

Evidently, the IDPs' representatives did not think it enough at this time to improve their clients' short-term situation, say, by seeking better living conditions in the IDP centers. Instead, they sought to ensure that their clients not be sent back to the mixed neighborhoods, which they saw as a source of danger and a symbol of low status. Their demand was that basic dwellings be built for them in Hadar HaCarmel; they refused to move to the tent encampments that had been offered as a stopgap. The refugees' delegates construed the separation from Arab Haifa as a done deal and, accordingly, felt that their housing problem should be solved in permanent, long-term ways that would keep them in the Mount Carmel area. One of the most prominent envoys of the organization of IDPs in Haifa, Gabriel Naqibli,[86] expressed this point of view. "The refugees," he explained, "have made up their minds not to return to the outskirts of the city, which are prone to the immediate menace of Arab rioting." David Bar-Rav-Hai of the Community Council, articulating the views of the entire panel, took the opposite stance: "Some refugees who are living on the edges of town will have to go back there because it's not in our interest to abandon crucial settled positions."[87] At the end of a protracted debate, Naqibli agreed to consider the possibility of provisional housing but only "in basic dwellings and on Jewish National Fund land." While not rejecting this demand per se, Bar-Rav-Hai insisted that the IDPs accept provisional housing as an interim necessity; only after this, he said, could the possibility of arranging permanent housing for those who could not return to their homes be addressed. The sides evidently accepted this compromise, with Naqibli winding up the meeting by promising to present the matters to those whom he represented at an assembly that evening.[88]

The Community Council soon realized that the crisis was not about to end even after a provisional arrangement for the IDPs appeared to have been found. The reason was twofold: a steady increase in the number of families that had to vacate their dwellings due to the escalation of warfare and the disconnection and divide that typified relations between the upscale population of Haifa and the inhabitants of mixed neighborhoods in the Lower City. As the Haifa IDP population grew with each passing day, it waited neither for instructions from its representatives nor for permission from the authorities. Entire families continued to break into schools in the city and disrupt studies.[89] The Jewish community activists in Haifa, aggrieved by what they saw, termed the refugee representatives' demands for permanent housing in Hadar HaCarmel "aggressive" and "intransigent."[90]

"It has been proved that the intention of some of the refugees is to sow chaos and generate unnecessary tension," charged Moshe Gutel Levin, chair of the Community Council and an esteemed figure in diverse Haifa circles. In this context, the possibility of sending in the Haganah was discussed but rejected by those who objected to the forcible removal of intruders as long as no alternative solution presented itself.[91] With no police or other legal authority in sight, the Situation Committee and the Refugees Bureau found themselves helpless against IDP aggression. As refugees balked at vacating schools that they had occupied, additional IDPs streamed into public places.[92] Policy makers gradually became aware of the impasse that had come about and turned their main attention to calming the tempers. To do this successfully, they had to maintain a dialogue with the refugees' representatives despite their disapproval of this body, toward which the Community Council members had developed grave suspicions.[93]

As the various provisional solutions were debated, progress was being made toward the creation of permanent housing. Some even proposed that the Refugees Committee (a reference to the IDPs' representative body) become a party to the permanent housing initiative, it being assumed that the IDPs themselves would have to commit to partial payment for any long-lasting settlement. Other voices on the Community Council, however, oozed contempt and condescension. One participant stated flatly that he pinned "no hopes on the arrangement of housing for this element, which can't be trusted to honor its obligations in terms of paying rent."[94]

The IDPs' self-representation in Haifa began to attract public interest when the press reported on an assembly that it had held, the resolutions that it had adopted (confiscation of rooms in large apartments inhabited by small families), and its demand to post delegates to any discussion about solutions.[95] Reports about tension between IDP representatives and establishment authorities continued to seep into the media, which accented the positive side—the very fact that the refugees had organized, to the betterment of their cause—while stressing the possibility that "the refugees' organization will serve individuals or groups of people who wish to exploit the refugees' plight for various causes other than the refugees' own wellbeing" (such as the secessionist movements or the communists). *Davar*'s editorial board called on the displaced population at large to disavow "cheap radicalism that aims not to accomplish anything real but only to stir up anger and cause panic."[96]

The IDPs' representatives found an original way to respond to this criticism in the print media; they distributed leaflets directly to the inhabitants of Haifa, warning them about the intention of collecting money from them for ostensible refugee relief without assurances from the fundraisers that the funds would really be used for this purpose: "Haifaites! They [the municipal authorities] are asking you to pay new taxes. They've told you that this money will be spent on housing for the refugees—to blot out the disgrace of having homeless people in our city. Have you given thought to how these public funds are being spent? What has the Community Council done for the refugees thus far?"[97]

Farther into the text of the leaflet, the IDPs' emissaries accused the Community Council of wasting public money on the construction of a tent village—"a Bedouin camp in a Hebrew city." Only the well-off, they alleged, would be able to receive permanent housing, leaving the large majority of refugees, composed of families of six or more, "to their fate!"[98] They described the public whom they represented as loyal citizens. These townspeople, the author of the leaflet rued, had been forsaken. In their appeal to fellow townspeople, the IDPs' representatives adopted an additional strategy. They emphasized the personal price that the residents of Haifa were paying for the absence of a solution to the problem: the disruption of studies. After all, according to the plan, the schools would be closed until the new school year.[99]

Thus, less than two months after they became homeless, the IDPs were already being represented by a recognized agency that comported itself vigorously vis-à-vis the local leadership that was tasked with dealing with their woes. This entity negotiated vigorously for new housing conditions and bargained over various solutions that it had been offered. It expanded its demands to include more than the alleviation of the distress that the state of emergency had created. They struggled, as they put it, for "our right to human life in the Hebrew state now being established."[100]

The public dispute between the IDPs and the authorities escalated another notch when Voice of Israel (VOI) radio devoted a special broadcast to the IDP problem. The Refugees Committee protested the program's "distorted view" of its "war for human housing." The public, the committee charged, was being presented as an enraged rabble that presented excessive demands and took no account of the country's bleak condition. The committee figured that the broadcast had been based on information that the Haifa Community Council had shared with VOI, and they demanded redress: "We are not an enraged rabble but an organized and disciplined public one that demands nothing 'excessive' but a minimum of justice and human consideration. We protest [the program's] unfair attitude expressed toward a public that was the first to respond to the national call and became the first casualty when the Yishuv came under attack."[101]

Criticized for the resistance that IDPs put up when ordered to vacate Yavne School, the envoys responded by accusing the Haifa leadership of using disproportionate force and causing the squatters physical and mental harm. They demanded an investigation of what had happened and the formation of a committee, on which the IDPs would be represented, to estimate damages. Then they placed on the table a practical proposal for the continuation of the joint work: the formation of an eight-person committee—four members of the community and four representing the IDPs—that would be empowered to debate and decide on any issue on the basis of an agreement in principle that the parties would determine.[102]

The antagonism between the refugees' representatives and the Community Council had long since overstepped the boundaries of the temporary distress that the emergency had brought on; by now it reflected class estrangement between lower and upper Haifa and the refusal of the inhabitants of the lower city to acquiesce in what they considered an attempt to exclude them from taking responsibility for their fate.

Internal Friction and Empowerment: The Maturing of the IDP Associations

Haifa

The second wave of IDPs in Jewish Haifa began in February 1948, as the intercommunal violence escalated and the fighting spread to additional parts of town. Now, people living on streets at the edges of Hadar HaCarmel abandoned their homes with permission. This outflow left some 500 families homeless in mid-winter, by which time most public places were packed with asylum seekers. Again the policy makers had to provide provisional housing and do so quickly.[103]

One solution was the placement of IDPs in hotels, which became possible due to cooperation between the Situation Committee and an organized body of hoteliers that offered affordable conditions, for this Situation Committee promised to pay for the rooms at the going daily rate in order to spare the hoteliers from massive losses.[104] Alongside systematic solutions such as this, impromptu ones, based on spontaneous settlement of refugees in schools, persisted as well. From the onset of the intercommunal violence to this time, IDPs in Haifa had commandeered eight public schools and approximately ten kindergarten classrooms, mostly at their own initiative. In early January, four additional schools were taken over, crowding an additional thousand pupils out of the classrooms. The seizure of Yavne School created special problems, because this institution relied on tuition payments; the suspension of studies there meant that the teachers stopped receiving their salaries.[105]

By late February, public reports about arrangements for Haifa refugees had taken an optimistic turn. *Davar* reported that 180 families could return to their apartments.[106] At a meeting with journalists, the Situation Committee's housing panel reported on developments in resettling the refugees and now mentioned, "with great satisfaction," cooperation with the IDPs' representatives, which, they hoped, would continue until all problems were solved. They followed this with a remark about the importance of imposing "internal discipline" to prevent ad hoc policy-making by individuals.[107]

The elation, however, appeared to be premature. As fighting in built-up areas in the Lower City escalated, including the detonation of car bombs (by both sides),[108] the IDP population grew steadily.[109]

In late February, a new associational player stepped onto the stage—a local committee chosen in secret elections to represent IDPs in the provisional camp on Mount Carmel. The new group introduced itself to the Community Council as an elected body and asked the council to recognize it as the sole agent for residents of the camp. It boasted a high level of functioning, having established a control committee and instigated an ongoing relationship with the Situation Committee.[110] Its initiatives included mediation between inhabitants in need and the Community Council authorities that ran the camp.

IDPs who had found housing in schools held a joint assembly that adopted a resolution as to who could represent them in the Central Committee of Haifa Refugees.[111] At this gathering, the clashing processes that were unfolding among this population rose to the surface—institutionalization and reinforcement of self-organization and official representation, contrasting with increasing inroads by criminal elements that attempted to take control of the allocation of places of shelter and profit from extortion and brokerage. In response to this challenge, the assembly authorized two representatives, David Vogel and Meir Nissan, to act on behalf of the refugee population vis-à-vis the Situation Committee "in dealing with rooms." In accordance with a resolution that they took for this purpose, they declared the withholding from two of their comrades all rights of representation before these institutions until the elections.[112] Vogel and Nissan claimed that the suspended members were suspected of profiteering from the allocation of rooms and bribing drivers who had been sent out to transfer home appurtenances. Evidence was presented to a representative of the IDPs who worked under the Situation Committee for a reexamination of the housing issue.[113] The testimonies he was given included personal stories of IDPs who were distressed by the criminality that had overtaken the matter of provisional refuge. The very fact that they disclosed their ordeals to their representatives attests to the extent of trust they felt toward their delegates and the immensity of the blow to public order that the town's humanitarian crisis embodied. For our purposes, however, the affair acquires its main importance by illuminating the turning point that was crossed in the status of the city's refugee committee—from a perceived burden on the authorities to a leadership auspice that was a full partner in the process. The committee's standing would be further validated in subsequent months, as spiraling warfare on the eve of the Haganah's conquest of Haifa on April 22 caused the crisis to escalate. By observing contacts between the committee and the refugee office in the spring of 1948, we also notice the expansion of the committee's responsibilities. This entity, which initially set out to deal with a spot humanitarian crisis, evolved into an agency that had the self-designated goal of rehabilitating its members in the long term by, among other things, thwarting the establishment of provisional camps and conditioning evacuation from places of refuge on permanent housing arrangements.[114]

Tel Aviv–Jaffa

In early March, entire streets along the "zipper" between Tel Aviv and Jaffa emptied out, and the vacated zone steadily widened on both the Arab and the Jewish sides.[115] Since the affected area was the manufacturing hub of the whole country, its paralysis, were it to last, would project on economic life at the national, not only the regional, level. Sniper fire in the area deterred delivery drivers from entering and brought traffic to the location to a nearly total halt. The outflow of population also exposed the warehouses, factories, inventories, and facilities to plunder and looting.[116]

From March onward, the municipality stepped up the pace of its evictions of IDPs from their places of refuge to regulated locations that it sponsored.[117] The formalization of procedures for the treatment of the crisis, however, did not prevent the emergency itself from worsening. As the fighting escalated and the dangerous frontier zones widened, additional thousands of people fled northward in search of refuge in parts of town that were safe from gunfire. The gap between the housing arrangements that city hall offered and the number of people in need of them grew and grew, even as the veteran IDPs' sanitary conditions (dire to begin with) steadily worsened and their provisional dwellings slowly became permanent.[118]

As the authorities institutionalized their handling of the crisis, those affected by it did the same. The IDPs' committees and joint council cemented their status as legitimate representatives of the internally displaced in Tel Aviv. Unlike what happened in Haifa, here, as the IDPs' power grew, so too did points of friction between them and the authorities, sharpening the disparities between the sides. A series of confrontations between the refugee committees and Haim Alperin led to harsh exchanges of words, with Alperin threatening to hold the committee members personally liable for their misdeeds. The General Council of Frontier Refugees reported these incidents directly to Mayor Rokach and demanded that he put his chief inspector in his place.[119] Alperin, asked to respond to the allegations of the IDPs' representatives, replied to each, listing case by case the misconduct of the refugees' leaders, including support for a wildcat invasion of a school, unauthorized construction, and threatening municipal workers. The members of the council secretariat, Alperin thought, should know their place, be mindful of their duty to serve the public that they represented, "and not present groundless demands."[120]

The affair surrounding the resettlement of IDPs in Jamusin provides a case study of the growing strength of refugees' local representation and, at the same time, its continued friction and power struggles with city hall. We now turn our attention to this local community, which in many respects is a litmus test for the IDP crisis and the centrality of this population's self-representation vis-à-vis the governing authority.

The Emergence of Local Leadership: The Case of Jamusin

The evacuation of Jamusin, an Arab village on the northeastern frontier of Tel Aviv along the southern bank of the Yarkon River, took place at an early stage of the hostilities due to an agreement between dignitaries of this village and Haganah officers in Tel Aviv. The initiative for this arrangement evidently had been taken by the dignitaries, who looked on as their village emptied of its own accord and wished to assure the possibility of returning to their lands and homes once the storm blew over. Thus, their representatives approached the Haganah and proposed the transfer of responsibility for the village lands to the Municipality of Tel Aviv "by leasing or in some other way."[121] Haganah representatives in Tel Aviv forwarded the initiative to their superiors, and the agreement was adopted. The responsibility for the location was then transferred to city hall, which made the village dwellings available to persons displaced from the city's frontier neighborhoods.[122]

The municipality was advised that it would be taking possession of the homes in Jamusin and would maintain a registry of the properties, cede them to refugees from frontier neighborhoods, and appoint a committee or inspectors to oversee the implementation of the accord.[123] Study of the pact indicates that the Jews who settled in Jamusin were not given carte blanche with the properties and that municipal representatives felt committed to the spirit of the agreement and may even have been afraid of future lawsuits in the event of damage. In addition, it is clear why the representatives of the security forces considered themselves the competent authority in imposing order in the village, interpreting the agreement with the village dignitaries, and overseeing its implementation by the new inhabitants. Now, however, an additional player stepped in—a Jamusin tenants committee headed by Menahem Cohen, whom we have already met as the head of the General Council for Frontier Refugees in Tel Aviv.[124] Members of this body in addition to Cohen appear to have been familiar neighborhood leaders. Moreover, several of them belonged to the Haganah, a circumstance that gave them confidence when they sat down with city officials to negotiate the regulation of their living conditions in the village. These opening terms were obviously a recipe for disagreements, tensions, and even eruptions of violence between the sides.

The committee and the municipality did conclude an agreement about the delivery of various services in return for taxes, and the tenants promised to refrain from expanding the houses. Before long, however, disagreements broke out between the parties, with the tenants claiming that the government was not doing its share and not allowing them to improve the buildings that they now inhabited. In their letters and petitions, which they addressed to the acting mayor, Eliezer Perlson, they complained that the city's garbage trucks were dumping their loads in the village and warned about the health hazard that this created. One letter contrasted their version of unauthorized construction with that of the municipal inspector, Alperin. Finally, the committee raised the question of its status vis-à-vis the community of tenants that it wished to represent. Alperin's contemptuous attitude, they charged, diminished their authority as a local leadership in the tenants' eyes, compromising their ability to assure "industrial quiet" in the village.[125] The panel offered to mediate between city hall and the civilians in Jamusin, many of whom were sullen and ready for a fight. Indeed, Perlson detected the advantages of the local association and instructed Alperin to meet with it. The outcome was a set of accords that established cooperation in tax collection, a ban on wildcat construction, and the demolition of add-ons that tenants had built on their own.

At this point, the versions of the events diverge. Alperin claimed that no sooner had water supplies to the village been arranged than Menahem Cohen and his associates presented new demands and conditioned the remittance of taxes on city hall's assent to them. Alperin was convinced that the committee, instead of wishing to play the mediator's role, was interested in strengthening its position and authority at the municipality's expense and aggrandizing itself by piggybacking on the conflict between the inhabitants and the city.[126]

To get to the bottom of the knotty relationship among the IDPs, the security forces, and the municipality in the events at Jamusin, one should be aware that all members of the Jamusin tenants' committee had been veteran activists on the Tel Aviv frontier neighborhood committees. Some even belonged to such panels at this very time and had amassed experience in contacts with municipal authorities in their attempts to obtain services for their neighborhoods, which abutted the Tel Aviv–Jaffa border. As a case in point, Ezra Haboura, one of the Jamusin tenants, was an important activist in the Kerem Hatemanim (Karton) quarter, a neighborhood on the municipal border between Jaffa and Tel Aviv where nearly all inhabitants had become IDPs.[127]

In the ensuing months, additional IDPs flowed into Jamusin, but living conditions there were not improved. Some residents lived in rickety shacks or structures that the Arab villagers had used as barns and stables. Although the construction of fifty rudimentary homes had been approved, these residents did not wait and began to build on their own, reigniting the controversy that had erupted between the tenants and the municipality two months earlier. Now municipal inspectors accompanied by police were attacked by residents and could return to the village only when escorted by armed Haganah soldiers. In the aftermath of these confrontations, the Jamusin residents stopped paying taxes and city hall suspended all the services that it had promised. Consequently, after a few days, the local committee announced its willingness to ensure that the illegal construction would stop and to act for the collection of municipal taxes, in return for which the village would be given infrastructures in education, health care, water supply, electricity hookups, and more frequent public transport.[128]

Apparently, the audacity displayed by members of the local committee in expressing demands and clashing with the city originated neither solely in the backing that they had initially received from representatives of the security forces there nor exclusively in the residents' experience in neighborhood politicking. It also reflected the expectations of their public (i.e., those who had found housing in the locality). These people expected their leaders to represent them vis-à-vis the authorities and presented them with grievances about their failure to perform as anticipated.[129] Even as they pressed the committee to show results, however, they recognized the limitations of its power. Indeed, their awareness of the committee's constraints apparently grew as Jamusin ceased to be frontline military base and became an inseparable part of Tel Aviv. In early May, a change in the committee's attitude toward city hall came into sight: the tenants' representatives began to display a wish to cooperate and even undertook to help maintain order in the village and strengthen relations with the various municipal departments. They also promised to prevent rogue construction of shanties and asked the Inspection Department to revisit its overall attitude toward the village. If this were done, they promised, they would "work hand in hand" with the municipal departments and support the municipality "as an organized and disciplined public should."[130]

Amid these negotiations and power struggles between the representatives—those of IDPs and those of the various authorities—another civic fracas erupted in view of the humanitarian crisis that internal displacement had brought about. The tussle was led by various groups in the city that felt harmed by the IDPs' takeover of their properties and of public buildings that were indispensable for routine urban life. Now we observe this parallel development.

The IDPs as a Threat: The Strength and Weakness of Anti-Refugee Pressure Groups

The first inflow of IDPs from frontier neighborhoods triggered immediate reactions among social and economic groups that felt directly affected by it. While the social tensions surrounding this episode have been covered elsewhere,[131] this chapter focuses on associational settings put together by those who were harmed by the IDPs' invasions and who sought to evict them from locations where they disrupted daily economic, religious, and educational life.

Several weeks into the intercommunal war, the Executive Committee of the Tel Aviv Chamber of Commerce held an initial discussion of the disorder and material damage that the invasions of merchants' offices and warehouses were causing. "Invasion has become a profession," several members of the chamber railed, charging that dubious elements—"sundry panderers and profiteers"—were exploiting the situation for gain and that refugees "are being paid [to] leave the places that they had invaded." The merchants termed what they perceived as "the plague of invasions" a threat to commercial life in the city at large. At a meeting of the chamber presidium, there was talk of organizing "joint public pressure by all institutions in the city."[132]

In Jerusalem, too, homeowners began to encounter the disturbing problem of intrusions. To tackle it, representatives of the Homeowners Association first approached the Community Council and described the predicament: the invasion of private homes by whole families. The Jerusalem envoys then demanded that the Community Council see to the eviction of squatters,[133] only to find the council in no rush to give the homeowners its backing.[134] The latter sensed the alienation of the former and blamed the municipal and defense authorities for the disorder that had come about, which included, among other things, intervention by armed strangers in defense of intruders.[135]

The victims of the intrusions regarded their professional bodies as their spokespersons vis-à-vis the authorities and turned to them for protection whenever their properties were violated. Thus, the Tel Aviv–Jaffa branch of the Hebrew Medical Association approached city hall on behalf of a member physician whose apartment had been invaded by IDPs.[136] The General Association of Merchants submitted a grievance on behalf of a café owner whose establishment had been raided by the internally displaced.[137] The Association of Artisans and Petty Industry demanded to know who would be held responsible for damage to the warehouse of an artisan in Haifa by armed persons who claimed that the place had been earmarked for expropriation.[138]

In Tel Aviv, the board of the Builders Association wrote directly to the mayor, demanding that IDPs be evicted from construction sites lest the entire industry grind to a halt.[139] The Tel Aviv board of the Association of Home and Property Owners demanded that the municipality act against the forced accommodation of refugees in private buildings with the help of armed young people who barged into homes and threatened their owners.[140] These few examples demonstrate the similarity of the responses of economic and/or professional stakeholder organizations to the internal-displacement phenomenon that affected their members for the worse.

Uniting behind their shared economic interest against a phenomenon that threatened their members' livelihood, the victim organizations met to discuss the accommodation of war refugees in private and public premises. They also set up a committee to coordinate the activities of the diverse economic bodies vis-à-vis the municipality in regard to IDPs and to promote appropriate housing solutions.[141] Moshe Naor emphasizes the public importance and political influence of these interest groups, all numbered among the Tel Aviv urban middle class, which held liberal attitudes toward the assurance of personal life and property.[142] As I show below, however, the seniority of these entities and their close relations with the local and national leadership gave them no edge over other supplicants.

The internal IDP crisis also triggered grave concerns about possible implications for the public's health. With so many people concentrated in makeshift housing that lacked essential sanitation, concern about the potential damage prompted interest groups that felt threatened on this account to organize in various ways. The result was a coalition of parents, teachers, and principals of schools where IDPs had moved in and studies had been suspended or disrupted. Sometimes the pressure was effective.[143] As the intercommunal war completed its second month, parents of students at Yavne School in Haifa held a special assembly to discuss the invasion of their school. Their institutions, and the religious schools generally, had been discriminated against, they claimed. According to their reportage, refugee incursions had left 700 children with no school to attend and doomed them to the danger of roaming around the increasingly violent city. The assembly authorized the school administration, the parents committee, and an expanded emergency council "to take all measures that they deem effective to liberate their school and resume studies."[144]

At the Takhkemoni religious school in Tel Aviv, parents threatened to suspend studies and declare a municipal tax strike.[145] The parents demanded that the Central Parents Committee protest by shutting down studies in all schools in town and mounting demonstrations. Representatives of the Parents Committee, taking part in the assembly, tried to soothe the tempers and promised that their full committee would act toward a solution.[146] The IDPs stayed anyway, and the parents agreed that their children would attend alternative schools in the afternoons.[147]

The multitudes of IDPs who had found housing in schools had indeed become a bothersome problem. Children whose studies had been suspended were roving the city streets precisely when the menace to personal security was greatest in open areas. Their parents, in turn, harried by the vicissitudes of the time, now had to solve education and employment problems as well, sometimes by absenting themselves from work. Local leadership in all three cities was aware of the implications of this disruption of routine life for the population that lived in relatively protected areas; such people could have continued to carry on normally, something that the city leadership valued immensely, and now they could not. As for solving the problem, the Tel Aviv Municipality had a structural advantage over the community councils that ran things in Jerusalem and Haifa. With its human resources and powers, it could, for example, post guards at school entrances to keep IDPs out and act to evict them from such schools as they had entered.[148] Even in Tel Aviv, however, many refuge seekers remained in schools and other municipal public buildings until the end of the intercommunal war and even afterward. The tension between them and their "victims" remained unsolved all this time.

The Orthodox developed a special sensitivity to the problem due to the disproportionate massing of IDPs in synagogues. When municipal inspectors visited the headquarters of Hapoel Hamizrachi (a religious Zionist organization) in Tel Aviv in their search for properties that might serve as provisional housing, an incident developed that ended with the smashing of windows in the building.[149] In response, the Orthodox in Tel Aviv organized a protest rally at which they implored the municipality to relocate the refugees from synagogues to vacant event halls, accusing the city of discriminating against their public's cultural institutions by putting them to disproportional use as refugee accommodations.[150] Ahead of the rally, as the municipality forbade the participants to march from the Great Synagogue to city hall, a delegation of religious public leaders formed to hold a discussion with the Tel Aviv Town Council, taking the opportunity to repeat their allegations about the infringement of synagogue activity due to the refugees' presence.[151]

The newspaper *Davar* showed no sympathy for the synagogue goers' protest:

"There are more than forty synagogues in Tel Aviv and they didn't open their doors to provide shelter and refuge for anyone. You call it public worship? . . . Prayer services in spacious halls that are empty and deserted most of the day and night, at a time like this and amid such an emergency, with the elderly and the very young massed outdoors, is not prayer [*tefila*] but folly [*tifla*]."[152]

Undaunted by the criticism, the synagogue committees continued to bombard city hall with requests to free their institutions from the IDPs' presence. Despite this heavy pressure, they were usually answered in the negative.[153]

Truth be told, the synagogues were not as exceptional as the Orthodox thought.[154] IDPs also considered informal-education and cultural buildings convenient if not legitimate targets for alternative housing for the duration. The synagogue committees' pattern of response was matched by educational and cultural bodies and organizations that found their premises clogged with the internally displaced. Even though one might expect them to be more condoning of the disruption of their routine lives, they tended to respond with frustration and to protest the suspension of their raison d'être precisely in wartime, when their activities for children and young people were even more important than in peacetime. Such was the tenor of a critical letter from the Hebrew Scouts Association in Haifa to the town's Situation Committee, in which the scouts demanded the eviction of IDPs from their club at the Alliance school. Now that the club was closed, explained Arie Kroch, head of the association, activity for hundreds of children was suspended precisely when more and more children's clubs were needed.[155]

In this and other cases, too, the press responded critically to the breaches of solidarity:

"Institutions and facilities for training, sports, and amusements. Institutions for the people—and they did not see that the houses and facilities must gather the inhabitants of the suburbs, refugees from fire and sword, and how at such a time cultural affairs and sports affairs and calisthenics and seminars for activists and counselors should be cancelled—with everything pledged to defense, protection, and refuge."[156]

The local authorities acted in various ways to alleviate what appeared to be an inevitable clash between interest groups that usually represented stronger segments of the public—business owners, liberal professionals whose children had been harmed by the shutdown of formal and informal education, and the religious, whose lives congregated around synagogues and institutions of devotional leadership.

The Haifa Community Council set up a "public panel for the resolution of housing disputes" in an attempt to steer the rivaling parties toward accords by means of dialogue, "dispel the bitterness that has amassed in their hearts, and ready the ground for the creation of decent neighborly relations as are befitting of civilized people."[157] In Tel Aviv, a detail of "mixed vigils for the maintenance of order in the street" was established in cooperation between the municipality and Tel Aviv Haganah command headquarters.[158]

As the war continued and no opportunity to send the refugees home presented itself, it was increasingly realized that the conflicts of interest would persist as long as internal displacement did, creating a major flash point of friction that brought the local leadership under pressure but offered no quick and easy solutions. Thus, when the heads of the Chamber of Commerce asked Mayor Rokach for an audience, he turned them down,[159] and even after five months of intercommunal warfare, the Association of Home and Property Owners (represented by Sa'adia Shoshani, a member of the town council) was as unable as anyone else to terminate the invasions of privately owned buildings. The homeowners, who were required to empty their cesspools and faced fines and prosecution for noncompliance, stood impotent against the strain that these facilities faced as the population of the courtyards for which they were responsible doubled.[160] In one sense, they succeeded where the Chamber of Commerce leaders had failed: they secured a personal meeting with the mayor himself. Even there, however, Rokach could only promise to establish "a joint public committee composed of representatives of the Municipality and the security forces, charged with putting the matter of the forcible invasions into order."[161]

The Orthodox circles, which were among the first to decry the invasion phenomenon, appointed a committee of agents from Tel Aviv synagogues to represent them. Receiving an audience with the mayor, they came away with a decision to establish a municipal committee with the participation of senior members of the town council. Beyond this sign of respect, however, the emissaries could not point to any real achievement.[162] Apparently, the envoys of the Orthodox, like the leaders of the town's economic elites, were forced by the ongoing humanitarian crisis to acknowledge the limits of their political power. Thus, synagogues remained important IDP destinations until the end of the intercommunal war.

As the lack of public conveniences forced people to relieve themselves in courtyards and public parks, the heads of the Tel Aviv–Jaffa branch of the Hebrew Medical Association and the municipal Hygiene Committee warned about the widening risk of epidemics. They demanded the immediate installation of emergency public toilets, assurances that refugees would use these facilities only, and inspection and cleaning of places prone to contamination.[163]

The opening of this discourse about the looming peril to the city on account of the IDP centers unlocked the tongues of the "victims of invasion," who now spoke overtly about the health hazard to themselves and, above all, to their children. They described IDPs as public menaces on account of the transmittable diseases that they carried: "We must note that some of the refugees are plagued with contagious illnesses such as boils, trachoma, and tuberculosis."[164]

Newspaper reportage about the decrepitude of the refugee centers became increasingly frequent. Journalists for *Yedioth Ma'ariv* visited these centers and returned with a warning: "Unless housing becomes a reality within a few weeks, the entire city may face the danger of severe epidemics." The journalist's attention was drawn by the hundred families that had been shoehorned into a rudimentary synagogue on Rabbi Kook Street, "a horrific spectacle" involving "exhausted people, dirty children, and limitless hatred for a city that's alienating itself." At Geulat Yisrael Synagogue, a large building and an important locale for religious services in Tel Aviv, IDPs were housed in the spacious sanctuary, the women's gallery, and the side rooms. Only two faucets were available to them, leaving no possibility of showering or maintaining a minimum level of hygiene. The townspeople "see this every day with their own eyes and quake with fear about what these conditions may cause."[165]

The municipality's steadfastness against the pressure did not emanate from a position of strength. The lack of housing opportunities for the swelling population of the homeless was a material problem that no pressure from interest groups could solve. After four months of futile efforts, an upturn in break-ins drove Alperin to the verge of despair: "They're invading everything: private homes, workshops, cellars, laundry rooms, between pillars of apartment buildings, etc., etc."[166]

The IDP Crisis: Over but Not Over

By the end of April 1948, once the Jewish conquest of Haifa was completed, a police station was established on Hamelechim Street in the Lower City; its first task was to impose order and, above all, to keep Jews and Arabs from looting.[167] Two days after the town was secured, the Situation Committee declared itself "the supreme civilian authority in Haifa" and defined its mission as the care of "all areas of civilian activity in coordination with the security forces." It promised to hand over its functions to the "competent authorities" gradually, once such were up and operating in town.[168] Two days later, the Jewish IDPs received a call to return to their homes.[169]

To prevent disarray in the confiscation of dwellings for immigrants, refugees, and miscellaneous institutions, it was decided to establish a special committee to deal with housing for both civilian-public and military needs.[170] Within a relatively short time, most of the IDPs—roughly 800 families in all—were sent back to their apartments or placed in housing in villages and neighborhoods vacated by their Arab residents.[171]

At first, some of the internally displaced refused to leave the private homes, cafés, civil-defense shelters, and laundry rooms that they had occupied during the intercommunal war. Also, some dwellings that IDPs left were seized by other IDPs or recently landed immigrants. Homeowners who returned to their dwellings sometimes encountered refusal to vacate them, bringing on violence. The Refugees Bureau sought to establish a public commission that would investigate each case and wield executive power to implement its decisions.[172]

Soon enough, in cooperation with the Haifa Refugees Committee, those involved managed to put the scheme into effect. Its successful and speedy implementation spared Haifa from a new potential catastrophe. Even before the last of the frontier-neighborhood IDPs could be removed from the schools, thousands of evacuees from farming communities in the Jordan River Valley streamed into the city. The children among them, along with their escorts, were placed in these venues.[173]

In Tel Aviv, some IDP centers began to empty out after approximately five months of uninterrupted crisis.[174] The solutions that had begun to appear, however, caused only more frustration among those left behind. Several despairing IDPs invaded the Inspection Department, and one of them assaulted Alperin—who, ironically, empathized with the attacker's distress: "I don't blame the man because I would have done the same if it were my family in the street."[175] New schools were overtaken by IDPs, and it was feared that studies would be disrupted after the Passover recess.[176]

On April 25, the Irgun launched a military operation to occupy Jaffa and eventually captured the mixed Manshiyye quarter. On the morning of the onset of the operation, the inhabitants of frontier neighborhoods who had remained in their homes were ordered to evacuate due to concern for their personal safety. Thus, as these neighborhoods indeed came under massive mortar attack, additional crowds of evacuees streamed toward the center of town.[177] On April 30, the villages of Salameh and Yazour, along the southeastern sector of the Jaffa–Tel Aviv frontier, were captured. Convoys of Arab refugees continued to stream eastward by motor vehicle and on foot along the Tel Aviv–Jaffa boundary as machine-gun rounds spattered the frontier neighborhoods and the military positions that had been set up in them.[178] On Saturday, Arab forces launched an offensive from Abu Kabir against Jewish-held positions at Giv'at Herzl in Tel Aviv, using automatic weapons and mortars.[179] With this, dozens of Jewish families joined the population of those in fleeing.[180]

On May 1, after about a week of intensive fighting, quiet descended on the Tel Aviv–Jaffa border area under an agreement with the British Army that allowed the latter to place forces in Manshiyye and make minor adjustments in the deployment of positions in the village.[181] The next day, the Tel Aviv Haganah commander declared the Arab parts of Manshiyye and Salameh a protected military zone, off-limits to all unauthorized persons.[182]

On May 12, the emergency committee that represented the Arab inhabitants of Jaffa met with the commander of Haganah forces in Tel Aviv in an attempt to reach a modus vivendi on the basis of the declaration of Jaffa as a noncombatant city. The commander advised them of the terms and allowed them to study them and respond.[183] Jaffa surrendered the next afternoon, and representatives of the emergency committee signed the accord.[184]

As the Arab outflow from Jaffa continued,[185] municipal officials began to weigh the return of the Jewish IDPs to the frontier areas. The conquest of Salameh, whence many of the attacks on Jewish frontier localities had originated, made it possible to send IDPs from the Hatikva, Ezra, and Yad Eliyahu quarters back to their homes.[186]

In late May, even though the city was absorbing a series of aerial bombardments, Alperin was finally able to report a significant decrease in the refugee population. Estimating the total number of IDP families, Alperin came up with some 1,100 and concluded that more than 1,500 had already gone home.[187] He expressed his hope that the rest would begin to do the same within a few days. A written directive was sent to the IDP centers, and an appeal was made to those living in areas where the hostilities had waned. Those who had resided at the edge of Manshiyye were not urged to return at this time.[188]

The challenge of one crisis had passed. However, its protagonists—the newly housed IDPs and the municipal and security authorities—would clash again in an attempt to ensure the attainment of their respective goals. The residents now focused on the revitalization of their old and new neighborhoods, whereas the representatives of the authorities, municipal and military, sought to complete the takeover of the areas previously under Arab control.[189]

The proclamation of statehood did little to change the reality on the ground. Gradually, however, it led to the entry of new players and the re-equilibration of forces between representatives of the pre-state local authorities (the community councils in Haifa and Jerusalem), the much more empowered municipality in Tel Aviv, and the institutions of the state, which had begun to make initial inroads in the urban centers. The refugee committees and the neighborhood panels (those of neighborhoods whose inhabitants had been displaced or resettled) did not disappear. They remained operative in the coming months, finding their way in the new organizational structure that the representatives of the state had just entered. The struggle now focused on regulating and institutionalizing the status of the new residents of the neighborhoods and villages to which they had been relocated, as opposed to daily survival in provisional centers. Interestingly, however, in most cases the people behind the associations identified themselves on the basis of the displacement experience that they had undergone. Many of them pointedly preserved their organizations' names, which included words that highlighted the experience of refugeeism—an ordeal that created a basis for organization both in political terms and in the associational entrepreneurs' collective identity.

Notes

1. Moshe Naor, *On the Home Front: Tel Aviv and Mobilization of the Yishuv in the War of Independence* (Jerusalem: Yad Izhak Ben-Zvi, 2009), 174–200; Arnon Golan, *Wartime Spatial Changes: Former Arab Territories within the State of Israel, 1948–1950* (in Hebrew) (Sede Boqer Campus: Ben-Gurion Research Center, 2001), 41–74, 98–133, 134–200, 236–56; Nurit Cohen-Levinovsky, *Jewish Refugees in Israel's War of Independence* (in Hebrew) (Sede Boqer Campus and Tel Aviv: Am Oved, 2014), 137–70.

2. Walter Kälin, "Guiding Principles on Internal Displacement," in *Studies in Transnational Legal Policy* 38 (American Society of International Law and the Brookings Institution, University of Bern Project on Internal Displacement, Washington, DC, 2008), 2.

3. Cohen-Levinovsky (*Jewish Refugees,* 12) counts roughly 25,000 in Jerusalem, 18,000 in Tel Aviv, 5,000 in Haifa, and 11,000 in rural areas.

4. Naor, *On the Home Front;* Golan, *Wartime Spatial Changes.*

5. Nurit Cohen-Levinovsky, *Jewish Refugees,* 137–70.

6. Stéphane Audoin-Rouzeau and Annette Becker, *Understanding the Great War* (New York: Hill and Wang, 2003), 84; Peter Gatrell, "Refugees and Forced Migrants During the First World War," in *Immigrants and Minorities* 26, no. 1/2 (2008): 82–110; Tammy M. Proctor, *Civilians in a World at War, 1914–1918* (New York: New York University Press, 2010).

7. Gatrell, "Refugees and Forced Migrants," 92; Stefan Goebel, "Schools," in *Capital Cities at War: Paris, London, Berlin, 1914–1919: A Cultural History, Vol. 2,* Jay Winter and Jean-Louis Robert, eds. (Cambridge: Cambridge University Press, 2007), 207.

8. Marc Vincent and Birgitte Refslund Sørensen, eds., *Caught between Borders: Response Strategies of the Internally Displaced* (London: Pluto, 2001).

9. Naor, *On the Home Front,* 173–4.

10. Report of the General Service, Israel Defense Forces Archives (hereinafter: IDFA), 140-8275-1949, April 7, 1948.

11. Benzion Nahmias, *Tel Aviv as a Front and Its Commander, Michael (James) Ben-Gal* (in Hebrew) (Tel Aviv: Friends of Haganah, 1998), 161. See also "From Today's News—Frontier Neighborhoods of Tel Aviv," IDFA, 136-8275-1949, December 6, 1947.

12. Benny Morris, *The Birth of the Palestinian Refugee Problem, 1947–1949* (Cambridge: Cambridge University Press, 1988).

13. Unsigned note to Taneh (code name for the Intelligence unit of the Haganah), re: Arab houses on the borders being used by Arab marksmen to fire continually into Jewish neighborhoods, IDFA, 136-8275-1949, December 9, 1947.

14. "Bombs, arson, stabbings, and gunfire in Haifa," *Davar,* December 8, 1947, 1.

15. Arnon Golan, "The Jewish Refugees in the War of Independence" (in Hebrew), *Contemporary Jewry* 8 (1993): 220.

16. Moshe Ehrenwald, "Civilians in the Northern Frontier Neighborhoods of Jerusalem," in *Civilians at War: Studies on the Civilian Society During the Israeli War of Independence* (in Hebrew), Mordechai Bar-On and Meir Chazan, eds. (Jerusalem and Tel Aviv: Yad Izhak Ben-Zvi, 2010), 150–77.

17. Golan, "The Jewish Refugees," 219.
18. Ibid., 220.
19. Yosef Ulitsky, *From Troubles to War: Episodes in the History of the Defense of Tel Aviv* (in Hebrew) (Tel Aviv: Haganah Headquarters Publishing House, 1951), 90.
20. "Log of Events," Kiryati, IDFA, 135-8275-1949, December 9, 1947.
21. Golan, *Wartime Spatial Changes*, 78.
22. List of refugee concentrations, accommodating refugees from the frontier, Tel Aviv Municipal Archives (hereinafter: TAMA), 16/156, December 14, 1947.
23. *"Be-shulei ha-devarim:* The Outcasts in Tel Aviv," *Davar,* December 7, 1947, 6.
24. Naor, *On the Home Front,* 178.
25. Decisions of the Sixth Council, Meeting 643, TAMA, December 7, 1947.
26. Naor, *On the Home Front,* 178.
27. "Log of Events," Kiryati, report from representatives of refugees in Kiryat Meir about armed Arab attack and reports about gunshots in the direction of the refugee camp near Sumayil, IDFA, 135-8275-1949, December 11, 1947.
28. Refugee Housing Department to L. A. Zelikowicz, Director of Housing Department, TAMA, 16/156, December 12, 1947.
29. Report of the General Service, IDFA, 140-8275-1949, April 7, 1948; the report mentions the prevention of an incursion at Bialik School on December 25, 1947.
30. Decisions of the Sixth Council, Meeting 647, TAMA, January 4, 1948.
31. Notice to Refugees, Circular no. 1, TAMA, 4/21a, Container 593, January 4, 1948.
32. "Making Arrangements for the Refugees in Haifa," *Davar,* December 10, 1947, 4.
33. My references to "Jewish community institutions in Haifa" and "heads of the Jewish community in Haifa" include two entities: the Community Council and the municipal Situation Committee. As Anat Kidron notes, both qualified as the "leadership of the Jewish public" in Haifa because in many cases, the same people sat on both panels. Despite the official division of labor between these entities, in this chapter I treat them as one and the same because in their activities and positions, they reflected the stance of the "institutional" local public leadership at large. See Anat Kidron, "The Committee of the Jewish Community in Haifa and Its Role in the Struggle to Shape Haifa's Civilian Character" (in Hebrew), in *Civilians at War,* Bar-On and Chazan, eds. (2010), 344, 349–50.
34. Report on Refugees Bureau Operations, Hebrew Community Council (Situation Committee), Haifa Municipal Archives (hereinafter: HMA), ID 4765 (File 00235/6), December 1, 1947–June 30, 1948.
35. Minutes of Situation Committee meeting, HMA, ID 5189 (File 00259/1), December 25, 1947.
36. Ibid.
37. Ibid.; Kidron, "The Committee of the Jewish Community in Haifa," 349–50.
38. Minutes of Situation Committee (small quorum) meeting, HMA, ID 5189 (File 00259/1), January 5, 1948. Several days later, this entity was expanded and renamed the Refugees Bureau. Kidron, "The Committee of the Jewish Community in Haifa," 333.
39. Minutes of Situation Committee (small quorum) meeting, January 5, 1948.
40. Ibid.
41. Ibid.
42. Situation Committee housing panel to Jerusalem Community Council, Jerusalem Municipal Archives (hereinafter: JMA), 4589/12, May 4, 1948 (review of housing panel

activities, December 1947 to date of report). Consensual arrangements between Jews and Arabs appeared in different stages of the intercommunal war (e.g., in an arrangement concerning housing in Jamusin, a village on the outskirts of Tel Aviv). (See pp. 43–46.)

43. Ehrenwald, "Civilians in the Northern Frontier Neighborhoods of Jerusalem," 156.
44. Ibid., 157.
45. Cohen-Levinovsky, *Jewish Refugees*, 145.
46. Maccabi Neighborhood Committee to Tel Aviv Mayor, TAMA, C 4/2209, December 12, 1947; details from interview with Yosef Cohen, Maccabi neighborhood representative, TAMA, C 4/2209, December 14, 1947 (3:00 p.m.); letter from Maccabi Barracks Neighborhood Cooperative Association to Eliezer Perlson, TAMA, C 4/2209, December 28, 1947.
47. Yehezkel Shoshani to Tel Aviv Mayor, TAMA, A 4/10, December 16, 1947.
48. "Tel Aviv—Residents of Frontier Neighborhood Demand Cancellation of Curfew," *Davar*, December 22, 1947, 3.
49. "Tel Amal Neighborhood Committee and Local Situation Committee," *Davar*, January 23, 1948, 9.
50. Summation of meeting with Yad Eliyahu neighborhood security committee (demobilized soldiers), IDFA, 49-321-1948, December 30, 1947.
51. Hebrew Neighborhoods Bloc in Southern Jerusalem to Jerusalem Hebrew Community Council, JMA, 4589/18, December 29, 1947.
52. Dromi (code name of Shalom Dror, commander of one of Etzioni Brigade' battalions) to Hashmonai (code name for Haganah intelligence in Jerusalem), report on events in Area 1, IDFA, 350-2644-1949, January 6–7.
53. Ernst Peretz to Peretz/Hashmonai, Daily Report, IDFA, 350-2644-1949, January 8–9, 1948.
54. Talpiot and North Talpiot Situation Committee to Dov Yosef, JMA, 4589/18, January 12, 1948.
55. Ibid.
56. Ibid.
57. Talpiot and North Talpiot Situation Committee to Dov Yosef, JMA, January 20, 1948.
58. Ernst Peretz to Peretz/Hashmonai, Daily Report, IDFA, 350-2644-1949, January 8–9, 1948.
59. Ibid.
60. Moshe Naor, *Social Mobilization in the Arab-Israeli War of 1948: On the Israeli Home Front* (London and New York: Routledge, 2013), 156.
61. "Tel Aviv—Taking Action for the Refugees," *Davar*, December 22, 1947, 3.
62. Report on Refugees Bureau Activities, HMA, ID 4765, Container 00235/6, December 1, 1947–June 30, 1948.
63. Jerusalem Hebrew Community Council Newsletter, no. 3, JMA, J2 3800, Container 4589/19, January 30, 1948.
64. Dishon (code name of Moshe [Misha] Eidelberg) to Kiryati, "Hashahar Association—Tel Aviv and Vicinity," IDFA, 100-321-1948, March 7, 1948.
65. Report on Refugees Bureau Operations, HMA, ID 4765, Container 00235/6, December 1, 1947–June 30, 1948.
66. Naor, *Social Mobilization*, 156–7.

67. Minutes of joint meeting of WIZO, OWM, and a representative of the Social Relief Bureau, HMA, ID 79089 (File 237/20), December 30, 1947; minutes of Committee of Women's Organizations for Refugee Affairs meeting, HMA, ID 79089 (File 237/20), January 12, 1948. For more on the women organizations' encounter with the distress of different sectors in society and an analysis of their role as mediators between marginalized strata of society and center of political power, see source below and chapter 6.

68. Paula Kabalo, "Leadership Behind the Curtains: The Case of Israeli Women in 1948," *Modern Judaism* 28, 2008: 16–7.

69. Devora Nosovietzky, "Mothers in the Rear," *D'var ha-Po'elet* (*Davar* women's supplement), February 5, 1948.

70. Nehama Hoffman, "On the Agenda—Hosting Refugee Children," *D'var ha-Po'elet*, March 16, 1948. See also Naor, *Social Mobilization*, 157.

71. Naor, *On the Home Front*, 180–1.

72. Rieger, director of Tel Aviv Municipal Social Work Department, to Municipal Treasurer. TAMA, A 4/21, Container 593.

73. Nosovietzky, *D'var ha-Po'elet*, 12. See, for example, Rieger, director of Tel Aviv Municipal Social Work Department, to director of Blobstein Orphanage in Ramat Gan, TAMA, Division 4, Container 593 (File 21a), January 1, 1948.

74. "WIZO's Wartime Activities and Emergency Measures," Central Zionist Archives (hereinafter: CZA), F/2215/49, September 1948.

75. Sue Lautze and John Hammock (1996). Coping with aid capacity building, coping mechanisms and dependency, linking relief and development. Paper prepared for the UN Inter-Agency Standing Committee Sub-working Group on Local Capacities and Coping Mechanisms and the linkages between relief and development, Lessons Learned unit Policy and Analysis Division, Department of Humanitarian Affairs, UN, 1996, p. 3.

For elaboration on the crisis capabilities discussed in this study, see the introduction.

76. This assumption is based on testimonies about the establishment of umbrella entities that were predicated on local representative bodies.

77. Nothing is known about the identity of the "refugee committees" of which the council was composed. Clearly, however, the council was established on the basis of local auspices that had already defined themselves as representatives of people who had found refuge in a specific building or street.

78. Frontier neighborhood refugee emergency. Secretariat of General Council for Frontier Refugees, Tel Aviv, to Mayor Israel Rokach, TAMA, A 4/20, March 5, 1948; Golan, *Wartime Spatial Changes*, 79.

79. I am unable to determine the identity of this local leader. He may have been the future Mapai member of the Knesset who, from 1949 on, headed the Tel Aviv municipal Neighborhoods Department.

80. Haim Alperin to Eliezer Perlson, TAMA 4/20B, February 22, 1948.

81. David Remez to Eliyahu Rosian and Gabriel Naqibli, Refugees Bureau, Hebrew Community Council, HMA, ID 5677 (File 00289/3), December 17, 1947.

82. Meeting of Refugee Committee representatives, HMA, ID 5189 (File 00259/1), December 29, 1947.

83. Ibid.

84. Report on Refugees Bureau Activities, HMA, ID 4765 (File 00235/6), December 1, 1947–June 30, 1948.

85. Minutes of Situation Committee meeting, HMA, ID 5189 (File 00259/1), December 25, 1947.

86. Naqibli was born in Palestine to a Jewish family in the ancient village of Peqi'in; he was the grandson of Baruch Naqibli, rabbi and ritual slaughterer of that community. According to his son, Gabriel was a member of the Haganah. His personal background found expression in the confidence that he displayed in his contacts with the establishment.

87. Meeting with representatives of refugees' committee, HMA, ID 5189 (File 00259/1), December 29, 1947.

88. Ibid.

89. Yosef Yanai, "Schools and Haifa and Tel Aviv During the War," in *Civilians at War*, Bar-On and Chazan, eds. (2010), 100–103; "What's Being Done for Refugees in the Frontier Neighborhoods?," *Davar*, January 16, 1948; "To House the Refugees in Haifa," *Hamashkif*, January 28, 1948.

90. Minutes of Situation Committee (small quorum) meeting, HMA, ID 5189 (File 00259/1), remark by David Taneh, January 8, 1948.

91. Minutes of Situation Committee (small quorum) meeting, January 8, 1948.

92. Minutes of Situation Committee (small quorum) meeting, January 13, 1948.

93. Minutes of Situation Committee (small quorum) meeting, January 8, 1948.

94. Minutes of Situation Committee (small quorum) meeting, January 13, 1948.

95. "Haifa: What's Being Done for Refugees in the Frontier Neighborhoods?" *Davar*, January 16, 1948, 9.

96. "*Be-shulei ha-devarim*: Frontier Refugees in Haifa," *Davar*, January 25, 1948, 4.

97. "Haifaites!," leaflet signed by United Committee of Haifa Refugees, HMA, ID 5677 (File 00289/3), January 25, 1948.

98. Ibid.

99. Ibid.

100. Ibid. See Orit Rozin's overview on immigrants in the first years of statehood. Rozin defines the demand to be heard as a "positive right." Orit Rozin, *A Home for All Jews: Citizenship, Rights and National Identity in the New Israeli State* (Waltham, MA: Brandeis University Press, 2016), loc. 2610.

101. Letter United Committee of Haifa Refugees, David Vogel, Arye Seidner, Moshe Musseri, and David Cohen, to Haifa Hebrew Community Council, HMA, ID 5677 (File 00289/3), February 3, 1948.

102. Ibid.

103. Report on Refugees Bureau Activities, HMA, ID 4765, Container 00235/6, December 1, 1947–June 30, 1948.

104. Rosenbaum, Organization of Hoteliers, Restaurateurs, and Café Owners in Haifa and Vicinity to Situation Committee, HMA, ID 5655 (File 00287/7), February 26, 1948.

105. Z. Carmi, head of Education Department, to Dr. Ben-Yehuda, director of Kenesset Yisrael Education Department, HMA, ID 4606 (File 00228/4), January 28, 1948.

106. "Haifa: About the Refugee Housing Program," *Davar*, February 25, 1948, 3.

107. Ibid.

108. Car bombs against the Jewish Yishuv were prepared in garages blown up in Haifa. *Davar*, March 1, 1948, 2; Tamir Goren, *The Fall of Arab Haifa in 1948* (in Hebrew) (Sede Boqer Campus: The Ben-Gurion Research Institute for the Study of Israel and Zionism, 2006), 116, 120; "Fourteen Arabs Killed and Dozens Wounded in Explosion in Haifa," *Davar*, March 4, 1948, 1.

109. Minutes of Situation Committee (small quorum) meeting, Abba Khoushy Archive (hereinafter: AKA), Situation Committee Correspondence, Minutes, and Reports, 1354631, A1/59:3, March 8, 1948.

110. Handwritten letter signed by M. A. Nissan and D. Peleg [apparently], no addressee noted, HMA, ID 5677 (File 00289/3), February 27, 1948. The members of this committee were Meir Azulai, Avraham Levi, and Haim Shehori. (Nothing about their professional or public activity, before or after the war, is known.) The control committee that they set up was composed of Shlomo Shalom and Moshe (Moise) Cohen (about whom, too, no information is available); Letter, Mount Carmel Refugee Camp Committee to Situation Committee of Haifa Community Council, HMA, March 16, 1948.

111. The members who received authorization to do this were Shimon Gavon, Shosha Aziz (or Izuz), Albert Mishan, Yaakov Stolzberg, Moshe Azar, and Avraham Suleiman. Handwritten letter, United Committee of Haifa Refugees to Situation Committee of Haifa Hebrew Community Council, HMA, ID 5677 (File 00289/3), February 29, 1948.

112. Ibid.

113. Handwritten letter, Meir Nissan to Situation Committee, HMA, ID 5677 (File 00289/3), February 28, 1948.

114. Resolutions of United Committee of Haifa Refugees, HMA, ID 5677 (File 00289/3), March 20, 1948.

115. "An Industrial Zone in the 'No Man's Land' of Neve Shalom," *Davar*, March 5, 1948, 5.

116. A. M. Chajes, Modern Flour Mill, to Security and Defense Headquarters, Tel Aviv, IDFA, 88-321-1948, February 15, 1948. Civil Guard Weekly Review, IDFA, 49-321-1948, March 5, 1948.

117. Alperin to Rokach, TAMA, 4/20 A, March 5, 1948.

118. Golan, *Wartime Spatial Changes*, 82; municipal secretary to secretary of Hapoel Hamizrachi, February 20, 1948; Zelikowicz to municipal secretary, March 30, 1948; Nadivi to Many, TAMA, 4/20 A, April 2, 1948.

119. General Council for Frontier Refugees Secretariat, Tel Aviv, to Rokach, signed by Rahamim Shalom and Hadi Menahem, TAMA, 4/20 A, March 31, 1948.

120. Alperin to Municipal Secretariat, TAMA, 4/20 C, April 14, 1948.

121. Polanim (Code name for Guard Force) to Tsefoni (code name of Shmaya Bekenstein, commander of Tel-Aviv Northern front), referring to a meeting that took place on January 18, 1948, IDFA, 151-8275-1949.

122. Tsefoni to Kiryati, January 26, 1948.

123. Tsefoni to Kiryati, IDFA, 151-8275-1949, January 28, 1948; Yam (Tsefoni) to the regional intelligence officer, (report on meeting with villagers from Jamusin), IDFA, 151-8275-1949, January 24, 1948.

124. Golan, *Wartime Spatial Changes*, 81–2.

125. Jamusin tenants committee to Perlson, TAMA, 4/20 A, February 22, 1948.

126. Alperin to Perlson, TAMA, 4/20 B, January 22, 1948; Kiryati to Acting Mayor, IDFA, 151-8275-1949, March 2, 1948.

127. Kerem Hatemanim Committee to Rokach, TAMA, 4/2209 C, March 9, 1947; Kerem Hatemanim (Karton) committee to Rokach, April 18, 1948.

128. Golan, *Wartime Spatial Changes*, 84. See also letter, Jamusin Village Committee to Alperin, TAMA, 4/20 C, May 3, 1948.

129. Jamusin Village Committee to Alperin, TAMA, 4/20 C, May 3, 1948.

130. Ibid.

131. Naor, *Social Mobilization*, 161–9.
132. Minutes of Chamber of Commerce Executive Committee meeting, Tel Aviv Chamber of Commerce Archives (hereinafter: COCA), book of minutes of Executive Committee meetings, December 24, 1947.
133. Dr. M. Pomerantz to Jerusalem Community Council, JMA, Community Council, Container 4589, Serial No. 18, CZA, 3800/1, Jerusalem Homeowners Association, January 5, 1948.
134. Dr. M. Pomerantz, to National Committee administration, Jerusalem, JMA, Container 4589, Serial No. 18, CZA, 3800/1, January 21, 1948.
135. A. Henigman, central committee of Association of Homeowners in Palestine, to Tel Aviv Municipality, TAMA, Division 4, File 20a, Container 593, February 1, 1948. See also letter from Sa'adia Shoshani, chair of central committee of the Association of Homeowners in Palestine, to Jewish Agency, IDFA, 86-6127-1949, February 1, 1948.
136. Medical Association to Municipal Housing Department, TAMA, 4/20 A, December 11, 1947.
137. Efraim Gosmann to Ben-Zion Argov, TAMA, 4/20 A, December 25, 1947.
138. Haifa Association of Artisans and Petty Industry to Situation Committee, HMA, File 00234/18 (4751), February 22, 1948.
139. Secretary of Builders Association to Mayor of Tel Aviv, TAMA, 4/20 A, December 18, 1947.
140. "What's Going on Around Us on January 22, 1948—For Members' Information," IDFA, 127-8275-1949.
141. Naor, *On the Home Front*, 192–3; TAMA, 4/20 A.
142. Naor, *On the Home Front*, 193.
143. Report on Refugees Bureau Operations, HMA, ID 4765 (File 00235/6), December 1, 1947–June 30, 1948.
144. Parents committee of Yavne Reali School and Haifa Religious High School—resolutions of parents' assembly, HMA, ID 228/8), January 25, 1948.
145. Naor, *On the Home Front*, 186.
146. "Tel Aviv: Takhkemoni Parents Demand Action," *Davar*, February 2, 1948, 3.
147. "Tel Aviv: Takhkemoni Children Go Back to School," *Davar*, February 8, 1948, 3.
148. Naor, *On the Home Front*, 187.
149. Zvi Bernstein, Hapoel Hamizrachi, to Acting Mayor Eliezer Perlson, TAMA, 4/20 A, January 9, 1948.
150. Naor, *On the Home Front*, 189–90.
151. Ibid., 190.
152. "*Min ha-tsad*—Accommodating the Refugees," *Davar*, January 18, 1948, 2.
153. Alperin to Eliyahu Hanavi Synagogue committee and Alperin to Shivat Tziyon National Religious Association, TAMA, 4/20 A, February 22, 1948.
154. Cohen-Levinovsky, *Jewish Refugees*, 158.
155. Arieh Kroch to Situation Committee, HMA, ID 4751 (File 00234/18), April 9, 1948.
156. "*Min ha-tsad*—Accommodating the Refugees," *Davar*, January 18, 1948, 2.
157. Public panel for the resolution of housing disputes to brothers Meir and Avraham Ozeri, Haifa, HMA, ID 5295 (File 00266/1), March 12, 1948.
158. Kiryati to Yoav, Talmon, Tal, IDFA, 88-321-1948, February 20, 1948.
159. Yitzhak Katz, secretary of Chamber of Commerce, to Rokach, TAMA, 4/20 C, April 2, 1948.

160. Zvi Gever, director of Association of Home and Property Owners, June 18, 1948. (The letter refers to the meeting that took place on April 20.)

161. Zvi Gever to Mayor Rokach, TAMA, 4/10 B, May 2, 1948. The document refers to remarks by Rokach at the meeting, which took place on April 20, 1948.

162. Zalman Shahor, chair of Tel Aviv Committee of Synagogues, via Shehori, to Rokach, TAMA, 4/20 B, March 18, 1948.

163. Dr. Neumann, chair of Tel Aviv branch of Hebrew Medical Association, and Prof. Klopstock, chair of Hygiene Committee, to Rokach, TAMA, 4/20 A, March 29, 1948.

164. Committee of Tel Aviv Workers Quarters G to Mayor, TAMA, 4/20 B, April 23, 1948; Committee of Workers Quarters E–F to Rokach, TAMA, 4/20 B, April 26, 1948; tenants of commercial building on Nahalat Binyamin Street to Mayor, TAMA, 4/20 B, April 12, 1948.

165. "Epidemic Hazard if Refugees are Not Housed: Thousands of Refugees Live under Sanitary Conditions that endanger Tel Aviv," *Yedioth Ma'ariv*, March 22, 1948, 2.

166. Alperin to Rokach, TAMA, 4/20 A, March 31, 1948.

167. Haifa Chief of Police to commander of Haganah forces in Haifa, AKA, 1356844, A1/103-5, May 1, 1948.

168. Summary of discussions at meeting of Situation Committee executive board, AKA, 1354631, A1/59:3, April 24, 1948.

169. "To Our Refugee Brethren," leaflet from Sephardi Community Council in Haifa, HMA, ID 4610 (File 00228/7), April 26, 1948. Refugees from frontier and mixed neighborhoods of Haifa, Haifa area commander, April 26, 1948.

170. Teneh, decisions of Situation Committee executive board at its meeting on May 10, 1948, AKA, 1354631, A1/59:3.

171. Overview of Refugees Bureau Operations in May 1948, HMA, ID 5815 (File 00298/4).

172. Ibid.

173. Report on Refugees Bureau Activities, HMA, ID 4765, Container 00235/6, December 1, 1947–June 30, 1948.

174. Alperin to Great Synagogue management, April 14, 1948; Alperin to Club Kadima management, April 14, 1948; Alperin to Tel Aviv Municipal Secretary, TAMA, 4/20 B, April 14, 1948.

175. Transcript of telephone call, Alperin to Tel Aviv Municipal Secretary, TAMA, 4/20 A, April 18, 1948.

176. Rosenbaum to Alperin, TAMA, 4/20 C, April 29, 1948.

177. *Min ha-na'ase* (Log of events), "Around Us: Irgun Operation in Tel Aviv and Its Outskirts," IDFA, 127-8275-1949, April 25, 1948.

178. *Min ha-na'ase* (Log of events), "Around Us: Conquest of Salameh and Yazour on the Jaffa-Tel Aviv Border," IDFA, 127-8275-1949, April 30, 1948.

179. "Salameh and Yazour are Occupied," *Davar*, May 2, 1948, 2.

180. Alperin to Mayor, TAMA, 4/20 B, May 2, 1948.

181. *Min ha-na'ase* (Log of events), IDFA, 127-8275-1949, May 1, 1948.

182. *Min ha-na'ase* (Log of events), order from Tel Aviv area commander, IDFA, 127-8275-1949, May 2, 1948.

183. *Min ha-na'ase* (Log of events), "Around Us: Jaffa Sues for Peace," IDFA, 127-8275-1949, May 12, 1948.

184. *Min ha-na'ase* (Log of events), "Around Us," IDFA, 127-8275-1949, May 13, 1948.

185. *Min ha-na'ase* (Log of events), "Around Us: On the Jaffa-Tel Aviv Borders," IDFA, 127-8275-1949, May 3, 1948.

186. "Refugees' Problems, Deliveries, and Robberies—At the Tel Aviv Town Council," *Davar*, May 3, 1948, 3.

187. Alperin to Mayor, TAMA, 4/20 C, May 21, 1948.

188. Alperin to Mayor, TAMA, 4/20 A, May 3, 1948.

189. *Min ha-na'ase* (Log of events), "How to Recognize Enemy Aircraft, IDFA, 127-8275-1949, May 15, 1948.

2

ECONOMIC WAR AND WAR ECONOMY

The Challenge to Business and Commercial Life

THIS CHAPTER TURNS THE SPOTLIGHT ONTO THE COMMUNITY of Jewish merchants and artisans, large and small, in Mandate Palestine and nascent Israel. It was a highly diverse socioeconomic population, with some members resting on stable economic foundations and possessing resources of their own and others barely making ends meet with the help of their small or family businesses. Despite this wide variance, many businesspeople had to cope with difficulties of a similar nature. The state of emergency took a particularly harsh toll on those whose livelihood depended on sustaining a business at a fixed location, as well as the kind that needed supplies of raw materials, basic commodities, and foreign currency for their diurnal operations. Commercial life predicated on free-market principles and routine import and export of goods sustained grave damage due to the war-induced crisis, placing the survivability of the merchant population, in all its complexions and strata, at risk.

This chapter looks into the coping mechanisms that the commercial community adopted in the first stage of the war. At that time, in addition to existential hardships flowing from the shortage of commodities and the disruption of supply, businesspeople had to adjust to the transition in governance from the British Mandate to the institutions of the Israeli state in the making. The chapter begins by reviewing the economic policies the British Mandate government invoked and their implications for management of the war economy by the Zionist National Institutions on the one hand and small and medium businesses in the Yishuv on the other. The organizing concept of the chapter is *occupational identity*—a common denominator around which persons of kindred economic interest gathered to assure the minimal conditions for their survival. The main intention of this chapter is to examine these proprietors' patterns of association at two levels of action. In the first, business owners associated under the umbrellas of large organizations in order to secure their status vis-à-vis the policy makers. The second level concerns small and local initiatives by persons who, sharing an economic interest, took bottom-up action to survive in view of the chronic shortages of goods, the unrelenting price controls, and specific damage to a given commercial sector. The chapter concludes with an overview of the war on the black market and on profiteering. Here, the involvement of civil organizations in the judicial system that was set up to wage this struggle is examined from two perspectives: that of those who fought the phenomenon and that of those accused of transgressing.

The economic policies of the Mandate government throughout most of that institution's term were typically laissez-faire until World War II, when the government's objectives shifted abruptly to mobilizing resources for the war effort and assuring the welfare of the civilian population. The result was far-reaching intervention in the economy, including the repeal of freedom of commerce and international payments in most systems of production.

Shortly after World War II broke out, the government froze inventories of vital commodities and empowered itself to set priorities for their use, to control foreign currency and its use, and to control prices. Its main lever of involvement was its control of imports, including, in greater part, food, livestock feed, and raw materials. This policy, partly carried forward in the years after World War II, directly affected the organization of the Yishuv's war economy during the War of Independence and was manifested in many operations that the Yishuv leadership undertook as early as the intercommunal war period.[1] The British policy also gave the National Institutions the legal and administrative infrastructure with which they could manage a centralized emergency economy.[2]

Governments at war do tend to intervene in setting prices, to the obvious disadvantage of those whose livelihood depends on selling price-controlled goods. For some of those who engage in buying and selling, war occasions dire uncertainty. For others, of course, it affords an opportunity to profit immensely as supplies of staples and raw materials shrink. Since one expression of this shortage is the development of a black market, outlaw traders may profiteer on an enormous scale. Merchants also suffer from the decline in customers' purchasing power and, of course, from military induction, which stymies their ability to run their businesses, which are often sole proprietorships.[3]

Studies on the hardships of daily life during World War I reveal that citizens do not believe they can or should pay an unlimited price for victory or peace.[4] In fact, it is claimed that at least two identities coexist in the minds and behavior patterns of ordinary people in wartime: national identity and occupational identity, the latter relating to their profession and employment.[5]

Determining an occupational identity that persists and influences behavior patterns and demands in wartime is a valid goal in respect to middle-class circles and private businesspeople whose livelihood is impaired by the war. In Israel's War of Independence, such an identity was blatantly evident in these circles specifically. The reason was that in contrast to the country's manufacturing economy, much of which belonged to the cooperative sector and based itself on regulated labor relations, merchants and artisans were susceptible to harm from war-induced economic ups and downs. The discussion that follows will bring this to light by tracing their collaborative responses, organizational initiatives, and attempts to protect and promote their interests vis-à-vis local and national authorities.

As Mandate rule disintegrated during the months of the intercommunal war, the National Institutions sought to impose an emergency economic regime that would allow them to organize food supplies and staples under a system of rationing and price controls.[6] Since the vestiges of British rule crimped the National Institutions' ability to apply such regulations, the Yishuv leadership went about it on the foundations of municipal government and the institutions of the Histadrut (labor) and private economies. In this context, it made consistent efforts to expand the swath of economic representation—as manifested, for example, in the wish to co-opt the Histadrut and private economies into the Emergency Economic Council that was intended to serve as an economic central command during the war.[7]

The Histadrut enjoyed quasi-governmental status, its elected representatives routinely taking part in decision-making entities. The private economy was less represented in these forums; it was more fragmented and scattered, and its members' needs often clashed with each other. Due to unbridgeable political and economic disputes, the intent to establish an emergency economic central command failed, even though both top-down and bottom-up efforts were invested in the cause.[8]

Consequently, a variety of representative bodies stepped forward to defend the private economy's interests vis-à-vis the National Institutions that managed the economic front in the war. Some were long-standing, institutionalized, and well connected; others reflected the vicissitudes of the time and had been set up pursuant to the secession or independent organizing of one economic branch or another that had been inseparable from some broader association until the war. These interest groups spoke on behalf of war casualties of a peculiar kind. Tracking their activity, one discovers, first of all, the deeper strata of the economic distress that the war had brought about. Beyond this, their activity reveals channels of mediation that interested individuals and groups in the Yishuv could invoke in their confrontation with the pre-state National Institutions. In a society where political affiliation was a familiar and legitimate path to influence, these associations represented their members' existential interests and not necessarily an all-embracing, comprehensive ideological worldview.

Interest Groups and Economic Policy-Making in Wartime—The National Level

An early initiative that sought to integrate representatives of professional organizations into economic policy-making in view of changes expected from the termination of the British Mandate and progress toward sovereignty occurred in late November 1947, even before the UN General Assembly adopted its partition resolution. Representatives of professional organizations in the private sector were invited to take part in an advisory committee on trade that the Jewish Agency Department of Trade and Industry set up. Participating in the inaugural meeting of this body were delegates from the Chamber of Commerce and the Association of Importers and Wholesalers in Palestine. The idea behind the panel was twofold: to help members of the Jewish Agency Executive who were responsible for economic affairs and to convey information about "the opinion, position, [and] wishes of circles that have an interest in the questions under discussion."[9] It was the very first meeting of this kind between the senior delegation of economic stakeholders and Yishuv policy makers, but the former left no doubt about their expectations of becoming part of the decision-making mechanism.[10]

A discussion on how to prepare for the accretion of stocks yielded various approaches. Whereas the head of the Jerusalem Chamber of Commerce proposed that his city's merchants be urged to stockpile goods themselves, others argued against individualized hoarding lest it lead to "mass eruption and panic," suggesting instead that the activity be regulated top-down by a "supreme institution" (i.e., a department or authority of the National Institutions).[11]

Members of the Tel Aviv Chamber of Commerce demanded an official and influential status on the committee. Some claimed that one of their own should serve as the deputy to Peretz Bernstein, head of the Department of Trade and Industry of the Jewish Agency.[12] Chambers of commerce had been established at the British authorities' initiative and functioned as members' organizations. Even though they acted autonomously in Tel Aviv, Haifa, and Jerusalem (and, until the intercommunal war began, in Jaffa as well), they cooperated under the Executive Committee of Chambers of Commerce and were often represented as a single entity vis-à-vis the authorities. Thus, the Tel Aviv–Jaffa Chamber saw itself as the representative of all merchants organized under chambers of commerce when it claimed the status of a policy maker and not only a nongovernmental or advisory player. The chamber expressed this stance by stating, "Trade [i.e., circles involved in trade] should demand its share in the Department from a *governing* perspective" (emphasis added). Therefore, the chamber believed it should insist on posting a deputy, as opposed to a mere "professional officer," to the committee as its representative. The chamber's own board, however, rejected this militant line and instructed members to bide their time because the matter concerned "provisional arrangements only."[13]

In its second meeting, the Advisory Committee turned its main attention to the state of food and fuel stocks. Mordechai Shatner, head of the Economics Department of the National Committee, described the difficulties that now beset the management of food supplies. While staples under British government control were recorded with the Food Supervision Department of the Mandatory administration, Shatner explained, the situation in stocks of other commodities was totally vague because they were in the hands of private merchants. Shatner did offer a conservative estimate of what was available: five to six weeks of food for people and livestock countrywide and only ten days' worth in Jerusalem. Therefore, he suggested that the committee strive to amass larger stocks of basic foods and that the merchants of Jerusalem join forces with the Hamashbir Hamerkazi cooperative, owned by the Labor Movement, in setting up a joint warehouse with a Jewish Agency subvention. In his approach, Shatner, the National Institutions representative, acknowledged the advantages of having delegates from the free market who would provide information that they possessed and the National Institutions officials lacked. Indeed, the Chamber of Commerce delegate shared inventory information with the rest of the Advisory Committee on the basis of his institution's investigation. Then, in view of this information and in a strong reflection of his commitment to those whom he represented, he requested import relief.[14]

The model that Shatner had in mind would leave trade in private hands but place it under the supervising and guiding umbrella of the National Institutions. Avraham Kahane, vice president of the Chamber of Commerce, found this disconcerting. While admitting that one could not rely solely on the private sector to assure sufficient stocks, he feared that "centralized buying" would impair "regular commerce."[15] As the debate wound down, the committee members were asked to submit a list of staples that could be imported outside the quotas, describe specific difficulties in importing foodstuffs, and present a program for the establishment of a central warehouse. Shatner expressed the hope that systematic contacts between the National Institutions and the entities that represented the community of merchants would continue.[16]

The merchants' delegates to the Advisory Committee were strongly urged by the National Institutions to mediate between the authorities and their ramified population of interested parties. They met, for example, with the "big grocers" and together worked up a list of vital foodstuffs that would later be shared with "the supreme institutions and the supervisor of food." Thus, a de facto "chain of command" came about from the grocers via their representative organization to the large trade organizations, ending at the Advisory Committee on Trade and the National Council.

The grocers judged the state of the stocks to be "all right; unless there's excessive hoarding, the stocks as they are will last until February." In respect to new import licenses, however, it was their impression that the Mandate government "won't make an effort to assure [adequate supplies of] staples."[17] This encounter between policy makers and people in the field, arranged through the mediation of the Chamber of Commerce, helped to define the goal—not to broaden the range of available commodities but to assure the continued issuance of import licenses so that basic items would continue to reach the country.[18] The consultation with the "field people" also softened the merchants' principled resistance to the formation of a central import agency. The wording adopted in this matter—the idea of "establishing a central company for the importation of vital foodstuffs during the transition period"—was favorably received and would soon be taken up for discussion.[19]

While the issue was pending, the Association of Importers and Wholesalers in Palestine launched an initiative involving the formation of a business firm, the Importers and Wholesalers Company in Palestine, Ltd., to handle all problems related to imports and distribution countrywide. The concept behind this was to give the firm the appearance of a public administration by co-opting representatives of two additional stakeholder organizations: wholesale merchants and the Chamber of Commerce. This, it was thought, would cement the new company's status as "an important player in regulating trade and setting prices."[20] The envisaged umbrella company would receive the merchants' import quotas and work with the institutions of state once the latter would take responsibility for imports. The firm was supposed to assure the share of private commerce in the import quotas.[21]

Even though the Importers and Wholesalers Company was the brainchild of the Yishuv importers' representative organization, and even though the Chamber of Commerce smiled upon the initiative, its members still had to give an accounting for their support of the "Import Monopoly Company," as one Chamber of Commerce veteran called it.[22]

The private initiatives notwithstanding, the National Institutions' tendency to intervene in import trade was not slow in manifesting itself. As Eliezer Kaplan, treasurer of the Jewish Agency, and Dr. Shaul Lifschitz, president of the Tel Aviv–Jaffa Chamber of Commerce, joined "a circle of friends for a glass of tea," the former expounded to the latter on the need to limit imports and create a mechanism "under the Jewish Agency" that would issue import licenses. Kaplan agreed to give the chamber limited entrée in this mechanism, within the framework of an advisory entity whose decisions would be accepted "if they fit the definition of the public welfare."[23]

The Yishuv's leading merchants were of course unsurprised by the surfacing of this question of import controls; their work, particularly with the Mandate government, had habituated them to it. However, the question of their collective involvement in the decision-making core—and the setting of limits to this involvement—had long been of concern to them and was an item on their agenda. Therefore, the leaders of the large organizations focused their attention on the responsibility of said advisory entity to allocate import licenses.[24] They agreed unanimously that the leading trade organizations—the Chamber of Commerce and the Association of Importers—should favor the establishment of the advisory entity and should join it.[25] Indeed, just a week later, Kaplan disclosed the intent to set up "an advisory economic committee under the emergency institutions." He clarified, however, that "*its power should be advisory and no more*" and stressed that both he and Bernstein were against giving it "broader powers."[26]

As the advisory committee went about its work, and perhaps in an attempt to coordinate the full set of economic actions and decisions that were needed in the transition period, discussions over the establishment of an emergency economic council—the Food and Supplies Board—commenced. The envisioned board would include, in addition to delegates from the National Institutions, representatives of all large economic entities in the Yishuv, private and cooperative alike, and local representative bodies including community councils and women's organizations—twenty-eight participants in all.[27] Those behind the move to broaden the economic delegature, Moshe Naor explains, were David Ben-Gurion and Kaplan, who sought to establish what one might call a war economic headquarters.[28] Underlying this gambit was Kaplan's premise that the Yishuv's civilian economic circles should be mobilized so that decisions on imports, trade, and price control could be made. Kaplan's expansionary approach, evidently shared by Ben-Gurion, ran into the opposition of circles in Ben-Gurion's party, Mapai, which frowned on the power that this entity would award to its middle-class non-Labor affiliates. Therefore, the Histadrut hurriedly set terms that would set its representation on the council at an assured minimum of 50 percent. In practice, almost every economic entity set up economic committees, introduced proposals for economic mobilization, and offered ideas about how to organize rationing and price-control mechanisms. The parallel existence of all these bodies accented the need for a cooperative arrangement among all levels of leadership—the National Institutions, municipal authorities, the Histadrut's economic constellation, and the private sector. Despite repeated efforts, however, the prospective partners were unable to surmount their differences, and the initiative never took off.[29]

A problem seemingly no less thorny concerned the extent of private-sector representation in decision-making bodies. While the cooperative sector clearly placed its deputation within that of the Histadrut and its central enterprises (Tnuva, Hamashbir Hamerkazi, and Solel Boneh), the private sector was badly fragmented. Thus, diverse entities, some organized on the basis of a specific economic branch and others on local foundations, demanded the right to participate in the policy-making organs and fumed loudly when their deputies were not invited.

Despite foot-dragging in the formation of the emergency economic council, or perhaps for this very reason, a new initiative now cropped up to assure information flow and coordination between the supreme institutions and the economic entities. The Economic Subcommittee (Subcommittee A) established a small forum to coordinate relations with the main bodies that represented the economic stakeholders. Centered in Tel Aviv, it included, in its innermost circle, the Chamber of Commerce, the Manufacturers Association, and the Histadrut, and in a more remote circle, the Artisans Center and the Middle Class Organization. The National Institutions' representative, Yitzhak Bavli, dealt with economic questions pertaining to the emergency and the transition period.[30] Bavli's message to the merchants was that the high institutions had no intention of meddling in trade; their only intention was "to help trade and industry ahead of the duties that they face." Among the problems Bavli listed as needing attention were stocks and supplies, crucial factories and warehouses on the firing lines, price controls, and assuring import-export activity in the event that military use of the ports would place these facilities off-limits for civilian trade.[31]

Where stocks and supplies were concerned, the subcommittee wrestled with a question of principle: Under what circumstances and to what extent should any provisional government be allowed to confiscate stocks for the Yishuv at large?[32] The panel also took up practical questions, defining what constituted stocks, setting minimum consumption of essential commodities, determining where stocks were located and how they were distributed around the country, and looking into possibilities of storage. In these and other matters, Bavli needed the cooperation of the economic stakeholders' representative bodies, with which he interacted on the basis of relevant areas of inquiry. In each of them, of course, the veteran private-sector business organizations—the Manufacturers Association, the Association of Importers and Wholesalers, and the Chamber of Commerce—were prominent.[33]

Amid all this, local public representatives, women's organizations, and economic interest groups partnered in the establishment of other entities. One such body was the Yishuv Supply Committee, which discussed the securing of stocks and prevention of profiteering.[34] At its first meeting, this panel addressed the need to draw up a list of foodstuffs for human consumption that were not under government control and livestock supplies that would have to be imported from then to year's end. Also discussing the need to plan the distribution of staples, the members concluded that municipal authorities should oversee the drafting of lists of consumers.[35] Yet another group began to operate at this time: the Experts Committee, established by the National Institutions to draw up a list of commodities that would be placed under public supervision and subjected to wholesale and retail price control.[36] None of these concurrent actions derailed the attempt to establish a supply committee. However, when this body finally held its first meeting and chose a representative subcommittee, it boasted only one deputy from the wholesale trade sector. The Chamber of Commerce grumbled about this and turned to Shatner, to no avail.[37]

Just then, the British government created a new situation by announcing the withdrawal of Mandate Palestine from the sterling bloc. The National Institutions accompanied this move with a unilateral measure of their own, setting aside the participatory democracy that they had tried to sustain to that point. [38]

Their concern was that the departing Mandate government would also walk off with the foreign reserves, creating a shortage of legal tender.[39] Haim Barkai terms the government's policy "chaos," explaining that it was a largely demonstrative measure and that "its immediate political purpose was to heighten economic uncertainty—and, accordingly, confusion."[40] Since import control was an important manifestation of British government involvement in Palestine,[41] the National Institutions hurriedly took steps that would secure their control of this sensitive domain, including the foreign reserves and their use. Thus, they rushed to announce the establishment of a Jewish Agency import-export department that would deal in "regulating and guiding foreign trade."[42] Any business that wished to import anything now had to approach the new department first, even though the Mandate government remained in power. To assure the implementation of this nearly unenforceable decree, the Jewish Agency executive stated that once the Mandate would expire, no import or export of goods would be allowed save with the department's prior approval.[43]

Thus, while preparing to petition the British authorities for a larger allocation of sterling for import purposes,[44] the leading merchants now had to contend with the establishment of an import-export department under the baton of the Yishuv's highest institutions. The department, imposed on them top-down, effectively circumvented the Advisory Committee, which had given economic stakeholders representation and had been expected to steward the process of setting up the department (and, from the perspective of private business circles, to assure their representation in the body that would hand down decisions on imports). Indeed, the representatives of the Situation Committee saw fit—for good reason—to apologize to the Chamber of Commerce and the importer delegates for "opening the Department without consulting with the Chamber and the other economic bodies." The government's announcement concerning import licenses, they explained to their peers, had forced the National Institutions to launch the new department preemptively; just the same, they would "welcome cooperation between the Chamber and the Association of Importers."[45] The merchants, however, had no intention of settling for cooperation or an advisory status. They considered themselves partners in policy-making, and many of them demanded demonstratively that their colleagues be annexed to the department or at least receive supervisory powers within the framework of the Advisory Committee.[46]

The president of the Chamber of Commerce reacted with greater militancy. He proposed that the chamber refrain from cooperating with the department until such time as the Advisory Committee would be established and activated. Many members seconded his view.[47] After argumentation, it was decided as a goodwill gesture to submit "the import applications [to the new Jewish Agency Department] on an exceptional basis" but not to continue doing so unless the Advisory Committee were established "in a composition and with the powers that would satisfy the community of merchants."[48] The Association of Importers and Wholesalers threw its weight behind the resolution later, assuring a unified front among the three representative entities of the wholesale sector.[49]

In addition to embittering the Jewish merchants by excluding them from the locus of decision- and policy-making,[50] the new procedure encumbered the process of obtaining import licenses and left the merchants fearful of severe cutbacks in the government's allocations of foreign exchange. This was the main reason for their opposition to the establishment of the new department, which, in addition to the awkwardness that it created, was staffed with professionally inexperienced bureaucrats. Its balky functioning led to lengthy queues and steadily escalating displeasure. Peretz Bernstein responded passionately to the merchants' announcement that they would no longer submit import applications in a centralized manner: "Your letter of February 29 caused me much anguish," he wrote. "I expected more understanding from the Chamber of Commerce."⁵¹ He then described the issue from the opposite perspective—Britain's unilateral ejection of Palestine from the sterling bloc three months before the end of the Mandate, the need to put the currency reserves to their worthiest use, and, in turn, the imperative of supervision and rapid response that prompted the decision to establish the department before the Advisory Committee was up and running.⁵² Essentially, however, Bernstein acceded to Lifschitz's demand and advised him that no further obstacles to the formation of the Advisory Committee existed.⁵³ The local chambers of commerce and the Association of Importers were asked jointly to post two deputies to the committee.⁵⁴

As for the composition of the committee, the formula adopted was that bruited by the Chamber of Commerce and delegates of the Association of Importers—two representatives for manufacturing, two for trade, and one for the cooperative sector.⁵⁵ In the meantime, pressure from the merchants and importers escalated, and grievances against the department for delaying the issue of import licenses amassed.⁵⁶ The work of the Supply Committee and the committee of experts also lagged, eliciting a threat from the Chamber of Commerce to suspend its cooperation with the department.⁵⁷

Succumbing to the pressure, Bernstein convened the Advisory Committee to the supervisor of stocks. Other participants in the meeting that ensued represented the defense forces, the National Institutions, and a welter of private trade, crafts, and manufacturing bodies. The engineer Yitzhak Bavli, of the Manufacturers Association, who in the meantime had been named supervisor of stocks for the Situation Committee, explained that the members of the Advisory Committee had been elected "on a personal basis; it is not intended that [they] should specifically reflect the views of the circles to which they belong."⁵⁸ Just the same, the conduct of the Chamber of Commerce's representative to the committee made it clear that the chamber was kept up to date and involved in guiding his activity and making sure that he expressed the chamber's positions officially.⁵⁹

The affair surrounding the Advisory Committee to the Import-Export Department aggravated the underlying suspicion that typified contacts between private-sector circles, foremost those involved in trade, and the National Institutions—soon to become the Israeli general-government sector. Behind the scenes, in fact, these matters had come up in the very first stages of the economic deployment. When Yitzhak Bavli was asked to draft a document containing an estimate of countrywide supplies of crucial commodities, he expected to obtain quantitative information from the economic entities associated with the private and cooperative sectors.[60] After meeting with their boards and committees, however, he deduced that even they could not force members "to divulge any part of their trade and business secrets."[61] The merchants and manufacturers, Bavli sensed, were implacably averse to sharing information about stocks and consumption "even with the highest institutions of the Yishuv." One of his first conclusions, therefore, was that the departments of the future Jewish government should make the centralization of information one of their prime duties and "should also be able to force individuals to reveal their business secrets."[62] For the time being, Bavli sought alternative ways to obtain a full picture that, although general, would be accurate enough for the Import Department to make its decisions on the basis of reliable reportage.[63]

The decision to name Arieh Shenkar, president of the Manufacturers Association, to the provisional government as an additional delegate from the General Zionists Party (the party that represented the middle class)[64] did not satisfy the large trade organizations and was ultimately rejected by Shenkar himself. Turning to Ben-Gurion on this account in a reflection of their self-perception as a sociopolitical sector and not only a group of economic stakeholders,[65] the organizations complained about not having found, among the candidates for the provisional government council, "even one who represents our public vis-à-vis these bodies."[66] Ben-Gurion, apprising them of the outcome of the Jewish Agency executive's discussion of their communication, reported that the executive had chosen not to grant representation to any economic organization, however large. "It seemed to the [National] Institutions that under the existing conditions, with the exception of the Sephardi community, only representatives of political organizations should be co-opted, as is the accepted practice in such institutions worldwide, it being assumed that most members of economic organizations belong to or vote for political parties."[67]

In addition to their effort to integrate into the economic policy-making bodies and obtain top-down recognition of their status as representatives of commerce as a distinct sector, the merchants' representative entities had to solve various bottom-up problems. Private proprietors often found themselves on the front lines after their commercial districts took direct hits. Examined below is the role played by the pattern of association on the basis of professional affiliation as a coping mechanism for these crises.

Self-Help: Advocating, Revitalizing, and Speaking Out

Casualties in Jerusalem: The Shama Commercial Center, Adjacent Streets, and Ben-Yehuda Street

The torching of Eliyahu Shama's commercial center in Jerusalem was a constitutive event that symbolized the eruption of the intercommunal war. It seems to have happened spontaneously, with an Arab mob breaking into the complex, setting fire to Jews' businesses, shattering their windows, and looting them. During the many hours of the mayhem, the British authorities sat on their hands except to prevent Haganah forces from entering the area and countering the rioters. Even before it was over, a representative body of merchants organized, visited the offices of the Jerusalem Community Council, and demanded that its leadership do something about it. One of those who spoke for the group, Meir Moshe Levi, accosted the councillors and snapped, "I hold you responsible because yesterday we wanted to move the merchandise out and they didn't let us." Members of the Haganah, it transpires, had visited the commercial center the previous evening and demanded that the merchants not clear out their shops and carry on as usual despite surging tension at the center, where Jewish-owned and Arab-owned businesses existed side by side.

Therefore, the Jewish tenants of the commercial center raged not only about the damage they had sustained but also about the reneging of undertakings by the central authorities, foremost the Haganah. "If you can't find a way to defend us, we'll do it ourselves," Meir Yosha[68] said, adding, "We pay taxes and we demand protection. We're willing to go to the [British] Commissioner."[69] Haim Salomon, chair of the Community Council, attempted to calm the tempers. While explaining that, yes, the British had promised to protect them, he noted, "This day is a failure for us. The fault, however, isn't ours and a warning about the situation that the whole world will hear should be sounded: to state publicly that we are willing to defend ourselves but are not being allowed to."[70]

The day after the riot, the merchants posted representatives to a Committee for the Reconstruction of the Commercial Center.[71] The National Institutions stepped in two days later. Two of their senior delegates, Izhak Ben-Zvi and Zerach Warhaftig, toured the charred compound and found forty torched shops and dozens of Jewish merchants loading the vestiges of their merchandise for relocation along with Arab merchants who were doing the same. The damage was estimated at half a million Palestine pounds. Some merchants were uninsured; many others carried coverage for fire but not for riots.[72]

The commercial center, which Menache Hai Eliachar called "the aorta of [Jerusalem] commerce," accommodated large and well-established businesses along with medium and micro merchants in all areas of trade. It abounded with familiar names on the local business scene. The center also had sundry workshops and, on the upper stories of most of its buildings, residential apartments.

The geographical location of the compound linked the Jewish neighborhoods in southern Jerusalem with those in the western part of town. Therefore, the impact of the attack on the center was much greater than the immediate economic blow to any particular business there. By implication, the shutdown of the center projected onto the strength of the Jerusalem Jewish community at large.[73]

Given the strategic location of the complex and the early timing of the incident, the various players responded quickly to the casualties' cries for help. Only three days after the events, an assembly took place at the Tel Aviv Hotel in Jerusalem with the participation, in addition to that of the affected merchants, of representatives of the National Institutions and the most important trade organizations: the Chamber of Commerce and the Jerusalem Labor Council.[74] The participants elected a committee to aid the casualties and promote the continued tenanting and reconstruction of the commercial center.[75] The living spirit behind this initiative was the aforementioned Menache Hai Eliachar—deputy chair of the Chamber of Commerce, a prominent figure in the municipal leadership, and the elected chair of the board of the casualties committee. In addition, the casualties themselves set up a subcommittee of experts and experienced members whom they chose on the basis of their areas of endeavor.[76] The Chamber of Commerce provided this entity with office space and secretarial services at no charge, sparing it much expense and giving it a stable basis on which it could act.[77]

A team that the committee appointed to investigate the damage presented its findings to the Yishuv committee for the casualties. Among other things, it sought £P50,000 in immediate support for what it estimated to be about one-third of the damage in ransacked merchandise only. This initial sum, the team explained, would serve as a first response and allow the casualties to restart their businesses and begin the rehabilitation work.[78] The appeal to the Yishuv committee was accompanied by a subtle threat:

unless the financial aid were forthcoming, the commercial center would be abandoned, shops on adjacent streets would also be affected, "and the borders of Jewish Jerusalem and the Yemin Moshe quarter and the Old City will empty out totally and the number of casualties will rise even more." The committee also warned about an upturn in despair and animus among the casualties toward "the defense forces that let them down and prevented them from acting on their own to save their property."[79]

These internal tensions and frustrations would resurface in every encounter between the casualties and the representatives of the Community Council and the National Institutions. Just the same, a large and accommodative body that would henceforth call itself the National Institutions and Chamber of Commerce Committee for Care of Casualties of the Events in Jerusalem took shape to represent the casualties' interests in an attempt to revitalize them and the commercial center with all possible celerity. To accomplish this, the merchants from the commercial center were given questionnaires on which they were asked to describe the damage they had sustained. The new committee counseled them on how to present complaints to the police and sue the British district commissioner for damage compensation. The complaints and suits were drawn up by the committee itself (via its lawyer, Yehuda Halevi); the drafting of damage assessments was divided among subcommittees.[80] Two weeks after the events, 111 people had filed complaints with the British police in Jerusalem.[81]

Despite the bustle that surrounded the work of the casualties' care committee in Jerusalem, the affected merchants continued to communicate intensively with other national players, venting their distress and warning against the national implications of the destruction of their premises. Their anguish was real; many had lost all their property, leaving high and dry numerous households that had depended on them, not to mention local residents who were now homeless. According to the numerical data that they gathered, the total tally of casualties of the incident—business owners, family members, and blue- and white-collar employees—exceeded 1,000, and the compensation that they demanded on this account was estimated at around £P240,000.[82]

The casualties' agents maneuvered among the various authorities, obtained permits to enter the closed compound, coordinated the onset of work in the area, and mustered initial funding from the National Committee. In their contacts with the authorities, the associates manifested their sense of self-efficacy in the authoritative tenor of their communication with the Yishuv-level entities, even setting a deadline for the honoring of their demands: "Therefore, we ask you to issue the requisite authorization this very morning."[83] To secure the National Institutions' support, the casualties committee also recruited the Citizens Union, a political entity that represented the urban middle class. Indeed, after representatives of the union described the merchants' distress to the Yishuv committee for the casualties, the latter decided to grant initial relief for immediate repairs and interest-free loans in urgent cases.[84]

In the meantime, the British maintained enough of a presence in the destroyed commercial center to limit free access to the area but not to prevent continued looting. Damage to shops and businesses persisted for weeks after the riot. The casualties committee sent protest letters to the British police—to no avail.[85]

At the meeting that finally took place with the head secretary of the Mandate government, Eliachar reported details about what had happened at the compound and "the merchants' demands to create the requisite conditions for their return to the location." Eliachar described the economic structure and demographic characteristics of the merchants, who, he said, had been living in the country "for more than centuries," and elaborated on the branches of trade and industry that had centered their activities at the complex and the disaster that this aggregate had sustained.[86] He described the financial damage and stressed the merchants' resolve to go back and revitalize the center. It was the authorities' duty, he advised the secretary, to compensate the victims and pay for the damage that had been caused to a lawful and law-abiding public. In addition, Eliachar presented a proposal from the casualties committee on how to secure the complex in the future: posting supernumerary police, establishing a local Jewish and British police station, banning the activities of the Arab guard detail at the approaches to the center, and sundry other practical suggestions that would beef up the British and Jewish presence and improve access to the affected area and adjacent city blocks. The head secretary promised to do only one of these things immediately—posting supernumeraries to the site. He would respond to the rest of it, he said, via the governor.[87]

The Mandate government responded to the merchants' demands in a manner that left much to be desired. It did not systematize security at the compound and appointed no Jewish supernumeraries, even though this had been promised explicitly. Therefore, Eliachar approached the district commissioner and again asked him to nail down the security arrangements before the British presence in the area would be terminated.[88] The district commissioner did not respond at first, and once he finally answered, he did so in vague terms. For our purposes, however, it is noteworthy that the letter indicates recognition of Eliachar's status as a local leader and, no less, of the nongovernmental association of commercial-center casualties as a body with which the Mandate government maintained direct contact. [89]

The casualty committee's activity was divided, as stated, between advocacy (attempts to mobilize authorities to provide financial and other relief) and internal measures—documenting the damage and promising to gather and process information for sharing with other stakeholders and assuring due compensation for the individual casualty. To take control of this activity, the committee appointed expert panels corresponding to the affected industries at the commercial center. A glimpse at the working procedures of the haberdashers' claims subcommittee attests to strong cooperation among all its members. Each victimized member was asked "to handle [his claim] on his own, following his conscience and discretion." The final compensation sum was set confidentially "in consideration of the opinion of all members and advisers of the committee." The method, the heads of the committee explained, was meant "to prevent grudges and complaints by anyone toward any particular member of the committee."[90]

All these efforts notwithstanding, a month passed, and the casualties remained in a dire state, their financial condition grim; some were forced onto the dole after losing their entire source of livelihood. The committee that represented them continued to badger high officials in the National Institutions and demand several tens of thousands of Palestine pounds in aid for revitalization work and easy loans. Representatives of the committee alleged that the British neglect of security at the commercial center reflected a "general worked-up plan" and insinuated a British intention of cutting off the bloc of Jewish neighborhoods in the southern part of town.[91] The casualties' approach emphasized the strategic importance of the compound: "The question facing the [National] Institutions is the fate of eastern Jerusalem."[92] Atop this foundation they developed their main message: reconstruction of the center as a comprehensive national objective as opposed to the narrow interest of those affected. "Construction against destruction, expansion against contraction, fortification and security against abandonment" was only one of the slogans that they put forward to express the grand goal that the reconstruction work should attain. The same was manifested in the casualties' willingness to set aside their personal needs for the general principle of revitalizing the compound by ceding their shops to influential public companies and entities such as Solel Boneh and Tnuva and allowing apartments to be built over their shops for demobilized soldiers' rent-free use. Concurrently, the casualties committee strove to arrange alternative premises for the destroyed businesses. The Romema neighborhood, in the western part of the city, was chosen for this purpose, and the Community Council's housing committee helped to reserve venues there. Only some of those affected, however, sank roots in the new location.[93]

At roughly this time, about a month after the commercial center had burned down and the area had deteriorated into a battlefield, the owners of businesses on adjacent streets realized that they, too, had to act to assure their survival. Thus, they called an assembly and elected a representative body that they titled, informatively, the Emergency Committee of Merchants and Residents on Princess Mary Street, Julian's Way, Storrs Avenue, and Central Building. This entity acted much as the committee of commercial-center casualties did; it gathered every scrap of information about property damage and its economic implications, produced a document that highlighted the residents' and merchants' personal distress and the national implications of the crisis, and circulated their report among various players. There was, however, a difference. The victims of the commercial center riot were represented by senior personalities who were firmly plugged into the Jerusalem leadership and connected with the National Institutions (e.g., Eliachar). Although they insisted that the complex be rebuilt and that the National Institutions take responsibility for ensuring this, they used somewhat cautious language. The newly organized group took a more militant line and posted a question mark over the future of the area.[94]

The businesses on the streets leading to the commercial center, nearly all of which were Jewish-owned, were in ghastly physical condition. Some had been damaged during the assault on the center; others had been savaged in the burglaries and looting that had followed. Business owners who attempted to carry on despite it all were also harmed because customers were avoiding the area in droves. Pressure on shop owners to stay open so as not to submit to violence was ineffective. The departure of many Jews who lived in the vicinity due to the deterioration of security also endangered these businesses' economic survivability. Hamekasher buses skirted the area.[95] Insurance companies canceled or refused to renew policies. Jewish guarding of the area was minimal and left parts of the vicinity unprotected.

All of this prompted the merchants and residents on the affected streets to ask an innocuous question: "Should we retain all of these territories no matter what, or should we not? Insofar as the answer is yes, we demand full assistance to revive the location . . . with Jewish pedestrians and traffic, constructive aid to the merchants who are sustaining the area, priority in orders from the [National] Institutions, pressure on the public to shop in this part of town, financial assistance in hiring people to guard [the area] at night, maximum beefing up of security forces, appropriate self-defense equipment when needed, and help in all matters that we find necessary."

The new association, like the committee of casualties of the commercial-center arson, stressed national recognition as a central stakeholder that instructed its members to keep their shops open despite the situation. It proclaimed its support of this response and of actions that would assure a steady flow of pedestrian and vehicular traffic—accompanied, however, by "appropriate security" that would make it possible "to maintain this part of the city [because otherwise] our situation today will be that of the city center tomorrow."[96]

Contacts between these groups of casualties, undertaken with the mediation and assistance of the Citizen Union vis-à-vis the Yishuv Rescue and Mobilization Fund and its representatives in the National Institutions,[97] paid off in the form of an immediate £P3,000 allocation for urgent assistance to those in imminent existential need and £P25,000 to organize aid in revitalizing the commercial center.[98]

Hope for the economic future of the commercial-center casualties flickered on January 21, 1948, when the National Committee and Idud, Ltd. (a financial-services company owned by the Jewish Agency) concluded an agreement with the Jerusalem branch of the Halva'a ve-Hisakhon Bank (a savings-and-loan institution) to create a special easy-credit fund for victims of the commercial center riot and other acts of mayhem in Jerusalem.[99] The requirement of guarantees, however, encumbered the issuance of the loans and effectively thwarted the aid as the casualties' representatives stood by helplessly.[100] The Jerusalem casualties committee, which continued to operate on a volunteer basis all this time, had also expected this source of funds to finance the mechanism that would deal with all the affected persons' affairs. Despite the agreement, this did not come to pass.[101] The interesting thing is that even after the contract concerning relief for the victims of the Jerusalem riots was signed and after the status and powers of the Yishuv casualties committee were set on firm ground, the casualties' own committee, a volunteer entity that had no official clout, continued to consider itself the leading champion of the casualties in Jerusalem. What is more, no one challenged this assessment or imagined that the committee's function as a driving force and an advocate had now come to an end.

Concurrently, the association that aggregated the merchants, shop owners, and businesspeople on Princess Mary Street and Storrs Avenue continued to operate and even gathered strength as it sought ways to revitalize commercial life on the affected streets. Its members continued to convene, hold internal consultations, and draft proposals and demands. One of the most consistent thoughts was to re-tenant the vacant shops and dwellings in the compound with persons displaced from other parts of Jerusalem.[102]

Ultimately, business owners from blocks neighboring the commercial center were incorporated into, and represented by, the general activity of the Casualties Committee.[103] In the final reckoning, the casualties committee estimated the number of persons affected and their dependents at 1,435.[104]

Another associational initiative by business owners who had sustained war damage took place after the aforementioned car-bomb attack on Ben-Yehuda Street on February 22, 1948. The attack, perpetrated at the initiative of Abdel Khadr al-Husseini, leader of the Arab combat forces in the Jerusalem area and by means of British deserters, exacerbated the problem of small businesspeople who lost their source of livelihood.[105] Even though the Community Council mobilized immediately to help the casualties and represent their needs before the high institutions, the victims established their own representative organization, held rallies, and expressed demands that their delegates presented to the Community Council's Situation Committee. It was not these envoys' idea to replace the community institutions; they did, however, consider themselves mediators or, one may say, mouthpieces of an interest group.[106] Due to the staggering extent of the damage and its implications for the entire area, physical reconstruction of the block began very shortly after the bombing under the supervision of the Community Council.[107] Despite the council's visible involvement in this work, the casualties committee continued to operate, meeting regularly with representatives of the council and apprising them of the difficulties attending to the victims' economic recovery. At one of these meetings, delegates from the casualties committee proposed that they take part in raising funds for victims' initial social relief "until appropriate resources are obtained from the National Institutions."[108]

The magnitude of the explosion and its toll—nearly sixty dead, dozens wounded, and buildings destroyed—prompted the Community Council to establish a special entity to deal with the implications: the Special Committee for Care of the Ben-Yehuda Street Casualties, some members of which were already active on the Casualties Committee.[109] The grants that the Ben-Yehuda casualties sought were divided into social aid and loans, and in all cases the casualties committee itself was asked to recommend candidates in writing.[110]

Unlike the precipitous collapse of the Jerusalem businesses, which was brought on by an extreme event that destroyed the enterprises' operating venue, the Lower City of Haifa experienced a slow but sure decline. Thus, the pattern of action there had two focal points: revitalization and self-help along with advocacy and prevention in order to forestall economic collapse. We will now contemplate the self-organization of the Lower City's Jewish merchants in view of the special characteristics of the crisis that had befallen them.

Jewish Merchants in the Lower City of Haifa

The aftermath of the partition resolution saw a surge in intercommunal tension in Haifa. The city's Arab population responded initially with strikes and demonstrations and subsequently with gunfire on Jewish transport and neighborhoods. The Jewish side responded with reprisals, and the city was drawn into a cycle of violence that lasted uninterruptedly until Haganah forces captured it on April 22, 1948. The violence was manifested in mutual exchanges of gunfire in the city's built area, particularly the Lower City—the quarter to which commercial and economic life drained. Reciprocal gunshots, explosions, and arson became increasingly frequent, despite repeated efforts by Jewish and Arab municipal leaders to work out agreements that would restore calm.

Two months into the intercommunal war, business conditions in the Lower City had deteriorated so badly that many merchants relocated to Jewish neighborhoods on the slopes of Mount Carmel. One important reason for the Lower City business crisis was the avoidance of the area by townspeople due to the danger that it now represented. The Haifa Community Council established a committee to deal with the Lower City's problems. The panel distributed a leaflet urging residents to continue to visit businesses, offices, shops, and workshops in the area, more often than before and "now of all times."[111]

Concurrently, the stakeholders themselves—Jewish business owners in the Lower City—organized and sent a signed petition to the Haifa Situation Committee asking them to force businesses that had left to come back.[112] Otherwise, they threatened to shut down their own enterprises in the Lower City.[113]

In late January, the Lower City merchants held an emergency assembly and decided unanimously to carry on in situ.[114] As security deteriorated further in March, however, a cloud of despair settled over them.[115] The town's leaders felt the pressure and, having an interest in retaining the Lower City's Jewish population, beefed up security in the Lower City and promised to give the area priority in personal and institutional shopping.[116] The Situation Committee, representing the National Institutions' authority in town, also intervened whenever a merchant or businessperson was known to be intending to remove his business from the area. Unequivocally it warned the potential escapee "in every possible way not to abandon his place in the Lower City."[117] One strongly doubts the effectiveness of such warnings, which lacked any mechanism of enforcement.

In the middle of this crisis, a soi-disant Public Office for Maintenance of Economic Life in the City of Haifa burst onto the scene. Its members circulated letters and leaflets taking a pronouncedly positive view of the defense forces and the municipal authorities. The odd wording of these communications, however, raises questions about the authors' identity and about the possibility that the missives camouflaged an initiative of the Community Council itself, even though no proof of this has been found.[118] In a leaflet to the townspeople, the office stated that its purpose in organizing was to maintain commercial life in Lower Haifa. Its materials included a flyer from the Situation Committee that listed the latter's activities on behalf of the Lower City: establishing a special subcommittee, assuring security, lowering public transit fares, demanding that businesses stay open until nearly sundown, and urging residents to participate in the effort to restore routine life in that part of town.[119] The volunteers disseminated a report to the effect that the Yishuv institutions intended to seize deactivated buildings and offices, hand them to others who would enter them immediately, and conduct inspections to make sure the businesses there were indeed active. They suggested a slogan—"Everyone should visit the City of Haifa [i.e., the Lower City commercial center] at least once a week"—and praised the stevedores at the port, who endured "all situations" and resisted the very thought of harming the Yishuv (by not going to work in a danger zone).[120]

The information in the Public Office's possession, its bombastic and propagandistic writing style, and its unreserved support of the Yishuv institutions and defense forces again make one suspect that behind this ostensibly volunteer organization stood the defense forces or the Community Council, which sought to enhance consciousness about the problem not only by issuing edicts and threats but also by generating public pressure and shaping sympathetic public opinion. As stated, however, this hypothesis is unsupported.

This notwithstanding, the Public Office's pro–Lower City campaign did not help to restore trust between the private merchants and the Community Council. In late March, when the Central Committee of the Haifa Hebrew Chamber of Commerce and Industry convened in special session to discuss the Lower City, the members grumbled about the authorities' indifference and neglect of the city, "the whole country's artery of life."[121] It was due to the authorities' inattention, they charged, that the city was emptying out. They likened the impending fate of the Lower City to that of the Shama commercial center in Jerusalem. Fueling the disgruntlement even more was the authorities' refusal to recognize them and their Chamber of Commerce as the representative agent of the Lower City. They demanded this recognition and summoned the city's Situation Committee to an urgent meeting at the chamber's offices.[122] The way the chamber approached the Situation Committee, the expectation that the latter would report to its offices on one day's notice, and the demand that it bring along representatives of the defense forces all reflect its status in its members' eyes. From their perspective, the chamber was an inseparable partner in managing the defense system on the local home front. No less, however, it attests to the immense responsibility that they felt toward their comrades and their profound sense of being on the front and on the battlefield. Accordingly, they asserted, "You [members of the Situation Committee] do not know the true state of affairs in this city. We hope that as a result of this meeting we will be able, by concerted efforts, to correct the situation and save the town."[123] Business owners who were clinging to their offices in the Lower City described the perception of emergency graphically: "The building has been bombarded into ruins . . . and we're almost the only ones in it. . . . No one's in control, no one's looking on."[124]

The Haifa Situation Committee then wrote to Ben-Gurion and alerted him to what its members had been told: the city was emptying of its Jewish inhabitants, and economic activity was crippled. If the Lower City had not been abandoned thus far, the authors of the letter continued, it was thanks to "the absolute prohibition that we imposed." The committee stressed its cooperation with the Chamber of Commerce in dealing with the matter but did not absolve the defense forces of criticism. "Things would not have reached this state," the authors of the missive alleged, "had the defense organization [the Haganah] devoted forces and attention to fortifying our standing in Lower Haifa as the importance of the issue entails."[125]

In a manifesto to public elements in the city, the Situation Committee implored them to shop and place orders with businesses and workshops in the lower part of town. This time they also promised to oversee the implementation of the edict.[126] In a separate letter, the Situation Committee turned to the neighborhood committees on Mount Carmel and in the nearby bayside suburbs, urging them, too, to set an example by giving the city's commercial and industrial enterprises first crack in procurements and orders. The committee also asked the neighborhood committees to refrain from serving institutions and businesses that had moved out of the city without proving that the Situation Committee had authorized them to do so.[127]

Just as civil organizing for the Lower City reached its peak, it appeared to become superfluous because the Jewish forces captured the town and ended the fighting. At the top of a document presented by the subcommittee on Lower Haifa affairs, the expression *No longer current* appears in handwriting next to the date, April 27, 1948.[128] Problems that had seemed insoluble vanished in one stroke. A comprehensive report put out by a self-styled committee for the Housing of Workshops, Businesses, and Warehouses, completed about two weeks after the conquest of the city, concerned itself with yesterday's problems. First among them was the task of clearing the residential areas on Mount Carmel of workshops, businesses, and storage facilities due to the risk of sanitary damage and discomfort occasioned by noise and fire hazards. Next came finding alternative venues for enterprises that could not return to their previous premises. Then appeared the main goal: securing recognition for a new committee that would oversee the relocation of workshops, businesses, and warehouses, designating a representative from the Situation Committee to liaise with it regularly, and—inevitably—creating the mechanism that the new committee would need for its work, all of which needed to be done urgently, so that the committee could get started. Again, nearly all of this had become unnecessary by the time the report was presented.[129]

Even as business proprietors began to associate on the basis of geographical commonality, special-interest associations of merchants and artisans in occupational sectors that had been harder hit than others due to the rationing and control policy began to sprout. The most salient of these initiatives were taken by those whose enterprises involved food.

Associationists, Confrontationists, and Secessionists—Autonomous Representation of Casualties in "Sensitive" Economic Sectors

As supply problems worsened, certain economic sectors faced increasingly acute particularistic challenges. Thus, although affiliated with large associations and entities, they no longer found this indirect representation satisfactory and demanded unmediated involvement in regulating affairs that pertained to their sector. It should be remembered that what they did was not exceptional; it was a modus operandi that sank ever-deepening roots as the war continued. What it meant was direct outreach by representatives of particularistic interest groups to municipal authorities and even, at times, the National Institutions. A partial list of these associations includes the Union of Margarine Manufacturers, the Union of Oil Manufacturers, the Palestine Pharmacists Federation, and the Milk Producers Union, not to omit the Journalists Association, the Organization of Small Public Car Drivers and Owners in Internal Service, and many, many others.

Due to the enormous scale of the phenomenon, this section generalizes by focusing on a representative and especially active sample of sectors—bakers, butchers, grocers, hoteliers, and restaurateurs.

The Bread and Baked-Goods Problem

In early November, the Mandate government reduced the stocks of wheat that it regularly distributed to the country's bakeries from enough for two weeks to enough for two or three days, making a bread shortage a near certainty. Transjordan stopped selling wheat to Mandate Palestine; at the same time, flour and bread were smuggled out of Palestine to Transjordan. At first, no one knew what to do about it. The matter was taken up for discussion at a meeting of the Emergency Supplies Committee, an adjunct of the Jerusalem Community Council. The vice president of the Jerusalem Chamber of Commerce, Menache Eliachar, proposed to call an assembly of the town's bakery owners and demand that they impose controls on sales of standard bread so that the commodity could not be transferred from the Jerusalem market. The reason offered, according to rumors, was that the drivers of bread delivery trucks were selling most of the bread allotted to them for distribution among shopkeepers to Arab go-betweens who paid them "special prices."

It was Eliachar's proposal that this control be applied via ration cards or by opening regional outlets that would sell bread to Jews only.[130] The Yishuv was heavily dependent on imported wheat, its economy providing only 10 percent of consumption.[131] The press occupied itself intensively with the question of bread supplies,[132] as did local policy makers. In Tel Aviv, municipal officials were perturbed about the lack of "any serious and effective supervision of mills and bakeries" and believed that for this reason, standard flour and wheat were being sold at jacked-up prices to Arab merchants and bakeries in Jaffa. The Jewish local authorities demanded the power to supervise the mills and distribute their output to the bakeries.[133]

The bakers, under pressure from all directions, demanded an increase in the price of standard bread, arguing that the price set by the Tel Aviv Municipality two years earlier no longer kept up with the wages they were paying. At the municipal Economic Department, it was believed that standard bread was running short in the market because the bakers were refraining from turning it out, forcing customers to buy much higher-priced rye and white bread.[134]

The shortage of flour and wheat cascaded onto a wide range of factories and businesses, which called on their own representative agencies or established new ones to assure the minimum allotment that they needed to survive the war intact. In the first few months of 1948, nearly all allocation was still performed by the Mandate government's food controller. Thus, the affected businesses sent envoys to the relevant departments of the National Institutions, which, they hoped, would forward the message to that official.[135]

In Jerusalem, the tension that pervaded relations between private merchants and the officials who represented the National Institutions surfaced in contacts between bakers' representatives and the Community Council concerning a debt that the latter had run up for the delivery of bread to the Old City[136]:

> To the same extent that a public institution demands cooperation by the individual, so is an individual entitled to demand that the public institution display an elementary understanding of him. We would like to hope that the

answers given us thus far concerning payment of the debt do not reflect the Community Council's view... The problem of the Old City and its unfortunate residents is a national public problem of the highest order and, obviously, only a public institution such as the Jerusalem Hebrew Community Council, the institution that ordered the bread from us, is responsible for paying the debt, and we should not be referred to other addresses.[137]

The event that sent the Jerusalem Bakers Union into high gear vis-à-vis the municipal and national authorities was the freezing of the price of flour. The bakers met with representatives of the Jerusalem Community Council's Situation Committee and sent a written message to Dov Yosef, the presumptive future commissioner of Jerusalem Affairs for the Jewish Agency. Rising production expenses, the bakers explained, should find expression in the price of bread; furthermore, due to insufficient quantities of white flour, less white bread was being baked, whereas the standard loaf did not allow them to turn a profit. The delegates from the Community Council retorted: "It's preposterous to raise the price of a commodity that's of utmost importance to the masses." Instead, they proposed to hike the prices of the kinds of bread that the rich consumed. The bakers, however, were producing less of the expensive bread in any case, and its price in the market was determined as a function of its consumption, which was steadily falling. This made the committee's proposed solution irrelevant for them. The bakers also argued that the fear of an increase in the price of standard (and lower-priced) bread was largely psychological and that the proposed upturn was too small to burden consumers' monthly budgets significantly. Per capita expenditure on other necessities, such as clothing and amusements, the bakers contended, had plummeted; therefore, an increase in the price of bread would do the household budget no harm. "You can't expect us to be the victim of the situation that has come about," they protested. "You can't expect the community of bakers to bear the burden in a totally disproportional way."[138] In addition, they wondered how so many products had gone up in price while bread stayed put and interpreted this as an attempt to obstruct their work. In their letters to Dov Yosef, they rejected the proposed new price of bread and, in effect, issued an ultimatum by requesting a response to their demands within several hours.[139]

The National Institutions Committee for Jerusalem Affairs turned down the bakers' compromise proposal.[140] This, plus the absence of direct dialogue in the exchange of demands—it had taken place by correspondence—caused a buildup of estrangement and tension that evidently led the bakers to raise the price of standard bread (and of white bread) beyond the increment that the National Institutions had set for them.[141] The negotiations with the bakers, although fraught and prolonged until the small hours of the night, did yield an agreement with the large bakeries in Jerusalem—Berman, Angel, and Ramat Rahel—and a decision that an audit committee would examine the bakers' charges of unfair treatment.[142]

Three Jerusalem dignitaries—Yitzhak Olshan, Mordechai Friedman, and Nehemia Salomon—were named to the bread audit committee.[143] Losing no time in meeting with representatives of the bakers and the Supply Committee, they concluded that the increase proposed by the Supply Committee already priced in some of the upturn in manufacturing costs. They noted, "In consideration of the situation and our comparison of the harm to the bakers as against that inflicted on of the Jerusalem public ... we find no justification in an increase in bread prices beyond that determined by the institutions' Emergency Committee for Jerusalem."[144]

In early March, further dwindling of flour supplies aroused growing suspicion among flour mill owners, bakers, and the municipal and national authorities.[145] The bread issue was especially sensitive; in fact, it did much to determine the national mood. When the newspaper *Davar* reported that the Tel Aviv Municipal Economic Department was abetting speculation in flour and bread, the town council convened to discuss the matter, and the department head, Moshe Chelouche, denied the accusation.[146] It was population growth in Tel Aviv and the massing of IDPs from the frontier areas, Chelouche claimed, that left flour supplies in the city a hundred tons short per week.[147] When *Davar* subsequently accused the flour merchants of profiteering under the protection of the city's Economic Department, the Chamber of Commerce fired off a protest letter to the newspaper against the "unfounded charges."[148]

About two weeks later, on April 11, the Tel Aviv Municipality issued Regulation No. 5 concerning flour and bread, the second appendix of a measure meant "to assure just distribution of controlled commodities." The rule required every importer, merchant, miller, and baker to present the food controller with full and accurate reportage on the quantities, movements, place of storage, and sale prices of all forms of grain, flour, or loaves of bread in their possession. Concealing or helping to conceal grain, flour, and bread and producing flour and mingling different kinds of flour in transgression of instructions from the competent authority were prohibited.[149] The crackdown was based on decisions of the Situation Committee for Control of the

Sale of Flour and Bread. Section 5 of the directive established flatly that any bakery that violated the rules would be shut down.[150]

Just then, Jerusalem faced another bread crisis over an issue that, according to the city's bakers, had been "dragging on since December" with no solution.[151] The bakers claimed to have agreed to charge a loss price on the basis of a promise of compensation and had hoped—and been assured—that the matter would be straightened out within a few days. Now, many weeks later, they were no longer willing to endure price discrimination, particularly since solutions in Haifa and Tel Aviv had been found. Therefore, they threatened not to return to work at the end of the Passover festival unless a fair price of bread would be set. The bakers' representative body proposed to meet with national officials but insisted that the encounter take place the day after the posting of the letter.[152] The Jerusalem Emergency Committee read out the bakers' letter the next morning and responded with a letter of its own, affirming that it would "not tolerate threats such as those in your letter."[153] A representative of the municipal bread committee spoke about the advantages of concentrating all baking work in a small number of plants and presented various pricing options, one of which, among the lowest, was accepted in the end.[154]

The Jerusalem Emergency Committee indeed devoted much attention to the bread question. Its members held a lengthy and detailed discussion about how different kinds of flour were mixed at the bakeries. This attested to the vast importance that they attributed to the matter and the immense knowledge that many of those dealing with it had amassed, even though they had probably never kneaded a portion of dough. The committee's decision reflected its wish to bring down the cost of making bread and defer to the bakers while causing no harm to consumers. Essentially, it allowed flour to skip the wholesale stage and move directly to five large bakeries that would be chosen for the purpose of "concentrating the baking work."[155] From the national authorities' standpoint, the bakers would be obliged "to supply bread to the townspeople, and if they prove unwilling to discharge this duty, we will seize all the bakeries and arrange the baking of bread by ourselves."[156]

Restaurateurs and Hoteliers

While allotments of food and basic commodities to households were regulated on the basis of more or less consistent criteria, caterers found themselves in a very dire state. Their services, considered relative luxuries, were given no preferential treatment, resulting in shortages of commodities crucial to them.[157]

In Tel Aviv, roughly 500 businesspeople who incorporated under an association of the hospitality industry, an adjunct of the General Federation of the Middle Class in Palestine, fell between the stools. No "efficient and just method for the apportionment of vital commodities in this city" had been established, they charged.[158] Meeting at their initiative with the acting mayor, Eliezer Perlson, in late February, they laid out their distress and offered practical proposals, including the allocation to eating establishments of a certain percent of relevant commodities that reached the city and the posting of representatives of hospitality-industry organizations, as observers, to the municipal Supply Committee. They also asked city hall to investigate an eatery that WIZO had set up at its club facility. The place, they claimed, had evolved into a restaurant that competed with their own establishments; they demanded action against it by the city. Most of their requests were turned down. Admittedly, it was decided to allot to eateries 10 percent of all commodities that were crucial to such businesses. This, however, the industry representatives retorted, was so insufficient relative to needs that it plainly ruled out any success on their part in resisting the black market, to which businesses were turning to assure their survival.[159]

In Jerusalem, the humanitarian crisis escalated in late March, as only one-third of the delivery trucks were able to make their way into the city. One of the local commanders warned of "food riots" in view of the city's absolute dependency on outside supply lines that, in nearly all cases, traversed Arab-controlled areas. [160]

In an attempt to place the distribution and use of staples under tougher control, hoteliers and restaurateurs were invited to post a delegate to the municipal Supply Committee. At this time, more than three months after the intercommunal violence erupted, most proprietors in these fields, lacking the most basic supplies and unable to operate, favored closing down. The only exception was the Labor Movement's workers' kitchen. Noticing this, a member of the Café, Hotel, Restaurant, and Pension branch of the Merchants Association, which now acted independently, proposed that they announce the closure of their business and post signs reading "Anyone who wants a decent meal should go to the workers' kitchen" and "We eat at the workers' kitchen, too." When the confectioners pleaded their case to the Situation Committee, they were told, "Flour is needed for baking only bread, not cake." This, the confectioners said, meant the eradication of the café industry. All they sought was a mere 3 percent of the flour quota in order to ensure bare survival. What emerged at their gathering was a sense of distrust toward the Community Council institutions generally and the supply regulators particularly. Some of those in attendance charged that each delegate to the Jerusalem Community Council agencies "is looking out for his interests or those of his organization only."[161] In response, the restaurateurs elected an envoy of their own and resolved that, barring an improvement in their situation within three days, all cafés and restaurants would shut down in collective protest. Violators, they added, would receive no share in future allotments.

Responding to the restaurateurs' demands, Zvi Lurie, a member of the National Committee, stood up and made a motion that confirmed the very phenomenon that the business owners warned against—the establishment of popular eateries by nonprofit organizations. These facilities, Lurie proposed, should serve two meals per day and receive priority in food supplies "before any shop, wholesale or retail, and before private restaurants and hotels." This, Lurie thought, was the best way to ration food and "fend off distress, semi-hunger, and physical depletion."[162]

Acknowledging that these eateries would charge less than cost, Lurie proposed that the difference be covered by a special social-relief fund. This, Lurie said, would create a more "handsome and effective" mechanism of social aid than an allowance "laid in one's palm."[163] These ideas, repeatedly bruited as alternatives to quota-setting for private restaurants in Jerusalem, generated tension and triggered a frontal collision between the restaurateurs and the chair of the Jerusalem Emergency Committee, Dov Yosef, after the latter had told them that all available flour was being used to bake bread.[164]

The confectioners were even worse off than the others. Their line of business, including cafés and cake shops, provided no fewer than 1,500 Jerusalemites with a living, and all were at risk of economic collapse. The confectioners called a meeting together with their employees and resolved that, in view of the ghastly situation, they should all turn out a standard cake such as that produced during World War II by British government edict.[165] They really used relatively small quantities of flour, sugar, and margarine in their work, and their output of cake not only fed much of the population but also "raised its morale," they added. Therefore, they demanded the repeal of the ban on cake-baking and a large enough allocation of ingredients to spare them and all subindustries dependent on them from having to close.[166]

Notwithstanding all the organizing, the efforts, and the delegations sent, the baking of cakes and rolls in Tel Aviv was halted in early May.[167] A week later, the Jerusalem Emergency Committee decided to set up public kitchens to distribute thousands of meals.[168] In this case, the main value of associating appears to have been the support that the associates provided each other and the venting of frustration that they achieved by holding meetings, producing petitions, and convening assemblies.

Grocers

In the first half of 1948, the Yishuv met only about half of the Jewish population's food needs. Steady supplies of 43 percent of food necessities, which depended on imports, became increasingly uncertain as ships refrained from putting into port and as storage facilities at the ports became hard to reach, impeding access to unloaded goods. Two-thirds of Jewish produce was comprised of agricultural commodities that were produced in shrinking quantities due to the state of war.[169] In response to the growing shortages of basic food, the supply mechanisms were placed under tougher and tougher control, affecting grocers in particular and inspiring them to organize separately from other food merchants.

The grocers evidently began to associate in the second month of the intercommunal war, when they set up a Situation Committee that demanded consideration of its members' views in setting prices and regulating supplies. These demands did not fall on attentive ears; in early March, the Supplies Committee published a rate sheet that included prices that, the grocers charged, would not cover even their routine business expenses. Outraged, they claimed that these conditions left them with two equally ominous alternatives—to go out of business or to become "'ostensible' profiteers."[170] Noting that general stores had been given priority in supplies,[171] the grocers suspected that the Supplies Committee intended to give all business to them. "Even the British authorities, known for their attitude toward the Yishuv, did not dare to abuse us so and even consulted with us in all matters."[172] The grocers' representatives thundered against this "misbegotten modus operandi, which will commit the whole Yishuv to the general stores, force people to queue at length, and destroy free commercial competition."[173]

The grocers' frustration escalated further when they discovered that they had been left out of the new matrix of supply institutions in Jerusalem, despite the inclusion of representatives of other specific industries such as the restaurateurs. Their envoys fumed over what they considered the deliberate marginalization of their collectivity. No other commercial and economic organization in Jerusalem represented them, they lamented, and any arrangement that overlooked them would be flawed, they warned.[174] Several days later, the grocers informed the Jerusalem Community Council Supply Committee that their delegate to the latter panel would be Moshe Bidlowski.[175] It is hard to tell whether the announcement was unilateral or coordinated. Undoubted, however, was their resolve to secure representation in the body that made policy in Jerusalem. Bidlowski was ultimately added to the Jerusalem Situation Committee's Supply Council, a new and broad-based entity that included representatives of particularistic interest groups.[176]

Grocers in Tel Aviv also stepped up their pressure, presenting the mayor with a proposal of their own for regulating the townspeople's food supplies. Their bid included clauses such as introducing ration cards, selling essentials in limited quantities to regular customers only, and—the main thing—co-opting a representative of their association onto existing committees and future bodies that would deal in food supplies. Ancillary demands followed, such as setting a fair retail markup, forbidding wholesalers to sell retail, including an envoy of theirs in legal proceedings against retailers accused of profiteering,[177] and, like their peers in Jerusalem, recognizing their status as their community's official representatives and confirming their right to participate in decision-making.

In Haifa, a Grocers' Union operated under the Haifa General Merchants Organization. In mid-April, it formed a new body that amalgamated all merchants in the grocery industry in Haifa: the Grocery Merchants Federation of the General Organization of Merchants in Haifa and the Vicinity.[178]

Even though few of these associational initiatives got very far in increasing supply quotas or influencing price-setting, they catapulted themselves to centrality in defending their members against attacks, defamation, and even prosecution on suspicion of profiteering. Their particularistic basis of association—affiliation with a specific trade or occupation—proved valuable as a representative and advocacy mechanism in countering what the private business community considered a disproportional attack on them by the authorities.

Fighting Back: Deflecting Accusations of Profiteering

Amid its efforts to overcome controls on the prices and distribution of foods and basic commodities, the mercantile community found itself under attack on an additional front: accusations of profiteering that besmirched the reputations of merchants in diverse industries. Even though the accusers clarified that theirs was not a *j'accuse* against the commercial class at large, the merchants found themselves on a collective defendant's bench. The charges, although always couched with reservations, were overt and explicit: "Lots of merchants are hiking prices to their hearts' content and exploiting every woe and hardship to raise prices or conceal goods in order to make a killing afterwards."[179] The man who said this on a radio broadcast, Mordechai Shatner, alleged that profiteering was undermining the Yishuv's resilience and called it "a mine that unconscionable people have planted in the Yishuv economy." It ought to be fought top-down and bottom-up, he advised.[180]

As the second month of intercommunal violence neared its end, reports appeared in Jerusalem about special tribunals that the Community Council had set up, on which merchant lawyers and "reputable people of other kinds" would be serving as judges.[181] At a session of the Tel Aviv Municipal Council, Deputy Mayor Perlson reported on the establishment of anti-profiteering courts, then being completed. A member of the council, Menachem Pitchon, called for a war on manifestations of profiteering but objected to "the persecution of commerce at large on that account."[182] Zvi Lubianker responded that while hounding merchants was the last thing on the council's mind, "It's a fact that some merchants have earned thousands of pounds in the past few weeks just by raising the prices of canned goods."[183] In Haifa, the Community Council's Situation Committee also mulled the establishment of anti-profiteering courts at this time and resolved to appoint two attorneys as court presidents who would take turns in managing trials, accompanied by two associates—one representing consumers and the other representing economic circles.[184]

Whenever the topic of war on profiteering arose, the merchants expressed feelings of mistreatment and ostracism. They hoped that their participation in drafting a blueprint for the regulation of supplies would assist them in refuting the "prejudice" by which merchants "by nature and very occupation [were seen as] dangerous speculator[s] who attract the rage of the simple man."[185]

The Better Business Association, self-defined as operating "under the patronage of the National Committee," countered blanket accusations of profiteering. Membership in the Association, based on organizational affiliation, included the B'nai B'rith Order in Palestine, the Manufacturers Association, the Homeowners Association, the Swiss-Palestine Chamber of Commerce, several lawyers, and a representative of the National Council. Its practical goal was war on corruption, in which rubric it included "profiteering and greed, false documentation of domestic produce, unfair competition, fraud, and exploitation of the weak."[186] The association also took action at the national level, linking the eradication of manifestations of corruption with the strength of the front: "If the home front isn't sound—the soldier in the farthest-away position will sense it."[187] However, it criticized the way the National Institutions were conducting the war on profiteering, accusing them of disproportionate action against agricultural product wholesalers and favoritism toward retailers in that field as well as producers and, particularly, manufacturers.[188]

The broad ambit of those who criticized the anti-profiteering courts indicates that the bias against this or that side was not as significant as estimated. Nevertheless, specific sectors that traded in the most vital goods did come under closer scrutiny than others. A quintessential example of the sense of persecution is that of the grocers and the bakers. When pressure in the war on profiteering was raised, the spotlight turned in their direction, of course. When the grocers' Situation Committee sought to post delegates to the Jerusalem economic institutions and the anti-profiteering courts, they were turned down, giving them a sense of having been wronged. The Yishuv was mired in a "profiteering psychosis," they charged, citing as proof the steep fines administered for every trifling infraction.[189] To eliminate the alleged injustice, they demanded that in every trial against a grocer there be seated among the judges someone intimately familiar with the profession and that every defendant be allowed to bring an advocate "from his profession." They proposed—or demanded—rules of jurisprudence, including a summons to trial that would itemize the counts in the indictment and, after the trial, a reasoned verdict spelling out how it might be appealed: "We state once again that a people that is preparing to establish its governing and judicial institutions cannot base them on an attitude of total disparagement of one of the Yishuv's [socioeconomic] classes, and *a fortiori* we must not fall into psychosis. Even when someone is charged with murder, [courts] allow dispensations in all aspects of self-defense and take care not to rush to judgment."

The steep fines, the committee warned, were driving many shopkeepers to economic ruin at a time when making a living in this manner was difficult to begin with. Therefore, the grocers' representative body threatened to close the shops in protest of the injustice to its members insofar as their demands remained unrequited.[190] To keep up the pressure, the grocers then remonstrated with the Jerusalem Community Council's Supply Committee, accusing it of warring against them, distributing bombastic propaganda about speculators, and conducting "unfounded trials" to prove the allegations.[191] When two bakers who had been caught selling short-weighted bread were fined £P300 each, their association accused the court of unprofessionalism. A baker, it contended, could not possibly weigh his product accurately; therefore, punishing him for a deviation of a few grams was "a malevolent and scandalous act." The bread makers threatened to turn off the ovens if the matter were not reinvestigated and backed this with a petition, signed by eighty-four of their number, that they presented to their organization.[192] The secretary of the bakers' organization asked the mayor of Tel Aviv to have an appeals committee review the proceedings and call experts "who are well versed in all processes of baking."[193] Until the completion of said appeal, he continued, the punishments should be suspended, and short-weighting and compromising on the quality of bread should not be defined as "profiteering."[194]

The pattern of speaking out, advocating, and demanding representation in policy-making forums found epitomic expression in this context of defending against accusations of profiteering. On this front, however, the struggle appears to have been directed at public opinion at large, as mirrored in the press and as it reached the policy-making entities by seepage.

In his investigation and analysis of the image of the speculator in World War I, Jean-Louis Robert finds an inevitable tension in wartime between consumers on the one hand and merchants and the propertied—producers, brokers, shopkeepers, and building owners—on the other. The media tend to treat consumers as a social monolith that has common interests—food, fuel, housing, and so on. They portray the consumer via the woman, the child, and the soldier's family, all in juxtaposition to one target of criticism: *the merchant*, a catchall term for anyone who profits in any way from the processes of commerce and distribution. Those associated with delivering and producing food, Robert notes, attract particularly emphatic criticism.[195] The web of defamations and attacks on the merchants of the Yishuv should probably be understood in the context of this broad phenomenon.

In this light, too, the economic interest groups, by organizing and speaking out against the attacks, should be viewed as employing a self-help mechanism and an instrument with which they hoped to alleviate the internal social tensions that are understandable in a war reality and not as entities that should be examined in terms of concrete achievements (i.e., policy change and representation).

Those discussed above, who associated on the basis of occupational or economic commonality, usually based their choice on existing organizational structures. The members of these entities had previously enlisted and incorporated; many of these bodies already had officers. They had tumbled into unique and specific crises due to physical damage to their businesses, emergency economic measures that crimped their ability to make a living, and the demonization of merchants as villains who put their interest over that of the public. It was these that yielded new associational initiatives or amplified those already extant.

In both cases, the new settings did not have to seek legitimacy and recognition as had the IDP committees. Business proprietors in commercial centers in Jerusalem and Haifa associated under chambers of commerce or merchants' organizations; grocers, café owners, and restaurateurs, in turn, were organized in recognized branches within umbrella organizations. This facilitated their interaction with authorities because their contacts sometimes had the umbrella organizations' verbal and practical backing. These prior affiliations found expression in steady broadening of the private business organizations' spheres of influence and their slow but steady penetration of various policy-making forums—in which, even if they did not always manage to exert influence, their voices were definitely heard.

Notes

1. Nachum T. Gross, *Not by Spirit Alone: Studies in the Economic History of Modern Palestine and Israel* (Jerusalem: Magnes and Yad Izhak Ben-Zvi, 1999), 221–5, 343.
2. Ibid., 344.
3. Jon Lawrence, "Material Pressures on the Middle Classes," in *Capital Cities at War: Paris, London, Berlin 1914–1919, Vol. 1*, Jay Winter and Jean-Louis Robert, eds. (Cambridge and New York: Cambridge University Press, 1997), 230, 246.
4. Ibid., 229; Jay Winter, "Paris, London, Berlin, 1914–1919: Capital Cities at War," in *Capital Cities at War: Paris, London, Berlin 1914–1919, Vol. 1*, Winter and Robert, eds., 17.

5. Ibid.

6. Moshe Naor (2006), "From Economic Globalization to the Austerity Front: Rationing and Price-Control Policy During the War," in *Civilians at War: Studies on the Civilian Society During the Israeli War of Independence* (in Hebrew), Mordechai Bar-On and Meir Chazan, eds. (Jerusalem and Tel Aviv: Ben-Zvi Institute, 2006), 189–213.

7. Ibid., 191.

8. Ibid., 192.

9. Meeting of Advisory Committee on Trade Affairs, an adjunct of the Jewish Agency Department of Trade and Industry, Tel Aviv Chamber of Commerce Archives (hereinafter: COCA), Chamber Relations With (File II), November 25, 1947.

10. Ibid.

11. Ibid.

12. He would become the first minister of Trade, Industry, and Supply in the Provisional Government of Israel.

13. Committee meeting, COCA, book of minutes of committee meetings, December 3, 1947.

14. Meeting of Tel Aviv members of Advisory Committee on Trade Affairs, an adjunct of the Jewish Agency Department of Trade and Industry, Central Zionist Archives (hereinafter: CZA), J1/6412, December 9, 1947.

15. Ibid.

16. Ibid.

17. "Shimon Allman's remarks at Chamber of Commerce meeting," COCA, Chamber Relations With: (File II), December 12, 1947.

18. Yitzhak Katz, Secretary of Chamber of Commerce, to Mordechai Shatner, head of National Committee Economics Department, COCA, Chamber Relations With: (File II), December 14, 1947.

19. Ibid.

20. Z. Suzajev, Acting President of Association of Importers and Wholesalers in Palestine, to Peretz Bernstein, Head of Department of Trade and Industry, CZA, S8/865, January 1, 1948.

21. Committee meeting, COCA, book of minutes of committee meetings, January 14, 1948.

22. Minutes of Presidium meeting, COCA, meetings of Chamber of Commerce Committee and Presidium before and after establishment of statehood, February 5, 1948, 15.

23. Committee meeting, COCA, book of minutes of committee meetings, February 12, 1948.

24. Committee meeting, book of minutes of committee meetings, February 2, 1948.

25. Ibid.

26. Minutes of Subcommittee A, Tel Aviv, CZA, J1/7070/1, February 20, 1948.

27. Meeting of Subcommittee A, Jerusalem, CZA, J1/6432, December 17, 1947; Dr. S. Rosenfeld, National Committee Economic Department, to Tel Aviv Municipality, Tel Aviv Municipal Archives (hereinafter: TAMA), Emergency Food Supplies 44–49, File 3048, Container 1207, January 8, 1948.

28. Naor, "From Economic Globalization to the Austerity Front," 191.

29. Ibid.

30. Chamber of Commerce meeting, COCA, book of minutes of committee meetings, January 14, 1948.

31. Ibid.

32. Yitzhak Bavli memorandum, CZA, J1/7070/1, January 28, 1948.

33. Ibid.
34. Meeting of Haifa Situation Committee, Haifa Municipal Archives (hereinafter: HMA), File 00234/1 (4728), January 18, 1948.
35. Meeting of Yishuv Supply Committee, Jerusalem Municipal Archives (hereinafter: JMA), Container 4589, Serial No. 20, January 22, 1949.
36. Mordechai Shatner to Deputy Mayor of Tel Aviv, Eliezer Perlson, TAMA, 4/38, Container 466, February 3, 1948.
37. Meeting of Chamber of Commerce, COCA, book of minutes of committee meetings, February 12, 1948.
38. The sterling bloc refers to the group of states and Crown protectorates that used the pound sterling as legal tender or pegged their national currencies to the British one.
39. Haim Barkai, *The Genesis of the Israeli Economy* (in Hebrew) (Jerusalem: Bialik Institute, 1990), 25.
40. Ibid.
41. Nachum T. Gross, "The Economic Policy of the British Mandate Government in Palestine (Part B)" (in Hebrew), *Cathedra* 25 (1983): 165.
42. Peretz Bernstein, "The Committee," COCA, Chamber Relations With: (File II), February 23, 1948.
43. Ibid.
44. Meeting of Chamber of Commerce Committee, COCA, Chamber Relations With: (File II), February 24, 1948.
45. Ibid.
46. Ibid.
47. Ibid.
48. Ibid.
49. Report by Z. Suzajev, Meeting of Chamber of Commerce Committee, COCA, Chamber Relations With: (File II), February 24, 1948.
50. Meeting of Chamber of Commerce Committee, COCA, book of minutes of committee meetings, February 24, 1948.
51. Ibid.; Shaul Lifschitz, President of Chamber of Commerce, to Peretz Bernstein, COCA, Chamber Relations With: (File II), February 29, 1948.
52. Peretz Bernstein to Lifschitz, COCA, Chamber Relations With: (File II), March 1, 1948.
53. Ibid.
54. Peretz Bernstein to Tel Aviv, Haifa, and Jerusalem Chambers of Commerce and Association of Importers, Tel Aviv, COCA, Chamber Relations With: (File II), March 2, 1948.
55. Minutes of Chamber of Commerce Presidium meeting, COCA, meetings of Chamber Committee and Presidium before and after establishment of statehood, File 15, March 7, 1948.
56. Memorandum from meeting at Jerusalem Chamber of Commerce offices, CZA, J1/7545, March 21, 1948.
57. Meeting of Chamber of Commerce Committee, COCA, book of minutes of committee meetings, April 1, 1948.
58. Meeting of Chamber of Commerce Committee, COCA, book of minutes of committee meetings, April 21, 1948.
59. Meeting of Chamber of Commerce Committee, COCA, book of minutes of committee meetings, May 5, 1948.
60. Consulting Engineer Bavli, "Import and Stock Problems and Purchasing Plans," Israel State Archives (hereinafter: ISA), Situation Committee files, Gimel 117/24, Division 41, March 25, 1948.

61. Ibid.
62. Ibid.
63. Ibid.
64. On the course of events that led to Arieh Shenkar's appointment and the rejection of the proposal, see Ben-Gurion to Golda Meir and Moshe Sharett, Ben-Gurion Archive (hereinafter: BGA), Correspondence Division, March 14, 1948.
65. Meeting of Chamber of Commerce Committee, COCA, book of minutes of committee meetings, March 3, 1948.
66. Letter Association of Farmers in Palestine, Tel Aviv Chamber of Commerce, Association of Importers and Wholesalers, General Association of Merchants, and Middle Class Organization to David Ben-Gurion, BGA, March 9, 1948.
67. Ben-Gurion to Association of Farmers in Palestine, Tel Aviv Chamber of Commerce, Association of Importers and Wholesalers, General Association of Merchants, and Middle Class Organization, BGA, March 10, 1948.
68. Elected in 1951 to the Jerusalem Municipal Council (representing the Herut Party).
69. Memorandum, Delegation from Commercial Center, JMA, 4589, Serial No. 18, CZA, 3800/1, December 2, 1947.
70. Ibid.
71. H. Salomon to chair of Chamber of Commerce, JMA, 4589, Serial No. 18, CZA, 3800/1, December 3, 1947.
72. Memorandum about the Commercial Center, signed by Izhak Ben-Zvi, JMA, 4589, Serial No. 18, CZA, 3800/1, December 4, 1947.
73. Committee for Care of Casualties of the Events in Jerusalem, CZA, S26/8176, December 16, 1947.
74. Y. Tehon, Palestine Land Development Company, and Menache Eliachar, JMA, 4589, Serial No. 18, CZA, 3800/1, December 8, 1947.
75. Letter from M. Eliachar, M. H. Ginot, and others, to Yishuv committee for casualties of the events (attn.: H. A. Grabowski), CZA, S25/8176, December 9, 1947.
76. Committee for Care of Casualties of the Commercial Center and the Vicinity, Draft Report (handwritten in English), CZA, S25/8176, May 9, 1948.
77. Ibid.
78. Letter from M. Eliachar, M. H. Ginot, and others, to Yishuv committee for casualties of the events (attn.: H. A. Grabowski), CZA, S25/8176, December 9, 1947.
79. Ibid.
80. Circular to Members, No. 1, JMA, Container 9, December 15, 1947.
81. Adv. Moshe Yehuda Halevi to Inspector of Police, JMA, Container 9, December 15, 1947.
82. Committee for Care of Casualties of the Commercial Center and the Vicinity, CZA, S25/8176, December 16, 1947.
83. Letter from Situation Committee and Reconstruction Committee to Grabowski, JMA, Container 4589, Serial No. 18, CZA, 3800/1, December 16, 1947.
84. G. Flash to M. Eliachar, memorandum attached to Flash's letter, JMA, Container 9, December 25, 1948; G. Flash to Committee, January 5, 1948, ibid.
85. Emergency Committee, JMA, Container 4589, Serial No. 18, CZA, 3800/1, December 17, 1947.
86. Unsigned and untitled report on meeting of delegation of commercial-center casualties with head secretary, CZA, S26/8176, December 29, 1947.

87. Ibid.
88. M. Eliachar to Jerusalem District Commissioner, December 24, 1947.
89. J. H. H. Pollock, District Commissioner, to Vice President, Jerusalem Chamber of Commerce, JMA, Container 4589, Serial No. 18, CZA, 3800/1, January 5, 1948.
90. Open letter from Committee for Care of Casualties of the Commercial Center and the Vicinity, JMA, Container 9, December 17, 1947. An identical letter was sent to members of the building merchants' vetting committee and to those representing machinery and metalwork merchants, watchmakers, jewelers, etc.
91. Neighborhoods such as: Talpiot, Arnona, Mekor Hayyim, and Ramat Rahel.
92. Committee for Care of Casualties of the Commercial Center and the Vicinity (signed by Eliachar) to David Ben-Gurion, CZA, S26/8175, December 30, 1947. A copy of the document with the same letter was sent to Haim Salomon, presidium of the Jewish Community Council, JMA, Container 4589, Serial No. 18, CZA, 3800/1.
93. Committee for Care of Casualties of the Commercial Center and the Vicinity, Draft Report (handwritten in English), CZA, S25/8176, May 9, 1948.
94. Report of Emergency Committee of Merchants and Residents on Princess Mary Street, Julian's Way, Storrs Avenue, and Central Building, undated but issued "a month after the events" (i.e., in late December), JMA, Container 4589, Serial No. 18, CZA, 3800/1.
95. The Jewish-owned cooperative that ran public transport in Jerusalem.
96. Report of Security Committee, Emergency Committee of Merchants and Residents on Princess Mary Street, Julian's Way, Storrs Avenue, and Central Building, undated.
97. See chapter 3, "Literally Abandoned to Starvation—The Bureaucratization of Relief and the Question of Responsibility for Soldiers' Families."
98. General secretariat, Mobilization and Salvage Fundraising Committee, to Jerusalem Casualties Care Committee, CZA, S8/834, January 25, 1948.
99. Document dated January 23, 1948, CZA, 9055.
100. Committee for Care of Casualties of the Commercial Center and the Vicinity, Draft Report, CZA, S25/8176, May 9, 1948.
101. M. H. Eliachar to P. Grabowski and Yitzhak Werfel, Jewish Agency, JMA, Container 9, February 11, 1948.
102. *Community Council and Situation Committee News* (in Hebrew, newsletter of the Jerusalem Jewish Community Council), no. 25, JMA, Container 4589, Serial No. 19, February 25, 1948.
103. Ibid.
104. Ibid.
105. T. (evidently Yakov Tehon) to Haim Salomon, JMA, Container 4589, Serial No. 18, CZA, 3800/1, February 23, 1948. The attack left fifty-eight people dead and thirty-eight seriously injured.
106. *Community Council and Situation Committee News*, no. 25, JMA, Container 4589, Serial No. 19, February 25, 1948.
107. Ibid.
108. Ibid.
109. Menache Eliachar, Dr. Amdor, Reuven Schreibman, and other noted activists on the Community Council and in Jerusalem public life (Daniel Auster, M. Baram, A. Levine, and J. D. Mann). The last mentioned was treasurer of the Community Council.
110. Letter, signature illegible, addressed to "here," in reference to Ben-Yehuda Street Casualties Committee, JMA, Container 4589, Serial No. 18, CZA, 3800/1, March 1, 1948.

111. Resolutions of Small Situation Committee, HMA, File 00234/1 (4728), February 2, 1948.
112. Signed and stamped petition from business owners to Haifa Situation Committee, HMA, File 00234/1 (4728), March 10, 1948.
113. Ibid.
114. "Public Office for the Maintenance of Economic Life in the City of Haifa," letter to Situation Committee (relating to merchants' assembly on January 29, 1948), HMA, File 00234/1 (4728), March 15, 1948.
115. Ibid.
116. Situation Committee plenary discussions, HMA, File 00234/1 (4728), March 15, 1948.
117. Letter, Situation Committee to Mr. Lifschitz, HMA, File 00231/13 (4675), March 24, 1948.
118. Public Office for Consultation and Maintenance of Economic Life in the City of Haifa to Haifa Situation Committee, HMA, File 00297/10 (5734), March 25, 1948.
119. Ibid.
120. Ibid.
121. Letter from Haifa Hebrew Chamber of Commerce to Haifa Situation Committee, HMA, File 00292/1 (5719), March 28, 1948.
122. Ibid.
123. Ibid.
124. Letter from Amir Supply Company of the Association of Jewish Farmers in Palestine, Ltd., to Haifa Community Council, HMA, File 00292/1 (5719), March 28, 1948.
125. A. Friedlander to David Ben-Gurion, HMA, File 00234/14 (4746), March 29, 1948.
126. Letter from Subcommittee for Lower Haifa Affairs, with address but no name noted, HMA, File 00259/22 (5210), April 7, 1948; "Internal Circular to All Committee Heads and Department Directors," HMA, File 00234/15 (4747), April 13, 1948.
127. Letter from Haifa Situation Committee to neighborhood committees—Bat Galim, Har Hacarmel, Neve Sha'anan, Kiryat Eliahu, Kiryat Bialik, Kiryat Haim, Kiryat Shmuel, Tel Amal, and Hadar Hacarmel, HMA, File 00234/14 (4746), April 18, 1948.
128. Ibid.
129. Dr. Gideon Kaminka to Haifa Situation Committee, HMA, File 00234/14 (4746), May 2, 1948.
130. Meeting of Emergency Supplies Committee with representative of Jerusalem grocers, JMA, Container 4587, Serial No. 13, November 9, 1947.
131. Dr. J. Fisch to Martin Lederman, Economic Bureau for Palestine, COCA, Chamber Relations With: (File II), November 20, 1947.
132. Ibid.
133. Matityahu Kalir, Tel Aviv Municipal Economic and Statistics Department, to D. Gefen, chair of Emergency Internal Executive Committee, TAMA, File 3048, Container 1207, December 12, 1947.
134. Ibid.
135. See, for example, Lahmeinu Cooperative Bakery of Consumers Unions in Tel Aviv and the Vicinity, Ltd., to Mordechai Shatner, CZA, J1/6412, January 4, 1948.
136. United Bakeries, Berman, Angel Keter, Ltd., to Jerusalem Jewish Community Council, JMA, Container 4585, Serial No. 17, January 6, 1948.
137. Ibid.

138. Jerusalem Bakers Union to Dr. Bernard Joseph (*sic*), Jewish Agency, ISA, Gimel, 275/9, January 25, 1948.
139. Jerusalem Bakers Union to Dr. Bernard Joseph, ISA, Gimel, 275/9, January 26, 1948.
140. Bernard Joseph to Bakers Union, ISA, Gimel, 275/9, January 27, 1948.
141. Letter signed on behalf of the Supply Committee, headed "Dear all bakeries," JMA, Container 4589, Serial No. 20, February 1, 1948.
142. *Community Council and Situation Committee News*, no. 5, JMA, Container 4589, Serial No. 19, February 2, 1948.
143. Yitzhak Olshan, at the time a well-known Jerusalem lawyer who upon statehood would become a Supreme Court justice and subsequently the second chief justice; Nehemia Salomon, a noted Jerusalem lawyer and a member of the Community Council's housing committee; and Mordechai Friedman, subsequently a member of the Jerusalem Municipal Council (representing Mapai).
144. Investigative Committee on Bread Prices to Jerusalem Situation Committee, JMA, Container 4589, Serial No. 20, February 3, 1948.
145. Shatner to Subcommittee A, proposal for supervision of foodstuffs in the interim period, CZA, J1/7070/1, March 7, 1948.
146. "Decisions of the Sixth Council at Meeting 660," TAMA, 2368, Meetings of the Sixth Council, March 21, 1948.
147. Ibid.
148. Minutes of meeting of Tel Aviv Chamber of Commerce presidium, COCA, March 25, 1948; meetings of Chamber Central Committee and Presidium before and after declaration of statehood, File 15.
149. "Regulation concerning Flour and Bread," No. 5, National Committee of Kenesset Yisrael in Palestine, TAMA, 3/14 / a/4, Container 466, April 11, 1948.
150. Ibid.
151. Jerusalem Bakers Union to Chair of Jerusalem Emergency Committee, ISA, Gimel, 275/9, April 28, 1948.
152. Ibid.
153. Jerusalem Emergency Committee to Jerusalem Bakers Union, ISA, Gimel, 275/9, April 29, 1948.
154. Jerusalem Emergency Committee minutes, ISA, Gimel, 274/1, April 29, 1948.
155. Jerusalem Emergency Committee minutes, ISA, Gimel, 274/1, May 6, 1948.
156. Jerusalem Emergency Committee (no personal signature) to Jerusalem Bakers Union, ISA, Gimel, 274/1, April 29, 1948.
157. Hotel Industries, an adjunct of the General Federation of the Middle Class in Palestine, General Federation of Merchants in Tel Aviv and Jaffa, to Eliezer Perlson, Acting Mayor of Tel Aviv, TAMA, 4/38, Container 466, March 3, 1948.
158. General Federation of the Middle Class in the Land of Israel, Organization of Cafés, Restaurants, and Sausage Stands, Tel Aviv, to Israel Rokach, Mayor of Tel Aviv, TAMA, 4/38, Container 466, March 8, 1948.
159. Ibid.
160. Benny Morris, *1948: A History of the First Arab-Israeli War* (New Haven, CT: Yale University Press, 2008), 111.
161. "General Assembly of the Café, Hotel, Restaurant, and Pension Industry," JMA, Container 4589, Serial No. 20, March 21, 1948.

162. Zvi Lurie to Mordechai Shatner, CZA, J1/7549/2, March 29, 1948.

163. Ibid.

164. Dov Yosef, *The Faithful City: The Siege of Jerusalem, 1948* (New York: Simon and Schuster, 1960), 149.

165. Jerusalem Café and Restaurant Owners to Supply Subcommittee of Jerusalem Situation Committee, ISA, Gimel, 276/1, March 31, 1948.

166. Ibid.

167. "Decisions of the Sixth Council at Meeting 669," TAMA, 2368, Meetings of the Sixth Council, May 2, 1948.

168. Jerusalem Emergency Committee minutes, ISA, Gimel, 274/1, May 9, 1948.

169. Moshe Naor, *Social Mobilization in the Arab-Israeli War of 1948: On the Israeli Home Front* (London and New York: Routledge, 2013), 63–4.

170. Administration of Jerusalem Grocers' Situation Committee to Supply Subcommittee of Jerusalem Emergency Committee, JMA, 4589, Serial No. 20, March 12, 1948.

171. These stores were not privately owned. Associated with the Labor Movement, most of them operated in collective and cooperative settlements.

172. Administration of Jerusalem Grocers' Situation Committee to Supply Subcommittee of Jerusalem Emergency Committee, JMA, 4589, Serial No. 20, March 12, 1948.

173. Ibid.

174. Jerusalem Grocers' Situation Committee to Jerusalem Community Council Supply Committee, JMA, Container 4589, Serial No. 20, March 26, 1948.

175. Jerusalem Grocers' Situation Committee to Jerusalem Community Council Supply Committee, JMA, Container 4589, Serial No. 20, March 30, 1948.

176. Haim Salomon, Jerusalem Jewish Community Council, to Jerusalem Grocers' Situation Committee, ISA, Gimel, 276/2, April 5, 1948.

177. Jerusalem Grocers' Situation Committee (signed by S. Ben-Gershon, B. Rubinstein, H. Rivlin, and S. Friedman) to Jerusalem Community Council Supply Committee, JMA, Container 4589, Serial No. 20, March 30, 1948.

178. General Merchants Organization in Haifa and the Vicinity, Grocery Branch, to Mr. Mandelblüth, Haifa Situation Committee, HMA, File 00234/18 (4751), April 13, 1948.

179. Mordechai Shatner, member of the National Committee Executive, ISA, Gimel 117/24, Division 41, January 10, 1948.

180. Ibid. In Shatner's opinion, the "civil war on profiteering," as he put it, should be spearheaded by women's organizations.

181. *Community Council and Situation Committee News*, no. 1, JMA, Container 4589, Serial No. 19, February 25, 1948.

182. "Decisions of the Sixth Council at Meeting 650," TAMA, 2368, Meetings of the Sixth Council, January 25, 1948.

183. Ibid.

184. Situation Committee plenary decisions, HMA, File 00234/1 (4728), January 26, 1948.

185. General Organization of Merchants in Haifa and the Vicinity, "Remarks on the Plan for Regulation of Supplies in the Jewish Yishuv," presented for study to the Economic Council, an adjunct of the Haifa Situation Committee, HMA, File 00234/18 (4751), February 22, 1948.

186. Abraham Landsberg, Better Business Association (under the Patronage of the National Committee), to Mayor Rokach and Acting Mayor Perlson, TAMA, 4/38, Container 466, January 25, 1948.

187. Ibid.
188. Ibid.
189. Jerusalem Grocers' Situation Committee (signed: S. Friedman, S. Ben-Gershon, H. Rivlin, B. Rubinstein) to Jerusalem Community Council Supply Committee, JMA, Emergency Supplies, Container 4589, Serial No. 18, CZA, 3800/1, March 4, 1948.
190. Ibid.
191. Administration of Jerusalem Grocers' Situation Committee (H. Rivlin, Y. Lubin, H. Gnessin, S. Friedman, H. Pasternak, B. Rubinstein) to Supply Subcommittee of Jerusalem Emergency Committee, JMA, Container 4589, Serial No. 20, March 12, 1948.
192. Peretz Bernstein to Tel Aviv, Haifa, Jerusalem Chamber of Commerce and Tel Aviv Association of Importers, COCA, Chamber Relations With: (File II), March 2, 1948.
193. The anti-profiteering courts operated alongside, and under the supervision of, the municipal authorities (in the case of Tel Aviv, the municipal legal department).
194. Bakers' Organization, an adjunct of the General Federation of the Middle Class in Palestine, to Tel Aviv Mayor Israel Rokach, TAMA, 3/14/a/4, Container 466, March 14, 1948.
195. Jean-Louis Robert, "The Image of the Profiteer," in *Capital Cities at War*, Jay Winter and Jean-Louis Robert, eds. (Cambridge and New York: Cambridge University Press, 1997), 119–21.

3

"LITERALLY ABANDONED TO STARVATION"

The Bureaucratization of Relief and the Question of Responsibility for Soldiers' Families

DOCUMENTED IN PREVIOUS CHAPTERS WERE PATTERNS OF RESPONSE that economic interest groups and committees of internally displaced persons invoked against the implications of the war. The families of the inducted did not replicate these patterns; neither they nor the inductees themselves were inclined to unite around their shared hardships in the first months of the fighting. The second part of the war—that following the proclamation of independence—saw the emergence of associations of mobilized soldiers' wives, bereaved parents, and, farther on, demobilized soldiers. In the earlier (intercommunal) phase of the conflict, in contrast, soldiers and their families spoke out mainly within circles of the military system and vis-à-vis the authorities. What is more, family members of inductees and of soldiers wounded in combat received no direct care by the nascent authorities of the state in the making.

Why did the families decline to press their case through associative patterns at this time? Given what we know about their subsequent initiatives,[1] the most reasonable explanation seems to be that the family members, like the inductees themselves, did not know how long they would be mobilized; therefore, they could not foresee the economic price that they would have to pay. Furthermore, the inductees—foremost those in the Haganah, who accounted for most of them—assumed that their families would receive lump-sum compensation in the event of their death because this had been the standard Haganah practice for several years.[2] Another model of support for inductees' families, well-known in the Yishuv, was the in-cash benefit that the British Army had introduced in World War II for Jewish inductees from Mandate Palestine. The message sent by this arrangement was clear: the inductee surrenders his time and is willing to offer up his life, and the recruiting entity sees to his family's needs as an expression of gratitude. The Yishuv's National Institutions kept this policy in place after World War II by assuming responsibility for the care of demobilized soldiers, disabled veterans, and bereaved families and by establishing various departments for this purpose under the auspices of, or as adjuncts to, the National Committee.[3]

British Army benefits for soldiers' wives and children were based on a fixed rate irrespective of the family's social situation. Indigent families received an extra sum from the Central Committee for Care of Soldiers' and Guards' Families and qualified for grants from an allocations committee that served as an auxiliary of the British military.[4] Dependency on benefits and grants, however, was slight, because British Army inductees were relatively well paid to begin with and could send some of their remuneration home to support their families.[5] Now, shortly after the onset of the intercommunal violence, the Yishuv Defense Committee policy makers sought to base themselves on these familiar patterns.

Reality, however, quickly proved that the current war had made the familiar models become invalid due to the steadily rising number of inductees and, no less, the large number of casualties—204 dead after one month of fighting[6] and nearly a thousand dead[7] plus some 1,500 wounded after four months.[8] To meet the needs of the enlistees and their families, those at the Yishuv's helm needed financial resources that they did not have and hoped to base themselves on donations from the Diaspora (foremost the North American communities). To accomplish this, they had to establish voluntary settings that would qualify for receiving donations. This chapter sheds light on the establishment of this auspice and, in particular, the role played by both the authorities of the state in the making and civil associations, particularly women's organizations. It also probes the differences that emerged between those who made policy and the volunteers who had to implement it.

It was the head of the Haganah National Command, Israel Galili, who first brought up the problem of paying inductees. At a meeting of the Yishuv Defense Committee only two weeks after the violence began, Galili reported on the general mobilization order for the ground forces, which was expected to bring in some 6,000 men, most of whom would probably have to spend more than three days on duty. "A man who's been posted for three days ought to get paid," Galili stated.[9] Moshe Svirsky, representing civilian circles in the Kofer Hayishuv administration (a Yishuv office for defense taxation) and the Mobilization Fund, advised those in attendance that the fund once had a committee that set levels of aid for families and proposed that it be reinstated. He also suggested that a budget panel under the Defense Committee be established to "create local resources" and "then ask important Diaspora communities to help us." David Ben-Gurion, responding, proposed that Svirsky and Levi Shkolnik bring a motion on "how to arrange a mutual commitment by everyone in the Yishuv to Jews who are wounded."[10] The attendees concluded the meeting by resolving to form two committees, one for budget and one to set soldiers' wages.[11]

A week later, Svirsky and Shkolnik presented the Defense Committee with their recommendations on compensation for wounded servicemen's families. The proposal, based on the accepted Haganah practice, envisioned a lump-sum grant of £P300 from funds that "the entire Yishuv" would raise. As for wages and payments for serving inductees, they resolved to pay inductees after three consecutive days on duty and to base the remuneration on an industrial laborer's wage, less a sum for the inductee's upkeep. The wage table thus produced took account of the inductee's marital status and number of dependents.[12]

As for the wherewithal with which the families of men killed or badly wounded in service would be compensated,[13] Berl Repetur of Ahdut ha-'Avodah, a member of both review committees (budget and wages) who had been appointed a week earlier, proposed the use of funds "from those for general Yishuv purposes and not at the expense of the organization's budget." Repetur even suggested that men "whose call-up would entail full payment" should not be inducted for the time being.[14]

Ben-Gurion harshly criticized Svirsky's and Repetur's recommendations. He warned against the implications of undertaking to adopt the Haganah format of monetary compensation, noting that the proposals overlooked those who would sustain severe or lifelong injuries. "This has just begun," he reminded those in attendance. "Our main concern should be the security of the living and not of the dead, and if things get hard, they might get very hard.... A hundred men or more may fall on one day. If we pass this law—the family will have a very strong claim, it'll be impossible to defer [payment of the benefit] until after the war."[15]

Ben-Gurion based his stance on American policy in World War II, which indeed deferred payment to fallen soldiers' families until the war was over. He also challenged the idea of trying to set the size of the grant without first specifying its financial source. Since the benefit would be paid to those wounded among all inductees, whose numbers were rising gradually, he expected the financial burden soon to become insufferable. Therefore, he insisted that priorities be set and then established them himself mordantly and dispassionately:

> I think saving the Yishuv comes before making families happy, and I think it irresponsible to make a decision on no basis, without determining where the money for it will come from. Either it'll be taken from the defense budget or they'll go broke and won't pay the casualties. It mustn't be done unless there is a *special source* [emphasis added]. We're endangering the Yishuv; we're sowing demoralization, we won't be up to it. It's enough that they lost their child; should they also be deceived? I think it mustn't be done; no such law should be adopted unless we make an arrangement that will assure that the decision is upheld.

Ben-Gurion's message was plain enough: compensation for bereaved parents should be paid from philanthropic sources (hence a special source, as opposed to existing budgets), conditioned on raising the funds, and should not be assured until such is done.

Galili, opposing, described the pressure that was arriving from the field: Commanders "are already bombarding us with demands for permission to tell their subordinates what the Yishuv's liability in this matter is. People are giving their lives, going into places of danger, and they want to be sure that if something bad happens to them their families' sustenance will be assured, at least somewhat."[16]

Fearing the implications of the soldiers' state of mind for military steadfastness, Galili urged his colleagues to decide quickly and advised those in attendance that the leadership and its institutions should have a higher level of commitment to people doing not compulsory but volunteer service. As a start, he asked the Defense Committee to approve immediate coverage of casualties' medical expenses. On this, Ben-Gurion backed him unequivocally.[17]

As for compensating casualties' families, a debate ensued: Should it be given to every family or only to those that lose breadwinners, and how does one define a breadwinner? Should the definition include teenage boys who would have helped to support their families at some later time had they not fallen in battle? At the end of the discussion, Galili was authorized to forward a message to commanders that family members of breadwinners killed in Haganah service would receive a subsistence grant of up to £P300 per decision to be made by "a competent Yishuv-level committee [i.e., a board under the National Institutions umbrella] that will be established for this purpose."[18] The "competent" National Institutions committee would determine the applicants' extent of eligibility and work up a plan including long-term medical assistance for casualties and assistance to their families and to inductees at large.[19]

The wording of the resolution included two novelties that would influence the treatment of casualties' families going forward: the establishment of a special committee for the care of inductees and their families and the setting of criteria for eligibility for financial support, as opposed to the automatic grant that the Haganah had given dead servicemen's families hitherto.

The early timing of the discussion and the permission given to representatives of the Defense Committee to recommend relief programs for families and casualties—less than two weeks after the intercommunal violence began—indicate that, indeed, it was widely assumed that the embryonic state authorities should be responsive to this aspect of the implications of the war. Furthermore, the fact that the matter was being deliberated and addressed was being passed on to inductees by their commanders and presented to the public as a consensual if not unanimous decision.[20] This presumably encouraged families of service personnel as well as soldiers themselves to behave more passively than other sectors that had been affected by the war by way of economic hardship or internal displacement.[21] Either way, inductees and their families refrained, for the time being, from establishing organizations or committees and did not find it correct to bring their cause to public debate or to promote it by lobbying the policy-making echelons.

Further indication that the *responsables* had placed the issue on their agenda may be seen in decisions at the district Haganah command level concerning inductees' and fatalities' families. The Haganah commander in Tel Aviv, for example, ordered the drafting of a proposal for "treatment and concern for family members of comrades who fell, were wounded, or were taken prisoner on duty."[22] Several bottom-up factors promoted this initiative, foremost the wish to prevent situations of indigence and dependency: "Woe unto us if we make our comrades or their families wander around, pounding on institutions' doors."[23]

As Ben-Gurion had warned in the initial discussion, however, all the programs that began to take shape for casualties and their families had no existing and secure financial sources on which to rely. The proceeds of the

Mobilization and Rescue Fund were not originally intended for the care of wounded servicemen or any health-related needs. The Mobilization and Rescue Fund was pledged to defense-related matters. The first fundraising campaign in this context, titled *For the Nation's Security*, took place during the discussion in the Defense Committee that had begun more than a week previously. Its target, raising £P500,000 from the Yishuv, was attained. Several months later, the fund undertook an additional campaign, this time more ambitious at two million Palestine pounds. This target, too, was achieved, but only after the campaign was prolonged to September 1948.[24] The proceeds of these drives were earmarked primarily for various aspects of war funding, including gear, food, miscellaneous expenses, and the development of domestic military production. The resources raised from affluent Diaspora communities, foremost in the United States and South America, were meant predominantly for military procurements abroad.[25] Thus, Ben-Gurion told the truth when he explained that economic support of bereaved families was not included in the budget raised from the Mobilization and Rescue Fund, which was pledged to war requisites.

By mid-December, the number of inductees serving day in and day out had risen to 6,000 and was expected to climb to 10,000. Now it was clear to the fundraisers that they lacked the resources to cover the needs. In this context, the concept of a special source was resurrected, this time by Meyer Grabovsky, a Mapai functionary and a member of the National Committee. Grabovsky's idea was to explore the extent to which "American Jewry is of a mind to plug this hole." He also proposed the launch of a new fundraising campaign immediately; otherwise, "there will be nowhere from which to appropriate the money for these needs."[26]

Others proposed that the Mandate government be held "materially responsible" for compensating those killed, as it had been during the Arab uprising of the previous decade. When members of the National Committee approached Golda Meir and asked her to take this up with the high commissioner, however, she refused, explaining that she would discuss "the most urgent points [with him]. I want him to stop the things that are *causing* [emphasis added] the demand for compensation."[27] David Remez concurred, opining that action to prevent fatalities—installing protective armor on cars, an expensive proposition—should come first and support for families should wait for later.[28] Meir's and Remez's responses suggest clearly that to regularize the support of inductees' and casualties' families, the official Yishuv authorities would need to give this cause priority over other urgencies. Otherwise, sources of funding would not be found.[29]

During the Defense Committee's deliberations in early January, Ben-Gurion addressed himself to what would be called "constructive assistance"—setting financial aid at a level that would facilitate rehabilitation and employment by keeping inductees' pre-enlistment jobs open for them. He also insisted that "wage-earning wives [should] engage in useful work." As for who should be in charge, Ben-Gurion wrote in his diary, "Much desired—a partnership among all circles."[30] Ben-Gurion's message remained consistent: the entity that would centralize support for families should represent the public in a broad way. His approach traced not only to political calculus but also, and no less, to the philanthropic source of the money and the wish to rally public opinion behind the policy that the envisioned public entity would make.

Yishuv public opinion, however, cut the national leadership no political slack. By the end of the first month of the intercommunal violence, the media already demanded the formalization of concern for widows and orphans. Specifically, *Ha'aretz* journalist Arieh Gelblum criticized the leadership for not helping casualties' families "whose reed of support has broken" to receive material aid. To correct this, he proposed the establishment of a relief fund for war victims to which casualties' families might apply.[31]

"What will become of those who made the dearest sacrifice?" asked the editor of the *Ha'aretz* women's and home supplement.

> It is society's duty to ask and investigate whether, in addition to the agony of the loss, there isn't something here of a material tragedy as well if the person killed had been a son who had been supporting his parents or a husband with a wife and children. Even if society cannot heal the wounds brought on by the psychological disaster, it should at least prevent the material disaster that accompanies the death of an adult son or a head of household.... A situation that forces the casualties of our war to become indigents who apply to welfare bureaus should not be allowed to come about.[32]

The writer also commented on the gender aspect of the problem, noting that only one-third of adult women "engage in labors that come with a wage" and that their jobs were usually less protected "at a time of economic crisis."[33]

The media's attention to the issue reflected the growing pressure that casualties' families were bringing against the authorities whom they recognized, foremost the Social Work Department of the National Committee, which passed it on to the leadership and demanded that the latter adopt immediate solutions until the committee could complete its "constructive" arrangement for families.[34] Grabovsky assumed that family relief would initially come from the welfare bureaus on the basis of their regular budgets. These bureaus, however, were too underfunded to meet the needs of widows with babies and young children "who were left without the bare basics."[35]

The matter remained unresolved even after two months of intercommunal fighting, during which time Ben-Gurion continued to receive demands for a response by means of a Yishuv-level committee. Yosef Y. (evidently Yosef Yizre'eli) and Levi (most likely Levi Shkolnik, subsequently Eshkol) presented Ben-Gurion with the need for "a committee to care for the inductee and his family: to arrange payment for soldiers' dependents (wives, parents), compensate bereaved families, care for the disabled, make arrangements for those discharged from service, and attend to the soldier's general welfare: newspapers, concerts, and so on."[36]

Yizre'eli proposed an organizational model that would be based on civilian activists from recognized volunteer organizations identified with the political mainstream and the National Institutions: the Women's Labor Council, Hadassah, the Maccabi World Union, the Farmers Association, and the Soldier's Welfare Committee. Ben-Gurion evidently had no objection to the idea in its general sense and to the centrality of representatives of volunteer organizations in it. However, he remarked in his diary, "This committee should be set up alongside the Defense Committee."[37]

Indeed, at the next meeting of the Defense Committee, Galili moved to establish a five-member public commission that would set levels of support for soldiers' family and help those who had been wounded and bruised.[38] It would engage in relief for inductees themselves; implement a policy of discounts for soldiers and their families for public transit, housing rent, admission to places of entertainment, and so on; and assure inductees' jobs and care for those discharged.[39] The members of this commission, Galili continued, should have amassed experience in dealing with inductees' families in World War II.[40] The Personnel Division at Haganah headquarters was already establishing facts on the ground by appointing the staff officer Eliezer Lipson "as a central address for casualties' families." Lipson's first task, Galili stated, was to assure "a respectful attitude toward the fallen." As matters proceeded, however, he also expected Lipson to deal with the question of family support.[41]

Galili's announcement drew questions about the status of the public commission, the establishment of which had been discussed on various occasions. Remez brought the matter to a head by wondering whether the idea was to hand responsibility to a soldier's welfare committee and not make it a "Yishuvic liability." By saying this, Remez was alluding to the National Committee for the Jewish Soldier, a long-standing and esteemed entity that had been established during World War II under Yosef Baratz.[42] Remez, chairman of the National Committee, reported on the welfare authorities' growing beleaguerment as they tried to serve the steadily rising number of casualties; he also asked how his colleagues intended to solve the money problem. Ben-Gurion called the spade a spade: "I understand that Remez is referring to compensation for bereaved families [and] the wounded. We won't make a decision about that. There ought to be a soldier's welfare committee ... that will look out for the soldier and his family. We won't define its purview. I don't know why there are grounds to oppose our setting up a public commission to take care of soldiers and their families."[43]

Reverberating in Ben-Gurion's remarks were the doubts that he had expressed in the first discussion about the viability of funding support at the requisite level and the need to resort to the aforementioned "special source" (i.e., Diaspora contributions that, under various countries' tax laws, could be forwarded only to nongovernmental entities, such as the Soldier's Welfare Committee).[44]

Subsequently, it was agreed that in the first stage, the Yishuv-level committee would deal with payments to soldiers' families.[45] This decision was pursuant to another one (concerning a set of rules for payments to Haganah inductees) in which each inductee's eligibility for payment and his family's eligibility for support would be determined on the basis of criteria that would take family composition and economic situation into account.[46] The rules did regularize soldiers' and families' eligibility but said nothing about casualties. In an instruction sheet for command staff on the front, distributed pursuant to Lipson's appointment, Galili announced the naming of "a special officer who will serve as a central address for our bereaved families." This made it Lipson's job to apprise families of their loved ones' death and stay in touch with them afterward. Lipson was also expected to review the bereaved families' economic circumstances and recommend necessary aid.[47]

The Haganah's standing procedures on serving notice had already begun to seep in. They included a form with guidelines on how to deliver bad news to casualties' families and on families' short- and long-term care. The clause relating to the care of the casualty's family specified the Casualties Department of the Personnel Branch as the entity responsible for dealing with "providing the casualty's family with all needed assistance where necessary."[48] Concern for inductees' families in the event of death included turning over their personal belongings to their families, paying out insurance proceeds and compensation to next of kin, and arranging family dispensations and discounts on taxes and childcare, as well as a statement addressing the family's sustenance. In the event of injury and disability, the department was to arrange for the casualty the possibility of "convalescence, recovery, receipt of insurance proceeds and compensation, job placement, etc."[49] Thus, entities at the end of the administrative chain, particularly those associated with the military, were signing agreements, laying down procedures, and making ad hoc appointments in one concrete field after another.

Ultimately, the Defense Committee established the Yishuv Inductee and Family Committee "alongside the defense institutions" (meaning it was aligned with but external to these institutions); its duties included "supporting the inductee's family in accordance with the rules for inductee payment and retention."[50] The announcement about the formation of the committee included guidelines for implementation—the distribution of a special questionnaire and forms that the applicant's direct commanding officer would have to fill out and approve. The officer was to instruct inductees "to report accurate details and [warn them] that every case [would] be investigated by a competent Yishuv institution."[51] Command staff was to advise all inductees of their right to apply for benefits but was not to "encourage" them to do so. In a circular attached to the letter, it was stated that "unlike the standard practice in other armies," family grants would be given only to inductees' dependents who needed it for basic subsistence, but the grant itself would be larger than the norm in other armies. These tenets, it was explained, reflected the premise that it is "just and correct to use the meager resources available to us to help those in need instead of dividing them up among everyone and leaving specifically the indigent in distress."[52]

To attain a just apportionment of resources, inductees and their commanders were asked to weigh carefully whether the family designated for support should really be on the Yishuv's dole. Accordingly, they were instructed to use discretion and apply only in cases of "unquestionable necessity."[53] To eliminate doubt, it was noted explicitly that "an inductee's wife and parents must make a living from their labor and only in cases where their unfitness for labor can be proved, or where concern for young children rules out the possibility of their working, may the inductee submit the appropriate form."[54] According to the circular, the Yishuv Inductee and Family Committee must arrange work for supported inductees' families through the general labor exchange wherever possible. Concurrently, command staff was advised that since only 20 percent of inductee families would be able to benefit from the support, the commander in charge should "ensure that the number of applications in his unit not exceed said percent." "Remember!" the author of the circular warned, "Unjustified applications may be severely harmful to our inductees' families and ultimately to our war effort."[55] The policy makers also took measures to rally public opinion behind the decision to apply selective support based on eligibility criteria. In *Davar*, it was stressed that "every Hebrew soldier" who was a sole or partial breadwinner "should be confident that after he exits his house to go to war, a public body will stand beside his family when it needs care."[56]

The Yishuv Inductee and Family Committee, headed by Georg Lubinski (Giora Lotan), went into action at the beginning of March from its office in Tel Aviv.[57] Baruch Rabinov, head of the Haganah National Command Finance Department, reported to Ben-Gurion about the availability of nearly half a million Palestine pounds for the upkeep of soldiers, "including families."[58] Much time, however, would pass before support for soldiers would become systematic.[59] Concurrently and irrespective of the allocation of payments, local chapters of the Yishuv Inductee and Family Committee began to come into being in order to implement the policy in specified geographical areas. One of the first initiatives in this context was the formation of a local committee (one could better describe it as a chapter) for inductees and families in Jerusalem, composed in a manner designed to reflect a broad ambit of local National Institutions activists: the local defense committee, the National Service Census Board, and the Committee for Care of Soldiers' and Guards' Families, as well as social workers.[60]

As progress in responding to inductees' families tarried, women's organizations stepped in as well. The Organization of Working Mothers (a Labor Movement entity that acted in coordination with the Women's Labor Council, an auspice of the Histadrut) pressed for a larger budget allocation from the National Institutions so that it could expand enrollment in its day-care facilities to "children of inductees and affected families."⁶¹ It was also women's organizations that exerted pressure to give inductees' wives broader employment opportunities,⁶² and the Organization of Working Mothers set up special offices to arrange work for women who were left without breadwinners and to place their children in day care so that they could hold down jobs once found.⁶³

The defense system, mindful of the women's organizations' experience, resources, and above all ample volunteer human resources, asked them to leverage the matter in an organized and centralized way under a subcommittee of women's organizations referred to as Eve's Task Force.⁶⁴ Those at the women's organizations did not always take a liking to this hierarchical approach and what they perceived as their being crowded out from leadership and policy-making positions. They realized, however, that their representatives should sit on these committees and seize the resulting opportunity to exert influence from the inside. "Now they're going to set up welfare committees . . . and *women should take part on the committees.*"⁶⁵ Beba Idelson, advising the board of the Council of Women's Organizations, repeated this at a general assembly of the council, stressing the importance of women's participation on the welfare committees that would be taking care of casualties' and soldiers' families.⁶⁶ Idelson apparently understood the nature of the moment, a transitional period in which volunteer entities and institutional and pre-governmental systems were intertwined and assimilated, and wished to make sure that she and her comrades would not be left out. In fact, women had long been involved in the local and district committees. The author of a circular sent out by the Yishuv Committee made the necessity of this membership clear: "If the Council of Women's Organizations is not represented on the local committees, someone from it should be added."⁶⁷

Despite this inclusion and the blurring of boundaries between autonomous and "institutional" (officially sponsored) volunteer activity, the women's organizations maintained their independence and allowed themselves to participate in the rising tide of public criticism of the failure, to that time, to set up properly the competent authority for the care of inductees' families. Thus, in an article in the *Davar* women's supplement, Nehama Hoffman of the Organization of Working Mothers welcomed the establishment of a "department" [*sic*] for this purpose but trenchantly rued the absence of such an institution at the time the battles began. She demanded the co-optation of women's organizations into the doings of the new entity in order to rid it of "the legacy of routine social work" and lend it "a national social complexion" and a spirit of "mutual aid." Implicitly she distinguished between bottom-up and "from the inside" social services and those of the top-down kinds—the sort that might inculcate dependency and hierarchical relations between benefactors and beneficiaries.[68]

Thus, while the various Haganah divisions were asked to report any vacancies in civilian wage-paying posts so that the jobs could be given to inductees' family members first,[69] the Council of Women's Organizations was already placing female members of casualties' families in enterprises that it operated—particularly in canteens and mess halls.[70] The Organization of Working Mothers, represented on the Histadrut's Women's Labor Council, had of course a structural advantage in regard to employment. Beba Idelson was central in this activity and managed, at the end of a process, to steer a resolution through the Executive Committee reserving "all service jobs under the autonomous management of [Histadrut] institutions . . . for inductees' families and disabled and demobilized inductees."[71] The resolution, adopted in late April, was preceded by months of letters to the Women's Labor Council from dozens of distressed women who had been economically harmed by their husbands' induction, as well as growing pressure on the council to enroll casualties' children in the settings that it operated. During these months, many women toppled into dire pecuniary hardship as promised payments failed to materialize and the partial advances that they received could not sustain even the humblest standard of living. At a meeting of the Executive Committee, Idelson told the story of a woman who had threatened to abandon her children or commit suicide unless her matters were set straight.[72]

Delinquency in payout of family benefits continued in April, the fifth month of the intercommunal violence.[73] The resulting frustration, growing to begin with, was additionally fueled by the bombastic rhetoric that accompanied the establishment of the Yishuv Inductee and Family Committee, stirring hopes that were quickly dashed.[74] *Ha'aretz* "knew" that special branches of the committee would be set up countrywide to manage the care of local inductee families. It also "knew" whence the committee would get its budget—from the Mobilization and Rescue Fund—and how large that budget would be (around £P100,000).[75]

The Yishuv Committee had indeed been active in March. By the end of that month, it had finished drafting rules that established criteria for benefits in reflection of the views and ideas that policy makers at various echelons had expressed. The new rules also gave inductees' relatives priority at the general labor bureaus and required employers of fallen inductees to hire their wives or one of their parents in their stead, where possible. The rules also laid down a mandatory procedure for the approval of benefits. It included investigation by the local committee, effected via a home visit by a staff member who was "knowledgeable in social investigations."[76] The authorities and "other interested parties" were to be represented on the local and regional committees. This wording cemented the participation of the women's organizations.[77]

The Jerusalem public began to notice the doings of its local committee in late March, when the panel announced reception hours. By that late stage, however—after four months of uninterrupted fighting—many wives had run out of patience. So often did they burst into the offices and disrupt the work that the committee requested, and received, help from a member of the People's Guard to maintain order.[78]

Observing the hardships that accompanied the Jerusalem committee's work, one gets an idea of the problematic nature of selective benefits based on prior investigation. The committee members found it difficult to supply "evidentiary" grounds for the support of applications when the inductees themselves were in a cutoff part of the city or out of town altogether.[79] They tried to expedite the process by allowing inductees' families to apply on their behalf,[80] thus skirting the problem that had come about when application forms dithered for months or failed to reach the committee at all.

As the months passed, however, the inductees sensed no real change in the care of their families. As one battalion commander wrote to his superior, "If this matter isn't cleared up, we'll get to a point where people will refuse to keep serving. I've already encountered people who've declared an extended symbolic strike to protest the way they're being treated. The final appeals committee has to be set up more quickly and the existing committees have to improve the accuracy of their reviews."[81]

Complaints about inductees' disgruntlement and growing indiscipline due to "disarray in support for parents and families" widened steadily and came up for discussion at a meeting of the Defense Committee.[82] "The disorder surrounding family benefits is starting to avenge itself on induction," charged Dr. Binyamin Avniel, chair of the National Service Census Board, demanding a quick fix.[83] The inability to commit to family benefits was central in delaying the decision to mobilize men who had families with children.[84]

"It's still premature if not impossible to review its work and the efficiency of what it's doing,"[85] wrote Shulamit Lev-Ari about the new committee in mid-April, five months into the fighting and after the Jewish side had sustained 895 dead and several thousand wounded.[86] Indeed, dependents' benefits remained in disarray in mid-April, three months after they had been promised to inductees who had been supporting parents or relatives.[87] Even such answers as had been received were incomplete, and many entailed resubmission due to lack of details, address problems, or even the infuriating explanation that the inductees' parents lived in "dangerous places," making it impossible to review their claims. In addition, more than 50 percent of applications (*not* counting those handed back due to missing details) were rejected.[88] Another aspect that had been overlooked when the criteria for relief were specified was the sudden impoverishment of Jerusalem inhabitants due to loss of livelihood. In one of many heartbreaking letters, Fritz Loewenstein, secretary of the Jerusalem chapter of the Yishuv Inductee and Family Committee, wrote to one such applicant, Dr. Hans Nathan, an inductee's father who had lost his sole source of income when the Ben-Yehuda Street bombing destroyed his business. Loewenstein, who was evidently acquainted with Nathan, had to reject his application because the reason for his loss of livelihood did not pass the test for benefits, which were reserved only for parents whose inducted children had supported them before the war.[89]

Masses of people were denied aid due to slipshod investigations, causing such displeasure among inductees as to have "a bad influence on the discharge of [their] duty," prompting requests to be excused from mobilization.[90] Evidently, one of the rationales for denying families access to the reception office was concern about "cleansing these support operations of the stigma of social assistance as far as possible." Therefore, it was also decided to pay family benefits by sending cashier's checks directly to beneficiaries' homes.[91] This rationale, however, as well as prodigious efforts to maximize justice in determining eligibility for support, were neither appreciated nor understood by the beneficiaries themselves as frustration over the distance between needs and response mounted steadily. Even when a local committee did its job and authorized benefits, payout was delinquent, and families recognized as eligible were unable to exercise their entitlements.[92]

Each of the auspices involved appeared to operate soundly; each ostensibly nailed things down, handed out information, maintained its professional cadres, and divided responsibilities between itself and its peers. Not one, however, seemed able to get past its intersection with the others. Thus, while local chapters railed against the central committee for not forwarding the funds that they needed to arrange family benefits, the central committee denounced the defense system treasury. Between the lines, one finds that communication between the central committee and Haganah units took place via the defense system treasury, and even a seemingly simple step such as handing out the forms got stuck along the way, resulting in repeated delays in payments to soldiers and their families.[93]

In late April, Avniel reported to Ben-Gurion about "months in which our fine soldiers put in full service and their families *are literally abandoned to starvation.*" This dilatory treatment eroded soldiers' morale, resulting in some even "running away from the camp because of it."[94] Avniel thought it better to pay several hundred families mistakenly than to drive "thousands of needy soldier families to hunger and demoralize soldiers and families collectively." He stated, "The situation is much worse than I have managed to express." Avniel, who as chair of the National Service Census Board had no ex officio responsibility for family benefits, felt it was his civic duty to warn against the foreseeable implications of the slow-paced treatment of such a sensitive topic.[95]

Care for Disabled Veterans and Bereaved Families

The cause of disabled veterans was initially marginal on the agenda of the Yishuv Inductee and Family Committee, which focused on arranging welfare payments to inductees' families. Disabled veterans were to switch over to the committee's care after convalescence so that they could be returned "to the path of working life commensurate with [their] situation, including protracted individual care, finding special sources of livelihood, constructive investments . . . and training for new work."[96]

In Jerusalem, the care of bereaved families and wounded soldiers' kin was deposited in the lap of Michal Feldman,[97] who for this purpose formed a special subcommittee that again found the going very tough in the absence of guidelines from the center. The frustration of those tasked with the treatment of this ultrasensitive matter is evident in a report from the secretary of the Jerusalem chapter to its Yishuv-level parent. In this document, variants on the expression *We don't know* recurs time and again:

> To this day we know nothing more about the question of compensation for bereaved families than that such a program exists or that benefits awarded

by ourselves are given at the expense of compensation. We do not know (a) whether every family will receive compensation or only those who need it; (b) whether every family will receive the same amount or whether the sums will vary in keeping with the circumstances of each case, particularly the social circumstances, and what the sum or sums will be; (c) roughly when it is thought that the compensation will be paid and whether they are thinking about giving the family a lump sum or whether we will provide supervision and guidance in the use of the money; (d) whether deceased who leave behind neither a wife nor children nor parents will receive no compensation, or will other relatives be sought? . . . I need not explain to you that it would be very important for us to know all these details because they often determine whether and how much to give.[98]

Groping through the mist of this uncertainty, the committee in Jerusalem processed 115 bereavement applications and awarded monthly benefits to thirty-six families "provided compensation is owed."[99] The volume of the data makes it clear that the committee did not deal with most cases of bereavement in Jerusalem at this time. Instead, it processed only those referred to it—"about one-third of all cases in the Jerusalem area," in the estimation of the committee members. This tally overlooked Jerusalem residents who fell elsewhere; the committee members had no official information about them.[100]

When the instructions from Tel Aviv finally arrived, they allowed no possibility whatsoever of support for childless widows. The members of the Jerusalem committee found this outrageous, noting that many soldiers' widows were wholly unprepared for the "war of existence" and had to learn an occupation in order to gain economic independence. Additional wives, they noted, were burdened with elderly parents who had until then been aided by their late husbands, making the requirement of being a "mother of children" often unjustified.[101]

Manifested here again is the gap between a local entity, in continual contact with a needy and vulnerable population, and the distanced perspective of a national-level committee. Those at the Jerusalem local chapter argued that the criteria for aiding bereaved parents should be broadened and not conditioned on age or state of health. They also urged the central committee to commit to financial support that would assure orphans' education and agreed unanimously that wives and, perhaps, parents should be given some benefit irrespective of their social situation and with no strings attached.[102]

The helplessness of the injured and disabled was also reflected in a letter from Avniel to Ben-Gurion:

We may not always be able to help the indigent and the helpless, but let there at least be an arrangement where the downtrodden and the injured will find an open door and an attentive ear to which they can pour out their bitter hearts and woebegone souls. This matters, too—after all, we cannot always give real assistance . . . we are approached by soldiers who sustained illness or injury in the course of duty and have no one to care for and stand by them in their distress and illness. We have no way of helping and no answer to offer. And when we refer them to the Soldier's Welfare Committee, again they find unwelcoming faces and also, sometimes, unwelcoming doors.[103]

The Widening Gap between Ideality and Reality— Aid to Inductees' Families and War Casualties on the Eve of Statehood

In early May, in a report to its parent committee on its work and future duties, the Jerusalem local chapter addressed the gap between needs and implementation. The rapporteurs had estimated, for example, that there would be 1,500 needy families of inductees in Jerusalem but received more than 2,000 applications for support. On May 1, approximately 2,000 partly mobilized men were switched to full mobilization, thus joining the population of those eligible to apply for support, their social needs permitting. The second mobilization was also different in its sociodemographic complexion; if the first inductees had been single and some supported their parents, now most were married and had children. In late May, when the data were presented, payments for April had not yet been fully made and added up to twice or more the amount that would be forthcoming.[104] Two weeks later, as stated, in view of the changes in the inductees' profiles, the irrelevance of this sum was clear to all.[105]

The Council of Women's Organizations expected the appointment of three of its members to the Yishuv Inductee and Family Committee to give it meaningful influence there. As it happened, however, many other bodies attained representation on this fifteen-person national body—a large and cumbersome ensemble in which the share of the women's coalition was narrowed.[106] In response, the council demanded the honoring of the initial motion, by which it would be given 50 percent of membership and be allowed to fill the post of coordinator at both the national entity and the Tel Aviv branch. Concurrently, the council approached Remez, who had established the committee in the first place, and demanded its place on it. Remez, responding at a delay, explained that the committee had not yet begun to function.[107]

On the eve of statehood, the Yishuv Inductee and Family Committee sent out a circular with working rules in regard to inductees' families and war casualties. Its authors reported that the Committee of General Labor Exchanges had adopted rules setting forth the rights of inductees' and casualties' families in queuing for jobs. The rules also spelled out the rights of soldiers discharged due to injury, those who had been incapacitated, and servicemen's widows and disabled veterans' wives who had become their households' sole breadwinners. The circular reported the establishment of a Yishuv-level welfare department for inductees.[108]

The Inductee and Family Committee appears to have geared up for regular activity only two days before statehood was declared. Six months of war, in which the number of inductees exceeded 42,000, had to pass before the institution began to function regularly.[109]

The first stage in coping with the direct agonies of military induction by the nascent institutions of state revealed the inductees' and their families' expectations of the establishment and induced the leading authorities to acknowledge their responsibility, however difficult, for implementing the policy decided upon. From the standpoint of community resilience and adaptation to a crisis, the situation described above concerns a more conservative case of humanitarian relief for a population in distress. It was not the kind of situation that helps to build capacity—identifying the elements of power in the community and making them a foundation on which to build social capital, from which steadfastness and adaptability may grow.[110]

The lack of genuine dialogue and interaction with the affected population, and the fact that the casualties themselves did not establish representative associations of their own to confront more institutionalized bodies, led to dependency on the relief mechanisms and discouraged capacity-building.[111] It is true that policy makers often expressed a diametrically opposite intent—the wish to make aid constructive and prevent the transformation of inductees' families into welfare cases, mainly by providing means of livelihood in exchange of mere welfare support—but the outcome did not square with the rhetoric. The selective method employed—establishing rigid criteria for aid and having the military system test eligibility on the basis of information received from caregiving agencies—often disrupted and short-circuited the relief process and aggravated the dependency of those in need of help on the entities that delivered it. The Defense Committee's decision to interact with the inductees and not with their families overlooked heads of household and denied them a partnering role in the relief processes that were intended for the families, or, to use Sue Lautze's and John Hammock's terminology, minimized their capacity-building process.

As demonstrated above, the authorities preferred to allow service to be delivered by a public committee that was not part of the pre-state authority structure but also did not authentically represent their client population. Paradoxically, this very factor, given the committees' structural weakness in financial resources and vagueness as to the limits of its powers, placed the inductees' families at an ever-growing disadvantage in their contacts with agencies that should have responded, however minimally, to their distress. It is altogether likely that this negative experience prompted soldiers' wives and, in their wake, demobilized soldiers and, above all, disabled war veterans to reject any attempt to mediate, inducing them to speak out by themselves, sometimes very aggressively. I will gauge this change in the modus operandi and the coping behavior of inductees' families and demobilized soldiers in part II of this book.

Notes

1. In regard to such initiatives by inductees' families and inductees themselves after discharge or injury, see chapters 6 and 7.

2. Moshe Svirsky's report to Yishuv Defense Committee, Ben-Gurion Archive (hereinafter: BGA), Protocols Division, December 18, 1947.

3. Shulamit Lev-Ari, "How the Yishuv Looks Out for Inductees' Families: Upon the Establishment of the Yishuv Inductee and Family Committee," *Ha'aretz*, April 12, 1948. Care of demobilized soldiers (mainly veterans of World War II) was the source of constant and perceptible tension between the Yishuv leadership and the Mandate government. According to Yoav Gelber, those eligible for government benefits received them at a delay, and most had to run a gauntlet of committees and clerks to determine the levels of demobilization allowances and grants that would be due. The handling of soldiers' assimilation into civilian life at the end of the war was similarly fraught with complexity and tension. Despite the many mishaps that attended demobilization and the process of caring for families, the Yishuv retained positive memories of the concern of the British government and army for their soldiers; indeed, this was the model that they now wished to apply in the context of the War of Independence. On the demobilization process and its attendant stresses, see Yoav Gelber, *The History of Volunteering, Vol. 4, British, Arabs, and Germans* (in Hebrew) (Jerusalem: Yad Izhak Ben-Zvi, 1984), 209–66.

4. M. Turnovsky-Pinner, "Grants for the Inductee's Family," *Ha'aretz*, May 20, 1948.

5. Ibid.

6. Yoav Gelber, *Independence versus Nakba* (in Hebrew) (Or Yehuda: Kinneret Zmora Bitan, Dvir, 2004), 63. The number of Palestinian Arab casualties was similar—208.

7. Ibid., 85; according to Gelber, the number of fatalities by early April was 895 on the Jewish side and 991 on the Palestinian Arab side. According to Benny Morris, *1948: A History of the First Arab-Israeli War* (New Haven, CT: Yale University Press, 2008), 112, there were roughly 1,000 Jewish dead by the end of March.

8. According to Gelber (*Independence versus Nakba*, 108), the count of Jewish wounded came to 1,384 by mid-March.

9. Defense Committee meeting, BGA, Protocols Division, Israel Galili remarks, December 11, 1947.

10. In addition to serving as treasurer of the Haganah, Levi Shkolnik (later Eshkol) was Ben-Gurion's aide on the Yishuv Defense Committee and head of the National Command Center, in which capacity he dealt with mobilization, supply, and procurement.

11. Defense Committee meeting, BGA, Protocols Division, December 11, 1947.

12. Defense Committee meeting, BGA, Protocols Division, December 18, 1947.

13. The term used in the discussion of wounded soldiers was *severely wounded*, presumably referring to those who were injured badly enough that they could not return to productive life and livelihood.

14. Ibid., Berl Repetur remarks.

15. Ibid., Ben-Gurion remarks. What he means is that if a decision on immediate compensation for every dead soldier's family were made, the Yishuv institutions would be obligated to each family irrespective of the number of casualties and the authorities' financial resources.

16. Ibid.

17. In the summarizing memorandum and after discussion, Galili worded the resolution as follows: "(b) We acknowledge that representatives of the Jewish Agency Executive and the National Committee administration will be added in order to produce a draft constitution that shall include a method of long-term medical aid for the wounded [and] aid for the families of those who were wounded or killed on their watch." Two months later, an agreement was also signed between the Haganah and the Histadrut's health fund (a health-care provider somewhat akin to an HMO) concerning an arrangement for inductees' medical insurance. See "Agreement between the Yishuv Security Organization and the Health Fund of the General Federation of Jewish Labor in Palestine concerning Medical Aid Arrangements for Inductees and Their Families," Israel Defense Forces Archives (hereinafter: IDFA), 33-481-1949; Galili remarks, Defense Committee, February 24, 1948.

18. Ibid.

19. Ibid.

20. "Those Aged 23–24–25 Report from Today in Tel Aviv: Inductees' Rights Equal to Soldiers' Rights," *Davar*, December 25, 1947, 1.

21. On the active response of civilians who sustained economic damage or displacement due to the war, see chapters 1 and 2.

22. To Kiriati (code name of Michael Ben-Gal) from Levi (Enshel Sachnai), IDFA, 27-321-1948, December 11, 1947.

23. Ibid.

24. Moshe Naor, *Social Mobilization in the Arab-Israeli War of 1948: On the Israeli Home Front* (London and New York: Routledge, 2013), 95–9.

25. Ibid., 103–5.

26. National Committee meeting, Central Zionist Archives (hereinafter: CZA), J1/7268, Meyer Grabovsky's remarks, December 15, 1947. Note that the *For the Nation's Security* fundraising campaign ended that very day.
27. Ibid., Golda Meir remarks.
28. Ibid., Aharon Remez remarks.
29. Ibid.
30. Ben-Gurion diary, BGA, January 2, 1948.
31. Arieh Gelblum, "Concern for Widows and Orphans to Be Systematized," *Ha'aretz*, January 9, 1948.
32. Shulamit (no last name given), "Insurance and Security for the Widow," *Ha'aretz*, January 27, 1948.
33. Ibid.
34. Rahel Cohen to David Remez (handwritten and not sent), CZA, J1/12420, January 21, 1948.
35. Ibid.
36. Ben-Gurion diary, BGA, January 30, 1948.
37. Ibid. The term *alongside* or *adjunct* was common coinage in the political constellation of the Yishuv. It related to voluntary organizations that enjoyed the patronage and backing of the recognized National Institutions and even acted on their behalf but were neither immanent to them nor funded by them.
38. *Public* is a term that was used at the time to denote what we refer to today as *nongovernmental*. The distinction between *wounded* and *bruised* is not clear. Galili considered the terms distinct, possibly denoting different degrees of injury.
39. Defense Committee meeting, BGA, Protocols Division, Galili remarks, February 3, 1948.
40. Examples given were Giora (George) Lubinski, director of the National Committee's Social Work Department and head of the division for families of soldiers and supernumeraries; Eliezer Perlson, deputy mayor of Tel Aviv and director of the municipal Health Department; Zelig Rusiecki, a Haganah veteran and a member of the National Committee for the Soldier; and others.
41. Defense Committee meeting, BGA, Protocols Division, February 2, 1948. According to Zehava Ostfeld, this announcement related to the establishment of the Casualties Department, at the head of which staff officer Eliezer Lipson was stationed as a liaison between the Haganah (later the IDF) and casualties' families. See Zehava Ostfeld, *An Army Is Born: Main Stages in the Construction of the Israel Defense Forces and the Ministry of Defense under David Ben-Gurion* (in Hebrew) (Tel Aviv: Ministry of Defense, 1994), 397.
42. Yehuda Slutsky, *History of the Haganah, Vol. 3, Part 1* (in Hebrew) (Tel Aviv: Am Oved, 1972), 722–5.
43. Remarks by Remez and Ben-Gurion's response, meeting of Defense Committee, BGA, Protocols Division, February 3, 1948.
44. Esther Suissa, "The Politics of Philanthropy: The Creation and Work of the Israel Education Fund, 1964–1967," Master's Thesis in Israel Studies, Ben-Gurion University of the Negev (2014), 38–40; Ernst Stock, *Beyond Partnership: The Jewish Agency and the Diaspora, 1959–1971* (New York: Herzl, 1992), 78–80.
45. Defense Committee, BGA, Protocols Division, February 3, 1948.

46. To Segal G., from Kiriati (the text in the document is stricken out), IDFA, 1–321-1948, February 6, 1948; to Staff C., from Kiriati, IDFA, 1–321-1948, February 6, 1948.
47. Hillel to Staff C., IDFA, 1–321-1948, February 9, 1948.
48. From Kenesset [Haganah], Re: Casualties (Provisional Instructions), IDFA, 1–321-1948, February 9, 1948.
49. "Casualties, Provisional Instructions," IDFA, 1–321-1948, February 9, 1948.
50. From Kenesset [Haganah] Personnel Division, to Staff C., IDFA, 330–2644-1949, February 25, 1948. See also Ben-Gurion's remarks at conclusion of meeting of Defense Committee, BGA, February 24, 1948.
51. From Kenesset [Haganah] Personnel Division, to Staff C., Ibid.
52. Ibid.
53. Ibid.
54. Ibid.
55. Ibid.
56. "Starting in March—Caring for the Inductee's Family," *Davar*, March 16, 1948, 1.
57. Kiriati from Utz (code name for Isar Ben-Zvi), IDFA, 34–321-1948, March 1, 1948.
58. Ben-Gurion diary, BGA, March 1, 1948.
59. Defense Committee meeting, BGA, Protocols Division, March 16, 1943.
60. Letter from G. Lubinski to M. Simon, Jewish Agency, Yishuv Inductee and Family Committee (established by the Yishuv Defense Committee), CZA, File 9274, March 4, 1948.
61. Summary of Organization of Working Mothers Department meeting, February 26, 1948, Labor Movement Archives (hereinafter: LMA), IV 250–49-39.
62. Ibid.
63. Devora Nusowieki, "Mothers in the Rear," *Davar* women's supplement, February 5, 1948.
64. Ahya to Levi (code names of nonidentified high-ranking officials at the Tel Aviv [Kiryati] Brigade), IDFA, 29–321-1948, March 2, 1948.
65. Minutes of Regional Meeting of Local Committees of Council of Women's Organizations (Tel Aviv, Dan Bloc, and Sharon), Tel Aviv, LMA, IV 250–49-30, March 8, 1948.
66. Ibid.
67. Circular 2/48, signed by Dr. G. Lubinski, CZA, File 9274, April 8, 1948.
68. Nehama Hoffman, "Up for Discussion: Hospitality for Refugee Children," *Davar* women's supplement, March 16, 1948.
69. General Staff/Personnel Division (signed by Tsefania on behalf of the division commander) to all divisions, IDFA, 9–321-1948, March 8, 1948.
70. To Kiriati from Ahya, Yishuv Inductee and Family Committee, IDFA, 40–321-1948, March 12, 1948.
71. Histadrut Executive Committee minutes, BGA, Protocols Division, April 21, 1948.
72. Ibid.
73. Ben-Gurion to Lubinski, BGA, Correspondence Division, March 10, 1948.
74. "Care of the Inductee's Family," *Ha'aretz*, March 16, 1948.
75. Ibid.
76. Proposed Rules for Benefits to Qualifying Families of Inductees, IDFA, 33–481-1949, March 23, 1948.
77. Ibid.
78. Ibid. Similar incidents occurred at the Tel Aviv Committee; see Naor, *Social Mobilization*, 53. In Haifa, it took until May to set up the local Yishuv committee for inductees.

79. Ibid.
80. Ibid.
81. Appeals committee for inductee support, letter from Battalion CMN to Kiriati, IDFA, 100-321-1948, April 1, 1948.
82. Administrative officer to Kiriati, IDFA, 100-321-1948, April 2, 1948.
83. Defense Committee meeting, BGA, Protocols Division, reportage Dr. Binyamin Avniel, April 13, 1948.
84. Shkolnik said at the meeting that he hesitated about these men because "We're not paying the families and it daunts me." Abravanel replied: "Mr. Shkolnik is right about the matter per se. The time hasn't come that we'll take people who've got families with children as long as we're are not paying out the family benefits." Ibid.
85. Shulamit Lev-Ari, "How the Yishuv Looks Out."
86. Ibid.; Gelber (*Independence versus Nakba*, 58), basing himself on British sources, numbers the wounded at more than 4,000 on both sides.
87. Headquarters to Kiriati, IDFA, 27-321-1948, April 14, 1948.
88. Ibid.
89. Dr. Fritz Loewenstein to Dr. Hans Nathan, CZA, 9274, April 23, 1948.
90. Ibid.; headquarters to Kiriati, IDFA, 27-321-1948, April 14, 1948.
91. Shulamit Lev-Ari, "How the Yishuv Looks Out."
92. Meeting of Yishuv Inductee and Family Committee (established by the Yishuv Defense Committee), CZA, File 9274, April 27, 1948.
93. Letter from Perlson and Lubinski to Moshe Tsadok (copies to Ben-Gurion, Galili, and Abraham Zabrasky), BGA, Correspondence Division, March 14, 1948.
94. Binyamin Avniel to Ben-Gurion, BGA, Correspondence Division, April 26, 1948.
95. Ibid. On the scope of demobilization in view of economic constraints, see Naor, *Social Mobilization*, 48–56
96. Shulamit Lev-Ari, "How the Yishuv Looks Out."
97. Farther on, Michal Feldman was named head of the Military Casualties Department of the Yishuv Inductee and Family Committee in Jerusalem and also served on a subcommittee of the Social Affairs Committee at the Office of the Jerusalem Military Governor.
98. Loewenstein to Yishuv Inductee and Family Committee, Jerusalem, CZA, 9274, April 27, 1948.
99. Situation report, Yishuv Inductee and Family Committee, CZA, 9274, April 19, 1948. (The date is garbled; the document is identified by its title: "Re: Bereaved Families.")
100. Loewenstein to Yishuv Inductee and Family Committee, CZA, 9274, April 19, 1948.
101. Loewenstein to Yishuv Inductee and Family Committee, CZA, 9274, April 27, 1948.
102. Y. Levin to Yishuv Inductee and Family Committee, Jerusalem, CZA, 9274, April 27, 1948.
103. Binyamin Avniel to Ben-Gurion, BGA, Correspondence Division, April 26, 1948.
104. Minutes, Yishuv Inductee and Family Committee, CZA, 9274, May 31, 1948; Dr. M. Simon to Meir Galadi, Yishuv Inductee and Family Committee, CZA, 9274, May 14, 1948; Dr. Loewenstein to Yishuv Inductee and Family Committee, CZA, 9274, June 13, 1948.
105. Minutes, Yishuv Inductee and Family Committee, CZA, 9274, May 31, 1948.
106. Leah Wilensky remarks, Council of Women's Organizations meeting, CZA, F49/2164, May 9, 1948.
107. Council of Women's Organizations, minutes of meeting, CZA, F49/2164, May 9, 1948.

108. Yishuv Inductee and Family Committee, Beit Hadar, Tel Aviv, Circular 3/48 (signed by Dr. Lubinski), IDFA, 46–7353-1949, May 12, 1948.

109. Amitzur Ilan, "Balance of Forces and Preparedness for War: The IDF and the Arab Armies in 1948," in *Israel's War of Independence 1948–1949 Revisited, Part 1* (in Hebrew), Alon Kadish, ed. (Tel Aviv: Ministry of Defense, 2004), 86.

110. Golam M. Mathbor, "Enhancement of Community Preparedness for Natural Disasters: The Role of Social Work in Building Social Capital for Sustainable Disaster Relief and Management," *International Social Work* 50, no. 3 (2007): 357–369.

111. Sue Lautze and John Hammock, "Coping with Aid Capacity Building, Coping Mechanisms and Dependency, Linking Relief and Development," paper prepared for the UN Inter-Agency Standing Committee Sub-Working Group on Local Capacities and Coping Mechanisms and the Linkages between Relief and Development, Lessons Learned Unit Policy and Analysis Division, Department of Humanitarian Affairs, United Nations Organization (1996), 4.

Figure 1. Children playing among the ruins in old Jaffa, Israel, 1948. Photo: Herbert Sonnenfeld. Source: Museum of the Jewish People at Beit Hatfutsot, The Oster Visual Documentation Center, Leni and Herbert Sonnenfeld collection.

Figure 2. Kindergarten for Children of Working Mothers, Tel Aviv, 1947. Photo: Herbert Sonnenfeld. Museum of the Jewish People at Beit Hatfutsot, The Oster Visual Documentation Center, Leni and Herbert Sonnenfeld collection.

Figure 3. Invalid Independence War veterans at the entrance to the Mugrabi movie theater that is playing the film *The Best Years of Our Lives*, Tel Aviv, Israel, 1950s. Photo: Leni Sonnenfeld. Source: Museum of the Jewish People at Beit Hatfutsot, The Oster Visual Documentation Center, Leni and Herbert Sonnenfeld collection.

Figure 4. Breathing fresh air during truce. The National Library of Israel. Source: Israel State Archives—Beno Rothenberg Collection.

Figure 5. Crowd near ruins. Photographer: Rudi Weissenstein. Source: The National Library of Israel.

Figure 6. Boy crying. Photographer: Rudi Weissenstein. Source: The National Library of Israel.

Figure 7. Laundry hanging outside shelter. Photographer: Rudi Weissenstein. Source: The National Library of Israel.

Figure 8. Queue for Water on Jaffa Street, Jerusalem. The National Library of Israel. Source: Israel State Archives—Beno Rothenberg Collection.

Figure 9. Ruins in Jerusalem. Source: Israel State Archives—Beno Rothenberg Collection.

Figure 10. Tel Aviv Central Bus Station bombed by Egyptian Air Force. Source: Israel State Archives—Beno Rothenberg Collection.

Figure 11. Tel Aviv frontier neighborhood from Haganah Post. Source: Israel State Archives—Beno Rothenberg Collection.

Figure 12. Tel Aviv bombed by Egyptian Air Force. Source: Israel State Archives—Beno Rothenberg Collection.

Figure 13. Water distribution in Jerusalem. Source: Israel State Archives—Beno Rothenberg Collection.

Figure 14. Woman reading list of fallen soldiers. Source: Israel State Archives—Beno Rothenberg Collection.

Figure 15. Displaced find shelter in house. Photographer: Rudi Weissenstein. Source: The National Library of Israel.

Figure 16. Displaced find shelter. Photographer: Rudi Weissenstein. Source: The National Library of Israel.

II.
ASSOCIATION AND SELF-HELP
IN A SOVEREIGN SOCIETY,
MAY 14, 1948–1949

4

THE DISPLACED COMMUNITIES REGROUP

THE ESTABLISHMENT OF THE SOVEREIGN STATE OF ISRAEL found the Jewish internally displaced persons (IDP) population in the midst of a struggle for survival. With nearly half a year of peregrination among places of refuge behind them, many now saw the state authority as the entity that would put an end to their humanitarian crisis. Accordingly, not only did the IDPs continue to struggle and organize for resettlement or return to their homes in the second part of the war, their exertions grew in intensity and complexity amid mounting confusion and frustration.

This chapter tracks the attempts of the Jewish IDP communities to return to ordinary life in mid-war, relying on representative organizations that in some cases now functioned as neighborhood committees. Many members of these communities did not return to their original neighborhoods, settling instead in abandoned Arab neighborhoods or villages. Accordingly, the chapter begins with a comprehensive account of the progression of the war that led to the Palestinian Arabs' flight from the country and continues by describing the realities of life in those geographic areas that now provided refuge to disempowered population groups, mostly Jewish. The chapter is divided geographically, mirroring the singular characteristics of each region that influenced the nature of the arrangements that the new residents of the former Arab areas concluded, or did not conclude, with the authorities charged with the care of these locations.

Three levels of change directly impacted Jewish IDPs' lives during the second phase of the war. The first and most important of them was the completion of physical separation of the Jewish and Arab populations in the formerly mixed areas. The separation had different characteristics in each of the cities of main concern in this discussion. These features were also influenced by a second factor that affected the fate of civilians—the intended status of the city under the partition plan: Jerusalem as an international city, Haifa within the territory of the Jewish state, and Jaffa as an Arab enclave in the heart of the Jewish sovereign area. The third determinant was the point in time and the circumstances of the consolidation of Jewish control in each of the cities, projecting onto the state of mind of each town's Arab inhabitants and affecting the waves of departure. In Haifa, the Arab leadership's decision to reject terms of surrender that had been offered, instead preferring to advise the inhabitants to leave, presumably influenced not only the Arab community in Haifa but also that in Jaffa, which would fall to the Jewish forces several days later. The evenly fought battles in Jerusalem, in contrast, encouraged expectations that Jewish control in parts of the New City would be temporary only.

However different the circumstances in each town were, the outcome of the decisive battles in each locality had much in common. Territories that a short time earlier had been considered combat fronts went over to Israel control, and residential areas that had been Arab-populated until recently emptied of nearly all of their inhabitants, leaving behind a physical space that the Jewish IDPs perceived as an immediate solution to their lengthy distress.

Before discussing the patterns by which the uprooted Jewish communities reorganized when they returned to their places of residence or moved into depopulated Arab neighborhoods and villages, I turn attention to the emptying-out of these localities.

Changing Landscapes: The Depopulation of Arab Neighborhoods and Surrounding Villages

The flight from the Arab quarters of Jerusalem and the surrounding villages gathered momentum between January and early April 1948. At this stage, the precipitants of this massive outflow resembled those that drove Jewish inhabitants of nearby areas from their homes—a combination of existential dread occasioned by the transformation of their neighborhoods and villages into war fronts and the accompanying loss of sources of livelihood.[1]

A matter of special importance in triggering Arab flight from Jerusalem and its environs was the massacre in the village of Deir Yassin, in which 100–120 people—around half of them armed and the remainder women, children, and elderly—were killed or murdered. For several weeks after the incident, the Arab media in Palestine and elsewhere reported and broadcast exaggerated and horrifying accounts of what had transpired there, hoping in this manner to prompt Arab governments to step up their involvement in the warfare. The immediate outcome of this media campaign was a frantic outflow of Arab villagers.[2]

Closely mirroring what happened on the Jewish side, the Arab inhabitants of western Jerusalem streamed eastward in search of temporary shelter in Arab-controlled parts of town or outside city limits.[3] When the British quit Jerusalem on May 14, Jewish forces captured parts of the city's southern and central sectors that had been British-controlled and pushed the Arab forces into the eastern sector. The Jewish momentum, however, was braked by the arrival of Arab Legion forces that took over the brunt of the warfare in the sector comprising the northeastern quarters of the city and in the Old City. The physical takeover of Arab neighborhoods by Jewish combat units precipitated the departure of the last of their inhabitants in the wake of the retreating Arab forces. Concurrently, inhabitants of the Jewish quarters in northern Jerusalem departed with greater and greater celerity. They were joined by residents of neighborhoods in the south and by inhabitants of the Old City, who were able to leave that precinct on the basis of a surrender accord that allowed women, the elderly, and children to depart after most of the men were taken as prisoners of war.[4]

In Arab Haifa, two parallel manifestations of population outflow emerged at the very beginning of the intercommunal war. Some Arab residents moved from the danger zone to other parts of town, as did their Jewish neighbors in the Lower City and its adjacent neighborhoods, whereas others left the city altogether. At the beginning of the military confrontation, migration among shelters was typical mainly of those living in the eastern neighborhoods of the city, where the warring forces clashed intensively. In the second and third months of the intercommunal fighting, when internal displacement spread to the western neighborhoods, Arab inhabitants as well as their Jewish neighbors found impromptu places of refuge, many doing so in churches and convents in the Christian quarter on the western flank side of the Old City.[5]

Some Haifaites who left the city at this time moved to other towns inland or to the cities of what would soon be known as the West Bank, while others crossed into neighboring countries. By early February, about one-fourth of Haifa's Arab population had gone. The exodus accelerated from then until April 1948, now including an organized initiative to extricate women and children and the establishment of marine routes of departure and escape. By April 22, when the decisive battle for the city erupted, the Arab population of Haifa was half of what it had been.[6] After the Jewish forces nailed down the victory and occupied most of the city, contacts ensued between the Jewish and Arab municipal leaders with British mediation. At the end of this interaction, the Arab delegation announced its rejection of the terms of surrender, demanding instead that the Arab population be allowed to leave the city safely and spurning Jewish and British attempts to dissuade them. In the following three weeks, Arabs continued to leave town. When the State of Israel was established, some 6,000 Arabs remained in Haifa, fewer than 10 percent of the original population.[7]

Much the same happened along the Tel Aviv–Jaffa frontier and in the northeastern suburbs of Tel Aviv. There, too, the departure of the British and the establishment of the State of Israel marked the final separation of population groups that had been spatially mixed. The outflow of Arab inhabitants of villages on the city's northeastern approaches occurred in the early stages of the fighting, sometimes on the basis of arrangements with the Jewish forces, as in Jamusin, and in other cases as the outcome of deliberate expulsions, as in Shaikh Muwannis.[8] In the northern precincts of Jaffa, those bordering Tel Aviv, much happened among members of both population groups. Jews and Arabs fled from their homes, turning these neighborhoods into depopulated war zones. At first, most displaced Arabs, like their Jewish counterparts in their respective urban precincts, remained in place and found refuge wherever they could. As the hostilities escalated, however, so did the tendency to leave.[9] From the middle of February until the introduction of longer-range weaponry, the outflow from the city gathered strength. By now, many preferred to leave by sea, considering the overland route too dangerous. In the days preceding the final Jewish attack on the city, beginning on April 25 and ending in early May, about half of the inhabitants remained. In the last week of April, however, as pitched battles ended with the conquest of the city by the Jewish forces, about two-thirds of the remaining inhabitants left by sea.[10]

Implications of the Demographic and Geopolitical Changes for the Jewish IDP Population

For the Jewish inhabitants of frontier neighborhoods in the major cities, the crisis of displacement did not end with the transition to statehood. The conquest of Jaffa and Haifa and the flight of their Arab residents, however, did have implications for the directions in which these towns' Jewish IDP populations flowed. Some of the IDPs wanted to go home, others stubbornly adhered to the impromptu shelters that they had found, and still others strove to find alternative housing and reestablish their communities. Alongside veteran neighborhood committees that spoke out on resettlement and the rehabilitation of damaged houses, committees of refugee neighborhoods now formed. These associations defined themselves in two ways: by their members' original geographic affiliation and by the displacement ordeal that they had undergone.

In the third week of May 1948, the Tel Aviv municipal Inspection Department estimated that of 3,500 IDP families, more than 1,500 had gone home and more than 600 others had been placed in Arab villages.[11] If so, many IDPs remained in provisional quarters. The longer they did so, the more friction built up between them and the homeowners.[12]

In the meantime, the shelling that had battered Jerusalem from mid-May onward left their destructive imprints on entire quarters.[13] As the siege on the city tightened and shortages of water, food, and fuel intensified, the town's northern neighborhoods almost totally emptied out, and IDPs thronged to centers that expanded steadily.[14] In early August 1948, the minister of Defense placed large swaths of Jerusalem and its surroundings under military rule. This terminated the activity of the Jerusalem Committee, as its responsibilities were transferred to the office of the Jerusalem military governor, although the person who headed the entity remained Dov Yosef.[15]

Another main player in Jerusalem's IDP affairs, the People's Guard, was inspired by the wish to maximize security and minimize the blight that the temporary DP centers were causing. The People's Guard described the displaced themselves as largely a passive collective—a thing that had to be moved from place to place in accordance with needs and possibilities.[16] Even though care of the town's IDPs had been tasked to additional institutional *responsables*—or due to the very proliferation of competent bodies—the agita of the displaced in Jerusalem persisted.[17]

As for Haifa, on July 1, the housing committee in this city became a government department, leaving moot the question of whether the Community Council should remain involved in housing affairs.[18] The ensuing debate revealed the difficulty in demarcating the powers of the various entities that operated in Haifa, and even their very necessity, during the transition period that presaged the new era of sovereignty. By majority vote and after loud disputation, it was decided to post a member to a public commission for the apportionment of dwellings that the governmental Housing Department would be constructing.[19]

Along with the gradual transfer of responsibilities to central and municipal government, the Haifa Community Council's Welfare Bureau continued to serve as an important service provider, foremost for immigrants and IDPs from frontier areas but also in additional neighborhoods where members of these two population groups were now being housed.[20]

Another Community Council auspice that remained active during part of the transition period was the Refugees Bureau. After Haifa was conquered, the bureau drafted a plan for the return and resettlement of the IDPs.[21] Those at the bureau believed that their relations with the IDPs and their representatives had been helpful in bringing the crisis to a successful end, with many of the displaced either returning to their homes or receiving alternative permanent housing.[22]

Now a new player stepped into the humanitarian crisis that the internal displacement had precipitated: the central government's War Casualties Ministry. Its involvement began to be felt in July or so, when its representatives visited Jerusalem to assess damage and allocate funds to those who had been harmed for initial repairs and purchase of essentials.[23] The ministry worked in coordination and cooperation with the Israel Emergency Damage Mutual Insurance Fund, Ltd., an intended principal address for those who had sustained property damage in the war. At a meeting between the ministry's director general and representatives of the fund, however, it transpired that the fund was covering only a small part of the property damage that had occurred.[24] In fact, the War Casualties Ministry preceded the other government offices in taking up the cause of rehabilitating war casualties.[25] The other offices—correctly, it must be said—saw themselves as being tasked with responding to the state of war itself, which had reached its climax due to the pan-Arab invasion that followed Israel's proclamation of independence.[26]

The War Casualties Ministry was in its infancy, barely getting organized and very far from being able to attenuate the burgeoning IDP crisis in any real way. Therefore, now as before, much of the activity was spearheaded by organizations that had been self-established by the most interested parties, neighborhood leaders and IDPs themselves, which now focused on attempts to rehabilitate their clients as quickly as possible. They usually interacted with local leadership, represented either by a municipality (in Tel

Aviv) or by government entities (e.g., the Jerusalem Committee, thereafter the military government administration, and the Haifa Housing Department). The process of transition gave the pre-state community organs in Haifa and Jerusalem a more focused role as mediators between citizens and state authorities. To some extent, too, it brought them closer to the civilian public that they represented and distanced them from the national authority that they purported to represent and in whose name they had acted before statehood.

Haifa

Government institutionalization of the Housing Department in Haifa did not suffice to assure order and sound management. The head of the department, David Taneh, had to close his office temporarily due to what he called the "chaos" that had overtaken the place.[27]

One of the characteristics of the transition period was the notion that the public should continue to address its demands and, above all, its criticism to the pre-state local authorities. Thus, residents of Haifa still held the Haifa Situation Committee responsible for housing and bombarded it with complaints, to its members' immense displeasure. The problem went beyond targeting a body that had been stripped of its powers. It included the suspicion, which steadily escalated in town, that transparent and agreed standards were not being applied in the management of housing at large.[28] Although the charges never appeared to be more than rumors, many members of the Situation Committee thought there was reason to relate seriously to "the unending slander of bribery and favoritism."[29] Members of the municipal leadership blamed the chaos, the crisis of confidence, and the suspicion of irregularities on the estrangement of the competent entity from the public that it was supposed to represent.[30] As they saw it, blameworthy for the situation were the excessive institutionalization of the entities that ran the city and, specifically, the entry of the central-government authority at the expense of the Community Council, which had represented the residents on a voluntary basis and had earned their trust for this reason.

Uriel Friedland,[31] responding to this criticism, argued that the problem itself had created a clash of interests between those in need of a solution and those who were supposed to provide it, be they community-based or authorized government bodies.[32] Taneh, treading delicately, confirmed some of the charges of disorder. Many people, he said, had hoped "to piggyback on the huge number of dwellings available for distribution." This, he continued, is why he had decided "to rid myself of responsibility for handing apartments out" and hand his authority back to the army institutions and the "Immigration Department."[33]

Some members of the Haifa Situation Committee were more occupied with absolving themselves of responsibility for the disarray than with eliminating it. "The public must be informed that the Situation Committee has nothing whatsoever to do with actions being taken in housing matters," they implored. Others, without belittling the importance of such a clarification, thought the Situation Committee should insist on its due share of the properties that were up for distribution. Thus, they believed, it would be possible to meet needs not related to the army or the immigrants, whom the locals saw as "interested parties" that did not have the welfare of the city and its inhabitants in mind.[34]

Notwithstanding the institutional changes taking place in the city, local leadership continued to operate in order to maintain the community's organizational network and make sure townspeople's voices would be heard and heeded in making decisions on the reorganization that the restoration of normal city life would entail. Accordingly, in July, the Situation Committee initiated meetings with representatives of neighborhoods and suburbs, at which the sides exchanged information and neighborhood leaders were given an opportunity to present their particular problems.[35] By then, the members of the Situation Committee realized that the entity within which they operated was expected to downsize itself as other public and municipal services came aboard. In the interim, however, before the new institutions could get organized and start to work systematically, the members considered themselves mediators between those in need and the state authorities.[36]

Eliezer Mollek, representing the Har Hacarmel quarter, reflected these expectations when he explained that the public still thought the Situation Committee (and the Community Council as a whole) should defend civilians' interests and offer itself as an address that could be turned to in the event of any infringement of rights. In Mollek's opinion, the Situation Committee should ensure that a matter as sensitive as the distribution of dwellings be in trustworthy hands; therefore, the decision to dodge responsibility for this delicate matter was mistaken.[37] Jacob Etkes of the Lower City reentered an earlier motion to set up an information bureau that the public could consult, adding that he had also heard the rumors about bribe-taking by the Housing Department's clerks. A Mrs. Hari, representing Kiryat Eliahu, noted that amid all these embryonic institutions, both civilian and military, "The simple citizen is orphaned and has no one to turn to if injustice occurs." The Situation Committee, she counseled, should represent the individual citizen's interest because the public trusts it and has endowed it with influence that it should wield. The committee, she said, should "defend the citizen's rights against infringement." Dr. Wiener of the German Colony complained about the neglectful treatment of citizens' standing. It is conventional practice worldwide, he said, that any expropriation, even if carried out by the military, takes place in cooperation with civilians' representatives; therefore, the army's powers in civilian domains should be constricted.[38]

The neighborhood representatives' rhetoric about the role of the public and the status of the townspeople relative to policy makers reflected the civilian chain of command in Haifa and the mechanisms that individual citizens could use to speak out and promote their interests and needs—from the neighborhood representative, to the community representative, and onward to government policy makers. The Situation Committee's attempts to shirk responsibility on the grounds of the official change in its status and the transfer of its powers and responsibilities to newly operative government entities were poorly received.

At a meeting of the Situation Committee's executive board, Taneh reported that he had set up a meeting with journalists to explain the existing arrangement in handing out dwellings.[39] Friedland's reaction to the advertising campaign mirrors the role of the Haifa neighborhood committees in the revitalization of the city: "A press conference is not enough to dispel the public's bitterness and suspicions. What's needed is a meeting of representatives of institutions and neighborhoods."[40]

It is of interest to note that the Haifa central refugees' committee disappeared at this time, and its activists were no longer mentioned in discussions or contacts among the diverse local authorities. This IDP leadership appears to have dissolved after its constituency basically did the same. Such was not the case in Tel Aviv, where IDP communities had been transferred to new or makeshift places of residence and brought the patterns of association and representation along with them.

Tel Aviv

As June 1948 went by, IDP families still languished in the stairwells of private and office buildings. Anyone who entered these buildings encountered them and their possessions, including beds and scattered cooking implements. The cesspools of the buildings overflowed continually due to the excessive burden, defying the municipal Sanitation Department's attempts to keep matters under control.[41] The Association of Home and Property Owners continued to represent its members, who had been adversely affected by the IDP concentrations, vis-à-vis the authorities.[42] The municipal Social Work Department mediated with the municipal engineer and shared with him lists of IDPs who needed home repairs so that they could return.[43] As it struggled to send the frontier neighborhood IDPs back to their homes, the municipality was also urged to continue caring for casualties of the shelling and assure them provisional housing.[44]

Neighborhood Committees and the Revitalization Process

The conquest of Jaffa brought a new problem to the surface: the status of the town's Jewish neighborhoods. Apart from the military and governmental bodies that dealt with the city's affairs, representatives of the United Committee of Jewish Neighborhoods turned their attention to the matter. The committee represented Jewish neighborhoods that belonged to Jaffa from the municipal standpoint, even though they had not enjoyed municipal services since the 1936 Arab uprising. The committee had been active throughout the 1940s, meeting the needs of inhabitants who fell between the stools. Due to their unique role, its activists acquired the status of a recognized and appreciated local leadership.

No sooner had the Israel Defense Forces occupied Jaffa than the committee demanded recognition as the representative of these townspeople and sought a formal relationship with the military government on the grounds of its being the civilian authority.[45] Its board decided to meet with a representative of the People's Administration (soon to be the Provisional Government) to assure itself that Jaffa would not be restored to the territory of the Arab state, that its Jewish inhabitants would not become citizens of such a state, and that Jews' property in Jaffa would be safeguarded. As it happened, the meeting took place a day before statehood was declared; afterward, many of the matters taken up there became utterly irrelevant.[46]

What did remain relevant even after the fall of Arab Jaffa was the demand of the old local Jewish leadership for recognition of its standing. This body of townspeople put forward its case on two grounds: the experience that its members had amassed over the years and an expression of appreciation for having "struggled and dealt with these matters and stayed on our watch" in tough times.⁴⁷

The cold shoulder that the United Committee received proved so frustrating to its members that some called for the body to be dismantled. Others opposed this, arguing that their association should continue to deal with everyday concerns. Therefore, the committee asked the government to make up its mind about their status and impose its decision on the Municipal Council. This idea, presented to Mayor Israel Rokach, was evidently answered in the affirmative. Just the same, more militant voices on the committee were heard, arguing that since city hall was belittling the neighborhoods' needs and the committee itself, the committee should maintain its independence. Those of this frame of mind also believed that once the borders of the state were finalized, Jaffa would be assigned to the Arab state; therefore, the Jewish townspeople should remain there and help to "Judaize" the town (and perhaps lead to its de facto annexation by Tel Aviv). Even though the committee members entertained two seemingly clashing trends of thought, they agreed about the contempt that, in their judgment, city hall felt toward the neighborhood residents.⁴⁸

The contacts between the United Committee's envoys and city hall yielded a meeting with the municipal Situation Committee, in the course of which the representatives of the Jewish neighborhoods in Jaffa noted the national importance of their quarters. After setting matters against this background, they asked to be represented in the municipal institutions commensurate with the number of delegates that they were owed in accordance with the size of the population that they represented.⁴⁹ As the meeting proceeded, the sides agreed that the municipality would set up a joint committee for the treatment of matters relating to hygiene, permits, and so on. The United Committee membership nominated five delegates to the new panel, and the mayor undertook to appoint members of the municipality to take part in the work.⁵⁰ Even before the Joint Committee got started, the mayor instructed the municipal treasurer to start collecting taxes from inhabitants of all neighborhoods.⁵¹ When the representatives of the neighborhoods protested against this change in their tax rates, Rokach made it clear to them that the matter would not be discussed because the extent and rates of taxes were "a general law for all residents."⁵²

In the ensuing months, the Joint Committee for the annexation of Jaffa's Jewish neighborhoods began to solidify. At the meeting with Rokach in July, it was evident that the local leadership was afraid to forfeit its community mechanisms and doubted the Jewish neighborhoods' ability to integrate into Tel Aviv unless it were allowed to mediate between the residents and the administration of the city.

Indeed, the very decision to establish a Joint Committee for annexation and to allow members of the United Committee to be represented on it reflected recognition of the Jewish residents of Jaffa as a community and not only as individuals. The committee was tasked with regularizing the residents' entitlements and adding their representatives to the town council.[53]

In addition to the more institutionalized activity of the United Committee, local entities continued to operate under revised formats and purposes. The leadership entities of neighborhoods that had been abandoned when the intercommunal war broke out now reactivated themselves as representatives of residents who had begun to return to their homes. New entities were set up in places where IDPs had been housed (usually abandoned Arab villages and neighborhoods) in order to assure the residents' status and the authorities' infrastructural and institutional care of these places. The schedule of meetings of the director of the Property Damage Department of the War Casualties Ministry demonstrates the recognized standing of the neighborhood committees and the role that the governing authority allowed these agencies to play as mediators and partners in the revitalization process. For example, the department director met with one committee from the Mahlul neighborhood and another from the Maccabi quarter to explain how the ministry would apply a means test for assistance in damage repair.[54]

The residents of the Maccabi Neighborhood Cooperative Association had settled the neighborhood back in the 1920s. During the war, much of the quarter had burned down. The residents left their homes, and many lost their economic underpinnings. In their appeal to Mayor Rokach, the Maccabi representatives stressed their national contribution, manifested both in residents' participation in the war (ending in some cases in death or injury) and in the economic price paid by residents who had been rendered homeless. This sacrifice entitled the inhabitants, in their own eyes, to special interest and aid in the reconstruction of their neighborhood. Therefore, they sought a meeting with the mayor.[55] After this request was turned down, the committee continued to apply pressure by sending letters to the prime minister and the interior minister, only to be told that their communications had been forwarded to the mayor. Seeing the committee's efforts dashed, they turned to the mayor again, expressing bewilderment about what they called "this weird estrangement from a neighborhood . . . whose only sin is its loyal service of the city" and demanding an urgent meeting to discuss the neighborhood's affairs.[56] When they finally met with officials from the housing department, they were given two options: expropriate some of the abandoned territory abutting the quarter or revise the neighborhood's parcellation.[57]

Another neighborhood committee that applied for special assistance as compensation for its residents' internal displacement was that of the New Shapira quarter. This body described the hardships that its clients had endured since the beginning of the intercommunal war. Given that their neighborhood had been on the firing line, they had fled from their homes and become refugees. What they sought now was not compensation in the form of alternative buildings and properties but an exemption from taxes for their term as IDPs. After all, during those months, their homes had been occupied by members of the defense forces, who had used them as an advance base. The inhabitants also asked city hall to go the extra mile in providing services to the locality and equalizing living conditions there to those accepted in the rest of the city in terms of sewage, lighting, street cleaning, and drainage of rainwater. The committee's letter, addressed to the mayor, was signed by the members and attached to a list of residents' signatures and addresses.[58] Reflected here again are familiar patterns of community self-organization. The enclosure of a page bearing the signatures of all members of the community, to be forwarded to the authority, had been a familiar modality of communication since the Ottoman era, used by Jewish and Arab communities alike.[59]

Another organizational initiative that based itself on familiar patterns and the reactivation of a preexisting body was pursued by the Committee of Mahane Yosef and Other Neighborhoods,[60] an entity that included the eponymous quarter along with Aharon, Ohel Moshe, Mahane Yehuda, Neve Tzedek, and Neve Shalom, all bordering Jaffa. Mahane Yosef had been established in the early twentieth century. Alongside its spacious and well-appointed dwellings, metal shacks and shanties had been constructed over the years, and various "backyard neighborhoods" had come into being next door. The united committee that represented the inhabitants of these neighborhoods had been set up at a general assembly of residents in 1946.[61]

When the war broke out, the inhabitants of these neighborhoods were the first to flee.[62] After Jewish forces conquered Jaffa, they began to return to and revitalize their homes. Many IDPs could not return because they had no homes to return to: "Those returning to their oases are immensely eager to rehabilitate. They use every corner of their buildings that isn't threatening to topple, but the destruction is immense . . . towering heaps of rubble . . . some vestige of a wall or a terrace dangling on a thread protruding here and there."[63]

The status of these neighborhoods was not regularized until late December 1948, when Jaffa was annexed to Tel Aviv. In and around Mahane Yosef, the inhabitants did not regard the municipal committee that the mayor had set up for these neighborhoods' affairs as their authentic representative; they continued to rely on their own panel.[64]

Erstwhile IDPs who had now settled or had been resettled on the outskirts of Jaffa and in abandoned Arab villages north of Tel Aviv quickly reconstituted themselves as organized communities. Although these were new associational initiatives that represented new residents' interests, they evoked the familiar pattern of local neighborhood association and used terminology suggesting that those associating, and the authorities, were aware of this pattern—an awareness that also, in various cases, rewarded them with "recognition."

Manshiya and the "Cardboard Box Quarter"

About a week after Jaffa surrendered, the government of Israel approved an allocation of land on the northern fringes of the city, near the railroad station, and in the southern part of the Manshiya neighborhood for residents who had fled from aerial bombardments and for recently arrived immigrants. Quickly, Jewish families and individuals began to invade the Manshiya area. They were families of inductees, IDPs from frontier neighborhoods, a few from Jerusalem, and others who sought an opportunity to improve their housing conditions.[65] In the first few days after the neighborhood was re-tenanted and with greater intensity after statehood was declared—at which time Jewish forces took over the entire area—looters spread across the quarter and made off with everything that could be moved: furniture of all kinds, housewares and kitchen implements, bedding, and anything else useful in quotidian life. Military forces rushed to the area and began to arrest the looters, firing in the air and even throwing "scare grenades." Brawls erupted between soldiers and looters, whose numbers included women and children.[66]

The municipal policy for Manshiya earmarked much of the neighborhood for demolition. The idea was to prepare these areas for annexation to

Tel Aviv so that a deepwater port and a transport system leading to it could be developed and also to obviate the possibility of Arab refugees' returning to their homes, it being assumed that the hostilities would resume. Another important consideration at Tel Aviv City Hall was to deter IDPs from squatting in the area and joining the indigent Jewish residents who were already there, creating a perpetual slum on the edge of town. The government backed this policy, largely for security reasons and to prevent the Arabs from coming back. Thus, the demolition of these quarters began apace.[67]

The official press release about the matter spoke of the demolition of "rickety buildings" that "endangered the public."[68] The demolition work, begun in mid-July and continuing until early September,[69] prompted residents near the Hassan Bek Mosque to form an association. They sent two representatives to the municipality, warning it not to blow up their own homes. The envoys, defining themselves as the "agents" of 300 families,[70] requested permission to enter houses "on the other side of the barrier" (i.e., in the area designated for demolition). The municipal secretary, meeting with them, said that city hall had room for their clients only in Salameh or Shaikh Muwannis; the representatives rejected both offers due to what they explained as a constraint occasioned by the local residents' workplaces.[71] Hearing this, the secretary referred them to "the state institutions that deal with housing in Jaffa."[72] The Manshiya residents' representatives evidently took this advice to heart and presented their predicament to the government minister Bechor Sheetrit, who was in charge of both Police Affairs and Minority Affairs.

Living in the neighborhood at that time were around 400 displaced families from frontier neighborhoods. The threat of demolition of the dwellings that they occupied was not accompanied by any offer of an appropriate alternative; in some cases, too, buildings were destroyed with their effects inside. The appeal to Sheetrit was signed by Emanuel Ben-Nissan,[73] who importuned the minister "in every possible way not to bring a disaster on us and leave our families, children, and wives in despair after having invested their last scanty resources in repairing the homes."[74] Ben-Nissan did not content himself with applying to Sheetrit; he sent copies of his letter to the mayor and a litany of government ministers—Defense, Welfare, Religious Affairs, Interior, and War Casualties—as well as the chief of the IDF General Staff. In his missive, he described the menace of the demolition of the homes where the frontier-neighborhood refugees had found shelter. He demanded a moratorium on demolitions until matters could be sorted out and added, at the bottom of the letter, that at a meeting with Haim Alperin, head of the municipal Inspection Department, his committee had been told in response, "We'll demolish anyway and you residents can go jump into the sea."[75] Ben-Nissan's letter was backed by action: the neighborhood representatives met with Sheetrit, who referred them to the inspector general of the police. When the committee members approached the latter, they were told that the matter lay outside the purview of the force because the demolition actions were being undertaken by the army and per instruction of city hall.[76] The Ministry of Minorities also forwarded the committee's communication to additional government agencies.[77]

Authorized by Sheetrit, the police inspector general met with municipal officials and handed them a request from the minister to postpone the demolitions. City hall insisted that the plan should be carried out as set forth. All of this, the municipality said, had been explained in so many words to the signatories of the residents' memorandum and to a delegation headed by Rabbi Emanuel Ben-Nissan. They were told to approach the contractor in charge of the demolition work, who had received instructions to help them find habitation in nearby buildings south of the Hassan Bek line.[78] Although the police supported the residents' request, the municipality refused to halt the demolition work due to the possibility of hostile activities that would emanate from the vicinity of the demolished buildings if such were allowed to remain. A safety argument was also raised (i.e., war-damaged buildings had to be knocked down lest they collapse).[79]

After meeting with the residents' representatives, municipal officials realized that those involved were several dozen families that had known about the intent to evict them. Just the same, they claimed, city hall did not reject their appeal and went out of its way to transfer them to "the care of responsible people who are searching for ways to house them in a nearby area that has not been earmarked for debris removal."[80] In the meantime, however, the demolition work went on, and people received notices of the intent to blow up their homes on only several days' notice.[81]

The inhabitants of Manshiya did not limit their activity to appeals to high government and municipal officials. As the demolitions proceeded, they hired a lawyer who approached city hall on their behalf and reminded those in charge that it was the municipality itself that had housed the people in that area. He also warned the city that "No one, even the municipality of Tel Aviv, is entitled to make its own laws and evict people from their homes by force or by threat of force, whether or not they are legal residents and whether or not the evicting agency is the legal owner of the property at issue." The attorney asked the mayor to cease the work at least until he could meet with him and discuss the situation thoroughly.[82]

City hall stood its ground, refusing to submit to the pressure, even when it emanated from high windows such as those of the minister of Minority Affairs and the army's national expropriation officer. The removal of buildings "in a dangerous demolition area," Rokach claimed, "is a matter of necessity that was decided upon in consultation with the government and the defense authorities." The mayor also repeated what he had said with the residents listening in—that they had known about the demolition plan in advance and should have left on their own.[83] Confronting city hall's intransigence, the local committee obtained a series of sympathetic responses from government officials. Even when a given government office had no authority in the matter, its representative either replied or referred its request for a reply to other stakeholders.[84]

As the struggle to thwart the demolitions continued, a new associative maneuver was launched by residents in a different part of Manshiya—the "cardboard-box quarter," the Jewish part of the neighborhood. They, too, had received eviction notices ahead of demolition. Unlike the tenants in the Hassan Bek area, however, they lived in the neighborhood and had bought their homes with their own money. Kharth al-Tanak (the "sheet-metal neighborhood," an alternative epithet for the cardboard-box neighborhood) lay on the municipal boundary between Jaffa and Tel Aviv, in the northern part of the Manshiya quarter, and was largely settled by Yemenite Jews.[85] Even before the war, a local committee had been lobbying to annex the neighborhood to Tel Aviv.[86] When the intercommunal war broke out, many residents of the quarter fled. Months later, returning after the conquest of Jaffa and the proclamation of statehood, they found some of their homes marked for demolition. In response, representatives of the neighborhood committee asked Rokach to intervene: "Please have mercy on scores of poor, large families that ask you to save them and not dispossess them of homes that they purchased with blood and money. Please do not cause them to despair; even when under gunfire they did not leave the area. . . . These are Jewish homes; do not destroy them. May God inspire you and the members of the Municipal Council to do us good and not harm."[87]

The pressure on city hall was heightened from an unexpected direction. A resident of the city, the architect and planner Eliezer Brutzkus, did not understand how the destruction of Manshiya squared with Jaffa's terms of surrender, in which the lives and property of that city's civilian population were assured. Brutzkus wondered how city hall would cope with the question of compensating Arab property owners for buildings demolished after the end of military action in the area and who should cover the cost of the compensation. What about the cost of the demolition work itself? And what example would they be setting for other communities (in Haifa, Tiberias, and Safed) if Tel Aviv were to demolish buildings of architectural, historical, and archaeological value and savage the country's landscape and cultural values? Brutzkus demanded that his remarks be presented to, and thoroughly discussed by, the Municipal Council.[88] The pressure appears to have paid off; an interministerial committee was set up, and a protracted legal discussion began that caused the demolition operations first to be postponed and ultimately terminated before they could be completed.[89]

One of the characteristics of this time of transition was the rapid pace of change and its immediate effects on the goals of the local civilian struggles. Such a process occurred in the case of Manshiya-Hassan Bek. After the residents of the area signed lease agreements with the municipal administrator of abandoned property and were dunned for municipal taxes, the residents' committee abruptly shifted gears. Now it demanded the same municipal services for its clients as those received by all residents of Tel Aviv, including "water, sanitation, and buses" and street signage in the area "for the mailman." The residents conditioned their willingness to pay taxes on the delivery of these services, conceding, however, that if city hall could not meet all the demands, it should at least see to sanitation "as quickly as possible because it is essential." The lack of it would be "responsible for the spread of various diseases, heaven forbid."[90] It is important to emphasize that Manshiya was not part of Tel Aviv when these events took place,[91] and the local committee continued, in effect, to mediate between a disadvantaged population of unclear status and an authority from which this population expected basic services. Only in May 1949 did the annexation of Manshiya to Tel Aviv take place.[92]

The case of the Manshiya neighborhood committees illustrates the role that a local association can play in allowing seriously disadvantaged residents of a frontier area to speak out to high-ranking national officials. It also demonstrates the responses of authorities at various levels and shows that, even when requests were not requited and the struggle did not end with full success, the residents' self-organization influenced the comportment of policy makers, who felt it necessary to respond and explain their policies.

Salameh

Salameh village, on the eastern flank of Jaffa, served Arab forces as a base for attacks on the Hatikva quarter and absorbed repeated Haganah reprisals on this account.[93] When the Jewish combat forces reached the area in the course of Operation Hametz (involving the encirclement of Jaffa and its severance from its rural hinterland), it was basically depopulated and fell without perceptible resistance.[94] The municipality of Tel Aviv saw the abandoned village as a potential source of housing for IDPs from the frontier neighborhoods; accordingly, it moved to tenant the village with members of this group shortly after it was conquered. It may have done so due to the continual friction that had existed at this strategic flash point. Alternatively, it may have seen an advantage in using this locality because of its proximity to the Yad Eliyahu neighborhood and the possibility of relying on that quarter's infrastructures.[95]

By the end of May 1948, some 200 families had moved into Salameh, and another 400 were thought to be on the way. The municipal inspector, Alperin, asked the mayor to apprise him of priorities in resettling IDPs there; should those housed in Tachkemoni School come first, or those squatting in building entrances? Salameh did not have room to accommodate all the IDPs, Alperin stressed, and the residents of buildings that the displaced had occupied were putting his department under immense pressure.[96]

In the meantime, lawlessness had become the rule in Salameh. Residents of the Hatikva quarter, perhaps avenging the bloody clashes that had occurred between the quarter and the village in previous months, circulated in the abandoned streets of the village, ripping out doors and windows and rendering dwellings uninhabitable for IDPs. City hall joined up with the security forces to impose control.[97] Alperin maintained contact with the Tel Aviv chief of police and reported to him about the pillage in Salameh and the sale of shutters, doors, and windows from village houses in the Bezalel market.[98]

Although most residents of Salameh were IDPs from frontier neighborhoods, recently arrived immigrants were housed there as well.[99] Thus, two classes of housing recipients took shape: immigrants, whom the authorities helped, and internally displaced persons, who had to fend for themselves. The latter found their voice in the newspaper *Ha-Mivrak*, the organ of the Jewish Freedom Fighters (Lehi, also known as Sternists), which expressed critical and oppositionist views. In an article titled "Partiality in the Housing of Refugees," the journalist B. Shotet stated that while "refugees from the [Holocaust] camps who made their way to Salameh receive a budget of IL 50 per family from the Jewish Agency to improve and repair the apartment for civilized habitation . . . the Manshiya refugees in Salameh have to make do with dwellings that they received as is. While refugees from the camps in that village . . . receive one dwelling per usually-not-extended family, the Manshiya refugees have to make do with one room per family, and their families, as you know, have lots of children."[100]

The IDPs' grievance, articulated by Shotet, was that city hall was discriminating against them in favor of recently landed immigrants from Europe. The mistreatment, Shotet contended, manifested not only in the allocation of different classes of housing to each group but also in municipal services. The frontier-neighborhood IDPs accused the municipality of not collecting their garbage while "the municipal street-cleaning service is hard at work" in the area inhabited by the "good refugees."[101] *Ha-Mivrak* blamed Municipal Inspector Alperin for what it called this deliberate discrimination. Alperin, Shotet noted, had a certain record as a graduate of the prestigious Herzliya Gymnasium and commander of the Civil Guard in Tel Aviv. This, Shotet ruled, made him "a member of the old boys' club." When the representative of "the Manshiya people in Salameh" visited Alperin, presented him with his allegations, and asked why a small family received a two-room apartment while a larger one got one room, Alperin replied "with a parable and a quip, flippantly retorting, 'If you give an animal two rooms, would it know what to do with them?'[102] Thus spoke Mr. Alperin . . . to the emissary of the perennially destitute and oppressed Mizrahi refugees, who sealed his lips, bottled himself up, and returned to his brethren embarrassed and head bowed."[103] Shotet was not astonished by the discovery of explicit and "contemptuous" discrimination; he considered it neither new nor surprising but part of "the social reality of our nation." He pointed to the internal division of the Yishuv between "the capital-Y Yishuv and everyone who's included under the term *'edot ha-Mizrah* (Jews originating from Muslim countries)—the good guys and our people on the one side and the bad guys, the nameless, on the other. . . . We have, however, naïfs who open their minds to the belief that with the ripening of statehood and the transition to sovereign independence, this contemptible, malignant, and horrifying raising of barriers within the nation must stop."[104]

Unlike the tableau that Shotet painted—a voiceless and disempowered mass of people—the documentation indicates that the Salameh B quarter, where IDPs from the frontier neighborhoods had settled, accommodated a collective that was aware of its rights and established a local committee as soon as the first of their number reached the location. Several months later, the immigrants who had been given housing there did the same. The municipality itself had promoted the election of the committees in Salameh and Shaikh Muwannis and intended that these panels should help it to interact with the respective populations.[105] As I have shown, however, the establishment of these local committees followed a familiar and routine pattern. Therefore, even though they showered the authorities with respect, it is not self-evident that the committees saw themselves as city hall's lackeys. Furthermore, their democratic practices allowed for new elections that resulted in the addition of new representatives, changing their nature and facilitating the formation of relations with oppositionist municipal players and critics of city hall, as I demonstrate below.

Immediately after it was formed, the Salameh immigrants' committee advised the mayor of the establishment of their new association. The notice, couched in terminology borrowed from Diaspora community structures, mentioned that the inaugural meeting had been devoted almost entirely— so the rapporteurs claimed—to thanking and praying for the heads of state (President Weizmann and Prime Minister Ben-Gurion) and all the ministers and soldiers. Then, turning to practical matters, the committee members concluded by expressing their wish that the mayor, "His Highness," would side with them and support the actions and efforts of "the public" to make up their shortfalls and meet their unrequited needs. The letter was signed by the secretary of the committee, Eliyahu Tepper, and its chair, Nahum Schneider. The panel already had an official rubber stamp, festooned with the expression *'Od evnekha ve-nibane* ("Again I [God] will build you and we will be rebuilt," patterned after Jeremiah 31:4).[106] The municipal secretary, replying to the letter on behalf of the mayor, congratulated them for their associative act.[107]

In late November 1948, amid fears that the various authorities were about to double their taxes, the erstwhile IDPs of Salameh B elected a new and militant committee under Menahem Hadi, formerly of Kerem ha-Teimanim and quondam leader of the General Council for Frontier Refugees. This measure received encouragement from Menachem Pitchon, a member of the Municipal Council and a functionary of the Tel Aviv Sephardi community (himself born in Turkey), which had extended its patronage to the IDP population in the villages and neighborhoods.[108] The committee was elected at the end of a general assembly of residents, during which the municipality's role in helping the frontier IDPs who had settled in the location was discussed. The assembly, attended by almost all residents, endorsed the existing committee and added six members, bringing the count to eleven; advised the mayor of the formation of the expanded body in an official letter; and asked him to recognize it as the representative of the population. The official name of the panel, as shown on its stamp (imprinted on the notice), was the Committee of Tel Aviv Frontier Refugees in Salameh Village. A copy of the notice of formation was sent to Pitchon. Plainly, this committee perceived itself as a full-fledged political entity.[109]

In January 1949, after Salameh was officially annexed to Tel Aviv, the IDPs committee presented Rokach with specific demands. One set concerned the improvement of municipal services in the village, including renovation of buildings ahead of the winter, enhancing medical services, establishing a child day center for working mothers, opening a welfare bureau for the many indigents in the quarter, assuring systematic public transport, bringing in telephone services, and putting up a police station in response to the village's high crime rate. A second cluster of demands had to do with the double payments that the residents were being asked to make: one to city hall and another to the administrator of Abandoned Property. *Make up your minds*, the committee demanded. The committee also demanded that the residents be treated like all other citizens of Tel Aviv, now that the village had been annexed to the city, and be relieved of the yoke of the municipal Inspection Department.

Rokach refused to recognize the committee and its demands, arguing that the annexation of Salameh to Tel Aviv had made the body unnecessary, just as there was no need for neighborhood committees in the city's veteran areas.[110] It seems that some residents of Salameh were themselves not supportive of the committee's activity, either due to their fear of city hall's response or because they were put off by the election of functionaries from a party that was identified foremost with the old-time Sephardi elite and did not represent the interests of Mizrahim at large.[111]

In any event, the Salameh committees crumbled under the weight of their interfactional disputes as the municipality fanned the flames of this discord to hasten their demise.[112] The internal intrigues in Salameh trickled into the Tel Aviv Municipal Council when the neighborhood committee sent a letter to the editor of *Davar* claiming that Pitchon, ostensibly "their man" on the council, had misrepresented the realities of life in their neighborhood and the foul relations that existed between them and the municipal inspector. The author of the piece in *Davar* mentioned an assembly that had been attended by people from Hatikva and Kerem ha-Teimanim who marched in with firearms and batons, all with the facilitation of Menahem Hadi, the mukhtar. The Salameh people, according to *Davar*, had eschewed the assembly altogether.[113] The committee of Salameh frontier refugees hurriedly issued a denial to the reportage in *Davar*, insisting that the villagers had indeed taken part in the assembly and had not perpetrated "acts of violence" there. At the village gathering, "Displeasure was expressed about the lies being disseminated by Menachem Pitchon, of the Municipal Council, about the village and against the committee."[114]

In May 1949, the Salameh B committee resumed its activity with the encouragement of Member of Knesset Moshe Ben-Ami of the National Union of Sephardim and Mizrahim. Again, however, the municipality refused to recognize the committee as the inhabitants' representative.[115] Menahem Hadi, chair of the village committee, perished shortly afterward when a wall collapsed on him as he visited a synagogue construction site in the neighborhood. His sudden death at the age of forty-four must have created a leadership void that vitiated the residents' representation and abetted the dissolution of the local committee.[116]

Jerusalem

The Military Governor's Council and the People's Guard in View of the IDPs and the Housing Challenge

When the shelling of Jerusalem began, many Jewish townspeople rushed to shelter in downtown buildings. Some of these new IDPs left these provisional quarters during the June 11–July 7 truce, but others remained in basements of unfinished buildings that had no sanitary provisions. The Jerusalem municipal health bureau, concerned about what this shortcoming might do to the inhabitants of the shelters and those around them, urged the police to evict the IDPs from these locations and send them back to their own neighborhoods or some other appropriate place. They also turned their attention to veteran IDPs—those who were evacuated during the intercommunal-war period and continued to live in schools that were unfit for permanent habitation.[117] The chief of police agreed to deploy his force for squatter eviction, but "only after the appropriate institutions arrange housing for these wretched refugees and if someone from the Jerusalem

Committee [then metamorphosing into the offices of the military government] files a complaint that some DPs are balking at leaving the shelters even after being offered housing."[118]

The People's Guard also pressed for a solution to the squatter problem, which its officials ominously termed "catastrophic."[119] A special desk at the headquarters of this organization was established to deal with IDPs, arrange their housing, organize them, and, eventually, send them home. This Refugee Housing and Organization Desk was headed by a municipal refugees officer, the well-known Jerusalem attorney Dr. Alexander Amdur, an old hand in dealing with internal displacement problems due to his involvement in the crisis surrounding the torching of the Shama commercial center.[120] In every location where IDPs had gathered, a "concentration commander," himself an IDP, was appointed "to be in charge of arrangements and of compliance with orders at the location."[121]

On July 13, when the resumption of shelling on Jerusalem ruptured the first truce,[122] a "fleeing frenzy" ensued.[123] Envoys from the People's Guard passed through the affected quarters, making contact with remaining residents and repeatedly assuring them that the municipal institutions were attending to their welfare and striving to improve security and housing in their neighborhoods. The residents, however, exhausted by the lengthy months of war, responded with irritation and bitterness, stating that mere words and promises could not alleviate their plight.[124] They asked the People's Guard representatives to pass on specific requests for the construction of protective walls and the delivery of sandbags to shelter pedestrians from snipers. These requests, they said, had been presented before and had gone unanswered; they could save lives and, above all, keep streets exposed to the northern front from emptying out. The People's Guard representatives were unable to influence the residents' state of mind because, as their commander attested, "We could not muster enough arguments to contradict their allegations." All they could do was report on the plight of "the few who stayed put," whose situation was "really bad due to the continual sniping," and to deflect the sense, which typified those affected, "that no one cares about these neighborhoods."[125]

The frontier quarters were also neglected in terms of care for damaged dwellings. The People's Guard compiled lists of buildings that had sustained harm during the shelling in July and forwarded them to the War Casualties Ministry, expecting engineers and building contractors to circulate among the ravaged premises and estimate the damage. It took the professionals until late September to visit the area and conduct their appraisal. What is more, the people affected—even those who wished to repair their houses at their own expense—were not allowed to meet with them. As winter approached, the People's Guard began to worry that these neighborhoods, their buildings perforated and their walls fissured, would not withstand the rain and that the scanty belongings that the residents retained would be ruined. The guard expressed the fear that people would break into dwellings elsewhere in Jerusalem "and won't want to leave them until they get satisfaction."[126]

What the People's Guard officials wanted from the military governor was to establish a permanent committee to deal with the frontier neighborhoods' affairs—a body that would visit the blighted areas, give moral support, listen as the residents described their needs, determine how bad security really was, and on this basis order residents to stay or to leave. They offered this committee their full assistance.[127] When the committee was set up toward mid-October, it did in fact cooperate closely with the People's Guard, and the latter, aided by its own field personnel, provided information and took an inventory of dwellings as a basis for action to solve the city's housing problem.[128]

Despite these structural redeployments, or perhaps because of these changes and the time they consumed, the last phase of IDP eviction was postponed, and Pini Barda, the People's Guard officer in charge of civilian care during the nine months of the war, announced her resignation. The responsibility for housing operations in Jerusalem was too much for her, she explained.[129]

Barda's resignation drew attention to the void that had come about in dealing with the town's housing casualties. The newspaper *Ha-Boker* enumerated "a lengthy series of institutions" that had been established to see to the future of the city—a military governor with a council at his side, a municipality and a municipal council, the Jerusalem Community Council with its array of public committees, a Jerusalem Development Commission that a delegation of government ministers had set up, a development corporation sponsored by the National Institutions, and another committee, appointed by the Jewish Agency. This proliferation of authorities and powers, however, *Ha-Boker* editorialized, made things "immeasurably more complicated" because each office "passes the buck."[130]

A sense of impatience settled over Jerusalem. A week after Dov Yosef announced that the German Colony would be opened up for refugee housing, the Agudath Israel newspaper *Ha-Yoman* remarked, "In fact, nothing has been done in the area to this day." That is, if something had been done, "the public does not know" about it.[131] *Ha-Yoman*, like the other print media, repeated the claim that "there's no one to talk to," because even though a Ministry of Housing existed on paper, its officials were "impotent" vis-à-vis the throngs that were beating a path to its offices. The editorialists demanded the expeditious launching of an extensive and comprehensive housing program. Each day without a solution to the problem, they pointed out, is harmful to the displaced, frazzles their nerves, "and amplifies disgruntlement and antipathy needlessly."[132]

Although Dov Rosen, commander of the Jerusalem People's Guard, rejected Pini Barda's resignation, he made it clear to Yosef that he could not continue doing so for long because the affairs of the IDPs in his city had become "quite exhausting," and the lack of central, competent, and adequately budgeted treatment was seriously encumbering the work and giving the public the idea that the matter was being neglected. Rosen recommended that the military governor appoint a refugees officer to represent him. If this were done, he continued, the People's Guard would place its volunteer forces and the existing public committee at the officer's disposal.[133]

The military governor set up committees to deal with social matters including IDP care, but none of those who dealt with the topic during the ten months of war on behalf of the People's Guard was invited to join them.[134] One of the problems these authorities faced was that the IDPs were refusing to leave their places of residence even after being offered alternative housing. Another was the difficulty that arose in expropriating unoccupied rooms. The People's Guard demanded greater latitude in the expropriation process on the basis of administrative orders. "There are people who have left town and aren't thinking about returning but aren't turning over their dwellings. We shouldn't protect their rights here. There's a way to punish these people: expropriation."[135] The commander of the People's Guard repeatedly insisted that the fiscal and public responsibility for solving the IDP problem in Jerusalem should not be foisted on his (volunteer-based) organization.[136]

In all these discussions, among the bevy of players who passed responsibility back and forth and scattered accusations in every direction, representatives of the IDPs neither participated nor are mentioned. This is not to say that IDPs in Jerusalem did not form associations. In the town's northern neighborhoods, various committees and a rich spectrum of charitable organizations provided relief services in mid-war.[137] Their absence in the People's Guard documentation suggests that the population of these quarters interrelated with other mediators that, to their minds, represented them (e.g., Agudath Israel or the Sephardi Committee). An exception in this context is the intensive associative activity that took place in the Katamon quarter after it was resettled with IDPs from the Old City.

Despite attempts to get the various entities to cooperate and coordinate their moves, the authorities continued to abrade and collide. In November, there were reports of intrusions by soldiers' families into vacant dwellings in the city without the involvement of the Housing Department in the considerations behind their tenanting. On the basis of information that reached the military governor, these break-ins took place with the knowledge of the welfare officers (of the army).[138] The IDP problem also affected the town's education system and perturbed those who headed it. Several days before the school year began, IDPs still inhabited schools and public buildings.[139] Some schools even filed complaints with the police against squatters.[140] In certain cases, the military governor had no idea that IDPs had settled in schools at all.[141] Only in December 1948, a year after the IDP crisis began, did reports begin to arrive about purging displaced persons from the last schools.[142]

The expropriation mechanism, rather porous in the absence of a government and in the midst of a full-blown war, now became more complex by undergoing institutionalization. Each expropriation launched by the office of the Jerusalem military governor entailed legal proceedings.[143] The change in procedures and the addition of new *responsables* in Jerusalem sowed confusion and aggravated the friction that existed to begin with. Institutions that approached the Housing Department while it was being set up or being transferred from the Community Council to the military governor's office received oral permission to enter vacant dwellings but were accused of breaking and entering once they did so. In some cases, different municipal authorities promised one dwelling to different institutions.[144]

Only in early December did the process of returning the IDPs to the neighborhoods of northern Jerusalem begin. As for those from the Old City, although the Jerusalem military governor's office had a special department for their care, Dr. Abraham Bergman, the town's new military governor, turned to the government and demanded that it assume responsibility for them.[145] The IDPs from the Old City sought alternative residential arrangements after the Transjordanian military occupation of the Jewish

Quarter made their displacement permanent. By resettling in the deserted Arab neighborhood of Katamon, they were able to preserve their community tapestry, even though the capture of many of their men had shattered their internal equilibrium.[146] In their patterns of self-association, the Old City Refugees in Katamon organization reflected the identities of both communities: the origin community (that of the Jewish Quarter) and that of the war experience, which coalesced around the ordeal of displacement. The voices of the associators of Katamon stood out in particular against the background of the "silence" of other IDP communities in Jerusalem.

IDPs in Katamon

The formation of community committees in Jerusalem's Katamon neighborhood came about against much the same background that spawned the residents' committees in Manshiya and Salameh. They were staffed by resettled IDPs who organized on the basis of prior community affiliations, their original places of residence in this case. Among the first to associate in the neighborhood were the Old City Refugees in Katamon, a group of some 1,400 people, mostly elderly, women, and children, who had been evicted from the Old City of Jerusalem after most of the men had been taken captive. Initially the group had been housed "hastily and with overcrowding" in the Katamon neighborhood, but members were later distributed among several dozen houses in the quarter.[147] The Department for Care of Old City Refugees in Katamon, an adjunct of the Jerusalem Committee (hereinafter: the military government council), was the entity that looked out for the needs of the evacuees, who had reached this place of refuge in utter destitution. It provided them with basic necessities, handed out food on the basis of special ration cards, and set up an old-age home, several schools, a few synagogues, and health-care facilities.[148] When the council began to prepare for a transition from distributing free food to in-cash assistance, the evacuees organized on their own, setting up a representative committee that demanded to be involved in the revitalization process and in setting criteria for resource allocation.[149] The department laid down criteria for assistance on the basis of an eligibility table but was given a much smaller allocation than it had requested—not enough even to match the grant given to soldiers' families.[150]

The relief mechanism was based on ration booklets that residents were supposed to receive through the mediation of the Ministry of Welfare (headed by Yitzhak Meir Levine of Agudath Israel). When rumors about the expected aid circulated, the residents evinced "much ferment" and held "tumultuous assemblies," at the end of which representatives of the refugees' committee visited the department and handed over a letter addressed directly to Dov Yosef.[151] In this communication, they protested the stinginess of the daily support that their constituents had been offered—110 mil per person per day, which was too little, they said, to sustain "minimal existence." They demanded that the Old City refugee families be treated like soldiers, noting that, after all, their husbands and sons had been taken prisoner. They also specified the living conditions that they needed, based on family size and their calculation of the monthly support that each family needed. Those able to work, they stressed, would gladly accept any job, but given the dismal job situation in Jerusalem, they demanded that the benefits owed continued to be paid until the workers received their first paycheck. The committee members posted their letter on August 3 and demanded an answer by Thursday, August 5. Namely, they gave Dov Yosef forty-eight hours to do as told or respond in some other way.[152]

The Department for Care of Old City Refugees' representative, Rafael Ben-Dor, receiving the letter from the heads of the residents' committee, Yehuda Alsheich and Naomi Serri, attempted to convince them that the arrangement offered to them was fair.[153] He failed, prompting the residents to boycott the relief mechanism and threaten to launch a hunger strike and to demonstrate. This made it very difficult to distribute the ration booklets. Ben-Dor then tried to toughen his stance, explaining that from the following Sunday onward (i.e., five days hence), the department would stop distributing food and leave those who lacked booklets "unable even to get bread." The committee representatives, in turn, "threatened to burn down the shops." The food they had received thus far, they alleged, was inadequate; fruit and vegetables were not being distributed to them as they were "in town" (i.e., in the IDP centers in central Jerusalem). In principle, the dispute did not concern the possibility of covering the cost of the food (100 mil per day); instead, it revolved around the size and composition of the ration. Implicitly, the department's representative agreed with the residents, since he himself had applied for an allocation of 130 mil per person per day.[154]

The department also asked the War Casualties Ministry to increase its evacuee relief because the assistance approved thus far was meant to meet nutrition exigencies only. The Old City IDPs had additional needs, having left their homes on the night of the surrender with neither belongings nor clothing. Therefore, the representative of the Department for Care of Old City Refugees in Katamon asked the War Casualties Ministry to take responsibility for providing basic necessities in view of the encroaching winter. The ministry also received an update about the IDPs' demands for compensation for damage to property, work implements and materials, household effects, clothing, and goods that they had owned in the Old City.[155] Lurking behind these matters was the steadily rising tension between the authorities' representatives and the evacuees. The department was concerned about the worsening relations and the evacuees' refusal to cooperate with and promote a rehabilitation process that would include opening businesses and developing new alternative sources of livelihood.[156]

After much effort and exertion, Ben-Dor concluded an agreement with the IDPs' committee: the sides agreed to close down the food-distribution center, and the average daily per capita allocation would be raised to 120 mil. The new arrangement, replacing the distribution of food with in-cash relief, went into effect on August 20.[157]

Regular elections for the Old City Evacuees Committee took place in February 1949, with the Department for Care of Old City Refugees in Katamon observing. Elected were Yehuda Alsheich, Baruch Amadi, Yitzhak Hazan, Yehuda Shoshan, and Avraham Yosef Mizrahi.[158] In accordance with the power of attorney that the residents' assembly had given its committee to add POW members once they were released, Yehuda Ovadia and Shlomo Min-Hahar were annexed to the panel as well.[159] The committee chose the latter as its chair and the former as the treasurer.[160]

Shortly afterward, another committee was set up alongside the Katamon Old City Refugees Committee to represent the residents' interests vis-à-vis the governing institutions. The new entity, defining itself as a provisional board that would serve until elections could be held, represented "the dispossessed of the Ashkenazi and Sephardi communities" who had been resettled in Katamon and offered its assistance to the various departments of the office of the Jerusalem military governor. In return, it demanded recognition as the authorized representative of the community in Katamon and urged Dov Yosef to instruct his people "to consult with our committee before making decisions that would affect arrangements in Katamon," such as food distribution, sanitation, housing, and opening of shops, to name only a few. The committee, in turn, promised to uphold public order.[161] Nuriel Shoshani chaired the committee, and Zusha Brandwein served as his deputy.¹⁶² They convened an assembly of neighborhood residents within a month, after having advertised the gathering by posting notices around the neighborhood. The advertisements, advising residents of an agenda that included elections, were signed by the Katamon Jewish Committee in the Holy City of Jerusalem.¹⁶³ Indeed, elections for the Katamon Jewish Committee took place at the assembly, and it was decided that the provisional committee would continue to operate as a permanent one.

The committee then served the military governor with official notice of its formation, as had been standard practice under the Mandate.¹⁶⁴ Soon afterward, the Katamon Old City Refugees Committee did the same, advising the governor of the general assembly that it had held on October 3, 1948.¹⁶⁵

Community versus State: Changes in the Perception of Community Resilience with the Advent of Institutions of State

The establishment of the State of Israel brought new elements and players into an arena that had been tenanted by community agencies that operated at various levels but had limited powers and resources. If during the intercommunal war the IDPs and casualties who belonged to this population associated mainly for confrontation with a local leadership (be it a community council or, in the case of Tel Aviv, a municipality), representatives of national leadership now stepped into the municipal field in the form of executive agencies and extensions of government ministries.

As one may see, the sovereign stage of the humanitarian crisis, played out against the backdrop of internal displacement in urban centers, was typified by confusion and redundancy of authorities and responsibilities. The local leaderships in Haifa and Jerusalem, operating within the framework of community councils but based on volunteer emissaries, continued to exist but were gradually forced to submit to the organs of state. Since the public continued to view them as natural addresses for their grievances, they evolved into mediators between the public and the state. In various cases, neighborhood leaderships reappeared in order to articulate the needs of residents who had been displaced from their homes and now wished to return to them. In Jerusalem, in contrast, an establishment organizational stakeholder that was also a voluntary one, the People's Guard, played a salient role by offering itself as an immediate address for residents who wished to express distress and speak out.

Ostensibly, this change should have strengthened social resilience, a phenomenon that, as Neil Adger shows, relies on "institutions for collective action, robust governance systems and a diversity of livelihood choices."[166] Indeed, among actions that are taken to cope with the vulnerability of communities undergoing self-revitalization following disasters, the research literature notes the dimension of national and international activity that includes building bridges among organizations in order to create integrated responses and horizontal civil-society networks.[167] The process of building these horizontal bridges, however, does not always yield cooperation and balance. Indeed, community organizations tend toward a factionalism and sectarianism that sometimes diminishes their constituents' ability to cope.[168]

These criticisms of grassroots and insider organizations that sprout amid a crisis and in response to it reinforce the model that Golam M. Mathbor proposes for the development of social capital, according to which, in the third and final stage, connections between communities and economic and public institutions should take shape. This, says Mathbor, yields optimum results in terms of both pre-crisis preparedness and post-crisis rehabilitation and recovery.[169]

In this chapter, one finds a reflection of all these tendencies—new IDP and resident organizations that defended their independence and status zealously, contrasted with the confusion that results from the state's entry into the arena with its representatives and its new organizational structures, seeking to instigate broader processes of reconstruction and problem-solving. Recounted above was the important role of go-betweens and mediators who were identified with the institutional structure of the Yishuv community that now, with statehood having been proclaimed, became even more intimate in serving constituents' needs versus a state establishment that projected estrangement. Such was the case of the Community Council in Haifa and the People's Guard in Jerusalem.

It is also of interest to compare the responses to the continued activity of the local community organizations. Tel Aviv City Hall reacted impatiently and moved to wipe these entities out. In Jerusalem, in contrast, patience seemed more the order of the day, and, as shown above, the residents of Katamon even got their way and received attentive treatment. Irrespective of the authorities' response to their associational initiatives, however, it seems that the IDPs plainly needed these local community representational networks and the relations that took shape between them and the fetal state authorities in order to attain social resilience.

Notes

1. Arnon Golan, *Wartime Spatial Changes: Former Arab Territories within the State of Israel, 1948–1950* (in Hebrew) (Sede Boqer Campus: Ben-Gurion Research Center, 2001), 30–1.
2. Benny Morris, *1948: A History of the First Arab-Israeli War* (New Haven, CT: Yale University Press, 2008), 127.
3. Itamar Radai, *A Tale of Two Cities: The Palestinian Arabs in Jerusalem and Jaffa, 1947–1948* (Tel Aviv: The Moshe Dayan Center for Middle Eastern and African Studies, Tel Aviv University, 2015), 162.
4. Golan, *Wartime Spatial Changes*, 32–34; Moshe Ehrenwald, *Siege within Siege: The Jewish Quarter in the Old City of Jerusalem During the War of Independence* (Sede Boqer Campus: Ben-Gurion Research Institute, 2004), chapter 9.
5. Tamir Goren, *The Fall of Arab Haifa in 1948* (in Hebrew) (Sede Boqer Campus: The Ben-Gurion Research Institute for the Study of Israel and Zionism, 2006), 191–3.
6. Ibid., 190, 193.
7. Ibid., 217–29.
8. Golan, *Wartime Spatial Changes*, 80–4.
9. Radai, *A Tale of Two Cities*, 200–1.
10. Ibid., 232–8.
11. Municipal Inspection Department to Mayor of Tel Aviv, Tel Aviv Municipal Archives (hereinafter: TAMA), C 4/20, Container 593, May 21, 1948.
12. See, for example, Tel Aviv City Hall correspondence with a homeowner whose properties had been invaded by IDPs: Yehuda Nadivi, Tel Aviv Municipal Secretary, to Mr. Zimmermann, 138 Allenby Street, TAMA, C 4/20, Container 593, May 23, 1948.
13. The shelling of Jerusalem began on May 16 and continued until June 11, when the first ceasefire went into effect. Many buildings were destroyed, others were damaged, and hundreds of civilians and soldiers sustained injuries: 1,222 civilians (204 dead and 1,018 injured), 248 soldiers killed in rear-guard battles, and 752 casualties overall, approximately one-fourth of the combat forces in the city. See Itzhak Levy, *Nine Shares: Jerusalem in the Battles of the War of Independence* (in Hebrew) (Tel Aviv: Ministry of Defense Publishing House, 1986), 260–1.
14. Minutes of Housing Committee meeting, Israel State Archives (hereinafter: ISA), Gimel, 276/2, May 11, 1948. The Jerusalem Council, under Dov Yosef, replaced the National Institutions committee as the supreme civilian authority in Jerusalem in late April.
15. "Agreement between Jerusalem Council, Central Emergency Authority, and Military Governor of Administered Territory of Jerusalem," signed by Haim Salomon for the Jerusalem Council and by Dov Yosef as military governor, ISA, 274/1, August 19, 1948.
16. M. Kersik, "Proposal for the Treatment of the Refugee Problem in Region 5" (handwritten document), Central Zionist Archives (hereinafter: CZA), J3/168, June 15, 1948.
17. Rabbi Yaakov Berman of Tel Arza (today's Aharon Street in Rehavia) to S. Patman, Director of Displaced and Dispossessed Persons Affairs, ISA, Gimel, 278/38 May 28, 1948.
18. Meeting of Haifa Situation Committee Executive Board, Haifa Municipal Archives (hereinafter: HMA), File 00232/16 (4698), June 21, 1948.
19. Ibid.
20. To Haifa Community Council Executive Committee from General Secretary of Community Council and Director of Welfare Bureau, HMA, File 00297/7 (5803), May 27, 1948.

21. Report on Refugees Bureau Operations, HMA, File 00235/6 (4765), December 1, 1947–June 30, 1948. The treatment of the new wave of IDPs, composed almost entirely of kibbutz members who had carried out an organized and coordinated evacuation, was different from that of those who had been displaced from urban frontiers. For elaboration, see Nurit Cohen-Levinovsky, *Jewish Refugees in Israel's War of Independence* (in Hebrew) (Sede Boqer Campus and Tel Aviv: Am Oved, 2014), 99–100, 163–4.

22. Overview of Refugees Bureau Operations in May 1948 and return of DPs, HMA, File 00298/4 (5815).

23. Yitzhak Werfel, War Casualties Ministry, to Jerusalem Council, Jerusalem War Casualties Department, ISA, Gimel, 278/38, July 1948.

24. The fund operated on a semiprivate basis with government support but did not cover all damage because no legislation mandating property insurance had been passed. See Director of War Casualties Ministry to Minister for War Casualties, ISA, Roll 51370/3, July 18, 1948.

25. Moshe Naor, "Post-War Relief and Rehabilitation: The Ministry for War Casualties, 1948–1951" (in Hebrew), *Cathedra* 138 (2011): 139–164.

26. For an overview on the fierce battles that were taking place at this time, see Morris, *1948: A History*, 180–263.

27. Situation Committee plenary meeting, HMA, File 00412/8 (8942), July 26, 1948. See also minutes of meeting with neighborhood representatives, HMA, File 00228/19 (4626), July 29, 1948.

28. Ibid.

29. Situation Committee plenary meeting, HMA, File 00412/8 (8942), July 26, 1948.

30. Ibid.

31. Uriel Friedland of Mapai chaired both the Haifa Situation Committee and (from 1942 onward) the Hadar Hacarmel Committee. See Anat Kidron, "The Committee of the Jewish Community in Haifa and its Role in the Struggle to Shape Haifa's Civilian Character," in *Civilians at War: Studies on the Civilian Society During the Israeli War of Independence* (in Hebrew), Mordechai Bar-On and Meir Chazan, eds. (Jerusalem and Tel Aviv: Ben-Zvi Institute, 2010), 360, 365.

32. Friedland remarks, ibid.

33. David Taneh remarks, ibid.

34. Ibid.

35. Meeting of Situation Committee Executive Board with representatives of Haifa neighborhoods and suburbs, HMA, File 00228/19 (4626), July 15, 1948.

36. Ibid.

37. Minutes of meeting with neighborhood representatives, HMA, File 00228/19, July 29, 1948.

38. Ibid.

39. Executive Board meeting, HMA, File 00412/8 (8942), August 8, 1948.

40. Friedland remarks, in Kidron, "The Committee of the Jewish Community in Haifa," 365.

41. Zvi Gever to Israel Rokach, TAMA, C 4/20, June 18, 1948.

42. Ibid.

43. S. Rieger to Rokach, TAMA, C 4/20, June 21, 1948; S. Rieger, Director of Social Work Department, to Municipal Engineer, TAMA, C 4/20, July 26, 1948.

44. Haim Alperin to Mayor of Tel Aviv, TAMA, A 4/20, July 22, 1948.

45. Interview with members of leadership of United Committee of Jewish Neighborhoods with B. Sheetrit, TAMA, A 4/2209, May 13, 1948.
46. Ibid.
47. Moshe Ben-Ami to Bechor Sheetrit, TAMA, C 4/2096, May 13, 1945.
48. Haim Rabin and Zvi Albrecht to Rokach, TAMA, C 4/2209, May 23, 1948.
49. D. M. Kalmus to Rokach, TAMA, C 4/2209, June 6, 1948.
50. "Joint Committee for Provision of Services for Residents of the Jewish Neighborhoods (formerly Jaffa)," TAMA, C 4/2209, August 12, 1948.
51. Rokach to Treasurer, TAMA, C 4/2209, June 10, 1948.
52. Rokach to Chair of Jewish Neighborhoods Committee, TAMA, C 4/2209, June 24, 1948.
53. D. Kalmus to Rokach, TAMA, D 4/2209, August 5, 1948.
54. Director of Property Damage Department to Director General, TAMA, D 4/2209, August 16, 1948 (meetings between July 29 and August 6, 1948).
55. Maccabi Barracks Neighborhood Cooperative Association, Ltd., to Mayor of Tel Aviv, TAMA, A 4/2209, June 5, 1949.
56. Maccabi Barracks Neighborhood Cooperative Association, Ltd., to Mayor of Tel Aviv, TAMA, A 4/2209, October 6, 1949.
57. Summary Note on Discussion at City Hall, TAMA, A 4/2210, January 25, 1950.
58. New Shapira Neighborhood Committee to Rokach, Mayor of Tel Aviv, TAMA, D 4/2209, December 20, 1948.
59. See, for example, Yuval Ben-Bassat, "On Telegrams and Justice: Petitions from Residents of Jaffa and Gaza to the Grand Vizier in Istanbul in the Late Nineteenth Century" (in Hebrew), *The New East* 49 (2010): 30–52.
60. In their title, they omitted the names of the other neighborhoods and identified themselves in this abbreviated manner.
61. Yosef Sa'ad to Rokach, TAMA, C 4/2209, July 28, 1946.
62. Committee of Mahane Yosef and Other Neighborhoods to Mayor Rokach, TAMA, C 4/2209, October 25, 1946.
63. Menahem Ben-Yosef, "The Neve Shalom Refugees Have Returned," *Ma'ariv*, June 2, 1948, 6.
64. Committee of Mahane Yosef and Other Neighborhoods to Mayor Rokach, TAMA, A 4/2210, May 16, 1949.
65. Arnon Golan, "The Reshaping of Erstwhile Arab Space and the Formation of Israeli Space (1948–1950)," in *Israel's War of Independence Revisited* (in Hebrew), Alon Kadish, ed. (Tel Aviv: Ministry of Defense, 2004), 916 (notes 52–3).
66. Report on Anti-Theft Operation in Manshiyye, signed by Yehu (code name for one of Kiryati's officers), Israel Defense Forces Archives (hereinafter: IDFA), 136-8275-1949, May 20, 1948.
67. Golan, "The Reshaping of Erstwhile Arab Space," 923–4, note 73; Arnon Golan, *Wartime Spatial Changes: Former Arab Territories within the State of Israel, 1948–1950* (in Hebrew) (Sede Boqer Campus: Ben-Gurion Research Center, 2001), 93–4. See also Or Aleksandrowicz, "Civilian Demolition: The Premeditated Destruction of the Manshiyya Neighborhood in Jaffa, 1948–1949," *Iyyunim Bitkumat Israel* 23 (2013): 274–314.
68. "Tel Aviv, Today and Tomorrow: Blowing Up Rickety Buildings in Manshiya," *Davar*, August 9, 1948, 3.
69. Golan, *Wartime Spatial Changes*, 94; Municipal Secretary, Press Release, TAMA, C 4/20, August 8, 1948.

70. One of them was the artist Chaim Sawicki, who was identified with the "secessionist" organizations (IZL/Lehi).

71. Municipal Secretary, Press Release, TAMA, C 4/20, August 8, 1948.

72. Record of telephone call to municipality, 10:25 a.m., TAMA, C 4/20, August 11, 1948.

73. A rabbi from a community originating in Iran who was closely associated with the Religious Zionist Hapoel Hamizrachi movement—a colorful figure and a man of strong public consciousness, sometimes described as a preacher or a prophet.

74. Emanuel Ben-Nissan, "Manshiya and Hassan Bek Refugees Committee," to Minister of Minorities and Police, TAMA, C 4/20, August 17, 1948.

75. Emanuel Ben-Nissan, "Manshiya and Hassan Bek Refugees Committee," to Mayor of Tel Aviv, Rokach, TAMA, A 4/2239, August 18, 1948.

76. Minister of Minorities, Bechor Sheetrit, to Mayor of Tel Aviv, Rokach, TAMA, C 4/20, August 19, 1948. See also Aleksandrowicz, "Civilian Demolition."

77. Y. Navon, acting Secretary General of Ministry of Minorities, to ministers of Defense, Welfare, the Interior, Religions, and War Casualties, and Municipality of Tel Aviv, TAMA, C 4/20, August 19, 1948.

78. Yehuda Nadivi to Ministry of Minorities, TAMA, D 4/20, August 19, 1948.

79. Yehuda Nadivi to Secretary General of Ministry of Minorities, TAMA, D 4/20, August 22, 1948.

80. Yehuda Nadivi to Ministry of Minorities, TAMA, D 4/20, August 25, 1948.

81. Emanuel Ben-Nissan to Rokach, TAMA, D 4/20, August 26, 1948.

82. Attorney Max Seligmann, on behalf of Neighborhood Manshiya and Hassan Bek Refugees Committee, to Mayor of Tel Aviv, TAMA, D 4/20, August 29, 1948.

83. Yehuda Nadivi to National Expropriation Officer, Israel Defense Forces, TAMA, D 4/20, August 30, 1948.

84. Haim Yefet, head of the Social Services Department at the Ministry of Welfare, receiving the committee's entreaty from several other players, saw fit to respond to the neighborhood people directly, even though their cause was outside his ministry's authority. See Haim Yefet to Rabbi Emanuel Ben-Nissan, TAMA, D 4/20, September 7, 1948. See also letter from attorney Asher Rosenblum, director of War Damage Department, War Casualties Ministry, to Manshiya and Hassan Bek Refugees Committee, August 27, 1948.

85. The "cardboard-box quarter," south of Kerem Hatemanim, had been under Jaffa municipal jurisdiction during the Mandate era. In the War of Independence, more than eighty-five residents of this neighborhood and Kerem Hatemanim were either killed or declared missing.

86. Letter from Kerem Hatemanim committee to Rokach, TAMA, C 4/2209, March 9, 1947.

87. Letter from Cardboard-Box Neighborhood Committee to Mayor Rokach, TAMA, D 4/20, September 3, 1948.

88. Letter from Eliezer Brutzkus to Mayor of Tel Aviv, TAMA, D 4/20, September 14, 1948.

89. Aleksandrowicz, "Civilian Demolition," 294–8.

90. Emanuel Ben-Nissan to Rokach, TAMA, D 4/2209, December 28, 1948.

91. "Tel Aviv Borders Expanded: Official Decision to Annex Frontier Neighborhoods Augments City's Population by 40,000," *Davar*, December 13, 1948, 1.

92. "When Will It Be Jerusalem's Turn? The Affair of the Expansion of Tel Aviv," *Herut*, June 10, 1949, 4.

93. Yosef Ulitsky, *From Troubles to War: Episodes in the History of the Defense of Tel Aviv* (in Hebrew) (Tel Aviv: Haganah Headquarters Publishing House, 1951), 107, 124.
94. Morris, *1948: A History*, 152–3.
95. Golan, *Wartime Spatial Changes*, 88.
96. Alperin to Mayor of Tel Aviv, TAMA, C 4/20, May 28, 1948.
97. Alperin to Chief of Police, TAMA, C 4/20, May 24, 1948.
98. Alperin to Chief of Police, TAMA, C 4/20, May 27, 1948.
99. B. Shotet, "Partiality in the Housing of Refugees: One Room—One Family in the Village of Salameh," *Ha-Mivrak*, 202, TAMA, C 4/20, August 11, 1948, May 27, 1948.
100. Ibid.
101. Ibid.
102. Ibid.
103. Ibid.
104. Ibid. Cohen-Levinovsky (*Jewish Refugees*, 157) describes the ethnic tensions between IDPs and authorities and between them and other Tel Avivians but finds groundless the view that all the refugees belonged to the Oriental communities.
105. Golan, *Wartime Spatial Changes*, 110.
106. General Committee of New Immigrants, Salameh Neighborhood, to Mayor Rokach, TAMA, D 4/20, October 21, 1948.
107. Nadivi to General Committee of New Immigrants, Salameh Neighborhood, TAMA, D 4/20, November 8, 1948.
108. Golan, *Wartime Spatial Changes*, 110.
109. Salameh Village Committee to Rokach, TAMA, D 4/20, December 3, 1948.
110. Residents of Salameh Village to Israel Rokach, and Committee of Frontier Refugees in Salameh Village (same signatories), TAMA D 20, January 11, 1949, January 13, 1949. Several signatories of the letters would become political activists (e.g., Yitzhak Simantov, a candidate on the Sephardi list for the First Knesset, and Efraim Mizrahi, a future activist in the Herut movement and, later, Mapai). Golan, *Wartime Spatial Changes*, 110–111, note 101.
111. Ibid., 111.
112. Ibid.
113. "Tel Aviv: Election Politics in Salameh Village," *Davar*, February 24, 1949, 3.
114. "It Never Happened," *Davar*, March 15, 1949, 4.
115. Golan, *Wartime Spatial Changes*, 111, note 102.
116. "Tel Aviv: Menahem b. Shlomo Hadi," *Davar*, June 10, 1949, 7. Hadi was eulogized as "one of the devoted activists in that location who dealt with the new immigrants' affairs, established educational institutions, and brought bus service to the village."
117. Dr. S. Ziman, Acting Chief Medical Officer, Jerusalem Health Bureau, to Jerusalem Chief of Police, Jerusalem Municipal Archives (hereinafter: JMA), 4589/10, July 29, 1948.
118. S. Sofer, Jerusalem Chief of Police, to Dr. S. Ziman, Acting Chief Medical Officer, Jerusalem Health Bureau, JMA, 4589/10, August 4, 1948.
119. To Benz (Ben-Zion Kaminsky) from Dov (evidently Dov Rosen, Commander of the People's Guard), CZA, J3/168, July 6, 1948.
120. See chapter 2; Jerusalem People's Guard Commander, "Instructions on Designating an Officer for Refugees," ISA, Gimel, 278/38, July 11, 1948.
121. Ibid.
122. "Those Were the Days," *Jerusalem People's Guard Collection* (in Hebrew) (1964): 46.

123. Commander of Jerusalem People's Guard Precinct 10 to Jerusalem Community Council Housing Committee, ISA, Gimel, 278/38, August 3, 1948.

124. Commander of People's Guard Precinct 10 (District 3) to Jerusalem Headquarters, ISA, Gimel, 275/19, September 26, 1948. Precinct 10 was part of District 3, which comprised the northern neighborhoods of the city—an area that had been suffering from mass abandonment since the beginning of the war.

125. Ibid.

126. Ibid.

127. Precinct 20 Commander to People's Guard Headquarters, ISA, Gimel, 272/5, September 26, 1948.

128. Minutes of Housing Committee Meeting, ISA, Gimel, 272/5, October 11, 1948.

129. Pini Barda to People's Guard Headquarters, Population Care Department, ISA, Gimel, 272/10, September 14, 1948.

130. "Six Institutions Deal with Jerusalem but No One Cares for Her," *Ha-Boker*, September 14, 1948.

131. "Give the Refugees a Place to Live," *Ha-Yoman*, September 15, 1948.

132. Ibid.

133. Dov Rosen to Dov Yosef, ISA, Gimel, 272/5, September 15, 1948.

134. Pini Barda remarks, minutes of Staff Meeting No. 8, CZA, J3/3, September 22, 1948.

135. Marani remarks, ibid.

136. Dov Rosen remarks, ibid.

137. Moshe Ehrenwald, "Civilians in the Northern Frontier Neighborhoods of Jerusalem," in *Civilians at War: Studies on the Civilian Society During the Israeli War of Independence* (in Hebrew), Bar-On and Chazan, eds. (2010), 161–2, 173–4.

138. Dov Yosef to District Commander, ISA, Gimel, 272/14, November 14, 1948.

139. Janowski remarks, minutes of first meeting of Jerusalem Military Governor's Council, ISA, Gimel, 273/1, August 31, 1948.

140. Rafael Koch, Torah u-Melakha School, Giv'at Shaul neighborhood, to Military Governor, ISA, Gimel, 273/1, November 23, 1948.

141. Military Governor Abraham Bergman to Principal of Girls' School A, Jerusalem, ISA, Gimel, 273/1, November 23, 1948.

142. Hannah Spitzer to Dov Yosef, ISA, Gimel, 272/21, December 6, 1948.

143. Military Governor Abraham Bergman to Principal of Girls' School A, Jerusalem, ISA, Gimel, 273/1, November 23, 1948.

144. Abraham Parshan to Yehosua Simon, Jerusalem Southern Region Authority officer, ISA, Gimel, 272/19, October 21, 1948.

145. Report from Jerusalem District Welfare Office, ISA, Gimel, 272/44, October 15, 1948.

146. Puah Steiner, *From the Midst of the Turmoil: Between the Walls of Jerusalem in the 1948 War* (in Hebrew) (Jerusalem: Tzviya, 1983).

147. Department for Care of Old City Refugees in Katamon, an adjunct of the Jerusalem Council, to Haim Salomon, Jerusalem Council, ISA, Gimel, 273/1, August 8, 1948.

148. Ibid.

149. Rafael Ben-Dor to Dr. Yosef (handwritten), ISA, Gimel, 273/1, August 3, 1948.

150. Letter from Department for Care of Old City Refugees in Katamon to Jerusalem Council, to Haim Salomon, ISA, Gimel, 273/1, August 8, 1948.

151. Rafael Ben-Dor to Dr. Yosef, ISA, Gimel, 273/1, August 3, 1948.

152. Katamon Old City Refugees Committee to Dr. Yosef (handwritten), ISA, Gimel, 273/1, August 3, 1948.

153. Son of Yaakov Alsheich and grandson of Yehuda Alsheich, prominent personalities in the Yemenite Jewish community in the Jewish Quarter. (According to certain documents, his father served as mukhtar and owned a popular café in the quarter.)

154. Rafael Ben-Dor to Dr. Yosef, ISA, Gimel, 273/1, August 3, 1948.

155. Director of the Department for Care of Old City Refugees in Katamon, to Haim Salomon, Jerusalem Council, ISA, Gimel, 273/1, August 8, 1948.

156. Ibid.

157. Rafael Ben-Dor to Military Governor (handwritten), ISA, Gimel, 273/1, August 19, 1948.

158. Evidently Rabbi Baruch b. Haim Amadi, whom the Jordanians had taken prisoner.

159. These two held leadership positions in the Um al-Jimal prison camp. Shlomo Min-Hahar, who served as treasurer of the committee for civilian affairs and the Jewish Quarter, represented the Old City prisoners in this camp; Yehuda Ovadia represented the Sephardim of the Old City.

160. Old City Evacuees Committee (Shlomo Min-Hahar, Chair; Yehuda Alsheich, Secretary; Yehuda Ovadia, Treasurer) to Jerusalem District Governor, ISA, Gimel, 272/36, February 28, 1949.

161. Letter from Katamon Jewish Committee (Avraham Nir Gaon, Treasurer; Eliezer Zvi Neiman, Secretary; Rabbi Shlomo Segal, Accountant; Aharon Bernstein, Accountant) to Jerusalem Military Governor, ISA, Gimel, 272/36, September 3, 1948.

162. Rabbi Zusha Brandwein was the brother of the Stretyn Rebbe in Jerusalem; he also owned a print shop.

163. "The Katamon Jewish Committee hereby invites all residents of the neighborhood to a general assembly on October 6, 1948, at 8:00 p.m., in Parkline Hall" (advertisement), ISA, Gimel, 272/36, October 6, 1948.

164. Katamon Jewish Committee to Jerusalem Military Governor, ISA, Gimel, 272/36, October 28, 1948.

165. Katamon Old City Refugees Committee to Military Governor, ISA, Gimel, 272/36, November 14, 1948. The assembly elected a committee for this entity: Rabbi Meir Hamo, Yitzhak Levi, Hakham Yohanan Netanel, Haim Maliah, Yehuda Alsheich, and Mordechai Yitzhak Amadi, with Rabbi Benzion Hazan elected as honorary president.

166. Neil W. Adger, Terence P. Hughes, Carl Folke, Stephen R. Carpenter, and Johan Rockström, "Social-Ecological Resilience to Coastal Disasters," *Science* 309 (2005): 1038 ("Social Resilience Including Institutions for Collective Action, Robust Governance Systems and a Diversity of Livelihood Choices").

167. Ibid., table 1 ("Bridging Organizations for Integrative Responses").

168. Olivia Patterson, Frederick Weil, and Kavita Patel, "The Role of Community in Disaster Response: Conceptual Models," *Population Research and Policy Review* 29 (2010): 137.

169. Golam M. Mathbor, "Enhancement of Community Preparedness for Natural Disasters," *International Social Work* 50, no. 3 (2007): 362.

5

EMERGENCY ECONOMY AMID EMERGENCY NORMALCY

The Quest for Regularization, Improvement, and Influence

On May 19, 1948, several days into statehood, the Israeli government declared a state of emergency and empowered itself to underwrite a process of economic mobilization.[1] The new centralized policy had direct implications for various economic interest groups, many of which had been active during the intercommunal war but now had to adjust to the new state bodies and policies. These groups and associations sought ways to access these nascent frameworks in order to try to influence policy makers and regulatory processes.

If the emergency economy projected onto all levels of the market, it did so to conspicuous effect vis-à-vis businesses based on trade in goods and immobile property. New import controls required merchants to obtain permits at every stage of the importation process, from foreign-currency allocation to specification of the nature and quantity of the goods at stake. Rationing policies established allocation priorities that took no account of businesses' needs. Enterprises that had operated in places that had become war fronts were forced to shut down for lengthy periods of time. Emergency regulations that dealt with the physical revitalization of affected areas imposed large deductibles on homeowners whose property and sources of livelihood had been destroyed by shelling and sniper fire.

These are only a few examples that illuminate the new challenge that private business owners in the urban centers faced. With the transition to sovereign life, they had to find ways to reach the new state authorities, attempt to influence them from within, and identify spheres of influence outside them to make sure that their needs and voices would be heeded amid the slow but steady process of restoring routine life and livelihood—even as the war continued.

This chapter centers on the give-and-take and bargaining and the agreements and disagreements that private business owners pursued in various fields, largely commercial, with the nascent government authorities. It begins with an overview of the state's economic policies and then takes a top-down view of the transformation of the Tel Aviv–Jaffa Chamber of Commerce into the mouthpiece of the country's business sector at large. It continues with bottom-up views of contacts between sundry business proprietors and the authorities who surrounded them and the extent of influence that those who associated had, or did not have, on the executive authority on which the recovery of their ability to make a living, and indeed to survive, depended.

By tracking the initiatives that merchants and business owners took in their contacts with government authorities, I uncover patterns of negotiation between sides that not only had contradictory goals at times but also adhered, ab initio, to clashing worldviews on the preferred way of managing the country's economy. Despite it all, these associates were the face of the business sector and the free market, representing a collectivity that played a crucial role in powering the national economy and thus held the success of the economic policy in its hands. Therefore, the channel of dialogue and coordination remained open even when the principals could not find a middle ground.

The State Takes Over: Tight Centralization and Control under an Emergency Economic Regime

The tussle began on May 6, 1948, on the eve of statehood, when the National Institutions imposed food import controls. Eliezer Perlson and Dr. Herbert Foerder, appointed to the posts of food controllers, derived their powers from the Jewish Agency Executive and its counterpart at the National Committee. The regulations required importers of basic foods to declare the goods, refrain from selling or transferring them without the controller's authorization, and keep accurate records of all food that came into their possession and any amount that they transferred to wholesalers. Noncompliance was an offense to be adjudicated before an anti-profiteering court on pain of penalties set forth in the emergency regulations for war on speculation, in addition to administrative measures that the food controller was allowed to invoke against offenders.[2] A newly established department for regulation of the distribution of imports instructed importers to apply separately for each commodity and put in a special request foreign currency.[3]

The rationing and price control of staples, along with the bureaucracy that was set up to administer them, were among the main expressions of the economic mobilization that accompanied the war.[4] Nevertheless, the principle of a planned economy was accepted within a context that transcended the state of emergency. If so, many in Israeli public life (and in its precursor, the Yishuv) trusted the policy and cooperated with it, at least at first.[5]

As the Yishuv braced itself for the expiration of the Mandate, an Office of the Controller of Imports and Stocks was set up under Perlson and Foerder. After independence and the state of emergency were declared, the minister of Industry and Trade, Peretz Bernstein, was empowered to apply emergency regulations in import-export, food control, and price control.[6] In late August 1948, a "council for war on the cost of living" was established under the Ministry of Industry and Trade and promptly set up four subcommittees—manufacturing, agriculture, retailing, and services[7]—to vet goings-on in supply and look into possible ways of improving and streamlining them. Participating on the council were representatives of the Tel Aviv Municipality and a skein of economic organizations: the Histadrut Executive Committee, the Manufacturers Association, the Chamber of Commerce, the Association of Importers, the Farmers Association, the General Merchants Association, Tnuva, and the Middle Class Organization.[8]

The cost of living indeed escalated rapidly due to constraints brought on by the circumstances—the lavish consumption of human resources by the military and mobilization, the dampening of output and product quality, and the destruction of farmland and raising of tariffs by the government. To bring prices down, people were urged to consume less and leave high-priced goods on the grocer's shelf; to wit, to mobilize the economy for the war effort, the government realized that greater concentration alone would not do. "The involvement and participation of society in the economic mobilization process" was needed as well.[9]

Cementing Relations between Private Trade Organizations and the Government: The Chamber of Commerce and Representatives of Importers and Exporters

In its members' eyes, the state in the making already had a ministry of industry and trade—the Chamber of Commerce.[10] Indeed, once statehood became a reality, the government empowered the chamber to apportion import quotas among merchants. To exercise this prerogative, the chamber formed import companies that were differentiated by types of commodities and authorized to dole out the quotas in their respective fields.

The Tel Aviv chamber, the country's largest and oldest, was the hub of national-level activity. Its members considered it the representative of the country's entire commercial sector.[11] Under this umbrella, varied and sometimes contrasting interests—of importers, wholesalers, retailers, banks, and so on—were represented.[12] In addition, the chamber posted envoys to committees and councils that served under the provisional government. Examples were the supply board that operated under the food controller, the Advisory Committee under the controller of stocks, the Labor Council under the minister of Labor and Construction, and the advisory committees on general and food imports under the Import-Export Department. To surmount the special hardships that the protracted state of war had brought on, the chamber set up a provisional situation committee, which delegates from the Association of Importers and the Union of Commissioners climbed aboard. This internal panel was expected "to deal rapidly with current trade issues that demand immediate solutions" and to thwart separate action by other commercial organizations for the same purposes.[13]

The lengthy state of war and the state institutions' birth pangs forced the Chamber of Commerce to assume functions that would normally be handled by competent state authorities. The chamber, for example, took action to salvage merchandise that had been impounded in Arab countries and for this purpose maintained contact with the International Chamber of Commerce, which it asked to intercede with the UN and the government of Egypt to have the goods released.[14] Similarly, it gathered information on goods ordered by Israeli merchants and held back in ports abroad in order to have them shipped to Israel en bloc.[15]

Within the chamber, a group of merchants whose goods had been seized in Egypt organized for a joint rescue action in which help would be sought from Israeli and foreign players.[16] The Chamber of Commerce, together with the provisional government, discussed renting cargo vessels to spring goods that had been impounded in ports of departure and those unloaded in ports of transit when the ships' access to Israeli ports had been obstructed.[17]

A special committee gathered material to determine what members were owed by Arab commercial circles with which they had interacted before the war; it also determined the extent of damage that the merchants had sustained in air raids.[18] Chamber representatives then met with Bernstein in an attempt to seek through his ministry an alternative way of compensating affected merchants (e.g., by drawing on assets derived from abandoned Arab properties). It was the chamber that undertook the gathering and centralizing of information on the extent and itemization of the sums due. Its estimate came to tens of thousands of pounds.[19]

Another matter that the Chamber of Commerce took up with the Israeli civilian and military authorities was the release of goods from warehouses at Jaffa Port and the consignment of Arab goods from Tel Aviv Port to the army or the government for sale under the auspices of a Special Sale Committee. Underlying this initiative was the loss of communication with Jaffa merchants whose goods had been stored at Tel Aviv Port; they had long since left the country.[20] The chamber's officials, noting the disarray that typified the sale of goods, insisted that they be represented on this panel.[21]

The matter of merchandise trapped in the ports of Jaffa and Tel Aviv was initially treated by the Economic Self-Defense Committee, chaired by Dr. Shaul Lifschitz, president of the Chamber of Commerce.[22] Here the merchants' envoys had to play a dual role: seeing to the merchants' needs vis-à-vis the authorities and wielding authority against the merchants themselves in view of the many burglaries that occurred at the warehouses in Jaffa and the market for stolen goods that this created.[23]

Even though the "chargé for foreign-trade problems" (akin to an undersecretary for commerce) at the Ministry of Industry and Trade, Hermann Hollander, came from a background similar to that of the merchants themselves,[24] commercial circles publicly criticized the government ministries' handling of import-export affairs. Complaints about pandemic protectionism in issuing import licenses were expressed overtly at a Chamber of Commerce conference, revealing the tension that prevailed between the traders and the governmental authority that was supposed to look after their interests.[25] The director of the ministry's import-export department, Dr. Müller, insisted on being shown the material on which the grievances were based and raged against the Chamber of Commerce for having shared the complaints with the public through the press without, he charged, having checked their veracity.[26]

The criticism that seeped into the public discourse turned into an indictment of the government's economic policy and "the comportment of all kinds of clerks, consultants, etc.," on whom import licensing depended. The term *protectionist economy* penetrated the discourse, and it was alleged that "the issuance of an import license depends on the mood and attitude of the clerk" and that "strong relations of many years' duration are very, very important."[27] A columnist for the newspaper *Ma'ariv* blamed profiteering in food on "fatal" errors that the government had made by thwarting food imports, creating shortages, and unleashing a flourishing black market. Prices, the journalist continued, were rising with each passing day, and the excuse given was that "imports have stopped"—whereas the truth was that not enough import licenses were being issued, and those issued were landing in profiteers' laps.[28]

In response to the merchants' complaints, the minister of Finance, Eliezer Kaplan, met with their representatives and agreed to consider dispensations for the importation of vital commodities on the basis of an agreed-upon list and as a nonrecurrent move in return for the investment of some of the hard currency that had been made available to local importers abroad. Kaplan's goal in making this offer was twofold: to get an idea of the amount of money that Israel residents were holding abroad and to encourage the importation of staples within a limited and predetermined period of time. In Kaplan's estimation, Israelis at this time kept some £5 million in Britain and another $5 million in the United States in private foreign accounts.[29] Hearing this, Abraham Zusman (A. Z.) Cohen, a veteran member of the Executive Committee of the Association of Importers and Wholesalers and an important Chamber of Commerce activist, remarked that all this currency might be in private hands but not in those of importers and merchants.[30]

The Chamber of Commerce's demand for involvement and representation in economic policy yielded practical results in the field of taxation. Delegates from the chamber were invited to sit on three taxation committees that the Finance Ministry had established—for direct taxes, tariffs, and municipal rates.[31] By seeing to this, Kaplan, several months belatedly, kept his word to the merchant community, making them full partners in the process of "exploring and studying the method of taxation" and admitting them to forums alongside manufacturers, labor officials, and tax experts.[32] This may have been a delayed response to public pressure from the Chamber of Commerce at an open conference that it had held, where Hollander's scheme to set up a centralized government import company had drawn criticism. According to the newspaper *Al Hamishmar*, Hollander termed the private monopoly in commerce an "economic cancer," whereas his critics decried his program for strangling private initiative.[33] Some speakers at the affair accused the government of pursuing an economic policy that "snuffs out private enterprise and private property."[34] The criticism and the attempt to generate public pressure did not have the hoped-for result in the short term. That is, the Income Tax Ordinance was passed in a format that doubled the tax burden and added a war tax set at 10 percent per year.[35] Afterward, however, responding to a crescendo of public comments and criticism, Hollander pivoted toward the chamber and the merchants at large, even beginning to meet regularly with representatives of the merchants' organizations but asserting that private enterprise should operate "within the framework of limitations that are essential under the special circumstances that the Government of Israel must contend with."[36]

As the commercial circles waged their struggle of principle, they formed a growing consensus about the "unruly situation at the government departments [that regulate] import-export and control of stocks." These departments, the merchants alleged, disallowed the importation of goods for no adequate reason and set prices arbitrarily and in disregard of the merchants' expenses.[37]

In various parts of the country, merchants' organizations took specific initiatives in response to needs occasioned by specific local conditions. In Haifa, for example, it was resolved on the eve of statehood that the Economic Department of the Haifa Situation Committee should establish a commercial partnership to buy and sell goods of Arab merchants who had fled the city, such goods now having been made available by the Administrator of Enemy Property. The proceeds were to be used to finance the commercial transactions of the local Economic Department.[38] Entering into the partnership would be private commercial groups from all business circles, on the basis of their organizations' consent, as well as cooperative commercial groups.

In Jerusalem, merchants mounted stronger pressure than elsewhere to lift the restrictions on commerce because the economy there was taking an especially severe battering. Their principal demands were two: lower the multiple taxes that the Jerusalem Committee had levied, and scrap the entire taxation method that was being applied in the city. The factor that influenced Jerusalem's dire situation the most, the merchants said, was the difference in commodity prices between this city and the rest of the country. When representatives of the local Chamber of Commerce met with Dov Yosef, they laid out their grievances in this matter, and Menache Eliachar, vice president of the chamber, offered an example from his own niche, the cigarette trade. Due to the price differentials in his commodity between Tel

Aviv and Jerusalem, Eliachar alleged, many Jerusalemites were obtaining their smokes from Tel Aviv, where prices were lower, resulting in the de facto smuggling of cigarettes from the former city to the latter. A decision should be made, Eliachar stated, about setting a standard price countrywide, including Jerusalem, for certain vital goods. The merchants also demanded the lowering of bus fares on roads leading to Jerusalem, because here, they said, lay much of the blame for Jerusalem's price disadvantage.[39]

Another arena of growing tension in beleaguered Jerusalem concerned private versus cooperative commerce. During the war, Hamashbir Hamerkazi (the Histadrut-owned central supplier for rural settlements) assumed responsibility for "general shops." The merchants' representatives alleged that Hamashbir Hamerkazi was treating them dishonestly and uncooperatively, refusing to give them their fair share in stocking these establishments. They then accused the Hamashbir Hamerkazi representatives, who also sat on the Jerusalem Committee, of exploiting their double role and prioritizing their political sector (the Zionist Labor Movement) over the others. Dov Yosef responded by criticizing the private merchants, claiming that "everyone in Jerusalem would starve to death" if the city "relied on free trade only." It was a fact, he continued, that even after numerous requests from the Jerusalem Committee, the free-trade consortium that he had proposed to set up in the city was not fully operative, forcing him to go to Tel Aviv personally "to find money and organize and arrange the purchases."[40] According to Yosef, when the Jerusalem Committee members saw that an organization of merchants functioned systematically, they supported the organization and gave it the right to make apportionments even though they could have handled it themselves, resulting in higher prices of staples due to the middleman's markup. So it was in the case of the cigarettes. Yosef decided that from the perspective of the public welfare, it would be better to continue distributing cigarettes the old way (i.e., via regular distributors), even if it meant slightly higher prices, because this would allow commerce to continue along "regular channels."[41]

He had no objection in principle, he stressed, to the merchants' continued activities and denied any intention on his part, and on the government's, of imposing socialist rule on the city's economy. Noting pointedly that the city had not yet emerged from its siege, however, he asked the merchants not to burden him with "unjust criticism." Had the city's economic affairs been given over to private commerce under the circumstances that prevailed three months earlier, "we would have been done for."[42] As for taxes, Yosef was compelled against his will to allow a new set of dispensations in response to the criticism he was facing. He dismissed the allegation that staples were costlier in Jerusalem than in Tel Aviv. He did undertake, however, to act vigorously to prevent smuggling and even to station police at the town entrance and advertise on the radio a ban on smuggling cigarettes.[43]

The Jerusalem merchants also vituperated over alleged irregularities and merchant-bashing at the municipal Supply Committee, a body that operated under the town's military government (established in August and replacing the Jerusalem committee). The chamber expected its representatives to be allowed to sit on the governor's economic committee and demanded stronger representation than that given the manufacturers.[44] In response to the pressures, the Organization of Wholesalers in Jerusalem joined the municipal military government organs that dealt with supplies and taxes.[45]

Another demand expressed by the Jerusalem Chamber of Commerce concerned import licenses, which, it claimed, left the Jerusalem merchants at a disadvantage that had to be regressed. Hollander agreed in principle to let the Chamber of Commerce distribute the licenses but only on two conditions: (a) that the merchants lodge no complaints about this practice and (b) that he receive proof that the chamber would allow any merchant to join without discrimination. Hollander explained that he would not allow a "state within a state [to exist]" in matters of domestic commerce."[46] Menache Eliachar assured Hollander that the members of his chamber were interested in working harmoniously with the institutions of state and might even accept some loss of "normal" freedom of trade provided the government cooperate. While refusing to accede to Hollander's "zero complaint" demand in the distribution of licenses, he assured the chargé that membership in the chamber was open to any "known and decent" merchant. Eliachar also affirmed the chamber's willingness to cede the distribution of import quota licenses to a commercial committee that would operate under the governor, provided said committee be considerate of recommendations that the chamber would tender.[47]

Hollander's mediation appears to have paid off. A secretary for commercial affairs was appointed under the military governor, and a commercial committee representing members of the Chamber of Commerce and the Merchants Organization was established. While not interfering in the merchants' choice of representatives, Hollander asked them to name "delegates who truly want to work for Jerusalem's well-being and not just babblers."[48]

Thus, although critical of its exclusion from the core of decision-making power, the Chamber of Commerce obtained broader and broader roles in the development of the country's economic institutions despite the growing economic concentration. In many senses, this concentration and the onset of bureaucratization in economic and commercial affairs stressed the comparative advantage of independent interest groups that could operate on the basis of their own resources and post representatives who had political and public experience in representing their community's interests. In many respects, the Chamber of Commerce now served as the voice of the merchants in cases that left them with feelings of discrimination in view of the many demands made of them during the state of emergency.[49]

Another problem that the chamber's emissaries now took up was the extension of military mobilization to heads of household and older age groups, given the calamitous economic effects of the new call-up policy on business-owning inductees. On various occasions, the possibility was raised of allowing representatives of the chamber and the Association of Importers to take part in a committee that would interact with the authorities "on the wishes of merchants who own vital enterprises and are liable to compulsory mobilization." The model envisioned was based on the previous practice at Histadrut-owned factories and firms.[50] It was the president of the Chamber of Commerce, of all people, who rejected the proposal, believing that it would trap the chamber in a vise and force it to accept almost any application presented.[51] After lengthy negotiations with the induction center and the minister of Trade, members of the Chamber of Commerce were placed on the appeals committee as the merchants' representatives.[52]

In its ongoing efforts to raise capital for private economic ventures, the Chamber of Commerce chose the option of reaching out to Jewish investors in affluent countries. The Economic Department of the Jewish Agency, headed by Meir Grossman of the Revisionist Movement, seemed like a natural partner for such a quest. In a meeting between Grossman and representatives of the Tel Aviv–Jaffa Chamber of Commerce, however, deputy president Avraham Kahane expressed a grievance: "The country needs foreign capital now but ... easy injection of capital into the country should not be expected as long as economic restrictions and political discrimination exist in Israel. The world has to be told that the totalitarian methods now in use will be repealed once the war is over; this would strengthen trust in a regime based on political and economic freedom in Israel."⁵³

Benjamin Scheinsohn, soon to become president of the Tel Aviv–Jaffa Chamber of Commerce, seconded Kahane's remarks: "Injecting foreign capital depends on trusting the political regime. The currency restrictions have to be lifted. . . . A counterforce of Diaspora Jewry can be activated against the Leftist pressure that's being felt in this country."⁵⁴ Grossman soothed the merchants by expressing the belief that the government would ease the restrictions in the realization that it needed capital. "The sector of the Left needs it, too," he added.⁵⁵ He then promised to include representatives of the trade institutions in an advisory committee that served the Jewish Agency Economic Department.⁵⁶

Ahead of the Constituent Assembly (First Knesset) elections on January 25, 1949, tension among these circles surged amid a wave of arrests of grocers on suspicion of profiteering and price gouging.⁵⁷ In tax collection, too, trust between the government and the commercial organizations deteriorated as merchants and businesspeople were ordered to surrender detailed information about their wealth. The Chamber of Commerce undertook to represent the arrestees and challenge the grounds for detentions.⁵⁸ Government concentration of imports intensified, with the army and the ministries launching overseas procurement operations without co-opting private enterprises.⁵⁹ These frictions appeared to clash with the merchants' expectations of becoming partners in the legislative and regulatory processes pertaining to commerce.⁶⁰ Gradually the chamber became an advocate for the merchant community as opposed to an executive or policy-making body. An amendment to its articles, approved after the First Knesset elections, reflects this emphatically: "It is the Chamber's duty to represent, vis-à-vis the authorities of the State of Israel and other authorities, the class of those who engage in commerce and allied industries; to enter into dialogue with said state authorities . . . and to express to them the stance of the community of merchants and those in industries related to commerce."⁶¹

Reacting to this change in the chamber's mandate, Kahane remarked: "It's impossible to turn [the chamber] into a lobby in search of [import] licenses; instead, it [should] be seen as a public agency that involves itself in matters of principle and cases of blatant discrimination against specific members." Sakharov urged his colleagues to stop thinking in terms of bygone concepts and "to learn from the Histadrut and come out in an open and revolutionary war against those who attack trade with the intention of destroying it."⁶²

The tension escalated further when Hollander resigned his post as director of the Trade Division at the Ministry of Industry and Trade against the background of the government's decision to reassign responsibility for trade affairs, including import licenses for food and other consumer commodities, to Dov Yosef, who in the meantime had been named minister of Supply and Rationing.⁶³ The president of the Chamber of Commerce, Lifschitz, expressed concern about the government's intention "to perform an experiment of which the merchant community may be the main victim." Their response to these developments was to send him to an event at the Trade and Industry Club in honor of minister of Finance Kaplan (who had just received the Industry and Trade portfolio). The idea was that Lifschitz should express in his welcoming remarks the merchants' concern for the fate of private trade in Israel "due to the government's economic policy."⁶⁴

Several days later, at the Trade Club in Tel Aviv, Lifschitz seized the opportunity. He expressed the hope that Kaplan, as the newly appointed minister of Industry and Trade, would bolster the ministry's relations with the chamber, "which have frayed recently." Dropping a hint, he stated that when funds had to be raised and compulsory loans prepared, it was indeed the minister's practice to invite representatives of commerce, but in ordinary times (when no capital-raising activity was at hand), "the Minister evidently feels no profound psychological need to be seen with and to convene with us."⁶⁵ Lifschitz tallied the merchant community's donations to the fundraisers and loans and reckoned them at more than IL 5 million, advancing toward IL 6 million. "Again we see clearly and conspicuously what can be attained by focused will, mutual responsibility, and self-organization." Lifschitz, however, frowned on the idea that cooperation between government and nongovernmental economic players should be restricted to raising money for the state's needs. Stressing that economic entities needed cooperation in many domains, he shared with those present the feeling, which had sunk roots, that "the government circles do not properly appreciate such cooperation" and reassured Kaplan that his community was "willing and ready to help."⁶⁶

Then, likening Israel's economic struggle to a military operation, Lifschitz stated, "We must win this campaign no less than we have to win on the battlefield." Comparing the merchant sector to "veteran soldiers in the economic war," he lamented what he termed the lack of perceptible encouragement from the "economic generalissimos." In Lifschitz's estimation, potential foreign investors would be deterred if they observed the government's attitude toward veteran domestic businesspeople. Addressing the government, he implored, "Encourage the manufacturer, the local merchant," and the foreign capital would surely come. Therefore, he urged the minister of Finance and his director general to cooperate with merchant collectivity, seek its advice, and put its capabilities, experience, and vigor to use "because woe unto us if these circles, builders and sustainers of the economy, falter in their morale and sink into despair and defeatism. The High Commander who is responsible for one of the mainstays of our national economy is trade. Only by fully mobilizing all forces does he assure victory."[67]

At the annual general assembly of the Tel Aviv–Jaffa Chamber of Commerce a month later, hundreds of chamber members and sundry public figures were joined by the minister of Supply and Rationing, Dov Yosef, and additional senior officials. In one of its resolutions, those assembled demanded the encouragement of private enterprise in all areas of life and alleged that the proclamations about socialist rule were frightening foreign capitalists and gravely undermining the country's ability to absorb immigrants. The assembly did not consider the austerity plan (announced a month earlier) an effective way to lower the cost of living. It demanded the establishment of a free-trade zone at one of the ports to encourage imports and place them in the hands of the "regular importer class." Emergency government controls, it insisted, should be applied only in consultation with professionals, and the government's advisory committees should include chamber representatives.[68]

One participant, relating to Dov Yosef's comments, said that the minister had uttered "things not of democratic governance but of dictatorship." Zalman Suzajev, president of the Association of Importers and Wholesalers, predicted that the government would "take one commodity after another out of the hands of private trade."[69] A journalist with *Davar* described the assembly's deliberations as "unilateral soul-searching." He mocked the lack of self-awareness among those at the assembly who had booed a merchant for attempting to examine the extent of his own class's responsibility for the plight of private commerce due to instances of profiteering and exploitation. The critic, the journalist continued, had provided details about price gouging but had been forced to quit the podium. Other speakers who verbally pummeled the government and its officials, in contrast, were allowed to continue undisturbed.[70]

At this time, the Chamber of Commerce had some 900 members and seventeen sections along with an Import Division. It had contributed IL 1,100,000 to the compulsory loan and IL 1,800,000 to the war loan. Even so, Lifschitz, claimed, the government treated the merchant collectivity like a stepson. Its programs, he charged, threatened personal freedom, menaced private enterprise, and patently sought to tilt the economy in favor of the cooperative sector. The government, Yosef responded, would support any decent merchant whom the economy needed.[71] By putting it this way, however, he issued a subtle critique of ostensibly indecent merchants, thereby fueling suspicions and estrangement that were surging to begin with. It appears that the Chamber of Commerce, which at the outset of the war had considered itself a partner in leadership and the economic struggle, was steadily shoved into the position of an oppositionist interest group vis-à-vis the government and its policies—an agent of advocacy whose voice rose just as steadily as its influence fell.

Striving for Normalcy: Goals of Associating After the End of Fighting in Urban Centers

Haifa's Merchants: The Struggle for Economic Revival

Several days after Israeli statehood was declared, a group of merchants whose businesses had been located in the Lower City organized and presented the town's Situation Committee with a petition of sorts, a document bearing its addressers' signatures. In it, the merchants urged the local leadership to restore commercial life in the Lower City by clearing Jaffa Street of its barbwire fencing and restoring transport from Hadar Hacarmel to the city proper.[72] The merchants' struggle to revive the Lower City had in fact begun more than two months earlier, during and after the battles (see chapter 2). Now, assuming that sovereignty did matter, the petitioners, accompanied by the Haifa Chamber of Commerce, noted that even though a decision had been made to concentrate the National Institutions' procurements with businesses and workshops in the Lower City, it was not being done in practice. Bus service to Jaffa Street had not been restored, and part of the street remained closed to pedestrian and vehicular traffic, impeding access to business centers in the area. Absent "immediate vigorous measures to revitalize these areas," the petitioners warned, "they will wither and the municipal leadership will be responsible for it—and who will pay for this sin?" Hence, the purpose of their appeal: "to call your attention to this situation and motivate you to take action."[73]

The Haifa Chamber of Commerce also attempted to promote the cause at the national level. Situating government offices in the Lower City, the chamber officials realized, would create an opportunity to proclaim in practice the restoration of economic activity in that part of town. They couched their view of the importance of the Lower City in national terms—access to the port and to Jewish-owned property, including real estate, banks, trading houses, and "the largest and most important" offices.[74] Despite the decision to give the Lower City priority in the placement of government economic offices, the Chamber of Commerce was surprised to hear that the Food Control offices would remain in Hadar Hacarmel, "ostensibly at the request of staff for its convenience, which we find wrong." This decision also seemed puzzling given that the Lower City was also home to the players with which the Food Control office was supposed to interact. In the chamber's thinking, the location of these offices was natural and warranted,[75] an idea they shared with Haifa's local leadership, which also repeatedly criticized the national and state institutions for continuing to avoid the area.[76] Nevertheless, despite pressure from all directions, national-level institutions moved slowly in returning to the Lower City. A month after statehood was declared and several months after the conquest of Haifa, they avoided the area, as did small businesses that had moved to Hadar Hacarmel during the intercommunal war.[77] The question that continued to occupy local policy makers was whether sanctions could be brought against them, as both private individuals and representative entities were demanding loudly.[78]

In the meantime, the grassroots initiative took a step forward when residents and merchants set up a joint committee in the "old commercial center" area and declared their intention of developing the location. They asked the Haifa Situation Committee to contact them on any topic related to the vicinity.[79] After waiting in vain for a response from the local and national leadership, they began to develop the commercial center themselves.[80] In some fields, however, the municipal authority's intervention was needed. The residents and merchants committee thus demanded the restoration of regular public transport by lowering fares, reinstating bus service to Lower City neighborhoods and from them to locations out of town, and adding bus stops throughout the area. Along with returning all government offices to the precinct, the panel expected the Situation Committee to threaten to reassign abandoned business premises to others unless their owners returned to and used them. Vacant shops that belonged to Arab merchants who had fled from the city, they continued, should be turned over to the indigent. Clearly, one can see that they acted on the premise that the Arabs who left the city would not return. This assumption proved correct except in minor cases of family unification, where repatriation was allowed.[81] The residents and merchants expected the Situation Committee to launch a campaign urging townspeople to visit the Lower City for business and shopping.[82] If their demands were not met and implemented within a week, the organized inhabitants of the Lower City warned, they would be unable to meet their tax and fee liabilities and would express their protest by closing all businesses and offices for three days. Attached to the petition were seventy to eighty signatures.[83]

At a plenary meeting of the Haifa Situation Committee, the chair, Uriel Friedland, read out the residents' demands and described what was being done to meet them.[84] A debate erupted over the question of forcing businesses and offices to return to the Lower City by edict. It being feared that such a decree was unenforceable and that the public would ignore it, several committee members preferred to pursue the same goal by means of information and persuasion.[85] Finally, the committee decided to draw up a list of residential and business properties that their owners had abandoned while relocating to other parts of town and afterward to appoint a small panel that would seek ways to persuade or compel them to return to the Lower City.[86]

The city leadership presented the Lower City entity with a report on its deliberations and described the modus operandi that it had chosen, focusing on mediation and conciliation between those behind the association and various municipal players and authorities. For example, the Lower City people's request to improve public transport was handed on to the Transport Committee, and, in regard to housing, the committee recommended continued contact with the provisional government's Housing Department. Finally, the local leaders asked the association of residents to prepare a list of businesses and offices that had been abandoned since the war broke out in order to "find a way to force the owners to return to the Lower City." In a nutshell, the Situation Committee promised to do everything it could to help everyone who had an interest in revitalizing the Lower City.[87]

Before testing the effectiveness of this local organizational initiative, one needs to determine how seriously the Haifa local leadership, the executive arm of the pre-state national institutions, took its moral and formal validity. The answer is reflected in how it dealt with matters. The Situation Committee invited the local entity to present its demands, then it put the questions up for discussion and resolved to forward the demands to various entities in Haifa. When the committee turned to these entities, it sometimes handed them a deadline for treatment and response. The documentation shows clearly that the Situation Committee's executive did not shirk responsibility, even when it submitted matters to the operative levels. Equally, however, it did not claim parentage of the initiative and emphasized the role of the grassroots association. For example, when members of the executive approached the Transport Committee, they noted that they did so pursuant to demands presented to them by "the committee of residents and merchants of the 'old' commercial center to revitalize the Lower City." In a letter to the coordinator of transport, the emergency committee's executive asked him to advise them within a week of actions taken and stressed that it was the Situation Committee's duty "to do promptly whatever it can to help revitalize the Lower City."[88]

In the resolutions of the Situation Committee's executive board, the commitment to the Lower City and its merchants was couched in plain and authoritative language: "The Situation Committee states that one method that may be immensely helpful in revitalizing and developing the Lower City is to place governmental and Yishuv institutions there. The Situation Committee *demands* [emphasis added] that all these institutions, which had been concentrated in the Lower City before the onset of the war, reopen their offices [there]."[89] The resolution included an appeal to the Housing Department and a demand for all requisite assistance and dispensations to obtain alternative suitable premises in the Lower City for institutions that, for whatever reason, could not return to their previous quarters. The board resolved to advertise its resolutions in the press, to turn to the Housing Department, now a government agency, and to make a one-off allocation of IL 50 for information and advertising "to instill awareness in the Haifa community of the national, political, and economic importance of the Lower City and of its appropriate place in the development of the city at large."[90]

Once this was done, the Situation Committee went back to the residents' and merchants' association and advised it of the measures that had been taken and which of their requests had not been met and why.[91]

At a certain point in time, the merchants' association was abolished and integrated into the Situation Committee. By doing this, they declared their confidence in the Community Council institutions, a body that before statehood was regarded as the authority and was now rapidly turning into the residents' mediator vis-à-vis the state's official authorities.[92] In late August 1949, some sixteen months after the end of the fighting in Haifa, the committee reported with satisfaction that the old commercial center was returning to "its old life."[93]

The Struggle of Homeowners to Fund Renovations and Shelters

The widespread damage to property—real property above all—exposed decision makers to pressure and became one of the first issues to be discussed in the transfer of powers from local authorities to the state authorities that succeeded them.

In Haifa, owners of damaged property pounded on the doors of the municipal Situation Committee, demanding a response. Consequently, the committee undertook to keep records of damage and offered itself as an address for information-sharing.[94] As a first step in this direction, it declared its intent to establish a special public subcommittee for "investigation and valuation" of the damage. It had no idea, however, of where to obtain resources for compensation and how much compensation it should offer; it also assumed no responsibility for the payout of compensation in any sum.[95] Attached to the group in addition to the Situation Committee delegates were public figures who represented property-owning circles in manufacturing, trade, and crafts.[96] In the first few months, the treatment of war casualties focused on those who had sustained physical injuries; no central entity was established to help people "whose entire property has been destroyed, burned, or looted due to enemy action." In the estimation of the Haifa Situation Committee, orderly record-keeping of damage would have a salutary psychological effect "as evidence of the state institutions' willingness to deal with the problem."[97] A delegation from the committee met with Yehuda Fishman-Maimon, minister of Religious Affairs and War Casualties, and shared with him the material that it had collected.[98]

In the meantime, applications for war-damage compensation were being hurled at the Haifa municipal leadership by individuals and groups that considered this body the address for their war-induced woes. The requests reflected the agonies that had overtaken the applicants, who had been economically viable until recently and were now emphatically not,[99] and it caused the leadership no little distress. The Situation Committee, as in the case of rehabilitating the Lower City, continued to deal with the confusion and lack of coordination that prevailed within government offices and the hardships this created for ordinary citizens who sought responses to their needs.[100] Thus, the Situation Committee presented the district commissioner (the highest local official representing the Ministry of the Interior) with the claim files that had been deposited with it, attaching legal opinions as to how the damage should be recorded. The Situation Committee members importuned the commissioner to quickly take responsibility for the problem, noting that it was worsening and "the affected public is stepping up its pressure."[101]

In Jerusalem, too, homeowners were under severe stress, and their local association pressed to convene urgently a national assembly of homeowners and additional circles to discuss their plight. The board of the Jerusalem Homeowners Association, protesting what it called "the imposition of arbitrary military rule, effectively a one-party dictatorship, on Jewish Jerusalem," warned the government that the ongoing mistreatment of its members, the builders of the city and bearers of the tax burden, was "making a mockery of all democratic concepts."[102] The Jerusalem homeowners demanded representation on all municipal bodies—the expanded city council, the board of the military governor, and all the rest—and democratic elections for each of them as promptly as possible.[103]

The board had also begun to think in national electoral terms. Therefore, it turned to property owners nationwide and urged them to prepare for elections to "the first Hebrew parliament, for active participation in these elections on an independent list and for the election of delegates to represent [our] public and fight for the classes of private enterprise in the Land of Israel."[104] It campaigned for the establishment of a national public fund for the repair of buildings in Jerusalem and countrywide "that were damaged by act of war and to encourage private construction."[105]

One of the problems still unsolved was that of the Ben-Yehuda Street bombing casualties. Although two entities—a special committee for Jerusalem casualties and another specifically addressed to their street—had seemingly given them priority in the economic revitalization work, half a year had gone by, and many loose ends remained.[106]

Damage to private sources of employment for craftspeople and merchants was a topic of cardinal importance in Jerusalem. People needed not only solutions to housing problems but also alternatives to the buildings where they had made their living. Here some individual victims turned to representatives in their professional field. The Jerusalem Association of

Crafts and Petty Manufacturing took up the case of a member named Meir Cohen, a watchmaker who had had to abandon his shop next to the Italian Hospital due to snipers, and that of a group of weavers who had had workshops in Batei Ungarn, Mea She'arim, and Beit Yisrael—neighborhoods that had become dangerous during the war and remained so in the autumn of 1948, even as routine life recovered elsewhere. The association's envoys made it their own business to search for alternative vacant quarters for their members.[107]

A relief loan fund for Jerusalem artisans and petty manufacturers affected by the war was also established at roughly this time. It came into being as an extension of the Fund for Casualties of the Events in Jerusalem, set up shortly after the intercommunal war began and in response to the Ben-Yehuda Street bombing.[108] The new fund gave economic victims the wherewithal to open shops in various parts of the city and start revitalizing their businesses by laying in stocks and repairing and replacing equipment.[109] The lender was the Palestine Union, Ltd., stewarded by a special committee established for the fund's purposes.[110]

The Jerusalem Homeowners Association sprang into action when the talk of expanding expropriations and passing legislation requiring homeowners to repair their dwellings gathered momentum. The homeowners' associational initiative largely coincided with the transfer of responsibility for municipal administration to the office of the military governor and the establishment of permanent entities to deal with the city's housing crisis. A mission from the association met with the deputy governor, Dr. Abraham Bergman, and the two mulled the governor's intention of expropriating buildings and land under Mandate emergency regulations that remained in effect. The mission called Bergman's attention to a clause in the regulations that entitled any party harmed by confiscation to turn to an appeals committee on expropriation and housing affairs. This panel had been established back in 1946 but was inactive; the association proposed that it be reactivated under the circumstances.[111]

Representatives of the Central Committee of Homeowners Associations in Israel were not invited to take part in drafting the emergency regulations based on the 1948 Law and Administration Ordinance[112] for the repair of war damage. Sa'adia Shoshani, the chair of the committee, was incensed about the omission: "We haven't the words to express our amazement and displeasure over the fact that those in charge of dealing with this problem did not see fit to approach and consult with us and at least hear our opinion about a matter of relevance to our constituents. One gets the impression that your office [the War Casualties Ministry] considers as war victims only residents of bombed or shelled houses and not the landlords who built them and invested the best of their strength and wealth in them, and yet require them to rebuild the ruins brought on by the war."[113]

Shoshani was aggrieved by the choice of the War Casualties Ministry, of all auspices, to disregard the existence of the very organization "that represents, in this case, the main interested parties in the matter under discussion." Accordingly, he demanded a two-week suspension of the promulgation of the regulations to allow representatives of his association to study the problem and present the minister with their remarks and proposals in order to prevent the introduction of a "law that is faulty, unjust, or unworkable because it lacks the experience and knowledge of those affected by it."[114]

One matter of particular concern to the Homeowners Association was the demand to build shelters. The Homeowners Association in Haifa, fearing that the cost of compliance would fall entirely on its members, hurriedly urged the Situation Committee to promise that it would devolve on "all residents of the buildings."[115] The Homeowners Association in Haifa, like its counterpart in Jerusalem, expressed dissatisfaction with the decision-making process in matters affecting its membership and complained that "the Situation Committee found it correct to decide on a matter pertaining directly to our public without consulting with our Association, the competent representative of the community of homeowners."[116] The Situation Committee responded to this sharply, claiming that the information on building shelters and charging homeowners for it had been sent on to the heads of the association "before any order was issued and not after the fact."[117] Even though the leaders in Haifa based their case on British law and specific precedents, their policy angered the Haifa homeowners, who complained of discrimination relative to homeowners in Tel Aviv.[118]

Eateries and Hotels—The Agonies of "Luxury Businesses"

The slight easing of tension in Haifa and along the Tel Aviv–Jaffa frontier after the Israel Defense Forces (IDF) secured these areas and imposed sovereign statehood found its way to Jerusalem gradually and hesitantly. Politically, Jerusalem remained "outside" the national borders and, in military terms, was still besieged and shelled.[119] With the establishment of the office of the Jerusalem military governor in late July 1948, however, the town's hoteliers and eatery owners hoped that now they had an address to turn to, one with powers. With the war decelerating, they thought, it might be possible to reopen the discussion over reestablishing normalcy, however partial, in their commercial life.[120]

The special body tasked with the affairs of restaurants, cafés, and hotels, operating under the Jerusalem Committee (soon to become the Council of the Military Government), was set up in coordination with representatives of the Organization of Cafés, Restaurants, and Hotels and may be regarded as the sole achievement of their advocacy efforts over a period of nearly six months. While regular contact with the town's leadership had not yet resulted in the release of essentials for their functioning, the discussions after the beginning of the second truce reflected a gradual sense of return to normalcy. Still, a pointed debate took place over the question of controlling the prices of staples, a discussion that may have reflected the siege mentality that still pervaded the city due to the siege in the present and trepidation about the future. The practical negotiations between the "food officials" and the food-service proprietors were ultimately resolved with the establishment of four price levels and detailed lists of products—"black coffee, coffee with milk ... honey cake with filling and icing, yeast cake with filling," and so on and so forth. This itemization attested that the cafés, restaurants, and hotels, which served luxuries based on vital foodstuffs, were still not fully welcome to return to business as usual.[121]

Nevertheless, the special panel not only ensured the control of supply and prices, it also encouraged the eateries to reopen by giving them an advance on their regular allotments.[122] Its members, including two representatives of the Organization of Cafés, Restaurants, and Hotels, were well versed in the minutiae of restaurant management and operation and made sure to present Dov Yosef with regular reports. Such reportage included information about the allocation of chickpeas, flour, and oil for the production of falafel in Jerusalem and the "smuggling of chocolate that caused loss of tax revenue and lawlessness." The topics covered included references to quantities of biscuits to be distributed, quantities and prices of carob, and the high price of ice cream "because the city still doesn't have any cones."[123] After lengthy deliberations, they agreed on prices that would be set for meals and even concurred that no beef or poultry would be served, except on Mondays and Tuesdays, until prices for meals containing these ingredients could be set.[124] It was this committee that approved the licensing of restaurants and cafés.[125]

The Organization of Cafés, Restaurants, and Hotels in Jerusalem now had to represent its members in solving another weighty problem—the plight of pension owners in outlying parts of town, whose establishments had been commandeered by the Israel Defense Forces to billet troops serving nearby. Protesting the losses in cash and kind occasioned by the soldiers' presence there, the proprietors summoned their representative association to present their distress to the Jerusalem Committee. The rate that the IDF paid them for billeting covered direct costs only; often the army's reps refused to pay bills presented to them or did so in arrears and dragged proprietors into creditor lawsuits. Billeted soldiers treated pension property contemptuously, removing furniture, beds, and bedding without proprietors' consent and leaving things in the yard. The army refused to allow owners to set aside a room in the building for the storage of equipment that the soldiers did not need. Often, divisional logistics officers set prices for billeting on their own, heedless of the proprietors' demands. When pensions accommodated soldiers without authorization, the army refused to pay for them. No one assumed responsibility for repairing or paying compensation for damage caused by soldiers—broken doors, shattered windowpanes, dislodged doorknobs, gouged walls, ruined furniture, and trashed gardens. Soldiers treated Jerusalem like "occupied territory" and pension property as "free for the taking," the proprietors complained.[126]

The representative organization of pension owners now demanded that the damage be valuated, that its members be compensated for it, and that the IDF pay for billeting its troops at the rate that the food controller in Jerusalem had set, on which the hoteliers had agreed to give the army a discount. Finally, they insisted that the IDF issue rules on billeting charges and use of facilities, require officers and soldiers to protect the property made available to them, and punish transgressors.[127]

Private Interests/National Interests

Associative conduct by people who had economic interests, for the purpose of defending themselves against harm to businesses and income, was much more widespread and diverse than the foregoing account suggests. Its genesis traces to two factors: the distress they suffered due to the war economy and centralized, rigid government control and the preexistence of an organizational infrastructure that would serve them. Most business owners already belonged to representative associations, namely the branches and sections of large umbrella organizations, such as the Chamber of Commerce, the Association of Merchants, and the Manufacturers Association. Now that these large entities were pursuing struggles of principle, their branches and sections set out on their own, establishing their own special emergency bodies. Their aims in so doing were to assure the ability of those with specific interests to minimize the damage that the inflexible policies were inflicting on them and to steward their members in the transition to acceptance of sovereign government authority and the attempts to restore partial normalcy and embark on revitalization. Interestingly, however, their autonomous activity did not come at the expense of their strong ties with the large entities. Workers continued to avail themselves of the Histadrut, merchants of the Chamber of Commerce or the Association of Merchants, and manufacturers and craftspeople of, usually, the Manufacturers Association. Thus, de facto, a chain of relations took shape that ultimately enabled representatives of economic interest groups to speak out, articulate their grievances, and put forward their claims to the highest levels of the Israeli governmental system—the ministries in charge and the ministers themselves.

In the background of these meetings stood each side's attitude toward the uniqueness of the state of emergency and the commitment of all parties to bear the burden. The interest groups' representatives made sure to present themselves as loyal patriots who agreed to do their share and pay the price of the state of emergency. Each portrayed its case as the drawing of a red line that, if breached, would render its constituents unable to continue shouldering the burden—setting in motion a cascade effect on the economy at large. From the point of view of those who associated on the basis of economic interest, their demands in no way clashed with the general welfare or the national calculus.

In many respects, one may regard these regular contacts with government authorities, established by private business organizations, as one of the earliest stages in the consolidation of relations between the "third sector" and government in Israel. The recognition that many of these organizations obtained—for themselves and for the cruciality of their members' business activity—placed them on a fast and relatively simple track to interaction and contacts with policy makers. Even if their wishes were often unrequited, in these contacts they managed to communicate messages and information that were taken into account, if not in grand and comprehensive policies, then in spot decisions and day-to-day conduct.

Notes

1. Moshe Naor, "From Economic Globalization to the Austerity Front: Rationing and Price-Control Policy during the War," in *Civilians at War: Studies on the Civilian Society During the Israeli War of Independence* (in Hebrew), Mordechai Bar-On and Meir Chazan, eds. (Jerusalem and Tel Aviv: Yad Izhak Ben-Zvi, 2006), 200–1.
2. "Food Import Control Regulations," *Ma'ariv*, May 6, 1948, 4.
3. Memorandum from meeting of Southern District Food Controller with representatives of City Hall, Tel Aviv Municipal Archives (hereinafter: TAMA), 38/4 (Container 466), May 14, 1948. "Import-Export Department—Notice no. 2 (May 28, 1948)," *Ma'ariv*, May 30, 1948, 3.
4. Moshe Naor, *On the Home Front: Tel Aviv and Mobilization of the Yishuv in the War of Independence* (Jerusalem: Yad Izhak Ben-Zvi, 2009), 63.
5. Nachum T. Gross, *Not by Spirit Alone: Studies in the Economic History of Modern Palestine and Israel* (Jerusalem: Magnes and Yad Izhak Ben-Zvi, 1999), 326. See also Orit Rozin, *Duty and Love: Individualism and Collectivism in 1950s Israel* (in Hebrew) (Tel Aviv: Am Oved, 2008), 22.
6. Naor, *On the Home Front*, 81; Situation Committee plenary meeting, Haifa Municipal Archives (hereinafter: HMA), 00232/15 (ID 4697), August 23, 1948.
7. Minutes of Chamber of Commerce committee meeting, Tel Aviv Chamber of Commerce Archives (hereinafter: COCA), August 25, 1948.
8. "Council for War on Cost of Living Goes into Action," *Davar*, August 22, 1948, 2.
9. Naor, *On the Home Front*, 71; Minutes of Chamber of Commerce committee meeting, COCA, August 25, 1948.
10. Interview with Ben Yakar, interviews with Chamber of Commerce members, COCA, Binder 10 (n.d., adjunct to another interview from November 1984, interviewer identity unknown).
11. Paula Kabalo, "Occupational Identity in Wartime—The Chambers of Commerce," in *Economy at War: Studies on Civilian Society during the Israeli War of Independence* (in Hebrew), Mordechai Bar-On, Itzhak Greenberg, and Meir Chazan, eds. (Jerusalem: Yad Izhak Ben-Zvi, 2017).
12. Interview with Ben Yakar, interviews with Chamber of Commerce members, COCA, Binder 10.
13. Tel Aviv–Jaffa Chamber of Commerce (undated document, placed with 1948 material), COCA, Binder 6; Tel Aviv–Jaffa Chamber of Commerce Archives, minutes of committee meeting, June 9, 1948; Minutes of Chamber of Commerce committee meeting, COCA, July 7, 1948.
14. "International Chamber of Commerce to Discuss Problem of Confiscation in Egypt of Goods Destined for Israel," *Ma'ariv*, June 3, 1948, 5; Minutes of Chamber of Commerce committee meeting, COCA, July 7, 1948.
15. Tel Aviv–Jaffa Chamber of Commerce (undated document, placed with 1948 material), COCA, Binder 6.
16. Minutes of Chamber of Commerce committee meeting, COCA, July 7, 1948; "20,000 Tonnes of Goods Destined for Israel Scattered in Various Mediterranean Ports," *Ma'ariv*, June 22, 1948, 4.
17. "Import Settlement: Government and Chamber of Commerce Discussions," *Ma'ariv*, June 23, 1948, 3.
18. Minutes of Chamber of Commerce committee meeting, COCA, June 2, 1948.

19. Minutes of Chamber of Commerce committee meeting, COCA, July 7, 1948; "Negotiations over Arabs' Debts to Jewish Merchants Begin," *Ma'ariv,* June 30, 1948, 7.

20. It is important to note in this context that as long as Arab merchants remained in Jaffa, attempts continued to carry out reciprocal swaps of goods—transfers of Arab traders' merchandise from Tel Aviv to Jaffa and that of Jewish merchants in the opposite direction. These contacts, naturally, ceased after the last Arab merchants in Jaffa left the city on the eve of its occupation by the Jewish forces, causing contact with them to be lost.

21. Minutes of Chamber of Commerce committee meeting, COCA, June 2, 1948.

22. Ibid.

23. Ibid.

24. Ofra Alyagon, "Herman Hollander's Forty Days," Ofra Alyagon Complete Writings, accessed February 4, 2019 (quotation from August 30, 2013), http://www.ofra-alyagon.co.il.

25. Tel Aviv–Jaffa Chamber of Commerce (undated document, placed with 1948 material), COCA, Binder 6.

26. Dr. A. Müller to Tel Aviv and Jaffa Chamber of Commerce, COCA, Binder 6, September 15, 1948; Yitzhak Katz to Dr. Müller, COCA, September 22, 1948.

27. David Ben-Yaakov, "Cost of Living, Finances, and Bureaucracy," letter to editor, *Ma'ariv,* September 29, 1948, 3.

28. Ibid.

29. Meeting with Mr. Kaplan and D. Horowitz, COCA, Binder 6, September 27, 1948.

30. Ibid.

31. Minutes of Chamber of Commerce committee meeting, COCA, October 27, 1948.

32. Meeting with Eliezer Kaplan, COCA, Binder 6, July 30, 1948.

33. "Chamber of Commerce Conference: Delay Decision on Raising Income Tax," *Al Hamishmar,* September 9, 1948, 2; "Council of State to Discuss Income Tax Bill Today," *Hatzofe,* September 9, 1948, 1.

34. "Chamber of Commerce Conference," 2.

35. "Doubling of Income Tax Approved: War Tax Imposed. Amendments to Tax Bill Will Reduce Income by IL 1,200,000," *Hatzofe,* September 17, 1948, 1.

36. "Government Attitudes toward Free Trade," *Hatzofe,* September 29, 1948, 3.

37. Minutes of Chamber of Commerce committee meeting, COCA, October 27, 1948.

38. Minutes of Meeting among Backers of Formation of Partnership for Purchase and Sale of Arab Merchandise, HMA, 00292/16 (ID 5734), May 10, 1948.

39. Minutes of meeting between Dr. Dov Yosef and Chamber of Commerce representatives, Israel State Archives (hereinafter: ISA), Gimel 1/273, August 15, 1948.

40. Ibid.

41. Ibid.

42. Ibid.

43. Ibid.

44. Minutes of meeting between Dr. Dov Yosef, Jerusalem Military Governor, and representatives of Chamber of Commerce, ISA, Gimel 1/273, August 15, 1948.

45. Inaugural meeting of Jerusalem Military Governor's council, ISA, Gimel 1/273, August 31, 1948.

46. Minutes of meeting at Jerusalem Chamber of Commerce between Dr. Hollander and Chamber of Commerce representatives, ISA, Gimel, 269/22, on September 17, 1948.

47. Ibid.

48. Ibid.

49. See, for example, Haifa Chamber of Commerce remonstrations against "room ransom" on businesses: Haifa and District Jewish Chamber of Commerce and Industry to Haifa Situation Committee, HMA, 00258/13 (ID 5179), June 22, 1948.

50. Minutes of Chamber of Commerce Committee meeting, COCA, July 7, 1948.

51. Ibid.

52. Minutes of Chamber of Commerce Committee meeting, COCA, July 25, 1948.

53. Minutes of meeting of joint presidiums, Chamber of Commerce and Importers Association, with Mr. Meir Grossman, COCA, Binder 7, Section 2, November 4, 1948.

54. Ibid.

55. Ibid.

56. Ibid.

57. See, for example, "Fine for Grocers Who Failed to Post Prices," *Ma'ariv*, October 10, 1948, 1; "Fined for Violation of Supervising Regulations," *Davar*, November 9, 1948, 3.

58. Minutes of Chamber of Commerce Committee meeting, COCA, December 8, 1948.

59. Minutes of Chamber of Commerce Committee meeting (with the participation of the Importers Association presidiums), COCA, December 22, 1948.

60. Ibid.; Minutes of Chamber of Commerce Committee meeting, COCA, January 19, 1949.

61. Minutes of Chamber of Commerce Committee meeting, COCA, February 22, 1949.

62. Minutes of Chamber of Commerce Committee meeting, COCA, March 30, 1949.

63. "Trade Policy to be Centralized at Ministry of Rationing," *Davar*, April 8, 1949, 8.

64. Minutes of Chamber of Commerce Committee meeting, COCA, April 5, 1949.

65. "To Strengthen Relations between Government and Merchants" (undated document), COCA, Binder 6. According to press reportage, this happened at a weekend event, placing it at April 8 or 9. See "We Won't Fight Cost of Living Unless We Hit Everyone without Exception," *Hatzofe*, April 10, 1949, 4.

66. "To Strengthen Relations between Government and Merchants," COCA.

67. Ibid.

68. "Jaffa Tel Aviv Merchants Protest Government's Economic Nonsense," *Herut*, May 13, 1949, 8.

69. Ibid.

70. "When Merchants Search Their Souls . . ." *Davar*, May 13, 1949, 8.

71. Ibid.

72. Haifa Old City merchants (many signatures attached) to Haifa Situation Committee, HMA, 00234/14 (ID 4746), May 24, 1948.

73. Haifa Chamber of Commerce and Industry to Haifa Situation Committee, HMA, 00234/14 (ID 4746), May 25, 1948.

74. Unsigned letter (accompanied by explanatory note from Haifa Chamber of Commerce) to Eliezer Perlson, HMA, 00234/14 (ID 4746), June 4, 1948.

75. Ibid.

76. Minutes of Council meeting, HMA, 00228/21 (ID 4629), June 9, 1948.

77. Yehoshua Meidav (Kropel) to Haifa Situation Committee, HMA, 00232/14 (ID 4696), June 15, 1948.

78. Ibid.

79. Committee of Old Commercial Center Residents and Merchants to Haifa Situation Committee, HMA, 00234/14 (ID 4746), June 18, 1948.

80. Committee of Old Commercial Center Residents and Merchants to Haifa Situation Committee, HMA, 00234/14 (ID 4746), July 2, 1948.

81. Jacob Tovy, *On Its Own Threshold: The Formulation of Israel's Policy on the Palestinian Refugee Issue, 1948–1956* (in Hebrew) (Sede Boqer Campus: The Ben-Gurion Research Institute for the Study of Israel and Zionism, Ben-Gurion University of the Negev, 2008), 323–36.

82. Letter from merchants in Lower City of Haifa (signed by the merchants themselves) to Situation Committee, HMA, 00234/14 (ID 4746), July 2, 1948.

83. Ibid.

84. Situation Committee plenary minutes, HMA, 00234/1 (ID 4728), July 7, 1948.

85. Ibid.

86. Ibid.

87. Haifa Situation Committee to Committee of Old Commercial Center Residents and Merchants, HMA, 00234/14 (ID 4746), July 11, 1948.

88. Haifa Situation Committee to Coordinator of Haifa Transportation Committee, HMA, 00234/14 (ID 4746), July 12, 1948.

89. Supplements to resolutions from Situation Committee meeting, HMA, 00234/1 (ID 4728), July 12, 1948.

90. Ibid.

91. Haifa Situation Committee to Committee of Old Commercial Center Residents and Merchants, HMA, 00234/14 (ID 4746), July 13, 1948; Haifa Situation Committee to Mayor of Haifa, HMA, 00234/14 (ID 4746), July 18, 1948; Resolutions of Situation Committee from meeting, HMA, 00234/1 (ID 4728), August 8, 1948; Situation Committee, Haifa, to Ya'akov Etkes, HMA, 00234/14 (ID 4746), August 9, 1948.

92. Committee of Old Commercial Center Residents and Merchants to Administrator of Arab Property, Haifa, HMA, 00234/14 (ID 4746), August 23, 1949. See also chapter 1.

93. Ibid.

94. Legal Subcommittee of Situation Committee to Haifa Situation Committee, HMA, 00230/166 (ID 4656), May 12, 1948 (appendix to letter sent to District Commissioner on June 20—see note 102).

95. Notice no. 2, HMA, 00230/16 (ID 4656), June 20, 1948.

96. Legal Subcommittee of Situation Committee to Haifa Situation Committee, HMA, 00230/16 (ID 4656), May 12, 1948.

97. A. Garbatski to members of Executive Board, HMA, 00232/16 (ID 4698), June 2, 1948.

98. Executive Committee minutes, HMA, 00234/1 (ID 4728), June 17, 1948.

99. See, for example, Adv. David Cohn to Haifa Situation Committee, HMA, 00230/16 (ID 4656), June 18, 1948.

100. Meeting of the Executive Board of Situation Committee with representatives of Haifa neighborhoods and suburbs, HMA, 00234/1 (ID 4728), July 15, 1948.

101. Situation Committee to Haifa District Commissioner, HMA, 00230/16 (ID 4656), June 20, 1948.

102. Jerusalem Homeowners Association Board, ISA, Gimel, 273/1, August 10, 1948.

103. Ibid.

104. Ibid.

105. Ibid.

106. Adv. Dr. Joseph Frank to Housing Committee, Jerusalem, ISA, Gimel, 272/14, August 13, 1948.

107. Jerusalem Association of Crafts and Petty Manufacturing to Crafts and Manufacturing Affairs Committee, ISA, Gimel, 272/14, September 14, 1948.

108. "General Overview for extraordinary meeting of representatives of institutions and banks participating in funds," Palestine Union Ltd., Jerusalem branch, Fund for Victims of the Events in Jerusalem, Loan Fund for Artisans and Petty Manufacturers Affected by the War in Jerusalem, Building Repair Loan Fund for War Victims in Jerusalem, Central Zionist Archives (hereinafter: CZA), J1/9034, October 1949.

109. Ibid.

110. Ibid.

111. Moshe Pomerantz, President of Jerusalem Homeowners Association, to A. Bergman, ISA, Gimel 272/14, October 15, 1948.

112. Section 9(b) of the Law and Administration Ordinance, 5708–1948, states, "Once an emergency is declared by the Knesset, the Government or any member thereof who is authorized for this purpose may establish emergency regulations insofar as he considers them beneficial for the defense of the state, public security, and the maintenance of supplies and essential services. Emergency regulations may amend any law, suspend its effect, or set conditions on it, save laws in which it is stated explicitly that they shall not be amended in said manner." See Shimon Shetreet, "Emergency Legislation in Israel in Light of Basic Law: Legislation" (in Hebrew), *Law and Government* 1 (1993), 433. Approval of Governance and Jurisprudence Ordinance, 5708–1908, Official Gazette no. 2 (in Hebrew), May 21, 1948.

113. Sa'adia Shoshani, Central Committee of Homeowners Associations in Israel to Minister for War Casualties, ISA, Gimel-Lamed 51370/5, December 12, 1948.

114. Ibid. The amendment to the Law and Administration Ordinance, 1949—Emergency Regulations (Repair of Houses Damaged by War) was published in *Official News Paper* 46: 143–6.

115. Homeowners Association to Haifa Situation Committee, HMA, 00231/5 (ID 4467), May 17, 1948.

116. Homeowners Association to Haifa Situation Committee, HMA, 00231/5 (ID 4467), May 30, 1948.

117. Haifa Situation Committee to Homeowners Association, HMA, 00231/5 (ID 4467), May 31, 1948.

118. Haifa Homeowners Association to Haifa Situation Committee, HMA, 00231/5 (ID 4467), June 6, 1948.

119. Motti Golani, "Jerusalem's Hope Lies Only in Partition: Israeli Policy on the Jerusalem Question, 1948–1967," *International Journal of Middle Eastern Studies* 31, no. 4 (1999): 577–604.

120. Minutes of meeting of Restaurants, Cafés, and Hotels Committee, an adjunct of the Jerusalem Committee, ISA, Gimel, 273/1, July 28, 1948.

121. Ibid.

122. Memorandum from meeting, ISA, Gimel, 273/1, August 5, 1948.

123. Memorandum from meeting, ISA, Gimel, 273/1, August 8, 1948.

124. Minutes of Military Governor's Supervision Committee for Restaurants, Cafés, and Hotels, ISA, Gimel, 273/34, August 31, 1948. The title of the forum changed when it started to operate under the military government; it now included the function of supervision, but its membership and structure remained as before.

125. Minutes of committee meeting, "Permission to License Cafés, Restaurants, and Hotels," ISA, Gimel, 273/34, October 31, 1948.

126. Organization of Hotels, Restaurants, and Pensions, Jerusalem, to Dr. Bernard Joseph, ISA, Gimel, 273/34, August 15, 1948.

127. Ibid.

6

SOLDIERS' WIVES AND A NONGOVERNMENTAL GOVERNMENT COMMITTEE FOR INDUCTEES' FAMILIES

The Question of Responsibility

WHEN THE ISRAEL DEFENSE FORCES (IDF) WERE ESTABLISHED and growing numbers of newly landed immigrants and heads of household were inducted, the IDF Manpower Division decided to establish a welfare service of its own. The founders of the service tasked it with the handling of inductees' personal problems in conjunction with the civilian welfare institutions.[1] The duties assigned to the new entity included personal social services for soldiers and their families; support services (such as visiting the ill and the wounded); rest and recreation, sports, and entertainment; canteens and snack bars; the special needs of religious soldiers; and more. The development of these social services, however, was delayed, mainly by shortfalls in budget resources and professional personnel. Thus, the IDF continued to avail itself of pre-state civilian entities—the Yishuv Inductee and Family Committee, the Soldier's Welfare Committee, and women's organizations.[2] The Council of Women's Organizations (CWO) was mindful of its responsibility for the well-being of soldiers and their families, a duty that did not disappear overnight when statehood and state mechanisms came into being.[3] As time clicked by and existential problems remained unsolved, however, inductees' wives began to weigh the formation of additional entities and to organize on a local grassroots basis. The resulting committees ultimately amalgamated under an umbrella that sheltered a broad spectrum of local associations and nationwide volunteer bodies. As this significantly gender-marked initiative progressed, the Soldier's

Welfare Committee reactivated itself on the basis of mutually affiliated local chapters. Its chair was Yosef Baratz, who had headed the committee during World War II.[4]

The Soldier's Welfare Committee and the various women's organizations collaborated with, and often operated under the auspices of, the military system, creating an example of cross-sector collaboration. This chapter focuses on this collaboration and the way those involved in it divided their duties and responsibilities. It begins by presenting the option of cross-sector cooperation and the special challenges that the Israeli case posed for those who cared to take that route. Coordination between volunteers and authorities to meet the needs of inductees' families and of soldiers' wives whose sources of livelihood were impaired took place along two parallel paths during the regular war: initiatives by women's organizations of both institutional and grassroots nature and recurrent attempts by the Inductee and Family Committee to systematize its activities and establish its credibility among beneficiaries whose resilience steadily dwindled as the war dragged on. The chapter proceeds along the axis between volunteers and bureaucrats, tracking the division of duties and collaboration between governmental service providers and those offering services on their own authority.

Volunteers and Bureaucrats: Division of Duties and Collaboration between Official Service Providers and Independent Counterparts

The concept of cross-sector collaboration entered the research literature on the third sector in the early twenty-first century. It denotes an organizational structure in which protracted interaction and exchange (sharing of information, resources, activities, and capabilities) take place among representatives of two or more sectors (governmental, third, business) for the collective attainment of an added-value outcome that the activities of only one sector cannot achieve.[5] Whenever a cross-sector encounter takes place, there is a strong probability of a clash or a rivalry between institutional logics due to each sector's different basic values. Therefore, to make collaboration possible, government must acknowledge that matters recognized theretofore as its own are now perceived as "general social problems that cannot be solved by political institutions alone; players from other sectors must also" be involved.[6]

The case described below was different if not almost opposite. First, the government's purview had not yet jelled. Second, other sectors (i.e., the sector of volunteer organizations in the inclusive and comprehensive conceptual sense of the term) preceded it in assuming responsibility for various aspects of the problem—mainly the treatment of specific social groups in need of aid. In the Israeli case, the state authorities in the relevant domain had not been established in a void; they had to cement their authority in a field that had already been occupied by diverse volunteer bodies. Particularly in this context of assisting inductees' families, it was the emphatic view among policy makers that reliance on the volunteer relief matrix should continue but that the matrix should be steered toward paths that the state considered crucial. In the policy makers' eyes, too, state coordination and supervision should be assured via the new authorities that were then taking their first steps. It is these relations, how they formed, and their short-term outcomes that this chapter will recount.

Cross-Sector Collaboration between Welfare Services and Women's Organizations

The army welfare service's responsibilities converged with matters of personal welfare, recreation, entertainment, sports, and canteens. This broad sphere of operations, totally integrated from May 1948 to the end of that year, impeded the development of social services in the Israel Defense Forces. The logjam eased gradually only after a network of town majors was set up and tasked with solving the problems of furloughed soldiers and coordinating the activities of committees that aided soldiers and their families.[7]

Even though soldiers had been alerted to the existence of the welfare services from their first days in uniform and were even urged to use them,[8] the desultory pace of organizational institutionalization was inconsistent with needs that, by the time the IDF came into being on May 31, 1948, had been building up after six months of warfare. Commanders warned that insufficient concern for individual soldiers and their families, reflected foremost in the families' worsening plight, was eroding soldiers' spirit.[9] In a meeting with the prime minister and defense minister, David Ben-Gurion, division commanders spoke of a "blow to morale" and "a crisis in all battalions because families are not being helped."[10] When these remarks were made, the fledgling state was in the middle of its first respite, a truce that followed six months of warfare. The Jewish combat forces had accomplished much in the month preceding the declaration of statehood, particularly in establishing control of urban centers and their connecting roads. However, on the night of May 14, when the British Mandate expired and the State of Israel had been declared, a combined offensive by five Arab countries' regular armed forces ensued, causing a stepwise increase in the warfare. The fighting now focused on the fronts whence the Arab expeditionary forces had attacked, and the first task at hand was to stanch the invasion. After some five weeks of difficult fighting, the sides accepted a ceasefire. Once this truce lapsed, within ten days the Israeli side switched from impeding the enemy to going on the offensive in order to give the nascent state defensible borders. The change in the nature of the fighting and its geographical foci created a clearer distinction between "front" and "rear." It now seemed to many of the fighters that while they continued to risk their lives and their families paid the economic price for their absence, the rest of the country was returning to normalcy, with many civilians picking up where they had been before the war, including in their amusements and social life. As demonstrated above, this image was far from reality. Nevertheless, it penetrated the inductees' discourse and sowed bitterness and frustration in the ranks, particularly among those whose families, or they themselves, were left without sources of livelihood.

The IDF Welfare Service did try to address the ongoing hardships and broaden its purview in regard to them. In early August, for example, it included the "partly" mobilized among those eligible for Inductee and Family Committee benefits and for compensation in the event of the inductee's death or disability.[11] Most inductees in this group belonged to the garrison force; they had not been recruited for combat units due to superannuation, poor health, or large families (defined as having more than two children). Some of them came from lower socioeconomic groups; even though they received benefits for their days in uniform, this did not compensate them from the blow to their employment because many were day laborers whose military commitment had made them less available to employers. In addition to this damage to livelihood, the partly mobilized were ineligible for discounts on health-care services, food, and cultural events. Their plight, however, had begun to attract attention after the press started publicizing it and demanding their inclusion in the rights that all other soldiers enjoyed.[12]

The daily burden of the material implications of the war was borne by the soldiers' wives, many of whom became targets for predation by their landlords. As their economic decline made it difficult for them to pay the rent, landlords often tried to evict them, sometimes by pressure tactics such as cutting off the electricity, triggering confrontations. Institutions and private individuals demanded, irrespective of the situation, that wives repay loans that their inducted husbands had taken. The wives responded resentfully, believing that they should be exempted in view of the anomaly of the events.[13]

Recently landed immigrants were another group that began to enlist with heightened intensity. With the establishment of statehood, immigrants who had been barred from the country as long as the British controlled the ports could now enter. The share of immigrants among inductees ramped from slightly over 4 percent in early June 1948 to twice the rate only one month later (8.99 on July 10) and doubled again by the end of 1948 to 18.32 percent.[14]

As they enlisted, the circles of inductees at large widened, adding growing numbers including heads of household to the subpopulation of inductees whose families' wherewithal took a beating due to the state of war. The immigrants were not only economically disempowered but also affected by adjustment difficulties of socioeconomic origin. Additionally, their plight impacted the independent organizational venture of the soldiers' wives.

Criticism of the army's paltry pay scale also seeped into the public debate. An artilleryman from the Negev sent a letter to the editor about soldiers' minuscule salaries, claiming that they failed to suffice even for the 1.5 agorot (an agora being the smallest denomination in Palestine coinage at the time, equal to ten mils, and a mil being one-hundredth of a Palestine pound) that, as one soldier said, would buy them "a glass of soda to drink." Uri Kesari reported the soldier's remarks in *Ma'ariv* and railed against the minister of Defense: "Does our soldiers' father—I mean the Minister of Defense—go to sleep with a clean conscience after he's been advised that a candidate for a martyr's death on the altar of the homeland didn't have, twenty-four hours ago, 1.5 *grush* [agorot] for a glass of soda? Isn't that a pleasure that any contemptible draft-dodger and every spoiled son of a speculator-father is privileged to enjoy without a moment's thought, legally and ten times over?!" In his letter, the soldier asked, "Where's the justice of civilians filling the cafés and swilling bottles of beer by the dozen while a thirsty soldier, in from the sizzling Negev on a day's furlough, doesn't have even a few grush to slake his thirst? . . . If the General Staff tells me money doesn't grow on trees and rifles come before riflemen, I'll tell them that one can still find a way to impose some kind of tax on all those luxuries that are flourishing on the home front."[15]

Only toward year's end, as the number of inductees reached 100,000 and the IDF Culture Service encountered other difficulties in dealing with the welter of welfare problems, did the General Staff decide to set up the Welfare Service as a freestanding entity under the Personnel Branch. When the service was inaugurated in November 1948—by which time the war was winding down—its responsibilities were also broadened to include helping soldiers to return to civilian life, meaning among other things responding to their housing and vocational training needs. This structure endured until June 1949, when the service was dismantled, and its duties were divided between the Personnel Branch and the Ministry of Defense.[16]

Care for Inductees' Wives and Children

The persistent vacuum in welfare services for inductees' families was filled largely, although not completely, by the activities of women's organizations. An important and visible area in which these organizations demonstrated their organizational and professional advantage was the placement of inductees' toddlers in care facilities. The organizations reached terms with the Yishuv Inductee and Family Committee on the maintenance of inductees' children in day-care facilities countrywide. The accord included a clause that allowed the women's organizations to bill the committee retroactively, indicating that children were indeed being enrolled in day care without guarantee of payment and that the women's organizations absorbed the costs of their upkeep for months. In the local branches of the women's organizations, the long-term solution—integrating women into the labor market—was increasingly acknowledged.[17]

To make this goal easier to attain and to smooth the clash between the responsibilities of soldiers' wives as mothers, de facto heads of household, and breadwinners, the Women's Labor Council aimed for an arrangement that would allow them to work part-time, four or five hours per day.[18] The council had amassed similar experience arranging employment for soldiers' wives during World War II.[19]

With the transition to regular warfare and the surge in mobilization of heads of household, members of the Women Workers Council began to pressure their organization to undertake the care of soldiers' wives once again. Now, however, leading members of the council demurred: this volunteer entity, with its limited capacity and resources, they argued, could not and should not assume this responsibility—it being "a general Yishuv problem entailing large resources and broad powers."[20] The establishment of the state, although having occurred only ten days earlier, had already transformed the way this nongovernmental organization (NGO) perceived its responsibilities. Now wary of taking on national missions, it preferred to appoint a delegate (Rivka Diamant, as it turned out) to liaise with the competent government players.[21]

The wives' distress mounted as the war dragged on, prompting them to visit the Yishuv Committee offices—local branches in particular—to demand the support that they had been promised. Budgeted funds, however, tarried in reaching the branches, and local workers faced the families empty-handed.[22] By the end of May, the Jerusalem local committee had received less than half of what it needed to serve an inductee clientele that had grown 2.5 times over during the month.[23] Frustration at the local branch intensified, as the staff felt that the Yishuv Committee, headquartered in Tel Aviv, was not doing enough to alleviate the Jerusalemites' distress. As the struggle to hold back the pan-Arab invading forces crested and mobilization expanded from day to day, the allocation to the Jerusalem committee stood at around 10 percent of what the committee needed.[24] The upturn in the families' distress was, of course, aggravated by the mobilization of men aged twenty-six to thirty-five, most of whom had families. Ostensibly, heads of household should have continued to receive their May salaries from their previous employers, but in Jerusalem, some 90 percent of the inductees were day laborers or owners of businesses that had been shuttered due to proprietors' mobilization. Their families were left with no source of income apart from the benefits that they had expected to receive from the local branch of the Yishuv Committee. In late May, however, the Jerusalem branch had not even begun to tackle the new needs, for which a budget twice as large was needed. The chair of the local committee let his frustration show: "It's inconceivable that we won't extend our aid to soldiers' families and parents and not help, at the very least to the limit of our abilities, to alleviate their dire condition. . . . We cannot carry on with our work unless they give us the resources we need."[25]

The Yishuv Committee, like the Women's Labor Council, went to lengths to arrange employment for members of inductees' families. To deliver this benefit—the solution that many of those involved in casework for soldiers' families preferred—employers' cooperation was needed. Again, however, implementation was delayed, even though the decisions in principle had been agreed upon and made.[26]

The branches of the Organization of Working Mothers were vigilant in this matter, sending reminders to public employers urging them to replace inducted employees with the employees' wives. They even promised to smooth the women's integration into the workplace by helping to train them.[27] However, even though many industries were short on working hands, the women found the breakthrough difficult due to the twelve-hour workday. An effort to arrange part-time employment was accompanied by contacts to assure the inductees' wives that their husbands' military salaries would not be cut off on this account.[28]

With the mounting difficulties in the background, inductees' wives in Haifa organized and held a rally where they described the plight that their husbands' mobilization had brought about. A memorandum to Dr. Giora Lubinski-Lotan of the Yishuv Inductee and Family Committee stated, "Many troubling facts that should terrify the listeners were noted [at the rally, such as] non-receipt of salary for two or three months if not longer." Another source of outrage among the women was the investigative vetting that they had to endure before qualifying for support. Their wish to organize under an entity of their own was mainly the product of their sense of weakness and impotence in contacts with the authorities. "No individual will manage to withstand the very numerous hardships." The picture described included treks "from place to place and office to office" that ended without a "satisfactory" response. The organizational initiative had the additional goals of providing support in case of disaster and easing the loneliness that beset recent immigrant women, "who should be helped before anyone else . . . by means of various kinds of mutual aid." On June 24, to translate their distress into action, the women of Haifa announced the reorganization of the Organization of Inductees' Wives.[29] The founding conference called for the establishment of a sliding wage scale for inductees' families and the total cessation of the investigation of members' eligibility for benefits. An inductee's wife "deserves her salary whether her parents can afford to support [her] or not. . . . An inductee's family must in no way be turned into a social object. The soldier is performing a pioneering war service of the highest order. He is removed temporarily from his job and his family must have economic security like the families of other workers who have remained in place." The women demanded that the salary be paid from the day of the husband's mobilization, without the exhausting red tape of filling out questionnaires "and interrogations and decisions by committees and appeals committees." The women demanded simplicity and order in the care of inductees' families.³⁰ Their approach was practical to a fault. They specified the level of pay that every inductee's wife needed in view of the number of her children. They also demanded special discounts for inductees' families in grocery stores; lowering of tuition payments, municipal taxes, and community fees; exemption from payment for childbirth; inexpensive convalescent centers for female members after illnesses; and home assistance in case of illness and immediate aid for the affected woman, including the placement of her children in care facilities. The more militant constituents also demanded the attachment of the salaries of persons liable to induction who were discharged for economic reasons and kept their pre-induction jobs or at least an assurance that such people would not receive more than a soldier's pay.³¹

Behind the angry, frustrated, and radical voices was a simple demand: the right to work and be self-supporting. "Inductees' wives should go to work immediately and support themselves by means of their labor. This is for two reasons: (a) many members will probably have to be their families' sole breadwinners; (b) one cannot live on army pay." At this juncture, they adopted the Women's Labor Council's call for the recognition of a half-day of work for inductees' wives. The organizers expressed the fear that "most members have not acquired a trade" and therefore found work hard to obtain, and even when they found it, their wages were too meager to support a family. The Organization of Inductees' Wives sought to solve this structural problem by creating rapid vocational training programs along the lines of those set up in World War II. Other items on the list of reforms that the women wished to promote included the possibility of layoffs and assistance to parents of inductees who were sole breadwinners. Finally, they demanded representation in the local institutions that gave care to inductees' families and legislation that would regularize the inductee's status and the state's responsibilities to him.³²

The pressure applied by inductees and their wives forced policy makers to revisit the method used to distribute benefits. By now, the IDF had been up and running for two months, violence had been under way for more than seven months, and mass mobilization was in effect. Even so, the support system had not managed to gain equilibrium and efficiency. Furthermore, questions of principle remained unanswered (e.g., should each inductee receive a standard unconditional benefit, as had been the British

Army's practice in World War II, or should a needs test be used?). The adoption of the former model would mean less support; the acceptance of the latter model would render some applicants ineligible. Another difficulty in applying the latter model was that many families had left their homes and were hard to track down. The rather common incidence of people having the same names had led to sundry mishaps, with some receiving benefits not intended for them, others double- or triple-dipping, and yet others getting nothing at all.[33]

Therefore, the Provisional Council of State (the country's first legislative authority) decided to reexamine the matter of support for soldiers' families and the financial implications of the attendant decisions by setting up a special subcommittee under its finance committee to explore options and propose a solution.[34] A tumultuous thrust and parry ensued in the council plenum when Saadia Kobashi, representing the Yemenite Association Party, challenged the addition of Rahel Cohen, a representative of the Women's International Zionist Organization (WIZO), to the subcommittee. This substantiated both the persistent blurring of boundaries between civilian non-parliamentary public activity and parliamentary political activity and women's personal involvement in this field. In response to Kobashi's demand to add a representative of the Yemenite-Jewish population to the subcommittee, Beba Idelson explained that Cohen had been chosen not due to her party affiliation but because of her professional experience as director of the social-service department of the National Committee, the pre-state executive entity in charge of internal affairs.[35]

As the national leadership debated (or fought over) the structure of the entities that would care for soldiers' families, the women's initiative gathered grassroots momentum. The women of Petah Tikva now joined those of Haifa in establishing an Organization of Soldiers' Wives. The new body began to operate independently and challenged the Women's Labor Council to deal with its existence. A view previously expressed by Beba Idelson took hold among members of the Histadrut Executive Committee: such an organization "should embrace all circles and not only members of the Histadrut."[36] However, seeing that facts were being created in the field (i.e., the organization was already operating on its own), the Women's Labor Council sought to secure its influence over them. To accomplish this, Idelson proposed that the Organization of Working Mothers annex itself to the new organization and that its leading core be Histadrut-affiliated. The politically savvy Idelson then set a goal for the organization: assuring the representation of inductees' families in the national institutions that cared for soldiers and their families.³⁷

Responding to what she considered a belligerent memorandum from the Organization of Soldiers' Wives in Haifa, Idelson chided the organization for having dispatched the memorandum on its own, without consulting with the Women's Labor Council. Although ostensibly upset about the contents of the memorandum, Idelson alluded to the main problem at the end of her letter: "Also, the very fact that you as a local organization are contacting, independently, a series of central institutions and even the Council of State seems totally unbecoming to us."³⁸ Then, convinced that the Women's Labor Council should step swiftly into the leadership vacuum that had come about in concern for inductees' wives, Idelson quickly seized the reins and instructed the local organizers to desist from appearing on their own before central institutions until "the matter is put onto a track and takes on an accepted form" (i.e., receives the approval of the Women's Labor Council).³⁹

The local initiatives, reflecting a common cause among inductees' wives from diverse social and political sectors, were now overshadowed by this move of the Women's Labor Council. In a communication with the superintendent of personnel for the Government of Israel, Idelson described the needs of inductees' wives as one element in a broad tableau centering on the question of "mobilizing women for the campaign" and attached a series of proposals for the integration of women into both the army and the civilian economy. Apart from enumerating the needs of inductees' wives, Idelson stressed the importance of recruiting young women for agricultural work so they would enjoy a "suitable and educational" atmosphere and offer "much assistance for agriculture." The participation in the labor cycle of mothers who were excused from military induction, too, would "alleviate the shortage of working hands." The memorandum proposed the possibility of part-time employment for mothers and pointedly recommended the opening of a network of afternoon preschools so that women could focus on their work. Continuing, Idelson asked to ensure adequate training for the new women workers and to develop special courses for them in areas that were considered men's at the time, such as metalwork, carpentry, plumbing, and electricity. Idelson then specified the desired constitutional patronage for the envisioned gender revolution in the workplace: a "constitution for the protection of women and youth."⁴⁰ She also proposed the establishment of an advisory council composed of women as an adjunct to the Ministry of

Labor, "to activate various public entities so that women's labor mobilization will succeed." Then, adopting a diplomatic tone and expressing herself in the plural, Idelson added her confidence that, as the representative of more than 70,000 working women and mothers, the Women's Labor Council would be represented on this panel "commensurate with our value and role in the workplace." In another version of the memorandum, someone added the following handwritten remark at the bottom: "We think delegates of WIZO and the Hapoel Hamizrachi women workers' organization should also be named to the council."[41]

By seizing the initiative in integrating women into the employment market, the Women's Labor Council abrogated the centrality of inductees' wives. It reframed the cause as a mission of principle, the goal being effecting women's economic integration and securing recognition of their role and share in the overall effort. This may have been an expansionary tactic, meant to underscore the potential contribution of women to the labor market; alternatively, it may have reflected deep-seated views on the supremacy of the obligation of "doing one's bit" over the right to present demands. Either way, it marked a change of tone and a revisiting of the perception of entitlement.

When delegates from the Women's Labor Council met with officials of the Ministry of Labor, they obtained a government commitment to support "a series of training enterprises for women workers, working mothers, and inductees' wives." The council now set to gathering information about employment opportunities in various locations countrywide; for this purpose, its delegates were asked to submit information about vocational training opportunities in each locality.[42] Later on, the council received an IL (Israel pounds) 1,000 loan from the Ministry of Labor to help equip sewing workshops.[43]

In an official circular under her signature, Bebe Idelson noted the "serious problem of looking out for inductees' families and assuring their rights" but termed the idea of establishing an organization of inductees' wives "a habit from the circumstances of the previous war." The Women's Labor Council, she explained, would not agree to be alone in accepting a decision concerning the very need to create such an organization under current conditions and to determine its path. Instead, Idelson clarified, the future organization should have a "comprehensive Yishuvic" (i.e., national) character. The thinking behind depriving the organization of Histadrut authority and auspices was to protect the Histadrut from "excessive responsibility for the fate of the inductee's family" and thwart "special organizing by non-Histadrut players for the purpose of weakening [the Histadrut's] influence." It was also decided that the organization would represent inductees' parents as well as their wives.

As for the goals of the organization, Idelson listed the development of mutual aid among inductees' wives, institutional care arrangements for children in need, promoting legislation concerning affirmative action in hiring for inductees' family members, obtaining representation on the newly established Inductee and Family Committee, devising a constructive program of arrangements for disabled war veterans, widows, their children, and parents of wounded persons, and even concern for the future of demobilized soldiers and their families.

Despite having stated in so many words that the organization did not belong to the Histadrut, Idelson noted explicitly the Organization of Working Mothers as "the public carrier that warrants the investment of energy and understanding in this problem of inductees' families." The message was clear: Histadrut organs should seize the initiative and take over the leadership of the Organization of Soldiers' Wives in order to forestall "the possibility of exploitation of the organization for inappropriate goals."[44]

That very day, the Women's Labor Council approached the Histadrut Committee for Inductees with proposals designed to facilitate the hiring of mothers who were soldiers' wives and even to encourage such women to take this step. The proposals included protection of the wage to which the soldier's wife was entitled due to her husband's mobilization, the creation of part-time employment opportunities on a half-day basis, participation in child upkeep expenses, efforts to expand job opportunities for soldiers' wives—including vocational training and vocational studies—and other matters.[45]

The authority and initiative that the Women's Labor Council projected under Beba Idelson were accompanied by disregard of repeated approaches by women in Haifa whose grassroots organizational initiative had prompted the Women's Labor Council to campaign for the care for soldiers' wives and families.[46] Only after the circulars were sent out and the contours of the operation spearheaded by the Women's Labor Council and the branches of the Organization of Working Mothers were presented did the women of Haifa receive a response. That is, the circular was sent to them along with a personal letter in which they were asked to consider themselves "an initiating group that, together with the Organization of Working Mothers in Haifa, will sustain the operation and determine the organization's methods going forward."[47]

The women in Haifa did not object to the demand that they subordinate themselves to a centralized authority; they even sent a letter in which they expressed satisfaction with the Women's Labor Council decision. Strenuously they denied any intention of taking "any action without consulting with the Women's Labor [Council] first" and explained that their memorandum had been based on remarks at an assembly of members and had been sent to all stakeholders to call attention to the quandary of the inductees' families. While expressing willingness to collaborate from then on, however, they disapproved of the conflation that the Women's Labor Council had created of the problems of inductees' wives and the hardships of inductees' parents. This, they feared, would subordinate the entire country to the organization that they wished to establish. The problem of soldiers' parents, they argued, was for the government to solve; the focal issue in that regard concerned the wages to which parents of only children were entitled. The wives' problem, they claimed, was more complex because it required a multidimensional support system that included arrangements for children while their mothers were at work and vocational training for the women themselves. This explains their request that the Women's Labor Council reconsider the inclusion of the parents in the organization.[48] This matter, as explained below, presented the organization's main policy makers with a difficult challenge. Ultimately, a compromise formula was found that assured the dominance of soldiers' wives as the main concern of the organization and left soldiers' parents, particularly mothers, within the organization's fold as well.

Now the Women's Labor Council established a special committee to coordinate action for soldiers' wives. Elected as its chair was Elisheva Kaplan, a prominent leader in the Women's Labor Council and the wife of Levi Eshkol, who was then assistant to the minister of Defense and subsequently the ministry's director general. Also joining the committee was Tsipora Laskow, a founding member of the World War II organization of soldiers' wives, and Riva Tabachnik,[49] Haya Gronich, and additional members from towns and several villages. The committee was defined as "internal and unofficial" due to its adamancy about not subordinating itself to the Histadrut. This obfuscation, however, did not satisfy everyone, and some still insisted that the organization join the CWO.[50]

The takeover of the Organization of Soldiers' Wives by the Women's Labor Council and the Organization of Working Mothers was emphatically advantageous in arranging employment. The members of the organization established relations with the Employment and Vocational Training Department of the provisional government's Ministry of Labor and Construction and reached agreement with it on an outline program for the training of women in needlework trades, including vocational guidance, equipment for workshops, expansion of existing enterprises and opening of additional ones, and forwarding of funds to workplaces that had begun to operate "by means of the Women's Labor Council."[51] Needlework and the enterprises that engaged in it were chosen due to their relevance for the army's needs; the choice was also consistent with the policy of the Employment Department of the Ministry of Labor and Construction, which encouraged the establishment of enterprises in these fields, especially in small localities. The workshops were intended primarily for the employment of inductees' wives and recent immigrants. The head of the Employment and Vocational Training Department instructed the central purchase committee to place as many orders with them as possible.[52] There was an additional advantage: the Organization of Working Mothers owned childcare facilities and the related organizational and professional infrastructure.[53]

The influence of the Women's Labor Council on the Organization of Soldiers' Wives was reflected in the organization's self-perception as an association of members tasked with finding solutions "in conjunction with the member, on whose shoulders the heavy burden of child raising, finding work, etc., rests." The emphasis was on collaborative action by members, not as passive subjects that others move across a chessboard but as full partners in finding solutions based on employment and a mutual-aid fund.[54] Riva Tabachnik, a member of the leading team of the Organization of Soldiers' Wives, had no doubts about the cruciality of her entity's relationship with the Women's Labor Council: "If we fail to organize the recently integrated women, it is feared that they will be influenced by players who are undesirable to us."[55] The activists understood the importance of the "generality" of their organization "just as the army is general." By implication, however, they knew that since they had officially declined to make the Organization of Soldiers' Wives a branch of the Histadrut through the offices of the Histadrut women's organizations, the Histadrut members who belonged to their organization would have to be "a serious player that will chart [the organization's] course."[56]

Who's Responsible? Debating the Duties of the Public Committee in Caring for Soldiers' Families

It was only at this advanced stage, by the end of July, with approximately 60,000 inductees comprising almost 10 percent of the country's Jewish population and the Organization of Inductees' Wives a fait accompli,[57] that Provisional State Council discussed the matter of inductees' families after its subcommittee presented its conclusions. The issue was introduced by Mordechai Shatner, a member of the Finance subcommittee, who noted that the question of support for soldiers' families had crowded out other urgent matters because of "its vast importance not only for tens of thousands of soldiers' families in Israel but also for our entire war effort."[58] At this time, the Yishuv Committee coordinated the care of 30,000 families of soldiers and disabled veterans. Given that the pace of mobilization had picked up just then and that a new inductee profile was placing people who had families in uniform, Shatner assumed that this number would eventually double.

The monthly financial outlay for this activity at that time was IL 70,000. To demonstrate to the council members what this sum meant, Shatner reminded them that it was equal to the budget that they had approved for all state services other than defense.[59] Due to a delay in allocating these funds in previous months, the July expenditure was IL 200,000. Shatner also mentioned the sum of IL 1.5 million that had been spent on security issues during a four-month period before the establishment of the state and contrasted it to the 1.3 million Palestine pounds that had been expended to meet the needs of soldiers' families during the four and a half years of World War II.[60]

So it was certainly an enormous problem. The first question that the subcommittee had to tackle was who was in charge of this activity. The members had no doubt about the answer: the state and the government were as responsible for soldiers' families and disabled veterans as they were for soldiers on active duty. Accordingly, the subcommittee's recommendations included a clause noting that "the government should be responsible for funding these activities." The minister of Finance had given the subcommittee a commitment to this effect as well.[61] To coordinate operations pertaining to soldiers' families, the subcommittee proposed the establishment of a special government department that would take matters in hand.

An interesting point in the subcommittee's proposal was a recommendation to keep the public committee (a nongovernmental entity supervised and led by the public) in existence and expand it to accommodate public and government forces. The Public Committee was intended to play an ombudsman's role vis-à-vis the government department. Shatner proposed the inclusion in the Public Committee of representatives of organizations of women, soldiers' families, and soldiers wives, "which, due to their mutual aid and their knowledge of matters in the field, can be very helpful in the activity." He also thought local authorities and other players should be represented.[62] By encouraging the Provisional State Council to co-opt nongovernmental civilian entities into the activity, Shatner and his associates expressed their confidence in these entities' professional caliber and, above all, recognition of their role as reliable mediators who could alert the authorities to realities and mediate between the establishment and the individual civilian in need. This, however, was only part of the story. No less than they wished to avail themselves of the NGOs' professional capabilities and advantages as civilian players immersed in their communities, Shatner and his associates, echoing on previous discussions, wanted to tap these organizations' financial resources and nongovernmental status for the cause. "These things have to be paid for. There has to be a way to receive money from abroad as well as funds that, for whatever reason, cannot be placed in the state exchequer but can and should enter the coffers of a public committee."[63] Simply put, the state needed an injection of financial resources that, due to tax laws and other regulations, it could not receive directly (i.e., donations from American Jews that would lose their tax-exempt status if put to political or military use).[64]

Shatner said it in so many words: "If we don't construct this thing in such a manner as to make it an instrument that, on the one hand, can receive money from the government and, on the other hand, can accept other funds from abroad that may flow to these purposes, we will, in my opinion, do an injustice to the soldiers' families and the others who need this financial aid, and we will bring these matters, which are very strained to begin with in terms of our financial ability, to a crisis."[65]

The subcommittee's proposal ultimately included the following: Point 1 recommended the establishment of a government department "for the affairs of soldiers' families and disabled veterans," its duties including oversight of activity; determining criteria for benefits; legislation and concern for supply, welfare, and health care; the education of inductees' children;

rehabilitation of disabled veterans; and the needs of war widows and orphans. Point 2 addressed itself to the duties of the Public Organization for the Soldier's Family, which would continue to oversee benefits to families and disabled veterans but would be reorganized to include government representatives as well; the Public Committee was to serve as an advisory body to the government department. Point 3 stressed that "the Government shall be responsible for the sums needed to finance the foregoing activities."[66]

Among the subcommittee members, there was also a minority opinion, expressed by Berl Repetur, a member of the Ahdut ha-'Avoda movement, a constituent of the Mapam (United Workers) Party. The dominant approach toward assistance for soldiers' families thus far, Repetur said, was philanthropic and not governmental. Decrying this approach, Repetur demanded that the government and the State of Israel not serve soldiers and their families "in a philanthropic manner" (i.e., through the offices of social-assistance agencies). Warming to his argument, Repetur asserted, "We cannot insist that the Hebrew soldier give his all in fighting, serving the war [effort] and carrying out our mission, unless we make fundamental changes in this respect."[67] Goings-on in Israel in recent months, Repetur claimed, added neither strength nor moral entitlement to the soldier and his role. Consequently, he ruled, the government should assume full responsibility for the institutions that should come into being and act vis-à-vis soldiers' families, "just as it is responsible for security on the ground, arms, fuel, and transport, and all other war-related needs." Repetur vehemently opposed the idea of ab initio reliance on financial aid from Diaspora Jewry for governing institutions in Israel—the idea "that we should, as it were, build our organizational institutions so that the Government of Israel won't be fully responsible for the human material that's carrying out the war." He urged the council to acknowledge that "the weight in the war depends on the person, his responsibility, and his existence." Therefore, responsibility for the soldier, his family, the disabled, the widowed, and the orphaned and for their rehabilitation after the war "is something that pertains to the state and the government. Consequently, all financial questions and relations should be solved within the ambit of full state responsibility, via the special institutions that the state will set up for this purpose." Here, Repetur noted an implicit contradiction in the subcommittee's statements. First, the subcommittee said that "the government should be responsible for the sums needed." In its recommendations, however, it wrote, "The Public Organization for the Soldier's Family should continue to pay benefits to soldiers' families and disabled veterans" and that the committee should be reorganized and augmented with government representatives.[68] The matters as they were worded in the report, Repetur claimed, did not clearly emphasize that the Government of Israel and the department it was about to set up should be the direct caretaker of soldiers, their families, and all related needs. Instead, he urged, the solution should be based foremost on legislation that would protect the soldier's civilian job and guarantee provisions and education for inductees' children and concern for the disabled "not philanthropically."[69] Therefore, Repetur proposed that the government establish a department to deal with all affairs related to soldiers' families, including orphans, widows, and wounded and disabled veterans, and that this body alone should coordinate, manage, and oversee all such matters. Repetur also moved that the government immediately pass legislation to alleviate the plight of inductees' families. The government department, Repetur proposed, would also commit to rehabilitation activities and help to wipe out debts that soldiers had accumulated due to the state of war. Repetur's proposal did have a nongovernmental aspect: the establishment of a body that would include "representatives of public organizations."[70]

The essential difference between Repetur's proposal and the subcommittee's was that Repetur held the government solely responsible for the soldier's family and its care.[71] His objections were reinforced by his party colleague Nahum Nir (Rafalkes), who pointed out that care for soldiers by means of "sundry institutions"—a constraint owing to the lack of a government—had not proved itself. Nir's remarks reflected the expectation of a change in the transition from Yishuv into state—from a public endeavor, largely based on kindhearted volunteers, to the state's recognition of its duty to care for soldiers, their families, and disabled veterans.[72] Nir insisted that the role of the public committee be defined precisely—would it serve as an advisory body, or would it continue to be the "paymaster"? He also saw a contradiction between the two: if it pays, "then it isn't advisory." The meeting adjourned without a vote.[73]

"Nixing a Philanthropic Approach to Care of Soldiers' Families," shouted *Al Hamishmar* in a headline. The attached article reported at length on Berl Repetur's objections to the motion tabled by the subcommittee and Mapam's countering motions.[74] Presenting the gist of the subcommittee's proposal, it quoted Shatner's justification for the need to have a public committee— its ability to receive philanthropic funds from abroad, without which the envisioned services would be hard to finance. *Al Hamishmar* extensively quoted Repetur's criticism and his alternative motion to the Provisional State Council, which would hold the government exclusively responsible for coordinating and managing affairs relating to soldiers' families (with the help of legislation) and rehabilitation.[75]

In the meantime, grassroots activity continued on July 29 as the Organization of Soldiers' Families held its inaugural meeting.[76] At this occasion, Elisheva Kaplan focused her remarks on her dispute with Idelson and the Histadrut Executive Committee concerning the centrality of the soldier's wife as distinct from his parents and other family members. "The main subject in establishing this organization should be *the soldier's wife*" (emphasis in the original), Kaplan ruled, explaining that the burden of the current situation rested on her "more than on the inductee's parents." By the time of the founding event, the organization had already recorded several achievements. Foremost among them was the establishment of relations with the Ministry of Labor in the provisional government, which promised to help both in finding work and in arranging vocational training ahead of work.[77] Idelson smoothed the contradictions a little. Yes, she conceded, the organization should embrace both wives and mothers but would be based on wives. Its principal role, she said, was to help the inductee's family sustain itself, "and only in this respect will it justify its existence." Therefore, it must be represented on all state committees that set wages, post delegates to the various relief funds, and develop diverse forms of mutual assistance along the lines of those followed in the previous war.[78] Idelson emphasized an additional important aspect of the organization's work: advocacy (i.e., reviewing the government's rules on inductees, determining their adequacy, and monitoring their implementation).[79]

Another question concerned affiliations between the organization with other organizations and entities that had begun to form at this time. Perhaps, Idelson noted, "it should be set up as an adjunct of the Soldier's Welfare Committee and the future institution of state that will take care of soldiers' families." Contrarily, however, Idelson saw no contradiction between such an affiliation and the continued intensive and central involvement of the Women's Labor Council, which considered itself "responsible for and willing to assist members in establishing the organization and guiding its activity."[80] Tsipora Laskow seconded her predecessors' approach, her remarks revealing a justification of sorts of the very need for such an organization: "Admittedly, there's a state and one might think it'll solve the matter, but one must bear in mind that the state is young and many questions remain that it cannot answer completely at the moment."[81]

This aspect came up again and again in the ensuing discussion, with the speakers feeling it correct to relate to the very "need to set up this organization." The point emphasized was that the entity that aids soldiers' families should be populated by "people from soldiers' families themselves."[82] It was broadly agreed that the organization should be independent and not a branch of existing women's organizations. "It should come into being spontaneously by women founders and not by any bodies or organizations."[83] By the same token, however, it was asserted that the governing authorities must be pressed to accept responsibility for aid and support for soldiers' families. The Yishuv Committee should no longer be in charge of these disbursements because, now that there is a government, it is no longer perceived as either relevant or competent.

Special attention was devoted to the matter of mobilized immigrants and members of their families. Immigrants' wives, Kaplan charged, "are pleased to receive government support and are not inclined to work." Other members stated the opposite, noting that the immigrants disapproved of their special treatment because it had turned them into welfare cases.[84] Only at the end of this debate did the discussants resolve officially to establish an Organization of Soldiers' Families (including soldiers' wives) as a pan-Yishuvic (i.e., national and not politically affiliated) organ under the care and direction of the Organization of Working Mothers.[85]

"The State Should Be Responsible for this Payment"

The debate over the treatment of soldiers' families ended without a resolution, and the Provisional Government rediscussed it several days later. The reins were now seized by the minister of Finance, Eliezer Kaplan, who expressed the dilemma that the earlier discussion had brought to light: "On the one hand, you want a special [governmental] department that will be responsible for the matter. On the other hand, you need a Yishuvic [public] committee that can receive financial resources for its operational needs." Kaplan then cut to the heart of the debate: "Should we accept the proposal about a department and a public committee that makes the payments or should we place direct responsibility in the government's hands, regardless of the risks?"[86] He proposed that a resolution be taken on the form of relations between the government and the public entity that would raise the requisite funds abroad; he also sought a resolution on the identity of the government ministry that would accommodate the department and the election of a chair for the public committee.

Again an argument broke out about the question of government responsibility, and Mordechai Bentov of Mapam joined the supporters of Repetur's objection and his demand that the government take sole responsibility for soldiers' families. "Any other responsibility, any other form of public responsibility," Bentov ruled, "lends the matter a philanthropic nature. It has to be done in the form of . . . government support; there is room for a public committee . . . with advisory powers."[87] In response, Ben-Gurion restated this in simple terms: the government would be responsible for soldiers' receiving what they were owed, but the committee that makes the payment would be a public one that could receive funds from abroad.

Summing up the meeting and disregarding the Mapam participants' reservations, the recommendation to establish a public committee as an adjunct to the department for care of soldiers' families was approved. It was also resolved that the government would be responsible for funding the activities and that the ministries of Finance, Defense, and Labor would prepare a program for the care of war veterans, widows, and orphans. The public committee would be tasked with offering each family a minimum payment.[88]

On the basis of this provisional government resolution, the discussion continued the next day in the Provisional State Council. In this forum, Ben-Gurion began by expressing his regret that the question of payments to soldiers' families had not been settled "in a fair and practical matter" thus far. It was not only a moral question and "a debt to the state's honor," he clarified, but also "a vital military question." After all, he explained, it is hard to demand that a person surrender himself, his "strength, time, and also life unreservedly, unconditionally," while being unsure that his wife and children, left behind at home, would be taken care of. Ben-Gurion also mentioned several cases of grave indiscipline that commanders had felt unable to counter "because they know why it happened: there is hunger in the soldier's home."[89]

Ben-Gurion then expressed dissatisfaction with the method being used to choose those eligible for support: "It is unfair to the soldier and unfair to his family." Now the government resolved, pursuant to the recommendations of a committee of review, that soldiers' families would receive regular payments automatically without any investigation and inquiry whatsoever, and Ben-Gurion asked the council to approve the new policy.

As for where the funding for this system might come from, Ben-Gurion alluded to the answer by pointing out that the army could not have been established and equipped had not been for the "extraordinary response" of world Jewry. Absent this response, "We might not have been able to endure this struggle and finance this war." The same rule, he said, applies to another item in the war budget—benefits for soldiers' families. "But in view of legal and political situations in other countries, particularly the most important countries [hinting at the United States without mentioning it by name], we have had to make arrangements so that the Government of Israel will not accept directly any sources from these fundraising mechanisms." Therefore, while affirming the principle of direct state responsibility for family benefits on account of the mobilization of family members, Ben-Gurion announced the decision that payment would be made by a public committee. The committee could always turn to the government in view of the latter's responsibility for all payments. "I stress," Ben-Gurion stated later on, "that the state is responsible for the entire budget that soldiers' families need," but it could also receive money from abroad.[90] Kaplan bolstered the persuasion campaign, repeating that the government was responsible de jure and would remain so even after various bodies in Israel acted to secure assistance from world Jewry. "These bodies, being public and independent, will have to reconcile their operations with regulations and directives that the Government will set forth."[91]

The motion that the government ultimately presented to the Provisional State Council included recognition of the entitlement of every soldier's family to a minimum payment irrespective of its situation and a larger one in case of need as determined by an investigation. In addition, it was decided to appoint a committee "to deal with these payments." Although the state would be responsible for all payments, "the committee shall have the right to obtain funds from additional sources for this purpose."[92] The provisional government passed the motion by a vote of twenty-three to five, with the dissenters voting in favor of Repetur's motion.[93]

The resolution concerning "care for soldiers' families" stated that the government, via one of its ministries, would establish a special department for the affairs of soldiers' families and disabled veterans. The department's duties were listed and included, mainly, "supervision of all activities on behalf of soldiers' families and disabled veterans, and centralization of material pertaining to soldiers' families and disabled veterans." The second clause designated the Public Organization for the Soldier's Family as the entity in charge of "disbursing benefits to soldiers' families and disabled veterans" and defined its status as "advisory." The third clause reaffirmed the government's responsibility "for funding the aforementioned activities as required."[94]

In practice, Giora Lubinski continued to run the Yishuv entity that by now had gradually evolved into a department or division of the Ministry of Defense. In his communications with the public, however, he continued to use the familiar title of the Yishuv Inductee and Family Committee.[95] In January 1949, the Ministry of Defense Division for Soldiers' Families, headed by Lubinski, went into action and systematized the payment of benefits to inductees' families.[96]

A Top-Down Public Committee and a Bottom-Up Organization of Inductees' Families: Two Formats of Nongovernmental Aid Converge

Amid the political debate over the composition, legitimacy, goals, and competence of the public committee, steps to consolidate and expand the Organization of Inductees' Families continued at the grassroots level. On August 25, inductees' families held an assembly in the city of Hadera with the participation of 200 wives and mothers. The participants resolved to establish an organization of inductees' wives in this town and elected a local committee.[97] The assembly authorized the committee to represent soldiers' wives vis-à-vis local and central institutions in all matters pertaining to inductees' families; it also determined that the family benefit was inadequate for basic sustenance and demanded an increase in it and other benefits. Soldiers' wives in Hadera repeated demands that counterparts elsewhere had expressed—for part-time jobs and what today would be called affirmative action in hiring soldiers' wives to fill them. The assembly gave special attention to the question of recent immigrants, resolving to be particularly mindful of the needs of families headed by inducted newcomers, foremost by developing mutual-aid mechanisms.[98]

The impetus for organizing at the local level appears to have come, among other things, from a discrepancy between commitments and proclamations about affirmative action and support for soldiers' families, on the one hand, and implementation on the ground, on the other. The termination of workers at a brewery in Rishon Lezion is a case in point. The laid-off workers wrote to Beba Idelson and sought her intervention. The voice of one aggrieved father, sent home jobless while his son had been posted to the battlefield, is plainly audible in the letter:

> Today I have a son who went off to induction on the first day of the war. He's at the front all the time and has survived by a miracle, may it only continue. Even though I have rights, I was fired with no consideration for my rights and for my son's induction, and my daughter was also partly mobilized. I ask you if for being parents, for raising such a generation as this, which knows how to stand up for itself, and for having come as far as we have by virtue of our children, we deserve to be fired. . . . The question is what the inductee's family is supposed to live on and where a father will get the wherewithal to help his son if they fire him. . . . Why is there no law for a state of emergency?[99]

The author of this lament mentioned three friends of his at the brewery who had been fired and who had sons in uniform. The son of one of them had been wounded and lost a leg. Beba Idelson forwarded the letter to the Histadrut Executive Committee and the Rishon Lezion Labor Council and asked them to investigate the matter and send the inquirers a response.[100] The correspondents had apparently chosen Idelson as the addressee of their letter because they identified her with the Organization of Inductees' Families. The structural advantage of this entity, precisely due to the dominance of the Women's Labor Council in organizing and leading it, was manifested again.

After the decision to establish the Organization of Inductees' Families was made and the founding assembly took place, local committees began to pop up all over the country, each undertaking to call assemblies of local women and appoint permanent delegations to the organization.[101] The Central Committee of the Organization of Inductees' Families approached local government players and continued to demand the assurance of a basic standard of living for the family and participation in child upkeep. Some of these demands were requited—the child benefit was increased, and participation in preschool fees was established. The organization also arranged a longer list of subsidized staples for families and maintained regular communication with the superintendent of rations. Sitting down with representatives of the Ministry of Labor and the labor exchanges, they discussed the passage of a labor constitution and the establishment of a special desk at the central labor exchanges to see to the employment of soldiers' wives. Budgets for vocational training for members who had become sole breadwinners were set aside.

The local committees established relations with local authorities and acted to assure the representation of their organization on the Public

Organization for the Soldier's Family.[102] Idelson envisaged an organization that would sit alongside the public committee,[103] while Elisheva Kaplan considered regulation and representation insufficient. She pressured her comrades in the organization to take action at additional levels, such as helping immigrant women and managing mutual aid. "There's no point in having an organization just to make demands of others," she asserted.[104]

Disgruntlement and day-to-day hardships prompted the women to step up their pressure. The Haifa branch of the organization, for example, demanded larger basic benefits for families and insisted that the disbursement of such entitlements be taken over by a government or military institution. On their list of recommendations for improvements, the women of Haifa included the need to set up consumer outlets with cut-rate staples, introduce vocational courses, and establish information systems that would convince members that it was important for them to accept jobs and that they could indeed support themselves. As an incentive, they proposed that members be totally exempted from taxes and payments such as water and electricity fees.[105]

Unique cooperation came about in Haifa between the associating soldiers' wives and welfare officers. The wives appear to have collaborated with the military system that had mobilized their husbands and received its support against the civilian bureaucrats whom everyone held culpable for the delays and their attendant damage.[106] The soldiers' wives in Haifa set up a mutual-aid committee and offered its services to the army welfare system, including support for inductees' wives in special situations such as illness, pregnancy, or postnatal status, and assistance for immigrant women whose husbands had been called up.[107] If so, something like a reversal of roles had taken place: instead of lodging claims against the military welfare system, they were offering to help the system in the capacity of a civilian social-service agency.

The ascendancy of the Organization of Inductees' Wives and its relations with governmental and military operatives was the product of the delay in establishing the department for care of soldiers' families and the public body that was supposed to be its adjunct. Representatives of soldiers' families expressed their dissatisfaction with the state of communication with the chair of the Defense Committee (a parliamentary committee of the provisional Council of State), David-Zvi Pinkas, who pressed the government on both the department and the composition of the public organization.[108] Pinkas viewed the large public committee "primarily as a crutch or a fig leaf for the Government. Namely, it was as though this money were being paid out from a quasi-charitable source—a necessary step for foreign-policy reasons—and it has an additional function: to give those among the public who had an interest in the matter a way to express their wishes."[109] As for the governmental department, Pinkas envisaged it as an executive agency, something like a military paymaster—a functionary that has to accept the decisions of the Defense Committee, an implementer, not a maker, of policy.[110]

Pinkas, having acted to secure the involvement and influence of the Defense Committee in regard to benefits for inductees' families, now wished to add Beba Idelson to the Defense Committee team that was instructed to draft the payment (benefit) regulations despite her many other public duties.[111] The blurring of boundaries between the governmental and the nongovernmental sector recurred: the same people held positions in both and were tasked with duties that, in certain senses, straddled the divide. As already mentioned, Beba Idelson, as chair of the Women's Labor Council, had been heavily involved in establishing and shaping the Organization of Inductees' Wives, an entity that engaged in advocacy and pressured government authorities to honor their commitments to soldiers and members of their families. The selfsame Idelson, however, represented Mapai, the ruling political party, on the Defense Committee of the provisional Council of State; this made her a de facto participant in the very establishment to which the women presented their claims. Pinkas appears to have been aware of this dualism and weighed the idea of exploiting it in order to attenuate the criticism. By adding Idelson to the Council of State subcommittee that would discuss the regulations on benefits to inductees' families, he would neutralize her ability to bring claims against the very entity of which she was a member. Pinkas's reasoning was obvious: to "soothe frayed nerves."[112]

Beba Idelson joined the veteran members of the subcommittee, Abraham Zabrasky and Repetur, and the three of them availed themselves of Baruch Rabinov, head of the Finance Division of the IDF General Staff. The details of their proposal, presented to the Defense Committee, included a benefit for inductees' wives who had no children, special supplements for each child, and a rent subsidy for those who qualified for it under welfare criteria. In addition, the committee recommended an exemption from taxes and tuition fees and the assurance of medical aid at no charge for soldiers' families.[113] Zabrasky referenced data on the latest rounds of mobilization, in which almost all inductees were heads of households. Noting this, he estimated the cost of implementing these recommendations at "a million and a half [Israel] pounds per month." Stating that the country "cannot afford any such outlays for long," he warned that a decision to award every family a standard benefit would harm the indigent above all.[114]

The moral dilemma that the policy makers faced was tellingly expressed by Meyer Grabovsky: "What's absolute justice, what's more just, to give everyone who's affected the same amount or different amounts to people who are differently affected?"[115] Grabovsky favored the one-size-fits-all approach; it required less bureaucracy and was less prone to abuse. Welfare investigations, he argued, were carried out not by philosophers but by "simple people" and were distressful to their subjects. Therefore, "automatic equality is more just than the harm caused by someone getting more."[116]

By the time this debate took place, the ministry's Finance Department had already made various decisions about special maternity grants, health insurance, tuition payments, and tax exemptions. With this in mind, Zabrasky asked, "Can we afford all this?" There was no need whatsoever, he reasoned, to give a bonus to women who were working and earning in any case. Idelson objected to this take on the issue. She reminded those in attendance that when a woman worked away from home, "Someone has to take her place while she's working. If her children are in day care, it costs lots of money. And if she's paying income tax as well, very little of her salary remains."[117] These remarks reinforced the stance of those who sought to pay severely diminished benefits to working women who had no children or whose children were above benefit-eligible age. A coalition began to form around this idea. Grabovsky, however, intervened in the debate and told the story of a recent immigrant woman whose husband had been mobilized. Working in a military chemical plant, he said, she was yellow from head to toe from filling bombs with lead. By what moral right did the discussants intend to deduct eight Israel pounds from her benefit while her husband might be killed at any moment and she might be pregnant? And what if she's supporting her parents?[118] After a lengthy and trenchant debate, a majority of those present voted in favor of paying 50 percent to a working woman who earned above a certain amount, on her own authority.[119]

In the ensuing debate, the discussants not only aired their worldviews but also revealed their familiarity with the hardships out there and the extent of their commitment to the groups and individuals who were paying for the head of household's mobilization in the coin of their daily lives. Just the same, disagreements about the state's responsibility lingered, as manifested in a debate that ensued over the name of the public (nongovernmental) Organization for the Soldier's Family and its composition. When Lubinski suggested that it be called the National Fund for the Care of Soldiers' Families and Disabled Veterans, a debate erupted over the components of this title and their meaning. One discussant proposed that the word *national* be deleted; another favored its inclusion. In response, Grabovsky explained, "Obviously the fund isn't governmental but it's set up so that Diaspora Jews can contribute to it. Therefore, it's a good idea to call it national, because it's applicable to the whole. There may even be anti-Zionists who'll contribute to this fund."[120]

In fact, the composition of the committee mirrored the status of the panel as an executive arm of the government. Apart from the threesome representing the Organization of Inductees' Wives,[121] all committee members were to represent the institutionalized political system (parties taking part in the governing institutions) and the state authorities. Despite this transparent structure and in disregard of the committee members' obvious connection with the political establishment, the chair of the Defense Committee stressed that the panel would be "a nongovernmental public body that isn't appointed by administrative action of the government" so that it could "serve as an address for the receipt of nongovernmental funds." While noting the committee's role as a recipient of philanthropic money, Pinkas stressed its responsibilities as an entity that would allow soldiers' families "to rely on a specific public commission that will take an interest in [their] fate."[122]

This additional function that Pinkas envisaged for the public committee, however, was already being discharged de facto by the women's organization. Indeed, this "body of interested persons," as it called itself, defined the presentation of problems and demands to the governmental and pregovernmental institutions as its objective, "so that together we may be able to find a way to alleviate the plight of the soldier's family."[123]

The Public Committee was finally activated at the beginning of December, when the war was largely over but the number of inductees was at its peak.[124] Mordechai Shatner, appointed to its chair, introduced it as the Central Committee for Soldiers' Families and himself as its head.[125] In one of its first moves, it established local committees and set up appeals committees.[126] The composition of the local committees reflected the Central Committee's guiding principle—a large majority representing political parties on the Council of State and two or three (female) representatives of the Organization of Soldiers' Families (the Hebrew text using the feminine pronoun), standing in different political constituencies. Places on the local committees were also reserved for representatives of the municipal authority. In all, the Jerusalem, Tel Aviv, and Haifa local committees were to have fifteen members; those in other towns were to have eleven.[127]

One of the first activities that the Central Committee undertook to examine and streamline was the receipt of in-kind gifts from abroad. In a report presented to the provisional government, the committee noted that shipments of food, clothing, and shoes from public bodies in other countries were not reaching the soldiers' families that needed them.[128] The committee released an official statement on this matter, protesting the "mistreatment of soldiers' families," urging the government and the Jewish Agency executive to take corrective action, and demanding the co-opting of a representative of the Central Committee in the distribution of these imports. The statement even carried a threat: "If things are not put right, the Committee will discuss the establishment of direct relations with institutions abroad."[129]

Nevertheless, despite the institutionalization and attempts to centralize the care of soldiers' families, the women's organizations still appear to have been the operatives closest to the field.[130] The establishment of a national committee for soldiers' families did not "disestablish" the Organization of Inductees' Wives in theory or in practice.[131] Indeed, the organization was the entity closest to the inductees' families; its representatives were the ones who reported to national players about delays in the distribution of family benefits.[132] Many requests in these matters were addressed to Elisheva Kaplan, who along with her work on the official committee, continued to support the Organization of Inductees' Wives and even helped the organization's branch in Hadera to raise seed money for a mutual-aid fund. Concurrently, however, she made it clear that the fund had to operate in conjunction with, and with the support of, all relevant local players—the municipal authority, the public committee, and economic entities. As the women's representative on the National Committee, Kaplan was able to promise "matching funds from the Central Committee" for any sum mustered locally.[133]

As the war wound down, the Central Committee focused on authorizing discharges from service on the basis of welfare-related needs and promoting the rights of demobilized soldiers at large.[134] As more and more soldiers were released, the committee decided on the establishment of bureaus to deal with them and the transfer of the demobilized soldiers to the care of the Defense Ministry's Rehabilitation Division.[135] Eventually, the local committees for soldiers' families operated rather systematically. In March 1949, their members were invited to a national meeting of the Central Committee, where the chair, Mordechai Shatner, presented a report accompanied by information from Dr. Lubinski, then director of the Division for Soldiers' Families at the Ministry of Defense.[136]

At the press conference that followed the meeting, Shatner, Menachem Pitchon, and Lubinski unveiled the new constitution that would govern benefits for soldiers' families. Israel, they claimed, was the second-best country in the world, trailing only the United States, "in caring for the economic, educational, medical, and other vital needs of inductees' families." They defined the budget for soldiers' families as "part of the defense budget" and noted municipal authorities' willingness to absolve the families of various taxes.[137]

The Central Committee for Soldiers' Families officially wound up its duties in April 1949, leaving routine care of inductees' families in the hands of the Ministry of Defense. Mordechai Shatner advised the minister of Defense of the change, defining the committee as having been "an advisory and supervisory public institution alongside the Ministry of Defense"[138] The letter also gave the background for the termination of the public committee's work: "With the establishment of the Knesset Labor Committee and the inclusion of the affairs of soldiers' families in its purview, the Central Committee believes that its role has ended."[139] The Central Committee expressed its hope that the Knesset would give both constitutions—that concerning benefits and that concerning appeals—the force of parliamentary legislation.[140]

In a letter to Elisheva Kaplan, Mordechai Shatner, the chair of the committee, emphasized the "harmony that prevailed among the committee members, irrespective of this or that party affiliation," and the close relations that had existed between the committee and the executive apparatus.[141]

It was not by chance that the notice concerning the conclusion of the work of the Public Committee for the Care of Soldiers' Families was served in the dying days of the war, as the final armistice agreements were being signed. The end of the war, however, did not mean, in itself, that the needs of the inductees and their families had been met. The epicenter of the civil struggle for the satisfaction of their needs now shifted from the families (chiefly, the wives) to the inductees themselves, who had become demobilized soldiers. They also rushed, before the war was officially over and even more vigorously afterward, to establish representative entities of their own and to demand that the authorities co-opt them into the policy-making process.

The associative acts of the demobilized soldiers (of their various kinds), however, contained an element of anger that largely ruled out the kind of cross-sector collaboration that had persisted as long as the soldiers' wives led the civil endeavor. As happened in many countries at the end of the world wars, demobilized soldiers in Israel found it difficult to return to their humdrum lives. By organizing into associations, they created settings within which they could express demands and even confront the authorities, which now stood more blatantly than before on the other side of the divide on an issue that should have belonged to the very core of the national consensus.

Notes

1. Zehava Ostfeld, *An Army Is Born: Main Stages in the Construction of the Israel Defense Forces and the Ministry of Defense under David Ben-Gurion* (in Hebrew) (Tel Aviv: Ministry of Defense, 1994), 435.

2. Ibid., 436.

3. Minutes of CWO board meeting, Labor Archives (hereinafter: LA), IV-230-6, May 16, 1948.

4. "A Soldiers' Welfare Institution Is Formed. Its Mission: Relief and Aid for Inductees and Their Families," *Ma'ariv*, May 10, 1948, 3.

5. Michal Almog-Bar and Ester Zychlinski, "It Was Supposed to Be a Partnership—Interrelations between Philanthropic Funds and Government in the Niv Venture" (in Hebrew), *Social Security* 83 (June 2010): 166. The definition is based on a diverse combination of research works that include, among others, John M. Bryson, Barbara C. Crosby, and Melissa Middleton Stone, "The Design and Implementation of Cross-Sector Collaborations: Propositions from the Literature," *Public Administration Review* 66 (2006): 44–55; and Beth Gazley and Jeffrey L. Brudney, "The Purpose (and Perils) of Government-Nonprofit Partnership," *Nonprofit and Voluntary Sector Quarterly* 36 (2007): 389–415.

6. Almog-Bar and Zychlinski, "It Was Supposed to Be a Partnership," 167.

7. Ostfeld, *An Army Is Born*, 436, 332.

8. Nahum, "Selected Relief Activities," *Ha-Metsuda* (Garrison Corps journal), 1, June 1948, Israel Defense Forces Archives (hereinafter: IDFA), 2-1147-2002.

9. Ostfeld, *An Army Is Born*, 436, 333.

10. Meetings with division commanders, Ben-Gurion diary, Ben-Gurion Archive (hereinafter: BGA), June 18, 1948.

11. Hadari, Staff orders, no. 39, IDFA 213-240-1954, August 2, 1948.

12. M. Meisels, "How Are the Garrison Corpsmen Doing? Veterans of the Ranks Demand Soldiers' Entitlements," *Ma'ariv*, September 2, 1948, 2.

13. "There Are No Laws that Protect Our Soldiers," *Ma'ariv*, August 8, 1948, 2.
14. Yaakov Markovitzky, "Foreign Recruitment in the War of Independence," in *Israel's War of Independence Revisited*, Vol. 1, Alon Kadish, ed. (Tel Aviv: Ministry of Defense, 2004), 532.
15. Uri Kesari, "The Shame of Our Soldiers," *Ma'ariv*, June 27, 1948, 3.
16. Ostfeld, *An Army Is Born*, 437.
17. Meeting of Organization of Working Mothers Secretariat, LA, IV-250-50-97, June 3, 1948.
18. Meeting of Women's Labor Council Coordinating Secretariat, LA, IV-230-97-5-A, May 20, 1948.
19. Ada Maimon, *Fifty Years of the Women's Labor Movement, 1904–1954* (in Hebrew) (Tel Aviv: Ayanot, 1955), 142–3.
20. Illegibly signed letter to Women's Labor Council, Tel Aviv, LA, IV-250-25-110, May 23, 1948.
21. Illegibly signed letter (evidently from Rahel Kleiman) to Rivka Diamant, LA, IV-250-25-110, May 24, 1948.
22. M. Simon, Local Committee for Inductees and Their Families, Jerusalem, to board of Mobilization and Relief Fundraising Organization, Central Zionist Archives (hereinafter: CZA), File 9274, May 24, 1948.
23. Ibid. See also minutes of meeting of Yishuv Inductee and Family Committee, CZA, File 9274, May 30, 1948.
24. In March, the committee received 800 Palestine pounds and needed 8,000; in May it received 3,000 pounds and estimated its needs at 30,000. Minutes of meeting of Yishuv Inductee and Family Committee, CZA, File 9274, May 30, 1948.
25. M. Simon to Dr. Giora Lubinski, Tel Aviv, CZA, File 9274, May 28, 1948.
26. Fritz Loewenstein to Gedalia Yaari, Jerusalem Labor Council, CZA, File 9274, May 17, 1948.
27. Organization of Working Mothers to Rehovot Labor Council secretariat, LA, IV-250-63-126, June 8, 1948.
28. Meeting of Women's Labor Council Coordinating Secretariat, LA, IV-230-97-5-A, June 15, 1948.
29. Memorandum from Organization of Inductees' Wives in Haifa, LA, IV-230-883-A, June 28, 1948.
30. Ibid.
31. Ibid.
32. Ibid.
33. Mapai Bureau meeting, BGA, July 6, 1948.
34. Meeting of Provisional State Council, 9, BGA, July 8, 1948.
35. Ibid.
36. Meeting of Women's Labor Council Coordinating Secretariat, LA, IV-230-97-5-A, July 11, 1948.
37. Ibid.
38. Beba Idelson to Organization of Soldiers' Wives, Haifa, LA, IV-230-883-A, July 13, 1948.
39. Ibid.
40. Beba Idelson to Menahem Bader, Israel Government Superintendent of Personnel, LA, IV-230-853-A, July 13, 1948.

41. Ibid. (and the same memo with the handwritten remark, dated July 14, 1948).
42. R. Gonskit, Women's Labor Council, to municipal women's labor departments and to "our members" at the labor exchanges, LA, IV-250-40-39, July 15, 1948.
43. Women's Labor Council to E. Bielecki, Ministry of Labor and Construction Employment Department, Provisional Government, LA, IV-230-853-A, August 5, 1948.
44. Circular signed by Beba Idelson, LA, IV-230-6-60, July 15, 1948.
45. Yishuv Committee for Care of the Inductee's Family, LA, IV-230-6-60, July 15, 1948.
46. Organization of Inductees' Wives, Haifa (signature illegible) to Women's Labor Council Secretariat, LA, IV-230-883-A, July 16, 1948.
47. Beba Idelson to Organization of Inductees' Wives, Haifa, LA, IV-230-883-A, July 18, 1948.
48. Organization of Working Mothers, Haifa to Women's Labor Council Secretariat, LA, IV-230-883-A, August 2, 1948.
49. Both were members of Ahdut ha-'Avoda movement, at the time a component of Mapam.
50. Meeting of Women's Labor Council Coordinating Secretariat, LA, IV-230.5–97, July 20, 1948.
51. E. Bielecki, Ministry of Labor and Construction Employment Department, to Women's Labor Council, LA, IV-230-853-A, July 26, 1948.
52. E. Bielecki to Central Procurements Committee, LA, IV-230-853-A, July 26, 1948.
53. Minutes of meeting of Working Mothers Organizations Department, LA, IV-230-6-60, July 28, 1948.
54. Ibid.
55. Ibid.
56. Ibid.
57. Amitzur Ilan, *The Origin of the Arab-Israeli Arms Race: Arms, Embargo, Military Power and Decision in the 1948 Palestine War* (New York: New York University Press, 1996).
58. Meeting 12 of Provisional State Council, BGA, Minutes Division, July 29, 1948.
59. Mordechai Shatner, a prominent Mapai member and central activist in the pre-state National Committee, was a member of the Public Services committee (a provisional council committee and thereafter a Knesset committee).
60. Meeting 12 of Provisional State Council, BGA, Minutes Division, July 29, 1948.
61. Ibid.
62. Ibid.
63. Ibid.
64. See Joseph Meyerhoff's testimony about the difficulties that American Jewish philanthropic organizations faced in 1948 due to suspicion that they were using the money for political purposes and military aid, two areas that were off-limits to tax-exempt (501c3) organizations. For these remarks and a description of the tax considerations and their effect on American Jewish philanthropy, see Esther Suissa, "The Politics of Philanthropy: The Creation and Work of the Israel Education Fund, 1964–1967," MA Thesis in Israel Studies, Ben-Gurion University of the Negev (2014); Meyerhoff, Oral History Division, the Institute for Contemporary Jewry, the Hebrew University of Jerusalem, 128–33 (1975): 27, 30.
65. Meeting 12 of Provisional State Council, BGA, Minutes Division, July 29, 1948.
66. Ibid.
67. Ibid.

68. Ibid.
69. Ibid. Berl Repetur made negative use of the concept of philanthropy as accepted in many Labor Movement circles. The concept suggested two things: a dependency and hierarchical relationship between donor and recipient and reliance on philanthropic funds from Diaspora Jewry, an act that was perceived per se as contrary to the enterprise of national revival in the Land of Israel, which should be based on a productive, self-sustainable society.
70. Ibid.
71. Ibid.
72. Ibid.
73. Ibid.
74. "Nixing a Philanthropic Approach to Care of Soldiers' Families: B. Repetur Objects to Motion by Investigative Committee on Ways to Help Families and Tables Mapam Counterproposal," *Al Hamishmar*, August 1, 1948, 1.
75. Ibid.
76. Minutes of founding meeting of Organization of Soldiers' Families, LA, IV-230-6-60, July 29, 1948.
77. Ibid.
78. Ibid.
79. Ibid.
80. Ibid.
81. Ibid.
82. Ibid.
83. Ibid.
84. Ibid.
85. Summary of resolutions taken at the founding meeting of Organization of Soldiers' Families, LA, IV-230-6-60, July 29, 1948.
86. Meeting of Provisional Government, BGA, August 4, 1948.
87. Ibid.
88. Ibid.
89. Meeting 13 of Provisional State Council, BGA, Minutes Division, August 5, 1948.
90. Ibid.
91. Ibid.
92. Ibid.
93. Ibid. See also "The Government Is Responsible for Funding Support of Soldiers' Families," *Davar*, August 6, 1948.
94. "Taking Care of the Soldier's Family," Israel State Archives (hereinafter: ISA), Gimel, 5663/24, August 8, 1948.
95. Circular from Yishuv Inductee and Family Committee. Until December 2, 1948, the circular was distributed by this committee (LA, 83-1344-1949). From the middle of December onward, approximately, a new entity appeared—the Ministry of Defense, Division for Soldiers' Families. The division was headquartered at the same place (Beit Hadar), and Lubinski held an important post in it, too, although he may no longer have been its chair. Circular 1/49, Minutes 2—Meeting of Appeals Committee of Headquarters and Tel Aviv Branch, LA, 75-852-1951, December 19, 1948.
96. Summary of meeting between Ministry of Defense, Division for Soldiers' Families, General Staff, Personnel Branch 3, Welfare Service, Registration Center, LA, 75-852-1941, March 31, 1949.

97. Comprised of Rivka Diamant, Mrs. Rotlevi, Haya Gronich, Rahel Shemesh, and Malka Kanner.

98. Organization of Inductees' Wives, Hadera, to Soldier's Welfare Committee, Town Major, Yishuv Inductee and Family Committee, and General Labor Exchange, LA, IV-250-25-110, August 31, 1948.

99. Beba Idelson to Histadrut Executive Committee and Rishon Lezion Labor Council, with letter from Aharon Jampulski, David Fecht, Aharon Calderon, and Zecharia Ratzon of Rishon Lezion to Beba Idelson, LA, IV-230/838-A, September 8, 1948.

100. Beba Idelson to Histadrut Executive Committee and Rishon Lezion Labor Council, LA, IV-230/838-A, September 8, 1948.

101. Document from Organization of Soldiers' Families, Haifa and the vicinity, Afula, Even Yehuda, Hadera, Kefar Sava, Ra'anana, Herzliya, Ramat Gan, Givatayim, Rishon Lezion, Holon, and Jerusalem, Provisional Central Committee, LA, IV-250-26-14, September 23, 1948.

102. Ibid.

103. Meeting of Coordinating Secretariat, Women's Labor Council, LA, IV-230-97-5-A, September 27, 1948.

104. Ibid.

105. Report on Regional Meeting, Organization of Soldiers' Wives, Haifa, LA, IV-230-883-A, September 11, 1948, circulated on October 11, 1948.

106. Ibid.

107. Organization of Soldiers' Wives, Haifa, to welfare officers, LA, IV-230-883-A, October 11, 1948.

108. Meeting of Defense Committee, BGA, Minutes Division, September 17, 1948.

109. Ibid.

110. Ibid.

111. Ibid. On the status of the Defense Committee, see Ostfeld, *An Army Is Born*, 765.

112. Meeting of Defense Committee, BGA, Minutes Division, September 17, 1948.

113. Meeting of Defense Committee, BGA, Minutes Division, September 24, 1948.

114. Ibid.

115. Subsequently Meir Argov. After the First Knesset elections, he chaired the parliament's Foreign Affairs and Defense Committee.

116. Meeting of Defense Committee, BGA, Minutes Division, September 24, 1948.

117. Ibid.

118. Ibid.

119. Ibid.

120. Meyer Grabovsky at meeting of Defense Committee, BGA, Minutes Division, October 8, 1948.

121. Meeting of Defense Committee, BGA, Minutes Division, October 8, 1948. In addition to these representatives, Elisheva Kaplan, a founding member and leading figure in the organization, was added to the committee as a representative of Mapai. Ben-Gurion diary, BGA, October, 29, 1948.

122. Remarks by David-Zvi Pinkas, Meeting of Defense Committee, BGA, Minutes Division, October 15, 1948.

123. Organization of Soldiers' Families, National Committee, to Minister of Defense David Ben-Gurion, Tel Aviv, LA, IV-230-6-60, October 28, 1948.

124. Around 100,000 inductees; see Ilan, *The Origin of the Arab-Israeli Arms Race*.

125. Central Committee for Soldiers' Families to Mapam Central Committee, LA, IV-230-6-103, December 5, 1948.

126. Central Committee for Soldiers' Families to Mapam Central Committee, LA, IV-230-6-103, December 5, 1948.

127. Ibid.

128. Mordechai Shatner, chair of Central Committee for Soldiers' Families, to Provisional Government of the State of Israel, ISA, Gimel, 5663/24, December 8, 1948.

129. Ibid.

130. Handwritten letter from Leah Balkin to Women's Labor Council, Tel Aviv, LA, IV-250-25-110, January 4, 1949.

131. Ibid.

132. Organization of Inductees' Families, Haifa, to Elisheva Kaplan, LA, IV-230-883-A, January 9, 1949.

133. Elisheva Kaplan, Women's Labor Council, to Committee of Organization for Inductees' Families, Hadera, LA, IV-250-25-110, January 13, 1949. See also letter from Elisheva Kaplan, Women's Labor Council, to the Central Committee for Soldiers' Families, Haifa, LA, IV-230-883-A, January 18, 1949.

134. Mordechai Shatner to David Ben-Gurion, ISA, Peh 3074/14, February 21, 1949.

135. Mordechai Shatner to Ministry of Defense, ISA, Peh 3074/14, March 1, 1949; the decision to establish the rehabilitation division was made in late November 1948, and the division began to operate approximately three months later (February 1949). See Review of Rehabilitation Division operations from March 1 to December 1, 1949, ISA, 248-580-1956.

136. Letter from Central Committee for Soldiers' Families to Women's Labor Council, Tel Aviv, LA, IV-230-883-A, posted on March 14, 1949.

137. "Israel—Second among World Countries in Caring for Inductees' Families," *Davar*, March 14, 1949, 4.

138. Central Committee for Soldiers' Families, Resolutions, LA, IV-230-883-A, May 2, 1949.

139. Ibid.

140. Ibid.

141. Mordechai Shatner, Central Committee for Soldiers' Families, to Elisheva Kaplan, LA, IV-230-883-A, May 19, 1945.

7

THE WAR VETERANS' CIVILIAN STRUGGLE

Discharged Soldiers and Disabled Veterans Confront the Policy Makers

THE FIGHTING BEGAN ITS HOME STRETCH IN THE middle of October 1948. From then to early January 1949, it saw Israel take control of the Negev and Galilee after driving the various Arab forces away from the country's frontiers. Diplomatic negotiations between Israel and its adversaries that had taken part in the war—Egypt, Transjordan, Lebanon, and Syria—began in the early months of 1949 and culminated in four separate armistice agreements that failed to produce a peace treaty but did bring the war to an official end.[1]

Demobilization began in January 1949 and lasted several months. The first government defined the reintegration of ex-soldiers into civilian life as a national objective and established a department for the settlement and rehabilitation of veterans in November 1948.[2] The state's involvement in demobilizing the soldiers and rehabilitating the wounded was manifested in a series of statutes enacted between May and September 1949 that gave veterans priority in hiring, business-development loans, housing and referral to rural settlement, and aid for those who had sustained war-related injuries.[3] The legislative proceedings and the process of implementation, however, proved to be time-consuming and bureaucratically cumbersome as the demobilized soldiers looked on with growing sobriety and then in alarm. Represented by a variety of committees and volunteer organizations, they soon channeled their frustration and anger into struggles and confrontations with the state authorities.

This chapter tracks associative initiatives of demobilized soldiers, which, like those of civilians, typically involved the particularistic formation of a group of individuals who had a shared interest or, perhaps one should say, a shared grievance. Here, as in other cases, the pattern of association was reminiscent of a pincer that reached from the bottom and from the top as small local initiatives, usually powered by radical elements in their camps, encountered national and more institutionalized ventures that sought to give their leaders entrée with policy makers and induce revisions of regulations and statutes.

Those behind these associations represented a broad spectrum of groups and interests and formulated their agendas accordingly. Some followed the conventional European pattern after World War II, setting up veterans' organizations to assure the representation of their broad interests as they reentered civilian life. Other represented the plight and distress of wounded and disabled veterans. Additional organizations, however, belonged to more distinct groups that for various reasons felt excluded from the nascent national ethos and sought to assure the recognition in material and, no less, in symbolic terms. All of the veterans' entities operated largely as membership societies and focused on advocacy alongside self-help.

The demobilized soldiers' associative activities helped them to obtain representation in various forums that discussed their affairs. By presenting their needs as sectorial interests, however, they concurrently triggered antagonism among policy makers, who saw no room for sectorial or "interest" representation of discharged soldiers—a social group for whose reintegration into society they, the policy makers, felt responsible.[4]

Disabled Veterans Organize

Among the first disabled veterans to associate were those staying at the army's rehabilitation center in Jaffa. The center, opened in August 1948, served its patients—mostly orthopedic casualties—as a temporary residence, a therapeutic center, and a labor exchange all at once. Apart from its lofty pretensions, the center's expansionary view of itself encountered difficulties at the level of implementation. Although it offered an abundant menu of vocational-training workshops, no one matched these activities with the patients' disabilities; therefore, they often offered no response worthy of the name. David Reifen, who headed the center, believed that the disabled should participate actively in their rehabilitation and saw their cooperation as a prerequisite for rehabilitation.[5] For this reason, he encouraged them to establish local and national committees to represent their interests vis-à-vis the authorities.[6]

David Ben-Gurion first became aware of goings-on in the disabled veterans' center in his meetings with the head of the Israel Defense Forces (IDF) Medical Service, Chaim Scheiber (subsequently Sheba), and Scheiber's deputy, Eliezer Levin-Epstein. About two months after the Jaffa rehabilitation center was established, with the war winding down, the two of them launched an effort to improve the supply of prostheses in the belief successful rehabilitation was unlikely if aids as basic as these were in short supply. The two presented Ben-Gurion with the idea of opening a branch of a British prosthesis factory in Israel and letting British experts set up a local production line in order to save on the immense costs of flying the disabled abroad for fitting.[7]

A delegation of eight disabled veterans accompanied Scheiber and Levin-Epstein to one of their meetings with Ben-Gurion, and they were given an opportunity to describe the distress attending to the matter. "They're demanding good [prosthetic] limbs, fast [delivery], and the establishment of a workshop to fix them," noted Ben-Gurion in his diary, suggesting that they appoint one of their number "to help me deal with the matter."[8] Even at this early encounter, the prime minister and Defense minister deemed the disabled veterans' delegation to be competent representatives of an interested party that should be co-opted into the decision-making and problem-solving processes. As I show below, these delegates were frequently replaced in the year that followed, but they repeatedly met with the minister of Defense, who devoted much attention to rehabilitation and the representative bodies that sprang up from below and from within to facilitate it.

The day after his first meeting with the "delegation of the disabled," Ben-Gurion sent two cables—one to the Jewish Agency executive in London, asking to see to the transfer from London to Israel of a branch of a factory for artificial limbs along with experts,[9] and one to Arthur Luria, the newly appointed consul general of Israel in New York and previously director of the Jewish Agency executive's office for United Nations (UN) affairs. Ben-Gurion asked Luria to make inquiries about prosthesis factories and whether it would be possible to move such a plant, experts and all, to Israel.[10]

That very day, another delegation of disabled ex-soldiers arrived for a meeting with Ben-Gurion and asked him to arrange, urgently, a trip to the United States for some 100 members of their population because they couldn't wait any longer. "That would be enormously expensive," Ben-Gurion warned his diary.[11]

At both meetings, the disabled veterans' envoys and Ben-Gurion appear to have opened a direct channel of communication. Indeed, two weeks later, they met with him again and now began to hint at their intention of launching a public struggle: "Bitterly they issued a veiled threat about bringing fifty [veterans]." They asked Ben-Gurion to have serious cases sent to the United States at once and asked what progress was being made in setting up the British factory locally.[12]

Addressing the Council of State about a month and a half later, Ben-Gurion called central attention to the problems of the disabled veterans and noted that the government could not afford the requisite housing and rehabilitation without help from the Zionist Organization. He also reported on progress in inviting experts in the manufacture of prosthetic limbs and described preparations for the training of disabled veterans in productive work.[13]

The growing awareness of the complex needs of the disabled—particularly those who had lost the use of limbs due to amputation or paralysis and needed special arrangements for housing and employment—lurked in the background of a tour that the IDF Medical Service conducted for military correspondents. The main stop on the field trip appears to have been the Jaffa rehab center, where the journalists visited workshops that manufactured provisional prosthetic limbs and employed disabled veterans, thereby also giving them vocational training. During the visit, the journalists were advised that the ministry of Defense had established a department for the settlement and rehabilitation of demobilized soldiers, headed by Yosef Gurion of Kibbutz Geva,[14] and intended to draft legislation that would require industrial plants to hire persons with disabilities.[15] Pursuant to the visit, the newspaper *Ha-Boker* harshly criticized the disabled veterans,[16] touching off furious responses from the latter and igniting the bitterness that had been building up for months. The writer accused some of the disabled of wishing to exploit their injuries "to extract assistance from the public" and likened them to an "Arab beggar who stands on a street corner and sticks out his trembling arm to all passersby."[17] In *Al Hamishmar*, a writer referred to a "committee" of disabled veterans to which journalists who wanted to have a word with the inhabitants of the facility were being referred. When the journalists met with "the coordinator of the committee, a tall, swarthy guy," he refused to speak with them "on one leg" (a pun denoting an ad hoc meeting and a sardonic reference to their physical condition) and proposed that they meet separately and hear the veterans' point of view.[18] Farther into the article, the writer quoted an official from the IDF Medical Service as accusing disabled veterans of seeking "to turn their disability into a tool to put to use." The *Al Hamishmar* journalist rushed to the disabled veterans' side, emphasizing, "Justice resides with those who sacrificed part of their body and their lives on the altar of victory, which entitles them not only to the nation's assistance but also to its appreciation."[19]

The piece in *Ha-Boker* slowly made waves in the internal discourse, made its way to the disabled themselves, and brought to the surface the resentment and frustration that had accumulated as the war moved toward its end.[20] The disabled veterans interpreted it as part of a campaign to defuse their struggle and even "delegitimize their demands."[21] Among those at the Jaffa rehabilitation center, it was widely believed that the article had been prompted by information from the authorities in charge of caring for their collective. Thus, it elicited hostility and suspicion toward the rehabilitation center, "its directors, bureaucrats, clerks, and hangers-on, and also those who 'deal with' arrangements [the Hebrew term is *siddurim*, meaning making arrangements for and, colloquially, "screwing"] for the disabled veteran."[22] Now that a government committee had begun to debate disabled veterans' rights, one such veteran, living at the rehabilitation center, used the center's newsletter to urge the committee members not to be rash in the legislative processes. The writer, identifying himself only as Uri, recommended that his comrades organize "in unison" and find "worthy representatives." He proposed the establishment of an association of disabled veterans whose envoys would sit down with the governmental committee on legislation and help it to find a just solution to their problems. He warned his comrades that their fate had been placed on the negotiating table and that they must unite and elect judicious and responsible representatives so that their stance would be taken into account. If hotheads set out independently and on their own counsel, he cautioned, their entire constituency would be harmed.[23]

Around the same time (December 1948), a soi-disant National Committee of Disabled Veterans of the Current War, Rehabilitation Center No. 1 (the aforementioned center in Jaffa), came onto the public scene and demanded representation of the disabled on all committees that dealt with their affairs.[24] Its goal was to enshrine in legislation the status of the disabled and their right to priority in housing, employment, and medical care, as well as financial compensation, plus preference in receiving business licenses and equipment. The list of benefits that the committee sought from the state on account of its constituents' incapacities concluded with study and advanced vocational training opportunities, free use of public transport, exemptions from national and municipal taxes, and free schooling for the casualties' children.[25]

Additionally, they alleged that the promises concerning the reserving of dwelling units in Jaffa were not being honored. They also protested the seizure of workshops and retail establishments in town that were supposed to be reserved for the disabled. The government, they demanded, must step in and make sure that the assurances were kept.[26] The committee attached to its declarative memorandum a letter that it disseminated to sundry politicians, describing the difficulties that the disabled war veterans were encountering in their contacts with state authorities: "We have spent months shuttling among departments and clerks to arrange elementary matters, to no avail. Sadly, the neglect exhibited by the bureaucrats who deal with our affairs is literally criminal. Many of our comrades remain homeless, their families languishing outdoors. On top of the situation, grave to begin with, bitterness is accumulating."[27]

The amputees set a very high bar by the standards of the time. The British and American armies first established rehabilitation centers in the 1930s and 1940s, but only in the latter decade did they begin to see employment and education affairs as part of the rehabilitation process. In the United States, the integration of disabled persons in the community came even later, in the 1950s and 1960s.[28] These rehabilitative practices penetrated Israel slowly; in the War of Independence, the main stimulus for change found expression, among other things, in placing casualties of a certain kind together in one location. This was the background for the establishment of the rehabilitation center in Jaffa, where limb amputees were brought, and the subsequent foundation of the center at Tel Hashomer, where casualties of spinal-cord injuries were sent. When the disabled veterans organized in December, they confronted authorities that were still groping to understand the basic concepts of rehabilitative medicine.[29] Also to be factored in were the awkwardness that typified the authorities generally and the difficulty of managing rehabilitation processes as fighting continued full speed in both the north and the south, all of which raised the threshold of stress and estrangement between the casualties and the authorities that treated them. This was clearly manifested at the meeting with the head of the Defense Ministry's rehabilitation department, Yosef Gurion,[30] and in the absence of Dr. Levin-Epstein, deputy head of the IDF Medical Service, with whom the veterans refused to meet.[31] Levin-Epstein lost their confidence because they suspected him, in his talk with the journalist from *Ha-Boker*, of criticizing them for ostensibly exploiting their disabilities for profit.[32]

In the absence of a central authority for the care of disabled veterans,[33] the ex-servicemen regarded the administration of the rehabilitation center in Jaffa as the address for their grievances and held it responsible for the denial of their demands and wishes.[34] David Shaltiel (commander of the Etzioni Brigade during the war and now head of the Inspection Division at the Ministry of Defense) pointed out an additional problem: the lack of a legislative framework was generating "exaggerated demands." This climate, Shaltiel argued, evolved due to the lack of permanent rules and regulations concerning the military status of the Rehabilitation Center itself.[35] Shaltiel criticized the center for not imposing military discipline and allowing outbursts to pepper life there: The patients "allow themselves to wake up whenever they want, eat whenever it's convenient for them, and leave the building whenever they feel like it. They live in a regime of pampering and license that allows psychological inhibitions to fall aside." Shaltiel went so far as to claim that the convalescents hounded the facility's professional staff with pressure and threats, forcing it to submit to any demand whether presented by "the committee" (scare quotes in the original) or by individuals who used rioting to advance their demands.[36]

The target of Shaltiel's criticism was the Committee of the Disabled, the very existence of which, according to Shaltiel, clashed with "military regimen and practice." Admittedly, Shaltiel continued, some of the disabled were "positive tenants" who cooperated with the institution's management, but others, whom he defined as "insurrectionists," set the "moral tone."[37]

While criticizing the amassing of excessive power by representatives of the disabled and decrying the lawlessness that prevailed at the rehabilitation center, Shaltiel expressed understanding of the tenants' disgruntlement, which he blamed on the scanty percent of the disabled who had found suitable housing and regular work. Their frustration only mounted when they watched the possibilities of housing in Jaffa dwindle as various authorities laid claim to properties and handed them out to other groups (immigrants or public officials). Shaltiel corroborated the disabled soldiers' allegations on this account by stating that members of their population had received housing on one occasion only—after they invaded, on crutches, a vacant building in Jaffa.[38]

Shaltiel then expressed his recommendations: A statute for disabled war veterans, or at least an interim announcement that would define their entitlements, should be drawn up. A set of permanent rules and regulations in regard to the rehabilitation center should be produced, and a commander should urgently be appointed. Conversely, the disabled should have no further discretion of their own and should not be allowed to strengthen their public standing. To attain this objective, he said, important military and governmental personalities should be convinced to stop receiving delegations of the disabled (and of disabled individuals) "except via their commander."[39]

Despite Shaltiel's criticism of the formation of the Committee of the Disabled and his recommendation to avoid contact with it, Ben-Gurion believed it correct to reply personally to the memorandum that the committee had sent him. "Even before receiving the letter," Ben-Gurion recounted to the convalescents' representatives, all departments of the Defense Ministry had been instructed to give the disabled priority in housing over immigrants, military institutions, soldiers' families, and others.[40] The Defense minister then gave them the latest news: his ministry's Rehabilitation Division was now dealing with determining the rights of the disabled and others who were being demobilized. Continuing, Ben-Gurion assured them that "no effort and correction will be spared to allow you to return to sound working and creative life as quickly as possible."[41]

Ostensible backing for Ben-Gurion's personal commitment was provided by Dov Shafrir, the custodian of Absentee Property, who stressed at a press conference in Jaffa that disabled veterans "are first in line to benefit from the Custodian's properties." Shafrir, however, also saw fit to explain that the disabled had been too late in presenting their housing demands: They did so "only in the past month; the apartments were already tenanted by then." Therefore, in his judgment, the solution needed to be sought in damaged dwellings that were being renovated and rehabilitated in "abandoned areas" (Jerusalem, Safed, and various Arab villages).[42] Shafrir's remarks masked what had really happened: apartments that had been promised to disabled veterans and earmarked for renovation due to their needs had been taken over by others, with his after-the-fact consent. An employee of the Medical Service, David Crohn, reported this and also recounted that several residents of the rehabilitation center had broken into houses in Jaffa after realizing that the authorities were unable to assure housing for them. Indeed, housing contracts had been signed between the office of the custodian and veterans who had been assigned dwellings that were supposedly vacant and in need of renovation to become habitable. On the basis of these contracts, rent payments were forwarded by the Ministry of Defense for the dwellings—after which, while visiting the sites of the break-ins, Crohn found the units occupied.⁴³

In another case, disabled-veteran squatters, acceding to a request by the military authorities, vacated a building that they had invaded because they were told that it had been designated for use as a military clinic. Several months later, however, seeing that military doctors with their families had been given housing in the building, they intruded again and clashed with military police, who after a daylong siege broke into the building and applied force against the resisting tenants. Four squatters were arrested, and one needed medical care after losing consciousness.⁴⁴ The Ministry of Defense sided with the MPs and decried the convalescents' takeover of the building, noting that it had indeed been given to the Medical Service and that the disabled veterans had been promised housing elsewhere. According to the Ministry of Defense, the MPs "had been compelled to use force but in view of the squatters' resistance they halted their operation to avoid making the clash worse."⁴⁵

As the crisis surrounding the invasion of the Medical Services building festered, representatives of the disabled soldiers met with Ben-Gurion and gave him their account of the event.⁴⁶ Ben-Gurion, "speaking to their hearts," as he told his diary, advised them "to refrain from acts of violence and be patient." Farther into the diary, Ben-Gurion noted with satisfaction that the disabled soldiers had left the building "peaceably."⁴⁷

As these envoys discussed their grievances with Ben-Gurion, several dozen amputee soldiers demonstrated next to the Knesset building and sent a delegation of their number to the office of the Knesset secretary, where they were received by the deputy speakers of the house, Nahum Nir (Rafalkes) of Ahdut ha-'Avoda and Joseph Burg of Hapoel Hamizrachi. Member of Knesset (MK) Nir suggested that the envoys appeal to members of the various parliamentary factions in accordance with their own partisan affiliations. This angered the members of the delegation, who protested that "the bullets did not differentiate among us when we were wounded."⁴⁸ After hearing from the convalescents about their urgent needs, the Knesset members asked them to commit their demands to writing and promised to distribute the text to all members of the parliament.⁴⁹

The violent brush with the military police in Jaffa brought the disabled soldiers' discontent to a new peak: "The authorities that shirked their duty to us have now burst into action, removing the disabled from the buildings violently, *with beatings to the extent of loss of consciousness!!!*" (emphasis in the original).⁵⁰

One of the main precipitants of the organized soldiers' foul state of mind was their suspicion of corruption in the allocation of housing. They protested this in their personal talk with Ben-Gurion and did so again to the elected officials whom they contacted several days later: "The apparatus of the disabled war veterans and the Custodian of Enemy Property is shot through with lawlessness. . . . There are cases of use of our names and forging of signatures to profiteer or to hand out apartments and shops to others." Consequently distrustful of the institutions that were supposed to take care of them, they continued relentlessly to demand the inclusion of their representatives on the committees that dealt with disabled soldiers' rehabilitation.⁵¹

It should be borne in mind that the disabled veterans in Jaffa demanded housing in a specific building for a reason: their need for special physical arrangements, such as proximity to public transport and lower-floor apartments. This, naturally, aggravated their sense of injustice when members of nondisabled groups were given priority over them for no discernable reason while they continued to languish in the rehab center.⁵² The soldiers' representatives felt it important to stress that they trusted the elected officials, whom they distinguished from the bureaucrats, terming the latter "the war-casualty apparatus." When approaching members of the house from both government and opposition parties, they stressed that they did not hold them responsible for the bureaucrats' rebuffs and scofflaw attitude. They expected the parliamentarians to transcend their political affiliations and to act "as one with our war and our suffering."⁵³

Less than a week after it received the delegation, the Knesset debated the Demobilized Soldiers (Return to Work) Bill, 1948/49, for its first reading.⁵⁴ Chapter III of the bill, which was passed into law about a month later and became effective on May 15, 1949, dealt with "the right to work of family members of deceased soldiers and disabled war veterans." Section 15 required factories to hire one family member of any person who had been defined as a permanent employee of the enterprise and had died or incurred disability in the course of military service. Chapter VI dealt with "disabled war veterans and rights of priority in hiring," and Section 31 laid the foundations of a quota system that would require every company with more than twenty people on its payroll to hire the disabled. The statute empowered the minister of Defense to force employers to hire disabled veterans and to reserve certain types of jobs in certain occupations for them. This section remained on paper only.[55] Regulations attached to the statute acknowledged the representative organizations and allowed them to sit on several panels that dealt with the entitlements of disabled soldiers, including individual cases.[56]

The organized disabled veterans, however, did not settle for advocacy vis-à-vis the elected echelon. Their representatives realized that they had to penetrate the public mind and use it to leverage influence; therefore, they sent memorandums and manifestos to newspaper editors, through whom they made inroads in the public discourse by means of articles and opinion pieces. In the public sphere, the newspaper *Herut* figured importantly in evoking the disabled veterans' quandaries. As an opposition paper, *Herut* had an interest in covering topics that it could use to criticize the government.[57] In *Al Hamishmar*, another opposition newspaper (due to Mapam's exclusion from the first governing coalition), Berl Repetur called for a review of "the apparatus [that acts] on behalf of the disabled veterans"[58]—the mechanism that the disabled deemed corrupt.[59]

Uri Kesari of *Ma'ariv* responded to the disabled soldiers' attempt to arouse public opinion: "I must say that public opinion seems somnolent in regard to these disabled soldiers." How could it be, he wondered, that a society that extols "the martyrs who fell and allowed the state to arise" would disregard these "dead men who had the luck to stay alive?"[60] Representatives of the disabled themselves turned to journalists, communicating the issue from their perspective and even escorting them on visits to the rehabilitation center and to properties that some of their number had invaded. Baruch Oren of *Herut* met with a member of the committee of the disabled at the Jaffa rehab center, who criticized Ben-Gurion for having "dodged all commitment." He stressed the nonpartisan nature of the association and expressed concern that its cause would become "a plaything among the parties" and then would be "totally lost."[61]

The crux of the rehabilitation that the committee's representatives sought was the opportunity to earn an income. The taxi industry was mentioned as a preferred occupation because in addition to income, it would enable people of limited mobility to obtain a motor vehicle.[62] The movie theater in Jaffa, too, could have been an excellent solution, but the authorities had consigned it and all such enterprises to a film-screening company for reasons that, the journalist hinted, were not on the up-and-up. In the appropriation of shops in Jaffa, too, the disabled veterans found irregularities that smelled of corruption. Several shops had been registered in the name of one veteran, even though he neither owned nor managed them. The impression was that false licenses were being issued in disabled veterans' names.[63]

The committee's representative then sent a message through the medium of the journalist:

> If you want to help, the best thing is to explain what we need.... Say that we're demanding to be included in all committees that deal with soldiers' rehabilitation and that we won't waive our rights. I know—they'll try to scatter us, wear us down, defeat us one by one until we sign away our rights. But you should know that none of it will help. We'll stand up for what we're owed and if they make the situation worse, you'll see a Tel Aviv that you won't quickly forget. Write whatever you want . . . but beware of one thing: don't make political "business" out of us.[64]

Indeed, Baruch Oren took the disabled veterans' cause under his wing. A patient at the Jaffa center showed Oren photographs taken at the clash with the military police. One of the policemen, the patient alleged, had threatened to evict him and the others by gunfire, but the veterans responded with contempt: "In the Negev and Jerusalem we stared down tanks with Sten guns. Here we'll stare down Sten guns with crutches." A military police jeep, he continued, had mounted the sidewalk and advanced toward them in order to scatter them; the driver would not have hesitated to run them over. Police began to rain blows with batons, "and we [did the same] with crutches and prostheses."[65]

Distrust and allegations of graft and protectionism became increasingly common among the disabled veterans.[66] Amid the escalating tension, daily brawls broke out between wounded veterans who waited for hours in the corridors of the War Casualties Ministry and ministry officials whom they perceived as responsible for their neglect: "A day doesn't go by without screaming and sobbing of the embittered and fate-stricken soldiers who, as a result of the horrors of the war, sustained frazzled nerves or lost hands or feet and now have to wait for hours to get their 60-grush-per-day basic subsistence that, by the way, doesn't suffice for a satisfying meal."[67]

A new entity calling itself the National Committee of Disabled Veterans Rehabilitation Center[68] responded to the criticism of the Jaffa facility by praising the work done at the center "to all the disabled veterans' full satisfaction."[69] Most of the disabled soldiers' responses, however, reinforced the manifestations of criticism and dissatisfaction. Here and there, additional local groups began to organize for action.[70]

The escalating protests of the disabled and the lively public discourse surrounding them served as a backdrop for the Knesset discussion of the second and third reading of the Demobilized Soldiers (Return to Work) Bill.[71] Now the disabled veterans, joined by demobilized soldiers in various locations, held a parade down the main streets of Tel Aviv that ended with a demonstration at the gates of the Knesset building.[72] The demonstrators were represented by motley organizations, some familiar and well established, such as the Union of Demobilized Soldiers, and others that were small, local, and unfamiliar.[73] Yet another joint association, which called itself The Organization of Demobilized Soldiers and Disabled and Wounded Veterans of the War of Independence, launched a sit-down strike at the casualties department in Jaffa.[74] A delegation of demonstrators was received by representatives of the factions of the parliament to hear out the demobilized soldiers' demands. Arriving at the meeting were Knesset members from the entire political spectrum. The soldiers' representatives demanded that their organization (presumably the largest and most solid of the entities involved, the Union of Demobilized Soldiers) be recognized and that the demands they had expressed at the assembly be met.[75] Thus, as ex-servicemen and disabled veterans massed at the Knesset from the outside and their representatives peppered public figures with their demands inside the building, the parliamentarians in the plenary chamber debated each other heatedly, the demonstrators themselves resting at the focus of the discussion.

Despite their efforts to avoid partisan labeling, the organized disabled veterans found themselves at the forefront of a political polemic, in which opposition parties embraced them and representatives of the coalition attacked them for this very reason, accusing them of pursuing hidden agendas. MK Meir Wilner (Maki, the Israel Communist Party), moved that the Knesset hold a discussion on the conduct of the military police and that the Knesset condemn what he called the "cracking" of skulls.[76] In response, Pinhas Lubianker (Lavon) accused Maki of inciting the soldiers to assault the police. "There's someone who's pulling the strings and directing them," he charged.[77] Lubianker based his allegations of organized incitement on the level of resources available to the demonstrators, which could only mean, to his mind, that they were being supported by powerful players: "Cars were rented for them and people came to work with hammers and rods."[78] Wilner responded to this by blurting "the Protocols of the Elders of Zion," to which Lubianker retorted, "They're the protocols of the youngsters of Maki." Wilner furiously responded: "That's a call for a pogrom against Maki."[79]

The government now enthusiastically adopted the hypothesis about a takeover by interested political opposition players of demobilized-soldier organizations generally and those of disabled veterans particularly. The Public Relations Division of the Ministry of Defense, in an official communiqué, claimed that on the very day of the demobilized soldiers' demonstrations in Tel Aviv and the sit-down strike at the rehabilitation center in Jaffa, a delegation from the Committee of Disabled Veterans visited the director of the ministry's Casualties Department and informed him that "the disabled veterans have nothing to do with these demonstrations and do not identify with the demonstrators' demands." According to Yosef Gurion, only thirty people had taken part in the sit-down strike, and even they were not "really [disabled] . . . This group was evidently appointed by certain elements."[80] These allegations made their way to David Ben-Gurion, who despite the Communist labeling, ostensibly meant to belittle the public importance of the strident self-organization, thought it necessary to respond to the matter by expediting the decision about payments to disabled soldiers and families of deceased servicemen.[81] But doubt began to creep into his references to the topic as well. Within two weeks, he used the expression *incited disabled veterans* in his diary.[82] He even went so far as to demand the closure of the center in Jaffa, claiming that "this group wants to oppose by force."[83]

The soldier-associates responded to the establishment's offensive by hitting back. *Ma'ariv* published an article that had in its center a photograph of a young man sleeping on a bench in a public park. The author of the piece reported having seen five doors in a corridor of a dilapidated building. On each of them, a scrap of paper bearing the name of the occupant had been affixed. On the second line was one word: *Invalid*. On the third line, in more boldfaced letters: "Invaders, it's your funeral! [literally: *your blood is on your head*]." One of them even added, "I was wounded in the head twice and I'm insane—look out!"[84]

When the journalist asked what kind of place he was visiting, his escort replied that the people at issue had squatted in these dwellings. Inquiring about the reason for the invasion, the newspaperman was told that it had been done to make it impossible for the custodian of Abandoned Property to assign the dwellings to people who already had apartments and shops. The rooms had no electricity, conveniences, or faucets. As the tour continued, the journalist was taken to a commercial area in Jaffa, where his escort showed him shops owned by business firms that had several other shops in Tel Aviv. "On what basis did they receive a shop here?" the escort asked. As the journalist did not know the answer, the escort answered for him: "*Protektsia*" (meaning *pull*). When the journalist reached the office, he found fifteen soldiers who had been waiting there for four hours, since 7:00 a.m. One of them said that he had been visiting this office for three months and always received the same answer: *We don't have a job for you yet*. Another told the journalist, "They'll tell you we're Communists and that it's just political calculus."[85]

The Disabled Veterans Law was debated by the Knesset in early September and passed in an expedited procedure.[86] The status of the disabled veterans' organization came up for discussion when MK Hannah Lamdan (Mapam) proposed that the law allow a representative of the soldiers' agents to sit on the appeals committee. "It would be good," she reasoned, for soldiers visiting the committee to plead their case "to find a friend on the committee."[87] Hearing this, Akiva Globman-Guvrin (Mapai) objected: "It's . . . a question of educating ourselves in civics. I ask where we will have come if a committee that's appointed by the Minister of Justice, and on which a judge, a public figure, and a doctor participate, can't be trusted unless we allow agents of interested parties to take part as well. It concerns not only this committee but similar committees as well."

Globman and others interpreted the demand of the casualties' representatives as an expression of distrust in the governmental system. From their point of view, now that sovereignty had been attained and an elected assembly had been formed, there was no further room for voluntary civil organizations in the decision-making process.[88] Nevertheless, the law as worded acknowledged the right of any individual who appeared before the appeals committee to be represented.

After the bill was passed into law, disabled soldiers gathered at the Knesset restaurant and spoke with Ben-Gurion about the way the statute had been worded.[89] According to a correspondent for *Ma'ariv*, Ben-Gurion promised to continue the conversation at Tel Hashomer Hospital: "I'll visit you in the hospital and there we'll talk it over and you'll beat me up," the prime minister concluded with a grin. "Why would we beat you up?" one of the attendees asked. "You won't literally beat [me up]. You'll present demands and I'll try to honor them," he commented.[90]

Indeed, more than a month later, on October 17, Ben-Gurion visited the hospital and met with disabled war veterans who were being treated in the paralytics/spinal cord injury ward. "Some have already been trained to use their legs somewhat," he noted in his diary. "Only a few grumble at the medical workers. A long talk with the disabled. They appreciate the army's comradely and humane attitude—but there are also complaints. Housing for those 120 who can already leave the hospital. Housing for disabled veterans generally."[91] The encounter, which surprisingly attracted little media attention,[92] became the constitutive event of the Organization of Disabled Independence War Veterans—the mainstream organization, the strongest one, and the one with the most support—which ultimately became the Organization of Disabled IDF Veterans that exists to this day.[93] It took place at Pavilion 19, where the paralyzed soldiers and those with spinal cord injuries were staying.

Amputees left the hospital gradually, commensurate with the pace of the arrival of prosthetic limbs. Paralyzed soldiers needed more time for rehabilitation, and their hospital stay was accompanied by a sense of uncertainty about their future, their motor limitations preventing most of them from returning to their prior homes and jobs.[94] By the time Ben-Gurion visited them, many had completed their medical care but could not be discharged because arrangements that would allow them to live independently outside the hospital had not been made. This projected onto the atmosphere of despair that prevailed in the building, manifesting inter alia in aggression toward the caregiving staff and blockage of the hospital entrance. The lengthy stay at Tel Hashomer ultimately inspired these patients to establish a representative body of their own that was eventually recognized by the Ministry of Defense Rehabilitation Division.[95]

The process that led to the formalization and primacy of the committee that took shape in Pavilion 19 was gradual and bumpy. At first, the members of the committee called spontaneous assemblies to which the disabled in the hospital were invited: "The building filled up with disabled [veterans] who were capable of arriving on their own, others who were wheeled in on carts, and a few who arrived on their beds."[96] Rafi Kotzer, "a moderate and level-headed kibbutznik" who had been elected chair of the committee of the disabled at Tel Hashomer,[97] stood out in the group that had coalesced. From the perspective of Kotzer and his comrades, this panel deserved primacy due to the size of the hospital and its large population of wounded and disabled veterans. By virtue of this primacy, Kotzer would eventually claim, "We were able to represent the disabled [veterans] vis-à-vis the institutions, the Ministry of Defense, and the IDF as well." The foregoing evidence about the scope and timing of the disabled veterans committees does not support this narrative. The most influential factor, it would seem, was the government officials' cumulative experience, which convinced the policy makers that the rehabilitation and convalescence process would do best if they would recruit these stakeholders for the cause. Otherwise, they would find the process difficult to implement. Two other factors were the extended period of time that the paralyzed soldiers spent in the hospital and the backing that the veterans in Tel Hashomer received from the IDF Medical Corps and its commanders, Drs. Chaim Scheiber and Baruch Padeh, who were intensively involved in the first stages of the disabled veterans' associative moves.[98]

When Ben-Gurion visited the hospital a month after the Disabled Veterans Law was passed, he was accompanied by the officials who were tasked with implementing the new statute—Dr. Scheiber, Yosef Gurion, and the chief benefits officer at the Ministry of Defense. The veterans described their distress and even presented a rehabilitation plan that they had outlined, including the allocation of a certain percent of every housing project for persons with disabilities. "Ben-Gurion listened attentively and asked all kinds of questions. . . . We had the feeling that we were dealing with someone who was willing to hear and to conduct an uninhibited and to-the-point conversation. . . . We came out more satisfied, calmer, and sure that we had an address to turn to."[99]

Ben-Gurion personally monitored the treatment of the problems that the disabled soldiers at Tel Hashomer had broached. True to his habit, he leaped into the thick of things where quantitative information was concerned: How many disabled veterans were demanding "immediate arrangements"? How many adapted dwellings could be set aside in housing developments that were under construction? Could squatting be approved after the fact in the absence of other solutions?[100]

As the housing and rehabilitation programs advanced toward implementation, Ben-Gurion met again with the representatives of disabled veterans in the company of high-ups at the Rehabilitation Division. It was evident by then that the organization established at Tel Hashomer was moving to the forefront, even though relations between its leaders and those of the Rehabilitation Division were at times conflicted and confrontational. The inclusion of the disabled in the discussion over their future was increasingly accepted as a done deal.[101] At roughly this time, the disabled veterans' organization also joined the Central Union for Demobilized Soldiers, an entity that had some 20,000 members.

The merger of the organizations gave the disabled veterans the patronage of an establishmentarian entity that the state authorities considered reliable and seemingly subordinated them to a more limited and conservative frame of activity. However, it also gave them an official public platform where they could make their arguments. Pressure from the political establishment to include them in the rehabilitation process, of which they were the objects, steadily rose. When Yosef Gurion attended a meeting of the Knesset Labor Committee to describe what his Rehabilitation Division had been up to, the members of the committee, particularly those from Mapam, asked the committee plenum to invite representatives of the demobilized soldiers and disabled veterans to join the discussion. Hannah Lamdan went one step farther, asserting, "There's no point in discussing the overview that we've heard without knowing what they themselves are demanding."[102] The Rehabilitation Division, she stated, is "totally impermeable to public influence." The (Labor) committee members, she continued, must be in legal contact with the soldiers and veterans at issue. Now that a consensually accepted Union for Demobilized Soldiers existed—"and I have not heard anyone disqualify it"—Lamdan demanded that "the allegations of the soldiers and the disabled vets" be heard.[103]

Lamdan then presented her fellow committee members with extensive information that she had gleaned from talks with demobilized soldiers and disabled veterans. The men were going through torments, she alleged, due to "inefficient arrangements." For example, she continued, disabled veterans had to report weekly to the hospital to receive aid, requiring them to queue at length each time. It was her impression that the Organization of Disabled Veterans was being led by "very responsible people who are stifling the resentment that wells up in them." The process could be improved immensely, she concluded, if the Rehabilitation Division would co-opt others, including the disabled veterans themselves, into its activity.[104]

Committee member Hanan Rubin, also from Mapam, took a similar approach. The Ministry of Defense or the Rehabilitation Division, Rubin thought, should set up a public commission to steward these activities. Rubin then mentioned the suspicions of corruption in the rehabilitation apparatus, surmising that some officials must in fact be on the take and demanding that they be not only summarily fired but also prosecuted.[105] Gurion responded tentatively about allowing interested civilians to take part in the decision-making processes. The Rehabilitation Division, he explained, was acting under the assumption that "there's no need in the State of Israel to continue the practice of having public commissions; instead, the Knesset committee should take their place."[106]

As for the outcome, however, the members of the associations prevailed. A coordinating committee that included representatives of the disabled veterans was already up and running at the Rehabilitation Division, a highly active entity that met several times each week. Despite this rapid institutionalization and accommodation of the status of the disabled veterans' representatives, however, Ben-Gurion noted, "Representation of the disabled in Israel is entirely in the hands of Mapam and the Communists and Rafi [Kotzer] is from Mapam."[107]

The Organization of Disabled Independence War Veterans ultimately joined the Union of Demobilized Soldiers as a special section. The merger, however, was incomplete, tentative, and short-lived. The section quickly became a separate division of the union and enjoyed far-reaching autonomy. In the ensuing years, steadily escalating friction between the autonomous division and the union led to the establishment of a separate organization of disabled veterans that registered itself as an association in early 1952.[108] The antagonism that marked relations between these associations indicate that while all demobilized soldiers had enough in common to cooperate, various groups among them had structural conflicts of interest that encouraged them to act separately in the conviction that their organization's central goal—fulfilling its members' interests—would be optimally attained outside the umbrella of the broad coalition. The separate initiatives that flowed from this premise evoked disapproval mainly in the oldest and most solid organization among all the entities that served ex-soldiers, the Union of Demobilized Soldiers.

The Union of Demobilized Soldiers

The Union of Demobilized Soldiers (known to its members simply as "the union") was established in World War II to represent members of the Yishuv who had enlisted in the British Army. When the war ended, it became an important player in rehabilitating and re-civilianizing the now-demobilized soldiers. Comprised of trained officers and soldiers, most of the union's members were inducted, and its activity ceased; it resumed only after the armistice agreements were signed and the IDF Rehabilitation Division came into being.[109] The reactivation found expression at a meeting of the union's central committee in June 1949, where representatives of its branches around the country convened.[110] In practice, local organized activity was already taking place in Ramat Gan, Netanya, and Safed.[111] In Haifa, for example, demobilized soldiers who were dissatisfied with the functioning of the town's rehabilitation office organized and elected a representative committee that began to take up housing issues.[112] Quondam soldiers also formed associations to promote economic initiatives.[113]

In the Knesset debate over the Demobilized Soldiers (Return to Work) Bill, members of the house opposed the inclusion of ex-soldiers' representatives on the executive bodies that would be set up, due to "the absence of an authorized organization of demobilized soldiers from this war."[114] Some 1,000 ex-soldiers and disabled veterans raised the gauntlet, convening at the Eden Cinema in Tel Aviv in response to a call from an entity that called itself the Initiating Committee of Demobilized Soldiers. The initiative spearheaded by this body appears to have included, apart from demobilized soldiers, disabled and wounded veterans. It amounted to an attempt to create an umbrella organization that would merge sundry associational ventures that were already up and running in Tel Aviv. These enterprises were united by two common causes—promoting housing and employment solutions for discharged soldiers and untangling the red tape that was thwarting members' return to normal life. Although the umbrella initiative seemed premature and organizationally shaky, the gathering produced a petition with an itemized list of demands for presentation to David Ben-Gurion and the government. It included affirmative action in civil-service hiring, legislation requiring employers to take on ex-soldiers, establishing cooperatives with the help of earmarked loans, setting up a separate labor exchange for former soldiers, expropriating spacious dwellings (unused Jewish-owned properties), and providing medical care and monthly support for one year as long as the former soldier was not placed in work.[115] The assemblage then set out on a demonstration parade along the main streets of Tel Aviv until it reached the Municipal Plaza, where it stopped for a series of critical speeches against city hall for its "inaction in looking out for the demobilized soldier." From there, the crowd continued to the Knesset, where a delegation of their number was received by the deputy speaker of the house, Joseph Burg, and the secretary, Moshe Rosetti. Afterward they met with parliamentarians from various factions, who promised to present their petition to the appropriate committee and see what could be done for them.[116]

In the meantime, the Demobilized Soldiers Union had mounted a comeback. Its representatives, depicting themselves as the successors of the veteran union (which would make them the envoys of an entity that had several thousand members), arrived for a meeting with Ben-Gurion, to which Yosef Gurion had also been invited. At the encounter, Ben-Gurion captured their demand succinctly—"They want a status in this country"—and, basing himself on their remarks, even spelled out the ways in which this status should manifest itself: representation of the union on the employment committees and at the Rehabilitation Division and priority for the immigrant soldiers in housing.[117] When Yosef Gurion objected to the representation of this voluntary organization in a government division, Ben-Gurion made a note to himself: "Rightly so." He added, however, that Gurion was "ready and willing to cooperate with the committee."[118] The union's self-perception as an umbrella organization that represented the full spectrum of demobilized soldiers' needs was reflected in its demand to arrange permanent employment for disabled veterans and its advocation for the special needs of former volunteer enlistees from abroad (Mahal) as well as demobilized immigrant soldiers (Gahal).[119]

The union's national founding conference took place two weeks later. There, while praising the IDF and affirming their commitment to those who had fallen, the members expressed dissatisfaction with actions taken to date in regard to legislation concerning rehabilitation and reintegration. They termed the statute that the Knesset had passed, the Demobilized Soldiers (Return to Work) Law, "a first and incomplete step on the road to ensuring the legal status of the demobilized soldier."[120] The parliament, the union lamented, had "totally ignored" amendments that they had proposed in regard to the law. The union commended the decision to set up a national authority under the Ministry of Defense for the care of ex-soldiers (the Soldiers Settlement and Rehabilitation Division) and proposed to cooperate with it.[121] By saying this, the union sent the government authorities a clear message: they would have to take the direct stakeholders—the discharged and disabled veterans—into account in any decision that would affect their status and entitlements.[122] "Not an Auxiliary alongside the Rehabilitation Division but an Autonomous and Active Entity," commented *Al Hamishmar* in the headline of its report on the conference.[123] By putting it this way, the newspaper's correspondent (and, evidently, important activists in the union) wished to disabuse readers of the notion that the ex-soldiers had set up an establishmentarian lapdog.

The union then urged all demobilized soldiers to join its ranks in order to maximize its public weight. They designated July and August as the months of the enrollment drive. Eligibility for membership was defined very broadly, including former British Army soldiers in both world wars, anyone who had served at least four months in the IDF, and anyone who had been wounded in action or discharged for reason of health as a direct result of their service, irrespective of how long they had served.[124] Elections for a conference of demobilized soldiers were called, and all eligible persons were encouraged to sign up and take part.[125] Even though the people behind this associative effort stressed their autonomous and critical posture vis-à-vis the state authorities, there is no ignoring the simple fact that the organizers invited Gurion himself to address the founding convention. There, he presented the achievements of his Rehabilitation Division and even "complained about the paucity of initiative on the part of the demobilized soldiers, whom [he called] human dust." The participants responded critically to Gurion's remarks, alleging (sarcastically) that the division was operating "in the finest ways of an appointed bureaucracy," unlike the institutions that had cared for discharged soldiers after World War II, which gave their clients the right of representation.[126]

Approximately a year after the warfare ended (December 1949), the union had established forty-five branches countrywide and swallowed up the Organization of Disabled Independence War Veterans.[127] Interestingly, while the union emphasized its inclusiveness as a coalition of associates and stressed its representation of the disabled veterans and their affairs, the disabled vets themselves disapproved of this embrace, considering it indicative of a caretaker approach.[128] Other associations of demobilized soldiers that had operated separately, in contrast, appreciated the advantage of setting up an umbrella organization that was headed by recognized representatives and untainted by a subversive and antiestablishmentarian image.[129] The subordination of local or special-purpose organizations to the union did not prevent particularistic associations from continuing to operate on their own, as I show below.

The union differentiated strictly between its functions and those of the Rehabilitation Division. In response to a question from the chair of the Knesset Labor Committee, its representative explained that it neither rehabilitated nor employed former soldiers but encouraged them to take part in "constructive projects and organizes them for housing, upholding of their rights, and interaction with the Rehabilitation Division."[130] In addition, the union emphasized that it was an "apolitical body" that accommodated former soldiers "from Herut [right-wing] to Maki [communist]."[131]

Addressing the Knesset Labor Committee, the union's envoy, Moshe Etzion (Gruenwald), expressed disappointment over the committee's "disregard of the soldiers' representative body in its discussions of their affairs."

What he meant was that responsibility for former soldiers' rehabilitation had been transferred to the Knesset Labor Committee nine months earlier, and no one from the union had been invited to address that entity all this time.[132]

Globman defended the committee, claiming, "Anyone, including a demobilized soldier, can approach the Labor Committee or any other Knesset committee, put in a request, express his opinion, say that this or that institution is acting against the interests of the demobilized soldiers, or express any other opinion. In such a case, the Knesset committee can decide whether or not to receive the person and hear him out."[133]

In the present case, too, Globman continued, the demobilized soldiers' representatives had not been ignored; they had not been invited to the discussions (on the Demobilized Soldiers (Return to Work) Law) solely because their request had arrived too late.[134] Globman proposed that representatives of the union be allowed to participate in ensuing discussions and be invited whenever matters of relevance to it were taken up for debate.

Yosef Gurion took stronger exception to the union's demands than did Globman. He thought it unsound to allow representatives of the ex-soldiers themselves to sit alongside delegates from the IDF on a committee that was drafting a bill pertaining to demobilized soldiers or disabled veterans. The soldiers' rights, he said, would be articulated by the army's delegates. Just the same, he was willing to invite representatives of the union to future discussions in matters of pertinence to its constituency.[135]

Here, the conformist and nonconfrontational approach of the Demobilized Soldiers Union found expression. Etzion distinguished between the union's demand for representation on the committees and the voicing of no confidence. The union, he explained, demanded representation due to its intimate connection with the matter and its ability to offer advice. For Globman and Gurion, however—speaking on behalf of the authorities—such a demand amounted to the recognition of an additional entity in the decision-making process.[136] Indeed, this is exactly what the union wanted: consideration of its views at the decision-making stage, not afterward. "I am of the opinion," Etzion stated, "that our Union, which already has a history, a great deal of experience, and a practical approach to all matters, can also make a contribution in . . . practical treatment of demobilized soldiers." By so affirming, Etzion made his perspective clear: the ambit of the union's involvement should exceed advocacy and should include delivering the service itself. Etzion did refrain carefully from dismissing the achievements of the Rehabilitation Division, stressing that the state was indeed doing something for demobilized soldiers under "intense financial pressure." Just the same, he asked the forum to allow him to present a list of unsolved problems and proposed that the union be recognized as yet another executive agency.[137] The union's hands-on experience gave it, according to its members, the right to demand "not to be a passive observer of goings-on, living by the mercy of this or that office, it must be a partner with a measure of authority."[138]

While Etzion, a Mapai member, attempted to toe an institutionalized and conformist line as best as he could, his union colleague, Kotzer, representing the association of disabled veterans and affiliated with Mapam, expressed himself much more bluntly: "Lots and lots of things are still not okay."[139] Explicitly mentioning the suspicions of corruption, he pointed to concrete examples in which abandoned property that could be adapted to the needs of the disabled were sold for money (i.e., for a bribe).[140] He drew a linkage between the employment problem and wage conditions, since many disabled vets were offered such paltry salaries as to deny them the right to an honorable living. The disabled veterans, Kotzer stressed, wanted not philanthropy but a systematic, rule-based solution.[141] Absent a response to their employment problems, Kotzer warned, his constituents might become "very dangerous."[142]

Yosef Gurion was taken aback by the critical tenor of the union representatives' remarks. He described himself as having encouraged the formation of the union and having entertained no disagreements with it until that meeting. He pointed to a long-standing and unbroken relationship with the union's representatives, including regular meetings where he had kept them up to date on activities at the Rehabilitation Division. What, he wondered, did the union have in mind by depicting the relationship as one between two rival parties—one presenting demands and the other "deficient in initiative, policy, and methods"? Gurion evidently traced Kotzer's criticism to political considerations. Kotzer denied it.[143] The government authorities' suspicion about the covert political interests of the demobilized soldiers' organizations surfaced again. This time, however, it centered on the most institutionalized association, one that took pains to keep channels of communication open and had not used provocative methods to apply pressure.

The standoff between the union and the Rehabilitation Division brought a question of principle to the surface: Who is authorized to represent the demobilized soldiers and their interests? As Gurion saw it, the Rehabilitation

Division represented not the state but the ex-soldiers in its capacity as their appointed custodian. Gurion, however, clarified that if the government of Israel decided "to impose public supervision over each division director—I'll do it, too." Gurion also noted the characteristics of the division's staff members, nearly all of whom were demobilized soldiers who were intimately familiar with the problems with the division's authority. Then he turned his attention to the union envoys, inviting them to refer members to the division for hiring and, in the same breath, criticizing the union's activists for being "totally divorced from the public." Namely, anyone whose problems were solved ceased to be active in the union, leaving behind only those who still believed they could gain in some way by belonging to it.[144]

Gurion also expressed criticism of the demobilized soldiers themselves, particularly those among the socioeconomically down and out (as his remarks suggest), who exploited the transitional period to improve their housing and broke "doors and windows" whenever their demand for a particular job went unrequited.[145] Every disabled veteran who wished to be treated as an equal in the workplace, Gurion exclaimed, should accept any job offered and prove themselves instead of adopting the position of "needing a caretaker."[146]

Attempting to calm the tempers, Etzion explained that his people had lectured to the committee about the empty half of the glass, not the full half, and had not intended to diminish their esteem for Gurion and the division. However, he fumed about the attempt to attribute political intentions to the union.[147]

Globman now assumed the mediator's role. Summing up the meeting, he described the goal as full cooperation, in which the Demobilized Soldiers Union would see itself not only as a plaintiff but also as a partner and the division, in turn, would understand the union's difficulties and bear them in mind. This stance, seeking to build a bridge between the sides in recognition of the union's legitimacy and responsibility, was seconded by Hannah Lamdan, who expressed her impression that "this is a responsible public representative organ that doesn't step forward to demand that the state give more than it can."[148]

Did the Demobilized Soldiers Union overreach by trying to function as an umbrella organization? According to Moshe Naor, the union failed the simple-outcome test (i.e., most demobilized soldiers did not join its ranks).[149] This demonstrates that, notwithstanding all its attempts to be inclusive, the union was limited in its ability to represent the full range of interests in play, at least in the crisis-intensive transition period. Consequently, many members whom it purported to represent preferred to join alternative settings, some of which eventually disbanded or subordinated themselves to umbrella organizations.[150]

Below we observe several of these initiatives in an attempt to broaden our understanding of the needs of small groups to have specific representation of their own.

Associations of Other Inductees: Secessionist Organizations, Overseas Volunteers, and Local Self-Organizations of Demobilized Soldiers

As stated, the Demobilized Soldiers Union was not the only entity that acted at the end of the war to represent and advance this constituency's needs. In the last few months of the war, even as the armistice negotiations continued, sectorial organizations representing ex-soldiers and identifying with various bodies or ideological movements began to crop up. Those behind these initiatives were usually motivated by the feeling of having been excluded from the national ethos, a sense of commitment to the memory of comrades who had fallen, and the need to help those who had survived but with disabilities. This part of the chapter gives an overview of several of these associations, some of which ultimately made their way to the national umbrella organization of demobilized soldiers; others maintained their independent status, and some simply ceased to exist after they got what they wanted.

In November 1948, as the war still raged although not on all fronts, the Herut movement in Jerusalem established an association called Gal (Wave) for assistance to disabled veterans of the War of Independence in Jerusalem. Gal appears to have been one of the first soldiers' organizations to put freedom of association in Israel to the test. When the head of the Jerusalem District Officer (Ministry of the Interior) received notice about its establishment along with its statutes, as required under the Ottoman Law of Societies that the British Mandate government had inherited, he forwarded the application to his superiors and to the Jerusalem military governor.[151] In this case, however, and in a departure from procedure, the minister of the Interior, Yitzhak Gruenbaum, intervened in the approval process by soliciting the opinion of the minister of War Casualties. He did note that while "the establishment of this association should not be prohibited" under the existing (Ottoman) law, its activities could be "guided."[152]

The legal adviser to the Jerusalem military governor objected to the registration of Gal on the grounds (or perhaps the pretext?) of its having the goal of "making a profit and engaging in trade"; therefore, it could not organize under the Ottoman Law of Societies. However, S. B. Yeshaya, a senior official at the Ministry of the Interior who was intimately familiar with the procedure for registering voluntary associations, defended the applicants on the grounds that the association was a legitimate venture that had social goals in mind.[153] The War Casualties Ministry, unimpressed with Yeshaya's stance, sided with the military governor in opposing the establishment of Gal "because its name is misleading and [its] goals are undesirable as long as there is no ordinance that determines the exact entitlements of war casualties in Israel."[154] Thus, the minister of the Interior, his doubts reinforced, decided not to allow the association to register itself "because its goals are contrary to the Ottoman Law of Societies."[155]

All these rationales were, of course, fig leaves for the real reason for frowning on this associational venture. Those behind it were former members of the IZL (Irgun Zvai Leumi, National Military Organization), an organization identified with opposition to the Yishuv's organized leadership. Just half a year before Gal applied to register, the IZL had been on the verge of a clash with the government of Israel against the background of its arms vessel, the *Altalena*.[156] The initiative of the former IZL members in Jerusalem, however, was not the only one. In the course of 1949, it became a phenomenon. Ex-soldiers who were affiliated with the opposition or had other special characteristics chose to oversee their comrades' rehabilitation by organizing on their own. Thus, the Society for the Rehabilitation of Freedom Fighters presented official notice of its formation in April 1949, signed by the senior personalities of the IZL—Ya'akov Meridor, Arieh Ben-Eliezer, Chaim Landau, Shmuel Merlin, Shmuel Katz, and Menachem Begin.[157] Its stated goals included "establishing a memorial to the fallen heroes and commemorating them; opening bureaus, club facilities, and libraries; organizing lectures, assemblies, and presentations; and acting for the rehabilitation of and assistance to demobilized and wounded soldiers—e.g., offering relief in honor of the families of the fallen, assuring assistance for the disabled and the casualties of the War of Independence in finding work and acquiring an occupation, establishing urban and rural economic enterprises, procuring basic housing, and cooperating with other societies that have similar goals."[158]

This initiative, like the one described above, aroused the suspicions of government officials in high places. Thus, the Tel Aviv district commissioner wrote hesitantly, "It seems to me that concern for the rehabilitation of the freedom fighters (i.e., soldiers in the War of Liberation) should remain within the exclusive purview of the Knesset and the government."[159] The commissioner added sundry administrative considerations that, to his mind, justified vetting the application for compliance with the letter of the law. His worries were soon eased by the Ministry's general administration, who promptly advised him that there was no reason to withhold routine confirmation of the receipt of the documents.[160] The Tel Aviv Subdistrict of the Israel Police, to which the notice about the establishment of the new association had been forwarded, also approved its registration.[161]

Notably, there was nothing unusual about passing such forms on to the police. It was a routine stage in the registration of Ottoman societies at the time, as evidenced by similar letters in which the police approved women's or immigrants' associations.[162] The establishment of separate associations for veterans of IZL and Lehi, however, was indeed unique. It reflected the reality that befell veterans of these organizations who had been wounded when the war was underway but before the Israel Defense Forces had been established, at which point their militias had been dismantled. Now, they encountered difficulties when they sought eligibility for assistance and, later on, for the benefits that disabled War of Independence veterans would receive under the recently passed Persons with Disabilities Law. It was in response to this situation that the establishment of associations of their own came about.[163]

In the case of the association of Lehi veterans, early evidence of their intent to associate independently appears in a report by the director of the War Casualties Ministry, Yitzhak Werfel, who met with representatives of Lehi in August 1948. Werfel heard from them about issues "pertaining to the war casualties in their ranks."[164] In December 1949, the Lehi Veterans Association, Committee for the Rehabilitation of Freedom Fighters in Jerusalem presented the Jerusalem district commissioner with notice about it having been founded. The application was sent on, in the accepted manner, to the Investigations Division of the Israel Police, which issued an unequivocal response: "We oppose the registration of this association because the Israel Freedom Fighters [Lehi] has been declared a terrorist organization under the 1948 Prevention of Terror Ordinance."[165]

The district commissioner, however, was in no rush to obey this instruction. Sensing the potential of a collision, he opined to his superiors that if the ministry refused to register the association, "as the police demand, our response will trigger questions and allegations about discrimination that might even reverberate as far as the Knesset." Conversely, he admitted, if the Ministry of the Interior saw fit to approve the registration of this entity, "We will enrage the police, who will argue, correctly, that if we will need to turn to them in regard to the association's activities, they will refuse to help us because they had opposed its registration from the outset."[166] The irony of the whole story is that while the bureaucrats in Jerusalem fretted over the question of registration, a Lehi veterans' association was up and running in Tel Aviv. In fact, the Jerusalem association was also a fait accompli; it was already looking after its members' rehabilitation and had long been interacting on their behalf with a bevy of authorities: the Soldiers Settlement and Rehabilitation Division, the Bureau of the Prime Minister, the Histadrut, the Labor Exchange, health-care providers, and welfare bureaus, to name only a few.[167] In other words, it operated overtly and even sought the establishment's support and backing. Over a period of roughly one year, some fifty people underwent rehabilitation and found work under the auspices of the association, which also provided members with legal, financial, and medical assistance and aided families of the fallen.[168] Only after doing this for many months did its members decide that the time had come to complete its registration and regularize its legal status.[169]

Ultimately, the commissioner again contacted the police and presented the applicants' version of their initiative, namely that their organization confined itself to social work and rehabilitation for its members, among whom were disabled veterans and families of the fallen. A similar association, he noted, was operating in Tel Aviv with government approval. If the application were rejected, he advised the police with emphasis, the matter might be taken to court.[170] The adviser's tenacity paid off: officials at the Police Investigations Division rediscussed the matter and decided not to oppose approval of the notice concerning the establishment of the association. Thus, yet another entity of demobilized soldiers, this one with a distinct organizational and local affiliation, was recognized officially and legally.[171]

Another fringe group of veterans that organized on its own was the Mahal (aka Machal) association, representing overseas volunteers. This time, the initial doubt about the initiative was expressed by the minister of the Interior, who approached the Ministry of Defense and wondered whether there was room for "an association that will unite people who came from abroad to join the Israel Defense Forces whether they are still in the ranks of the army or have been discharged."[172] According to its statutes, the association was composed of members who had come to participate in the War of Independence. The founders defined their association as apolitical and its purpose as the unifying of all IDF volunteers who had come from abroad, still serving or not and irrespective of their country of origin, language, party, class, or gender affiliation. The association had come into being "to represent the interests of the overseas volunteers, to help them with housing, getting settled, and integrating into civilian life in Israel."[173]

The Ministry of Defense opposed the application, convinced that "the association's main goal is a cover for dubious political activity."[174] In its investigation, the ministry found that the five members of the association's secretariat who had signed the application were "of East European origin and several are known to be activists in Communist circles." They also related that at a meeting between Gruenwald (Etzion), secretary of the Demobilized Soldiers Union and someone representing the organization of overseas volunteers, "the latter turned down Gruenwald's requests for a list of registered members of the association on the pretext that their technical secretariat was not yet operative." One member of the applicants' association, Wili Cohen, who had signed the application as a member of its secretariat, had reached Israel with the Czechoslovak Brigade; by the time the application to form the association was submitted, he had applied to return to Czechoslovakia. On the basis of these findings, the Ministry of Defense inferred that the association existed "on paper only."[175]

"Overseas volunteers" were defined by the Personnel Division of the IDF General Staff as "individuals who came to the country for the purpose of enlisting in the army and helping to establish the state during the war, with the intention of returning to their countries after the end of the war."[176] Yaakov Markovitzki notes that, in fact, members of Mahal were classified as such on the basis of promises from representatives of the IDF and the Ministry of Defense that they would enjoy special conditions during their service and, at the end of the fighting, would be sent back to their countries of origin at the expense of the Israeli defense system.[177] Much friction existed between the Mahal soldiers and the military system and the native inductees. Part of the problem originated in cultural and mentality differences, such as disputes over unpaid wages and service amenities or charges of inappropriate placement. Other tensions originated in political and ideological considerations.[178] The Czechoslovakian Brigade, for example, had never been activated as an organic unit due to, Markovitzky claims, concern that this assistance from fellow Jews was part of a

Soviet-communist conspiracy to make deeper inroads in the country as the War of Independence wound down.[179] These suspicions fit well with those concerning the organizing of disabled veterans and demobilized soldiers, it being feared that they intended to create provocations and enjoyed the support of political players who had a stake in having this done.[180] Markovitzki offers another possible explanation for the suspicion and estrangement that typified the Israelis' attitude toward the overseas volunteers: the effect of national pride. Viewed in this manner, the Israeli leadership wished to belittle the value of the assistance that it had received from abroad in prosecuting the war; the volunteers' departure would make it possible to put their contribution out of mind and refrain from "cultivating the memory of their assistance and contribution to the war effort."[181]

The Ministry of the Interior, mulling whether to approve the registration of the overseas volunteers' organization, repeated what was already known at this time. First, the Ottoman Law of Societies said nothing about approving or registering the association. Second, the government is rarely able to withhold confirmation of the receipt of documents and is unlikely to have this power even if the association's goals contravene the provisions of the law.[182] In this case, as before, it was the stance of a district commissioner, this time in Tel Aviv, that tipped the scales. Like his counterpart in Jerusalem, he refused to accept verbatim the negative recommendation that he had received, arguing that he saw no possibility of not confirming the receipt of the documents unless a police investigation concluded that the association's goals were illegal or contrary to the Law of Societies.[183] The commissioner stood his ground and got his way,[184] even though the ministry brought pressure on him not to approve the association in view of an internal report about its members that had come into its possession.[185]

Amid all this, a Demobilized Officers Housing Association came into being for the purpose of "organizing those who live in the so-called 'Officers' Neighborhood' in Sarona and ensuring sound order there." Those behind this initiative, specifying the exact location of the land in Sarona on the basis of block and parcel numbers, stated that it was their intention to develop the neighborhood in terms of its utilities and services and to establish assistance funds and financial institutions for their members' benefit.[186] Yet another association of soldiers that formed for collective housing purposes was the Demobilized Soldiers Housing Committee, established by thirty-five families while the war was in progress. The committee represented ex-soldiers who lived near Petah Tikva and served as an alternative municipality of sorts. Its purpose in applying for registration was to obtain the power to charge dues.[187] These are only a few of the local and focused initiatives by demobilized soldiers for purposes of housing, settlement, economic interests, and, of course, specific ideological and group affiliations, as in the cases of the "secessionist" organizations' veterans and the overseas volunteers.

In the ensuing years, demobilized soldiers of various affiliations and groupings would act to set up associations of their own. The responses to such initiatives, as well as their motives and the entities' subsequent activities, transcend the boundaries of this study. However, the phenomenon as such, as well as its scale, indicate that subgroups of army veterans felt that the large national settings did not properly represent their interests and also, perhaps, their singular war experiences.[188] Those behind these initiatives put the Israeli establishment's patience to the test; not only did they wish to associate for purposes that were ostensibly (or supposedly) being dealt with by the state, they also revealed fissures in the values of solidarity and mobilization that they themselves, as "1948 warriors," were supposed to symbolize more than any other group in Israeli society.

One may hypothesize that some of those who took exception to the associative initiatives felt that the initiatives as such amounted to an indictment or criticism of the state authorities. Conversely, however, it is interesting to see that those associating saw no contradiction between their willingness to lay down their lives for the state and their demand that this state recognize their particularistic interests and their right to voice them and, by so doing, to represent themselves. After the fact, it may be correct to view the associative ventures of demobilized soldiers of various kinds—from the organizations of disabled veterans via the Demobilized Soldiers Union to the small contrarian associations—as a transitional stage on the path to citizenship, in which associating played a mediating role that also allowed special-interest groups to speak out against the functioning of the state. Concurrently, it gave them a place in the public sphere where they could continue to preserve their identity as soldiers while behaving like civilians.

Notes

1. Benny Morris, *1948: A History of the First Arab-Israeli War* (New Haven, CT: Yale University Press, 2008), chapters 8–10; Yoav Gelber, *Independence versus Nakba* (in Hebrew) (Or Yehuda: Kinneret Zmora Bitan, Dvir, 2004), chapter 12.

2. Moshe Naor, "The 1948 War Veterans and Postwar Reconstruction in Israel," *Journal of Israeli History* 29, no. 1 (2010): 48.
3. Ibid., 49–50.
4. Daniel Nadav, *The Ministry of Defense Rehabilitation Division, 1948–1998: Rehabilitation of IDF and Defense System Disabled Veterans and Survivors, Fundamentals and Changes* (in Hebrew) (Tel Aviv: Ministry of Defense Documentation and Historical Research Unit, 1999), 221, 224.
5. David Reifen, overview of rehabilitation center, Rehabilitation Center Newsletter, Israel Defense Forces Archives (hereinafter: IDFA), 282-129-1951 (n.d., adjunct to documents from December 1948).
6. Nadav, *Ministry of Defense Rehabilitation Division*, 220.
7. David Ben-Gurion diary, Ben-Gurion Archive (hereinafter: BGA), Diaries Division, September 20, 1948.
8. Ibid.
9. Ben-Gurion to office in London, BGA, Correspondence Division, September 22, 1948.
10. Ben-Gurion to Arthur Luria, New York, BGA, ibid., September 22, 1948.
11. Ben-Gurion diary, BGA, Diaries Division, September 22, 1948.
12. Ben-Gurion diary, BGA, Diaries Division, October 7, 1948.
13. "Government's Plans for Care of Disabled and Demobilized Soldiers," *Al Hamishmar*, November 19, 1948, 6.
14. Former head of a committee that had dealt with the discharge of Yishuv soldiers from the British Army in World War II.
15. "Soon to Be Established: Factory for Prosthetic Limbs," *Al Hamishmar*, December 22, 1948, 1.
16. "Rehabilitation Center Restores Disabled War Veterans' Ability to Work and Make a Living," *Ha-Boker*, December 22, 1948.
17. Rehabilitation Center, *Ha-Boker*, quotation from letter to the editor, "Disabled Veterans' Protest," signed by "a disabled [person]," *Al Hamishmar*, December 23, 1948, 2.
18. Zvi Amitai, "The Other Side of the Coin: A Visit to the Rehabilitation Center," *Al Hamishmar*, December 24, 1948, 2.
19. Ibid.
20. Uri, untitled article, Rehabilitation Center Newsletter, IDFA, 282-129-1951. (The newsletter is undated but was evidently produced in December 1948, concurring with publication of the article in *Ha-Boker*.)
21. Avraham Efraima, "Disability as a Source of Pride and . . . Livelihood," Rehabilitation Center Newsletter, IDFA, 282-129-1951. (The newsletter is undated but was evidently produced in December 1948.)
22. Ibid.
23. Ibid.
24. National Committee of Disabled Veterans of the Current War, Rehabilitation Center No. 1, IDFA, 282-129-1951, December 30, 1948.
25. Ibid.
26. Ibid.
27. Ibid.
28. Avraham Ohry and A. Shaked, eds., *Introduction to Rehabilitation Medicine* (Tel Aviv: Israel Ministry of Defense, 1990), 100.

29. Ibid., 99.

30. Yosef Gurion, "Overview of Rehabilitation Division Actions," submitted to the Labor Committee of the Knesset, IDFA, 248-580-1956, December 27, 1949.

31. Levin-Epstein was the deputy of Dr. Chaim Scheiber (subsequently Sheba), director and founder of the army's medical service. See also Daniel Nadav, "The Beginning of Rehabilitation of Casualties in Israel's Wars," 'Alei zayit ve-herev 4 (2002): 275–299.

32. Handwritten note headed "rehabilitation center," with the name "Reifen" recorded (evidently alluding to information communicated by telephone or orally by David Reifen), IDFA, 282-129-1951, December 31, 1948. According to the contents of the note, the militant disabled veterans at the Rehabilitation Division were represented at this time by Yaakov Mizrahi. In his diary, however, Ben-Gurion listed other names: Avraham Mizrahi, Yaakov Skowronin, and Yaakov Tzadok.

33. Since the decision to establish the central authority was made only in late November, it had not yet become relevant from the veterans' standpoint at this time.

34. David Shaltiel to Minister of Defense and Chief of IDF General Staff, IDFA, 282-129-1951, January 2, 1949.

35. Ibid.

36. Ibid.

37. Ibid.

38. Ibid.

39. Ibid.

40. Ben-Gurion to National Committee of Disabled Veterans of the Current War, Israel State Archive (hereinafter: ISA), Gimel, 5659/1, January 7, 1949.

41. Ibid.; Moshe Naor, "The 1948 War Veterans and Postwar Reconstruction in Israel," *Journal of Israeli History* 29, no. 1 (2010): 50.

42. "Control of Abandoned Property: Press Conference with D. Shafrir," *Davar*, January 7, 1949, 4.

43. David Crohn, letter to no specific addressee, IDFA, 282-129-1951, December 31, 1948.

44. "MPs against Disabled Soldiers Who Invaded Government Officials' Apartments in Jaffa," *Herut*, March 18, 1949, 6.

45. Ibid.

46. The representatives were Avraham Singer, Yaakov Skowronin (number 130 on the Herut Party list for the First Knesset), and Yaakov Tzadok (whom Ben-Gurion called "Bavli" in his diary).

47. Ben-Gurion diary, BGA, Diaries Division, March 17, 1949.

48. "Disabled Soldiers Demonstrate at Session of Knesset: Deputy Speaker of Knesset Refers Them to Party Representatives," *Herut*, March 18, 1949, 6.

49. Representatives of Disabled Veterans of the Current War, letter signed by Yaakov Rubowicz (subsequently a founding member of the Organization of Merchant and Artisan Demobilized Soldiers and Disabled War Veterans), Bella Schub, and Yaakov Skowronin to members of the First Knesset (posted from Rehabilitation Center No. 1, Jaffa), ISA, Gimel 5659/1, March 20, 1949.

50. Ibid.

51. Ibid.

52. Ibid.

53. Ibid.

54. "Knesset Takes up the Demobilized Soldiers Bill: Returning [Them] to Work, Treatment and Employment of the Disabled, Housing for Demobilized Soldiers," *Hatzofe*, March 22, 1949, 1.

55. Nadav, *Ministry of Defense Rehabilitation Division*, 101–2, 179–88.

56. Ibid., 219.

57. "Disabled Soldiers Demand Protection of Their Rights," *Herut*, April 5, 1949, 4; "Disabled Soldiers Demand Their Rights," *Hatzofe*, April 5, 1949, 4.

58. Berl Repetur, "Our Duty to the Demobilized Soldier," *Al Hamishmar*, April 5, 1949, 2.

59. Ibid.

60. Uri Kesari, "Twilight Flickers: The Disabled Are Representatives of the Deceased!" *Ma'ariv*, April 11, 1949, 3.

61. Baruch Oren, "You Have Two Hands, You Have Two Feet," *Herut*, April 15, 1949, 2.

62. Very few Israelis owned a car at the time; having a vehicle for professional use would go far toward solving the mobility impediments of the disabled.

63. Baruch Oren, "You Have Two Hands, You Have Two Feet," *Herut*, April 15, 1949, 2. See also M. M., "The Wounded Did Not Cry Out—but the Disabled War Veterans Are Crying Out for Lack of Care and Aid," *Ma'ariv*, April 26, 1949, 3.

64. Oren, "You Have Two Hands, You Have Two Feet," 2.

65. Baruch Oren, "Israel's Disabled War Veterans and the State of Israel's Government," *Herut*, April 18, 1949, 2.

66. "Prosthesis and Protection: Impressions of a Visit to Institutions and Enterprises of the Demobilized Soldiers Rehabilitation Division," *Ma'ariv*, June 12, 1949, 2.

67. Michael Levi, "How They're Looking Out for Disabled War Veterans," letter to the editor, *Al Hamishmar*, May 13, 1949, 6. Levi himself was wounded in the war.

68. The previous committee at the rehab center was titled the National Committee of Disabled Veterans of the Current War, Rehabilitation Center No. 1. Although the entities' names are very similar, they appear to have been competing entities that represented different attitudes toward the struggle of the disabled.

69. National Committee of Disabled Veterans, Rehabilitation Center, "Israel's Disabled War Veterans and the State of Israel's Government," letter to the editor, *Herut*, April 22, 1949, 5.

70. "Assembly for Disabled War Veterans" (concerning a gathering of disabled war veterans in the Northern District at the auditorium of the Haifa Technion), *Al Hamishmar*, April 6, 1949, 3; "Jerusalem: Committee of Wounded Soldiers," *Al Hamishmar*, August 5, 1949, 9.

71. By this time, disabled veterans from World War II were also taking part in the soldiers' protests. See, for example, "Dramatic Demonstration by the Disabled in Tel Aviv: Amputees Demand Their Rights," *Herut*, April 27, 1949, 4; Demobilized Soldiers Bill Passed into Law, Effective May 15," *Al Hamishmar*, April 26, 1949, 1.

72. "Incited Demonstrations," *Hatzofe*, May 19, 1949, 1.

73. "Demobilized Soldiers Demonstrate in the Streets of Tel Aviv," *Davar*, May 19, 1949, 5.

74. Ibid., 4.

75. "Demobilized Soldiers Present Their Demands to Knesset Factions," *Al Hamishmar*, May 19, 1949, 4.

76. "Behavior toward Demobilized Soldiers and Political Censorship in Knesset Debates," *Al Hamishmar*, May 19, 1949, 1.

77. Ibid.

78. "Flash Photos from the Knesset Hall and Backrooms," *Herut*, May 19, 1949, 4.
79. "Behavior toward Demobilized Soldiers and Political Censorship in Knesset Debates," *Al Hamishmar*, May 19, 1949, 1.
80. "The Truth about the Disabled [Veterans'] Demonstration," *Hatzofe*, May 25, 1949, 4; "The Truth about the Disabled Veterans' Demonstration," *Davar*, May 25, 1949, 1.
81. Ben-Gurion diary, BGA, Diaries Division, May 20, 1949.
82. Ben-Gurion diary, BGA, Diaries Division, June 2, 1949.
83. Ibid.
84. Dan Diner, "People without an Address: Scenes of Demobilized Soldiers' Distress," *Ma'ariv*, June 2, 1949.
85. Ibid.
86. Disabled Veterans Law, 5709–1949 (first discussion), *Divrei ha-Knesset*, Session 76, September 5, 1949, 1572–3; Disabled Veterans (Benefits and Rehabilitation) Law, 5709–1949 (second and third discussions), *Divrei ha-Knesset*, Session 79, September 8, 1949, 1633–6, 1644.
87. Lamdan remarks, *Divrei ha-Knesset*, Session 79, September 8, 1949, 1633–6, 1644. (Notably, Hannah Lamdan, a member of the Ahdut ha-'Avoda faction, eventually returned to her home party, Mapai, from which she subsequently seceded to Rafi under Ben-Gurion.)
88. Akiva Globman remarks, *Divrei ha-Knesset*, Session 79, September 8, 1949, 1639.
89. "Military Training and Agricultural Training: The Two Fundamentals of Our Standing Army, Rehabilitation of War of Independence Disabled Veterans from the Ranks of the Underground as Well," *Ma'ariv*, September 9, 1949, 2.
90. Ibid.
91. Ben-Gurion diary, BGA, Diaries Division, October 17, 1949.
92. "Prime Minister Visits the Ill and the Disabled," *Hatzofe*, October 18, 1949, 1.
93. Yosef (Yoske) Lautenberg and David Green, eds., *Giborei Ha'il, the Full Story, the Organization of Disabled IDF Veterans, 1948–1998* (in Hebrew) (Tel Aviv: Green Publications, 2005), 15.
94. Geula Paran, "The Spirit Entered Them and They Came to Life. They Stood Upon their Feet: The Development of the Rehabilitation Medicine in Israel as a Reflection for Changes in Israeli Society, 1948–1974," PhD Dissertation, Bar-Ilan University (2014), 86–87.
95. Yosef Gurion remarks to Knesset Labor Committee, ISA, Kaf, 23/7, January 2, 1950; Paran, "The Spirit Entered Them," 87.
96. This account of formation of the organization appears in the festive album that marked its fiftieth anniversary. In fact, all the evidence indicates that the organization had been founded in late 1949. If so, the jubilee album actually marked the forty-ninth anniversary, because the more significant earlier association was that at the rehabilitation center in Jaffa, elaborated upon above.
97. A member of Kibbutz Sha'ar Hagolan and the first commander of the Golani Brigade commandos, he chaired the Organization of Disabled Veterans for a year and went on to be an activist in the Hakibbutz Ha'artzi kibbutz movement and the Mapam Party.
98. Lautenberg and Green, *Giborei Ha'il*, 15.
99. Ibid., 16.
100. Ben-Gurion diary, BGA, Diaries Division, October 20, November 16, and December 5, 1949.
101. Ben-Gurion diary, BGA, Diaries Division, December 5, 1949.
102. Knesset Labor Committee, ISA, Kaf, 23/7, January 2, 1950.

103. Ibid.
104. Ibid.
105. Ibid.
106. Knesset Labor Committee, ISA, Kaf, 23/7, January 2, 1950.
107. Ben-Gurion diary, BGA, Diaries Division, January 8, 1950.
108. Nadav, *Ministry of Defense Rehabilitation Division*, 222–3.
109. Meeting of representatives of the Central Committee of Demobilized Soldiers in Israel with the chair of the Knesset Labor Committee, ISA, Gimel, 6154/16, December 18, 1949.
110. Central Committee of Demobilized Soldiers Union, resolutions adopted at conference, ISA, Gimel 6154/16, June 28, 1949.
111. "Safed: Demobilized Soldiers' Organization Established in Safed," *Davar*, May 25, 1949, 4.
112. "Haifa: Demobilized Soldiers Committee in the Bay Area," *Davar*, June 26, 1949, 4.
113. "Organization of Demobilized IDF Soldiers Who Own Looms Established," *Davar*, April 17, 1949, 3.
114. "Demobilized Soldiers Law Approved: Most 'Civic' Factions Abstain," *Davar*, May 25, 1949, 5.
115. "Demobilized Soldiers Demonstrate in the Streets of Tel Aviv," *Davar*, May 19, 1949, 4.
116. Ibid. A description of this event, with emphasis on the role of disabled veterans and their organizations in the demonstrations and demands, appears on page 262 (this volume).
117. Ben-Gurion diary, BGA, Diaries Division, June 9, 1949.
118. Ibid.
119. "Soldiers' Representatives Demand that Prime Minister Expedite a Solution to Housing Distress," *Davar*, June 12, 1949, 4.
120. Central Committee of Demobilized Soldiers Union, June 28, 1949.
121. Ibid.
122. Ibid.
123. "Demobilized Soldiers Union Central Committee Resolves: Not an Auxiliary alongside the Rehabilitation Division but an Autonomous and Active Entity," *Al Hamishmar*, June 29, 1949, 1.
124. Central Committee of Demobilized Soldiers Union, June 28, 1949.
125. "Demobilized Soldiers Union Central Committee Resolves," 1.
126. Ibid.
127. Meeting of representatives of Central Committee, ISA, Gimel 6154/16, December 18, 1949.
128. Nadav, *Ministry of Defense Rehabilitation Division*, 222. Indeed, the alliance soon crumbled: the disabled veterans seceded and established an organizational autonomy that they have maintained to this day.
129. Letter from Inspector A. Kramer to Haifa District Governor, ISA, Lamed, 63/18, May 16, 1949; Central Committee of Demobilized Soldiers Union, June 28, 1949.
130. Meeting of representatives of Central Committee, ISA, Gimel 6154/16, December 18, 1949.
131. Ibid.; Nadav (*Ministry of Defense Rehabilitation Division*, 222) quotes Moshe Rashkes in this context.
132. Meeting of representatives of Central Committee, December 18, 1949. See also Inspector A. Kramer to Haifa District Governor, ISA, Lamed, 63/18, May 16, 1949.
133. Ibid.

134. Ibid.
135. Ibid.
136. Ibid.
137. Meeting of Knesset Labor Committee, ISA, Kaf 23/7, January 9, 1950.
138. Ibid.
139. Ibid.
140. Ibid.
141. Another union representative charged that demobilized soldiers were encountering a *social work* attitude. This term was widely invoked as the opposite of a constructivist approach to rehabilitation, one leading to autonomy as against dependency. See Knesset Labor Committee, ISA, Kaf, 23/7, January 10, 1950.
142. Meeting of Knesset Labor Committee, ISA, Kaf, 23/7, January 9, 1950.
143. Ibid.
144. Ibid.
145. Ibid.
146. Ibid.
147. Ibid.
148. Ibid.
149. Naor, "1948 War Veterans and Postwar Reconstruction in Israel," 54.
150. In regard to representing other groups, see, for example, Moshe Rashkes, Demobilized Soldiers Union, Disabled Independence War Veterans Division, to Secretariat of Cooperation Center, ISA, Gimel, 5429/1, October 19, 1950. On the durability of specific organizations of demobilized veterans from the War of Independence, see Naor, "1948 War Veterans and Postwar Reconstruction in Israel," 55.
151. S. B. Yeshaya, Jerusalem District Officer, to General Administration Division of Ministry of Interior and Jerusalem Military Governor, ISA, Gimel, 2196/7, November 1, 1948.
152. Yitzhak Gruenbaum to Minister for War Casualties, ISA, Gimel, 2196/7, November 25, 1948.
153. S. B. Yeshaya to General Administration Division, Ministry of the Interior, Tel Aviv, ISA, Gimel, 2196/7, December 9, 1948.
154. Asher Rosenblum, Director General of War Casualties Ministry, to Minister of the Interior, ISA, Gimel, 2196/7, December 10, 1948.
155. Y. Kissilov, Director of General Administration Division, Ministry of the Interior, to Jerusalem District Officer, ISA, Gimel, 2196/7, January 6, 1949. The Ottoman Law of Societies prohibited "any society . . . contrary to the provisions of the law, public morality or with the intention of disturbing the peace of the country or aiming at disintegration of the State, or changing the form of the ruling Government, or causing dissension among different communities, and it is prohibited to establish political societies under the title of races and nationalities."
156. An arms vessel that sailed to Israel at the initiative of the IZL and approached the coast several weeks after the proclamation of statehood. In the absence of an accord between the IZL and state leaderships on the apportionment of the weapons and the IDF's exclusive control of the cargo, the government of Israel under Ben-Gurion decided to blow up the ship. Nineteen persons—three IDF soldiers and sixteen IZL fighters—were killed in the incident.
157. "Notice of Formation of Society," ISA, Lamed, 93/40 and Gimel, 2196/5 (n.d., adjunct to documents from April 1949).
158. Statutes of the Society for the Rehabilitation of Freedom Fighters, ISA, Lamed, 93/40.

159. Superintendent of Tel Aviv District to Minister of the Interior, ISA, Gimel, 2196/5, April 21, 1949.

160. Deputy Director Y. Gubernik to Tel Aviv District Commissioner, ISA, Gimel, 2196/5, May 2, 1949.

161. Tel Aviv Subdistrict headquarters to Criminal Investigation Bureau, ISA, Gimel 93/40, May 13, 1949.

162. Paula Kabalo, "Constructing Civil Society: Citizen Associations in Israel in the 1950s," *Nonprofit and Voluntary Sector Quarterly* 35, no. 2 (2006): 161–82.

163. Nadav, *Ministry of Defense Rehabilitation Division*, 238–40; Letter from Natan Yelin-Mor to Ben-Gurion, ISA, Gimel, 5428/4, May 1, 1950; *Divrei ha-Knesset*, Session 79, September 8, 1949, 1638.

164. Letter from Director of War Casualties Ministry Yitzhak Werfel to the Minister, Rabbi Y. L. Hacohen Fishman, ISA, Roll 51370/3, August 13, 1948.

165. Yitzhak Ben-Ari, Head of General Investigations Division, to Jerusalem District Commissioner, ISA, Gimel, 2196/7, June 9, 1950.

166. Jerusalem District Commissioner Avraham Biran to Director of Ministry of Interior Administration Division, ISA, Gimel, 2196/7, June 19, 1950.

167. Ibid.

168. Letter from Lehi Veterans Association to Jerusalem District Commissioner, ISA, Gimel, 2196/7, June 20, 1950.

169. The legal status that the association would gain by registering would allow it to have a bank account, charge dues, and, of course, represent members vis-à-vis judicial authorities.

170. S. B. Yeshaya to Israel Police National Headquarters, ISA, Gimel, 2196/7, July 3, 1950; Tel Aviv District Commissioner to General Administration Division, ISA, Gimel, 2196/7, July 28, 1950.

171. S. B. Yeshaya to Jerusalem District Commissioner, ISA, Gimel, 2196/7, September 4, 1950; and N. Stavi, Assistant to the Inspector General, Israel Police, to Ministry of Interior Administration Division, ISA, Gimel, 2196/7, August 25, 1950.

172. Director General, Ministry of the Interior, to Director General, Ministry of Defense, ISA, Gimel, 2196/10, May 3, 1949.

173. Foreign Volunteers Association—Statutes, ISA, Gimel, 2196/10 (n.d., adjunct to documents from April 1949).

174. Gubernik to Ministry of Justice, ISA, Gimel, 2196/10, August 29, 1949.

175. "Re: Overseas Volunteers Association," attached to letter from Jacob Pat, Ministry of Defense, to Director General, Ministry of the Interior, ISA, Gimel, 2196/4, June 6, 1949.

176. Yaakov Markovitzky, "Machal—Overseas Volunteers in Israel's War of Independence," in *Israel's War of Independence Revisited*, Vol. 1, Alon Kadish, ed. (Tel Aviv: Ministry of Defense, 2004), 539.

177. Ibid., 540.

178. Ibid., 547.

179. Ibid.

180. "Behavior toward Demobilized Soldiers and Political Censorship in Knesset Debates," *Al Hamishmar*, May 19, 1949, 1.

181. Markovitzky, "Machal," 549.

182. Y. Gubernik to Ministry of Justice, ISA, Gimel, 2196/10, August 29, 1949.

183. Tel Aviv District Commissioner to General Administration Division, ISA, Gimel, 2196/10, July 6, 1949.

184. General Administration Division to Ministry of Justice, August 20, 1949; director of ministry of justice to General Administration Division, Ministry of the Interior; Y. Gubernik, Deputy Director of a General Administration Division, Ministry of the Interior, to Tel Aviv District Commissioner, September 8, 1949, September 2, 1949. All correspondence is in ISA, Gimel, 2196/5.

185. Y. Kissilov, Director of General Administration Division, to Tel Aviv District Commissioner, ISA, Gimel, 2196/5, June 21, 1949.

186. Demobilized Officers Housing Association, an Association of Disabled Veterans in Israel. See also letter from Israel Police, Criminal Investigation Bureau, to Tel Aviv District Headquarters, Criminal Investigation Department, May 9, 1949, and "Association of Disabled Veterans in Israel," undated but with documents from May 1949, ISA, Lamed, 93/40.

187. Letter from Demobilized Soldiers Housing Committee near Hadarga, Petah Tikva (the suburb of Petah Tikva where Kefar Ma'as was established), to Ministry of the Interior, ISA, Gimel, 2196/5, January 13, 1950.

188. See, for example, "Alliance of Soldiers from the National Military Organization [IZL]," ISA, Gimel, 2196/11. (The entire file contains documents from the year 1952 and deals with this association only.)

CONCLUSION

As scholarly attention to the nonmilitary aspects of Israel's War of Independence expands and intensifies, new heroes step onto the research stage: settlers in frontier areas, senior officials of the National Institutions and the fledgling state, soldiers' families and those who commemorated the fallen, urban and rural leaders, and, of course, a welter of diverse civic associations. The litany of such organizations comprises powerful establishmentarian entities as well as grassroots and at times ad hoc initiatives. This study joins the steadily growing corpus of nonmilitary works that concern themselves with war. At its center stands this organizational array of civic and voluntary entities that represented sectors and subgroups in the Jewish population of pre-independence and formative Israel as they coped with the blow occasioned by the war that engulfed them from late 1947 to early 1949.

The role of anonymous stakeholders in history—those pawns whose faces and names are blurred even in mid-event and swiftly fade afterward[1]—often remains concealed from the observer's eye. In those trying times, while still astride the stage of the historical events, these unwitting heroes are mired in their struggle for survival and cannot afford to waste even a moment on a public-relations campaign that would highlight their activity and contribution. Once the tumult ebbs, they must pledge their psychological and material resources to the reconstruction of their lives and routines. Still, even though their role does not sink into the collective consciousness, not all of them remain mute. Some speak out by turning to policy makers or the media as the events proceed. Others write memoirs that afford a belated glimpse at what they experienced. In both cases, however, the emphasis is usually personal and specific; it fails to provide inclusive and comprehensive information about the essence of the function that organizing citizens discharged as they struggled to cope with the crisis situation.

This gap between understanding the past from the point of view of policy makers or cultural elites and its representation as a personal and particularistic experience, which makes it hard to view reality in its broader and more comprehensive contexts, is filled largely by the mechanisms of human association. The stakeholders' organizations that were formed for the purpose of serving and representing their members constitute, in their essence, a bridge between the anonymous individual's experience and the circles from which he or she seeks relief. This kind of mediation took place throughout the War of Independence in response to the implications of the war for day-to-day life. As the process unfolded, the voices of ordinary civilians were heard, expressing along with their personal distress that of the rest of their community, and, above all, the hardships and struggle that were their lot and, at the same time, their proactive approach to this hardship and their unwillingness to be passive and static in view of their plight. By choosing the coping mechanism of self-associating, they demonstrated their capabilities for action and indeed became a force to be reckoned with.

If so, the purpose of choosing civic association as an axis for retelling the plot of Israel's War of Independence is to propose a path of research by which one may understand the depth of the war experience as it was undergone by the variegated community mosaic that makes up a society. The understanding thus attained attaches to any war, and not necessarily a war in Israel and not necessarily the War of Independence. As demonstrated in the literature, along this avenue one may shed light on the way people cope with a catastrophe of either human or natural provenance.

The study presented above analyzes the events of the Israeli War of Independence (a term that differentiates between the sides in how they experienced the war) as a humanitarian crisis characterized by the devastation of quotidian life, loss of sources of livelihood, displacement and separation from the familiar community tapestry, and carrying on amid protracted uncertainty. Those who experienced the war had to contend with its implications as it proceeded and create paths to rehabilitation and recovery afterward. The word *crisis* in this context is used as Daniel P. Aldrich defines it: "Collective events that—at least temporarily, and often for years afterwards—suspend normal daily life routines owing to widespread damage."[2]

By contemplating civic associations in the War of Independence from the standpoint of coping with a far-reaching crisis, one extends the discussion to new conceptual and theoretical domains: ways in which communities cope with crises and, foremost, studies that track the functioning of social networks and civic associations in order to explain why one group displays resilience while another evidences weakness and fragility.

Resilience is a concept that occupies researchers of humanitarian disasters and crises as well as relief organizations and agencies. After many decades of focusing most attention on matters of physical and pecuniary revitalization, a new insight dawned: the solution to the riddle of resilience lies not at the material level but on more abstract planes that pertain to relationships among members of the wounded community and its organizational structures. Aldrich's comprehensive comparative study, which matches Tokyo's 1923 earthquake as a historical case study with current disasters, offers compelling findings that show the centrality of social networks and connections (among individuals and groups) in powering rehabilitation processes after disasters and crises—no less, and perhaps more, than material resources.[3]

Derived from this perspective is the concept of community resilience, which Connie P. Ozawa defines as a community's ability "to respond to unexpected and unwelcomed events in ways that enable groups and individuals to work together to minimize the adverse consequences of such crisis."[4] A resilient community, it follows, draws its strength and stability from its members' social capital—a concept that captures the phenomenon of social networks and the norms of trust and reciprocity associated with them.[5] "When such elements exist," Golam M. Mathbor states, "better preparedness and superior ability to respond to the disaster and its implications effectively are assured."[6]

The current study tracked the doings of voluntary stakeholder associations that gathered around a common denominator for a joint purpose and, in so doing, gave rise to norms of trust and reciprocity. Despite the vast differences among the dozens of settings that were chosen in this book, they shared three dimensions of action irrespective of their purviews, their degree of organizational institutionalization, and their members' socioeconomic origins.

A central aspect of these associations' activity is their representative and mediating role vis-à-vis the sovereign and pre-sovereign governing authorities. Chambers of commerce and the Association of Homeowners—entities with political pretensions that considered themselves representative of a powerful socioeconomic sector—took part in this kind of activity. So did committees of united internal displaced persons in Haifa and of tenants in the vacated Palestinian neighborhoods in Jerusalem (Katamon) and Tel Aviv (Manshiya and Jamusin). In all these cases, the leaders of the associations undertook to represent their members in policy makers' forums at both the national and the local levels. Often, too, they aspired to permanent representation that came to pass in some cases and fell through in others. In all instances, representatives were chosen among the membership in some manner and a mechanism of accountability to members was created in order to advise them of the outcomes of negotiations with the authorities and of goings-on among policy-making bodies in which the agents took part.

Researchers who examine the implications of civic association for civilian resilience point to the representational aspects and the internal governing mechanisms of the association as empowering factors for members—a school of democracy, one may say, that gives its students tools with which to cope at the civil and political levels.[7] The findings of this study substantiate this determination.

The second characteristic shared by all the settings examined in this study is the objective of strengthening and broadening members' grasp of relevant information. The information-gathering function at issue here is bidirectional, flowing from the inside out and from the outside in. Internal information relates to the extent of destruction and damage that members of the organization sustained; it is gathered for the purpose of being shared in order to obtain relief. External information is composed of regulations and orders that affect the associating group and that indicate where it may apply for aid. In this context, one may draw a line between two committees—that of the Ben-Yehuda Street casualties and the organization of soldiers' wives in Haifa. The first collected information about the extent of members' monetary and property damage and advised members of the operations of the funds that had been set up to help them by extending short-term loans or assigning alternative venues for their damaged businesses. The latter body located inductees' wives who needed financial aid and vocational training and shared information about employment opportunities and eligibilities that had been established for inductees' families.

Expounding on the effects of civic association on individuals, Mark E. Warren notes the roles of associations as "collectors, organizers and conduits of information that educate individuals about matters relevant to them. Information empowers citizens to demand transparency and public accountability."[8] The information that social networks deliver, Aldrich states, makes it possible to surmount "collective action problems" and helps members to cope with the uncertainty that typically accompanies disasters. Often the information available to social networks is unavailable to the government because its source is the casualties themselves.[9]

The third characteristic, a crucial one in the context of the War of Independence, is the possibility that civil associations afford their members a chance to sound their voices—both in the public space (i.e., through the media) and in closed settings that include writing letters and sending them to public figures. This enunciation is manifested in press coverage of members' distress, the outdoor notices that they posted, and the willingness of the associates' addressees to reply and respond to the hardships and requests expressed in the missives, irrespective of the petitioners' identity and the contents of their communication. These patterns of action, which Orit Rozin generalizes as "the right to be heard or to be heeded,"[10] recurred up and down the roster of associates—internally displaced persons (IDPs), disabled veterans, economic casualties, neighborhood committees, and inductees' families.

Rozin ties together the discussion of the right to be heard or heeded, as manifested in Israel's early years, by speaking of "the pursuit of recognition"—"a positive right, requiring society and policy makers in particular to make an effort to listen." This cannot be assured by law or constitution. The demand for the fulfillment of "the right to be heard" reflects a profound need for belonging, consideration, respect, and appreciation on the part of society and its policy makers.[11]

A clear and consistent line may be drawn between the patterns evinced by those who spoke out during the War of Independence and those that Rozin detects and reveals in sovereign Israel's early years. The similarity does not end with the methods adopted by individuals and groups that demanded to be heard. It manifests in the ethnic and class diversity of those doing the speaking and in the response to their voice by media and policy makers alike. To get to the bottom of this phenomenon in its Jewish-Israeli context, one must, it seems, plunge into earlier realms of history—the settings of Jewish life in the various Diaspora communities and the patterns of citizenship that took shape there. This, of course, is the concern of another study.

From the affirmative presented above, obviously one may adduce the negative—tasks that are customarily assigned to community associations at times of crisis but were basically overlooked in the War of Independence. Women's organizations did provide various vital services in part (e.g., clothing, food, childcare, and housing). Often, however, the services were delivered under the auspices of a local or national leadership, so that in the recipients' eyes they were given by "the authorities."[12] Additional voluntary entities that operated under the auspices of "the authorities"—the People's Guard and the General Service[13]—guarded damaged neighborhoods, provided first aid, and had vital equipment delivered. They, too, however, operated on behalf of the fighting forces and with their patronage;

therefore, their ministrations were correctly perceived as the doings of "the authorities."[14]

A possible explanation for the relative paucity of such service activities among civic associations in the War of Independence is that local or national leaderships were never totally absent at any of the focal points of crisis described in this study. Thus, despite the leaderships' cumbersomeness, inefficiency, and resource limitations, no vacuum took shape in the chain of command that led from the affected individual to the governmental authority. One may also hypothesize that the authorities' proximity to those affected made it easier for associates to address their requests to powers that, at least in theory, if not in practice, had the resources that were needed. This nearness was twofold—physical (geographic closeness of local offices of community councils, municipal departments, and divisions of the National Institutions) and symbolic (belonging to the same community of residents). This often resulted in personal acquaintance and yielded information about what the National Institutions and their appendages—situation committees, special committees, the municipality of Tel Aviv, and the Jerusalem and Haifa community councils—dealt on a regular, if not a daily, basis with in the implications of the war for civilian life.

Another question evoked by the study of civic association in the War of Independence concerns the potential adverse implications of community resilience for the resilience of the population at large. The possibility of such a failure has been pointed out both by scholars of civil society and by researchers of humanitarian disasters and crises.[15] It is captured in the imbalance between the collective of citizens who form associations—the community that is aware of its entitlements and has the ability to engage in associative action, choose its representatives, and make its voice heard—and the nonassociated public: passive, disadvantaged, incapable, and above all lacking the means for collective action.

A pervasive assumption among researchers in this field is that those associating belong to social strata that are "strong" to begin with—well educated, economically solid, and socially well connected. One often finds relations between these characteristics and origins or, in common locutions in the Israeli context, intra-ethnic affiliation and longevity in the country.

Attempting to answer this question, this study ran into a methodological catch-22: the more it focused on those who associated and acted, the more it overlooked those who did not. Consequently, it could not characterize the damage inflicted by those who associated on others. An additional and special difficulty encountered in this context was the inability to track the activities of associative settings in the ultra-Orthodox neighborhoods of Jerusalem, despite widespread testimonies about the existence of such settings among that population group. The difficulty traces mainly to the separate channels of communication that the ultra-Orthodox used (via the Eida Chareidis or Agudath Israel, for example) and the community's avoidance of direct contact with the National Institutions.[16] Another group absent in this study is the Palestinian population of Jaffa, the Arab neighborhoods of western Jerusalem, and the Lower City of Haifa. Although there is reason to assume that internal association occurred among this population before it was displaced and left the country,[17] documentation on a scale that would allow thorough and consistent comparative examination of this activity is not as yet available. Since this population, however, interacted with its own authorities and not vis-à-vis the (Jewish) National Institutions and their appendages and experienced the war from the other side of the divide, it entails its own separate and thorough research. Such research is waiting to be done, and I contend, on the basis of the current study, that the researcher who would manage to track down associative mechanisms and characteristics in the Palestinian refugee camps may fill gaps in our understanding of the unfolding of the Nakba.

What the current study can provide is an analysis of the characteristics of those who formed the associations that were chosen for inclusion in this book due to the salience and intensity of the founders' activities. It is not argued that this study covers all civic associative endeavors on the Jewish side. It does, however, encompass a broad and representative range of community associators who were driven to act by and for themselves in response to the extent of harm that they sustained.

Were they all members of the veteran middle class? Were most of them of European origin? Were they largely male? Were the inhabitants of long-standing, well-off neighborhoods represented first and foremost? Did they hold political party and movement membership cards and thus were represented in the decision-making centers?

The answers that this study offers are clear. Those associating came from a very broad ambit of social sectors—from the well-established urban business class to the population of craftspeople, petty merchants, and temporary workers. Consequently, they represented a range of educational and socioeconomic backgrounds. Some of their family names indicate origins in Syria, Iraq, Yemen, and other non-European extraction, even though most of the Yishuv population was of European provenance. (Mass Jewish immigration from Islamic countries would not take place until the end of the war and, with even greater intensity, in the 1950s.)

In most cases, the associates' partisan affiliations are hard to determine because they tended to reject categorically any attempt to attribute covert political intentions to their activity. The associations of the disabled and the committees of IDPs in Haifa and Tel Aviv are cases in point. Elsewhere, there were partisan connections and even political aspirations that were clear to everyone. Members of the soldiers' wives and women's organizations, for example, openly maintained their movements' partisan links but operated under an umbrella that took this into account. Such was also the case with the association of homeowners, which declared its intent of running for elections and exerting influence inside the tent.

Some of those who formed associations did belong to the Yishuv's social elites. Many of the disabled war veterans, members of the "1948 generation," fall into this category. Nevertheless, when one follows the struggles and the rhetoric of associates who belonged to the older and more connected groups in the Yishuv, one does not find a demand for priority and entitlement by dint of social position. Importantly, too, all of those associating, irrespective of their position at the socioeconomic starting gate, were directly affected by the state of war and resorted to the instrument of association to cope with the crisis. Thus, irrespective of the circles from which they came, the war toppled them into distress with which they sought to cope via the tool of association.

A sociological indicator of all the associations apart from those of women and of soldiers' wives is the almost total absence of women at the level of internal leadership. Here and there, a woman is mentioned in the context of a committee of IDPs or an association of micro-business owners. These women's names, however, always come up in isolation; rarely are they personalities who spearhead struggles or speak for an entire interest group. This is probably an indication of male dominance in the public sphere of the time. It indicates not that women were absent among the associates but only that they usually acted behind the scenes and not at the front of the stage.

Another question that the study brings to the fore concerns the accepted image of Yishuv society as a mobilized one and the tendency to link the level of commitment and mobilization to achievements in the war. Can the particularistic community initiatives examined in this study be seen as early indications of fissures in the national collectivism of the Yishuv era? Does the profusion of civil associations imply a lower level of solidarity and shakier social cohesion than have been assumed? The answer to both questions appears to be yes. This does not refute the familiar basic premise about the Yishuv that it had a broad national common denominator in its commitment to the overarching goal of the Zionist Movement: establishing Jewish sovereignty in the Land of Israel. Nevertheless, a close observation of a given reality, as would be done by zooming in on a photograph, reveals gray spots. These spots, invisible in a distance shot, become people who have clashing interests when observed from up close and in focus. Indeed, there were various conflicts of interest that impaired solidarity; there were even blatant demonstrations of a lack of solidarity. It happened when groups organized for action against the IDPs and when vendors of certain goods clashed with manufacturers or consumers of the same goods. The extensive documentation about the struggles and collisions among groups of associates and between them and representatives of the authorities do reveal cracks in the Yishuv's front of solidarity. Although the existence of these clefts is known from previous studies, their possible effects on social cohesion in a state of emergency have been examined only in a limited scope and context.[18]

The answer to the first question also seems simple and unequivocal. The images of the Yishuv as a collectivistic and mobilized society overstate the case and do not square with the particularistic outlooks that typified the stakeholders. Such a question, however, is tested not in the range of colors that one proposes to include in the prism of Yishuv society but in the outcome. Did this multiplicity of shades and contrasts erode the community resilience of the Jewish population in the War of Independence? Or might it be the other way around—did it provide the civilian casualties of the war with coping tools that empowered them and gave them channels on which they could take action and speak out?

The plain facts known to us are the following: Those who brandished the tool of civil association expressed resentment and protest, established channels of dialogue with the authorities, and also, in many cases, made inroads in secondary policy-making settings and impeded the advancement of policies to which they objected. In greater part, however, their distress persisted throughout the war, and their basic problems defied solution until the hostilities ended, and even then, they were requited incompletely.

Further research should, of course, examine the revitalization and rehabilitation processes, some decades long, and contemplate some of the basic problems that arose during the war and under its circumstances and the way they evolved over the years—questions of locating provisional and permanent housing for the IDPs, rehabilitating the disabled, placing the economy on solid footing, and compensating business owners for lost income.

The question of the importance of civic associations in influencing the course of the war remains moot. The answer may be based, at the most, on circumstantial evidence and findings from corresponding studies. Even so, the importance and contribution of this study goes beyond zero-sum considerations such as these.

My premise, which this study does promote, is that the associative life of the Jewish community during Israel's War of Independence offers a case study of an importance that transcends the time and place of the events. By tracing the typical complexions and patterns of the associative enterprise in this specific war, one may propose patterns of activity for societies that find themselves in crisis. Even if such patterns of self-instigated action may not always yield the hoped-for results, they provide casualties of disaster with an instrument or a bridge with which they may challenge the situation imposed on them, as passive victims, and become active casualties whose voices are heard—stakeholders and community members who have a say and whose distress neither blurs their identity nor renders them into passive objects on history's chessboard.

Notes

1. Sebastian Haffner, *Defying Hitler: A Memoir (Geschichte eines Deutschen)*, Oliver Pretzel, trans. (New York: Picador, 2002).

2. Daniel P. Aldrich, *Building Resilience: Social Capital in Post-Disaster Recovery* (Chicago: University of Chicago Press, 2012), loc. 188 (Kindle edition); Henry W. Fischer, *Response to Disaster: Fact Versus Fiction and Its Perpetuation* (Lanham, MD: University Press of America, 1998), 3.

3. Aldrich, *Building Resilience,* loc. 70, 76, 175 (Kindle edition).

4. Connie P. Ozawa, "Planning Resilient Communities: Insights from Experiences with Risky Technologies," in *Collaborative Resilience: Moving through a Crisis to Opportunity,* Bruce E. Goldstein, ed. (Cambridge, MA: MIT Press, 2012), 19.

5. Robert Putnam, *Bowling Alone: The Collapse and Revival of American Community* (New York: Simon and Schuster, 2001), 19.

6. Golam M. Mathbor, "Enhancement of Community Preparedness for Natural Disasters: The Role of Social Work in Building Social Capital Sustainable Disaster Relief and Management," *International Social Work* 50, no. 3 (2007).

7. Archong Fung, "Associations and Democracy: Between Theories, Hopes and Realities," *Annual Review of Sociology* 29 (2003): 520; Mark E. Warren, *Democracy and Association* (Princeton and Oxford: Princeton University Press, 2001), 74; Joshua Cohen and Joel Rogers, "Associations and Democracy," *Social Philosophy and Policy* 10, no. 2 (1993): 289.

8. Mark E. Warren, *Democracy and Association* (Princeton: Princeton University Press, 2001), 71–2.

9. Aldrich, *Building Resilience*, loc. 895–906; 1088, 1089 (Kindle edition).

10. Orit Rozin, *A Home for All Jews: Citizenship, Rights and National Identity in the New Israeli State* (Waltham, MA: Brandeis University Press, 2016), loc. 378–83 (Kindle edition).

11. For discussion of this concept and the research literature dealing with it, see Rozin, *A Home for All Jews*, loc. 2615–22 (Kindle edition).

12. Under the heading of *authorities*, I also include, apart from the National Institutions (and their successors, the offices of the provisional government) and the municipalities, the community councils, which served as leaderships in the cities, and the Haganah—the militia that was subordinate to the National Institutions. Due to this subordination, the public perceived them (correctly) as representatives of the authority, even though they operated on a voluntary basis.

13. See introduction, pages 11, 13–14 (this volume).

14. On the activities of the People's Guard, see pages 149, 167–172 (this volume) and Moshe Naor, *Social Mobilization in the Arab-Israeli War of 1948: On the Israeli Home Front* (London and New York: Routledge, 2013), 38–42.

15. For example, Joshua Cohen and Joel Rogers, "Associations and Democracy," *Social Philosophy and Policy* 10, no. 2 (1993): 295–6. For example, Aldrich, *Building Resilience*, loc. 1153–9, 1516–28 (Kindle version).

16. Moshe Ehrenwald's studies shed light on these population groups and, foremost, on their leadership and their relations with the authorities but have little to say about autonomous organizational settings. See, for example, Moshe Ehrenwald, "Civilians in the Northern Neighborhoods of Jerusalem," in *Civilians at War: Studies on the Civilian Society during the Israeli War of Independence* (in Hebrew), Mordechai Bar-On and Meir Chazan, eds. (Jerusalem and Tel Aviv: Ben-Zvi Institute, 2010), 161–2; and Moshe Ehrenwald, *Siege within Siege: The Jewish Quarter in the Old City of Jerusalem During the War of Independence* (Sede Boqer Campus: Ben-Gurion Research Institute, 2004).

17. See, for example, Ellen L. Fleischmann's study on Palestinian women's associations during the British Mandate period: Ellen L. Fleischmann, *The Nation and Its "New" Women: The Palestinian Women's Movement, 1920–1948* (Berkeley: University of California Press, 2003).

18. See, for example, Tammy Razi, *Forsaken Children: The Backyard of Mandate Tel Aviv* (in Hebrew) (Tel Aviv: Am Oved, 2009); Deborah Bernstein, *Women on the Margins: Gender and Nationalism in Mandate Tel Aviv* (in Hebrew) (Jerusalem: Yad Izhak Ben-Zvi, 2008). An exception is Naor's work, which does look into some of these rifts (mainly those caused by socioeconomic inequality) and their impact on solidarity during the war.

BIBLIOGRAPHY

Introduction

Aldrich, Daniel P. *Building Resilience: Social Capital in Post-Disaster Recovery*. Chicago: University of Chicago Press, 2012.
Bandora, Albert. "Exercise of Personal and Collective Efficacy in Changing Societies." In *Self-Efficacy in Changing Societies*, Albert Bandora, ed. Cambridge: Cambridge University Press, 1995.
Bar-On, Mordechai, and Meir Chazan, eds. *Civilians at War: Studies on the Civilian Society During the Israeli War of Independence* (in Hebrew). Jerusalem and Tel Aviv: Ben-Zvi Institute, 2006, 2010.
Bar-On, Mordechai, and Meir Chazan, eds. *Politics in Wartime: Studies on the Civilian Society During the Israeli War of Independence, Vol. C*. Jerusalem: Ben-Zvi Institute, 2014.
Ben Pazi, Shmaryahu. "The Citrus Harvest and Its Impact on the Intercommunal War During the Winter and Spring of 1948." In *Civilians at War: Studies on the Civilian Society During the Israeli War of Independence* (in Hebrew), Mordechai Bar-On and Meir Chazan, eds. Jerusalem and Tel Aviv: Ben-Zvi Institute, 2006.
Ben Pazi, Shmaryahu. "Not by Bread Alone: The Cereal Market During the Intercommunal War." In *Civilians at War: Studies on the Civilian Society During the Israeli War of Independence* (in Hebrew), Mordechai Bar-On and Meir Chazan, eds. Jerusalem and Tel Aviv: Ben-Zvi Institute, 2010.
Cnaan, Ram A., Carl Milofsky, and Albert Hunter. "Introduction: Creating a Frame for Understanding Local Organizations." In *Handbook of Community Movements and Local Organizations*, Ram A. Cnaan, Carl Milofsky, and Albert Hunter, eds. New York: Springer Science and Business Media, 2008.
Cohen-Levinovsky, Nurit. *Jewish Refugees in Israel's War of Independence* (in Hebrew). Sede Boqer Campus and Tel Aviv: Am Oved, 2014.
Ehrenwald, Moshe. *Siege within Siege: The Jewish Quarter in the Old City of Jerusalem During the War of Independence*. Sede Boqer Campus: Ben-Gurion Research Institute, 2004.
Eshel, Tzadok. *The Hagana's Battle for Haifa* (in Hebrew). Tel Aviv: Ministry of Defense, 1978, 1998.
Fine, Jonathan. "The Impact of the War on the Establishment of the Government System of Israel, 1947–1949." In *Civilians at War: Studies on the Civilian Society During the Israeli War of Independence* (in Hebrew), Mordechai Bar-On and Meir Chazan, eds. Jerusalem and Tel Aviv: Ben-Zvi Institute, 2006.
Fung, Archon. "Associations and Democracy: Between Theories, Hopes and Realities." *Annual Reviews of Sociology* 29 (2003): 515–539.
Golan, Arnon. *Wartime Spatial Changes: Former Arab Territories within the State of Israel, 1948–1950* (in Hebrew). Sede Boqer Campus: Ben-Gurion Research Institute, 2001.
Greenberg, Itzhak. "Military Recruitment of Manpower for Vital Services and Economic Enterprises." In *Civilians at War: Studies on the Civilian Society During the Israeli War*

of Independence (in Hebrew), Mordechai Bar-On and Meir Chazan, eds. Jerusalem and Tel Aviv: Ben-Zvi Institute, 2006.

Haffner, Sebastian. *Defying Hitler: A Memoir (Geschichte eines Deutschen)*. Oliver Pretzel, trans. New York: Picador, 2002.

Justino, Patricia. *War and Poverty: IDS Working Paper* 2012, no. 391. Institute of Development Studies, Conflict Violence and Development Research (April 2012): 11–2.

Kabalo, Paula, and Alon Lazar. "Jewish Social Entrepreneurship in Jerusalem and Jaffa, 1880–1914." *Giving, Thematic Issues in Philanthropy and Social Innovation* 2 (2008): 151–68.

Kabalo, Paula. "The Historical Dimension: Jewish Associations in Palestine and Israel, 1880s–1950." *Journal of Civil Society* 5, no. 1 (2009): 1–20.

Kidron, Anat. "The Committee of the Jewish Community in Haifa and its Role in the Struggle to Shape Haifa's Civilian Character." In *Civilians at War: Studies on the Civilian Society During the Israeli War of Independence* (in Hebrew), Mordechai Bar-On and Meir Chazan, eds. Jerusalem and Tel Aviv: Ben-Zvi Institute, 2010.

Lautze, Sue, and John Hammock. "Coping with Aid Capacity Building, Coping Mechanisms and Dependency, Linking Relief and Development." Paper prepared for the UN Inter-Agency Standing Committee Sub-Working Group on Local Capacities and Coping Mechanisms and the Linkages between Relief and Development, Lessons Learned Unit Policy and Analysis Division, Department of Humanitarian Affairs, United Nations Organization (1996): 3.

Levy, Itzhak. *Jerusalem in the War of Independence* (in Hebrew). Tel Aviv: Ministry of Defense, 1986.

Mathbor, Golam M. "Enhancement of Community Preparedness for Natural Disasters: The Role of Social Work in Building Social Capital Sustainable Disaster Relief and Management." *International Social Work* 50, no. 3 (2007): 357–69.

Morris, Benny. *1948: A History of the First Arab-Israeli War*. New Haven, CT: Yale University Press, 2008.

Naor, Moshe. *On the Home Front: Tel Aviv and Mobilization of the Yishuv in the War of Independence*. Jerusalem: Ben-Zvi Institute, 2009.

Patterson, Olivia, Frederick Weil, and Kavita Patel. "The Role of Community in Disaster Response: Conceptual Models." *Population Research and Policy Review* 29 (2010): 129.

Putnam, Robert. *Bowling Alone: The Collapse and Revival of American Community*. New York: Simon and Schuster, 2000.

Rozin, Orit. *The Rise of the Individual in 1950s Israel: A Challenge to Collectivism*. New England: Brandeis University Press, 2011.

Salamon, Lester M., and Helmut K. Anheier, "In Search of the Nonprofit Sector II: The Question of Classification." *Voluntas* 3, no. 3 (1992): 267–309.

Slutsky, Yehudah, ed. *History of the Haganah, Vol. 3, Part II* (in Hebrew). Tel Aviv: Am Oved, 1973.

Vincent, Marc, and Birgitte Refslund Sørensen, eds. *Caught between Borders: Response Strategies of the Internally Displaced*. London: Pluto, 2001.

Warren, Mark E. *Democracy and Association*. Princeton and Oxford: Princeton University Press, 2001.

Yaron, Michal. "The Roles and Activities of Women in the People's Guard [Mishmar ha-ha-'Am]." In *Anthology of the People's Guard [Mishmar ha-'Am] in Jerusalem, 1947–1949* (in Hebrew). Jerusalem: Mishmar Ha'am Activists and Organization of Hagana Members, 1965.

Yosef, Dov. *The Faithful City: The Siege of Jerusalem, 1948* (in Hebrew). Tel Aviv: Schocken, 1960; (in English): Simon and Schuster, 1960.
Ziv-Av, Nahum. "Towards a Popular Organization." In *The Book of the Hagana in Tel Aviv* (in Hebrew). Tel Aviv: Hagana Foundation, 1957, 140–43.

Chapter 1

Audoin-Rouzeau, Stéphane, and Annette Becker. *Understanding the Great War*. New York: Hill and Wang, 2003.
Cohen-Levinovsky, Nurit. *Jewish Refugees in Israel's War of Independence* (in Hebrew). Sede Boqer Campus and Tel Aviv: Am Oved, 2014.
Davar (Hebrew-language newspaper).
Ehrenwald, Moshe. "Civilians in the Northern Frontier Neighborhoods of Jerusalem." In *Civilians at War: Studies on the Civilian Society During the Israeli War of Independence* (in Hebrew), Mordechai Bar-On and Meir Chazan, eds. Jerusalem and Tel Aviv: Ben-Zvi Institute, 2010.
Gatrell, Peter. "Refugees and Forced Migrants During the First World War. *Immigrants and Minorities* 26, no. 1/2 (2008).
Goebel, Stefan. "Schools." In *Capital Cities at War: Paris, London, Berlin, 1914–1918, Vol. 2*, Jay Winter and Jean-Louis Robert, eds. Cambridge: Cambridge University Press, 2007, 188–234.
Golan, Arnon. "The Jewish Refugees in the War of Independence" (in Hebrew). *Contemporary Jewry* 8 (1993): 217–242.
Golan, Arnon. *Wartime Spatial Changes: Former Arab Territories within the State of Israel, 1948–1950* (in Hebrew). Sede Boqer Campus: Ben-Gurion Research Center, 2001.
Goren, Tamir. *The Fall of Arab Haifa in 1948* (in Hebrew). Sede Boqer Campus: The Ben-Gurion Research Institute for the Study of Israel and Zionism, 2006.
Hamashkif (Hebrew-language newspaper).
Kabalo, Paula. "Leadership Behind the Curtains: The Case of Israeli Women in 1948." *Modern Judaism* 28 (2008): 14–40.
Kälin, Walter. "Guiding Principles on Internal Displacement." *Studies in Transnational Legal Policy* 38 (2008). The American Society of International Law and the Brookings Institution, University of Bern Project on Internal Displacement, Washington, DC.
Kidron, Anat. "The Committee of the Jewish Community in Haifa and Its Role in the Struggle to Shape Haifa's Civilian Character" (in Hebrew). In *Civilians at War: Studies on the Civilian Society During the Israeli War of Independence*, Mordechai Bar-On and Meir Chazan, eds. Jerusalem and Tel Aviv: Ben-Zvi Institute, 2010, 343–379.
Minutes of Situation Committee (small quorum) meeting, March 8, 1948. Abba Khoushy Archive, Situation Committee Correspondence, Minutes, and Reports, 1354631, A1/59:3.
Morris, Benny. *The Birth of the Palestinian Refugee Problem, 1947–1949*. Cambridge: Cambridge University Press, 1988.
Nahmias, Benzion. *Tel Aviv as a Front and Its Commander, Michael (James) Ben-Gal* (in Hebrew). Tel Aviv: Friends of Haganah, 1998, 161.
Naor, Moshe. *On the Home Front: Tel Aviv and Mobilization of the Yishuv in the War of Independence*. Jerusalem: Ben-Zvi Institute, 2009.
Naor, Moshe. *Social Mobilization in the Arab-Israeli War of 1948: On the Israeli Home Front*. London and New York: Routledge, 2013.

Proctor, Tammy M. *Civilians in a World at War, 1914–1918*. New York: New York University Press, 2010.
Rozin, Orit. *A Home for All Jews: Citizenship, Rights and National Identity in the New Israeli State*. Waltham, MA: Brandeis University Press, 2016.
Ulitsky, Yosef. *From Troubles to War: Episodes in the History of the Defense of Tel Aviv* (in Hebrew). Tel Aviv: Hagana Headquarters Publishing House, 1951.
Vincent, Marc, and Birgitte Refslund Sørensen, eds. *Caught between Borders: Response Strategies of the Internally Displaced*. London: Pluto, 2001.
Yanai, Yosef. "Schools and Haifa and Tel Aviv During the War." In *Civilians at War: Studies on the Civilian Society During the Israeli War of Independence* (in Hebrew), Mordechai Bar-On and Meir Chazan, eds. Jerusalem and Tel Aviv: Ben-Zvi Institute, 2010.
Yedioth Ma'ariv (Hebrew-language newspaper), March 22, 1948.

Chapter 2

Barkai, Haim. *The Genesis of the Israeli Economy* (in Hebrew). Jerusalem: Bialik Institute, 1990.
Gross, Nachum T. *Not by Spirit Alone: Studies in the Economic History of Modern Palestine and Israel*. Jerusalem: Magnes and Yad Izhak Ben-Zvi, 1999.
Gross, Nachum T. "The Economic Policy of the British Mandate Government in Palestine (Part B)" (in Hebrew). *Cathedra* 25 (1983): 135–168.
Lawrence, Jon. "Material Pressures on the Middle Classes." In *Capital Cities at War: Paris, London, Berlin, 1914–1918*, Vol. 1, Jay Winter and Jean-Louis Robert, eds. Cambridge and New York: Cambridge University Press, 1997, 229–254.
Morris, Benny. *1948: A History of the First Arab-Israeli War*. New Haven, CT: Yale University Press, 2008.
Naor, Moshe. "From Economic Globalization to the Austerity Front: Rationing and Price-Control Policy During the War." In *Civilians at War: Studies on the Civilian Society During the Israeli War of Independence* (in Hebrew), Mordechai Bar-On and Meir Chazan, eds. Jerusalem and Tel Aviv: Ben-Zvi Institute, 2006.
Naor, Moshe. *Social Mobilization in the Arab-Israeli War of 1948: On the Israeli Home Front*. London and New York: Routledge, 2013.
Robert, Jean-Louis. "The Image of the Profiteer." In *Capital Cities at War: Paris, London, Berlin 1914–1918, Vol. 2*, Jay Winter and Jean-Louis Robert, eds. Cambridge: Cambridge University Press, 2007.
Winter, Jay. "Paris, London, Berlin, 1914–1919: Capital Cities at War." In *Capital Cities at War: Paris, London, Berlin, 1914–1918*, Vol. 1, Jay Winter and Jean-Louis Robert, eds. Cambridge and New York: Cambridge University Press, 1997.
Yosef, Dov. *The Faithful City: The Siege of Jerusalem, 1948*. New York: Simon and Schuster, 1960.

Chapter 3

Davar (Hebrew-language newspaper), December 25, 1942, March 16, 1948.
Gelber, Yoav. *Independence versus Nakba* (in Hebrew). Or Yehuda: Kinneret Zmora Bitan, Dvir, 2004.
Gelber, Yoav. *The History of Volunteering, Vol. 4, British, Arabs, and Germans* (in Hebrew). Jerusalem: Yad Izhak Ben-Zvi, 1984.
Ha'aretz (Hebrew-language newspaper).

Kadish, Alon, ed. *Israel's War of Independence 1948–1949 Revisited, Part 1* (in Hebrew). Tel Aviv: Ministry of Defense, 2004.
Lev-Ari, Shulamit. "How the Yishuv Looks Out for Inductees' Families: Upon the Establishment of the Yishuv Inductee and Family Committee." *Ha'aretz* (Hebrew-language newspaper), April 12, 1948.
Mathbor, Golam M. "Enhancement of Community Preparedness for Natural Disasters: The Role of Social Work in Building Social Capital for Sustainable Disaster Relief and Management." *International Social Work* 50, no. 3 (2007): 357–369.
Naor, Moshe. *Social Mobilization in the Arab-Israeli War of 1948: On the Israeli Home Front.* London and New York: Routledge, 2013.
Ostfeld, Zehava. *An Army Is Born: Main Stages in the Construction of the Israel Defense Forces and the Ministry of Defense under David Ben-Gurion* (in Hebrew). Tel Aviv: Ministry of Defense, 1994.
Slutsky, Yehuda. *History of the Haganah, Vol. 3, Part 1* (in Hebrew). Tel Aviv: Am Oved, 1972.
Stock, Ernst. *Beyond Partnership: The Jewish Agency and the Diaspora, 1959–1971.* New York: Herzl, 1992.
Suissa, Esther. "The Politics of Philanthropy: The Creation and Work of the Israel Education Fund, 1964–1967." MA Thesis in Israel Studies, Ben-Gurion University of the Negev, 2014.

Chapter 4

Adger, W. Neil, Terence P. Hughes, Carl Folke, Stephen R. Carpenter, and Johan Rockström. "Social-Ecological Resilience to Coastal Disasters." *Science* 309 (2005): 1038.
Aleksandrowicz, Or. "Civilian Demolition: The Premeditated Destruction of the Manshiyya Neighborhood in Jaffa, 1948–1949." *Iyunim Bitkumat Israel* 23 (2013): 274–314.
Ben-Bassat, Yuval. "On Telegrams and Justice: Petitions from Residents of Jaffa and Gaza to the Grand Vizier in Istanbul in the Late Nineteenth Century" (in Hebrew). *The New East* 49 (2010): 30–52.
Cohen-Levinovsky, Nurit. *Jewish Refugees in Israel's War of Independence* (in Hebrew). Sede Boqer Campus and Tel Aviv: Am Oved, 2004.
Davar (Hebrew-language newspaper), August 9, 1948, December 13, 1948, February 24, 1949, March 15, 1949, June 10, 1949.
Ehrenwald, Moshe. "Civilians in the Northern Border Neighborhoods of Jerusalem." In *Civilians at War: Studies on the Civilian Society During the Israeli War of Independence* (in Hebrew), Mordechai Bar-On and Meir Chazan, eds. Jerusalem and Tel Aviv: Ben-Zvi Institute, 2010.
Ehrenwald, Moshe. *Siege within Siege: The Jewish Quarter in the Old City of Jerusalem During the War of Independence.* Sede Boqer Campus: Ben-Gurion Research Institute, 2004.
Golan, Arnon. "The Reshaping of Erstwhile Arab Space and the Formation of Israeli Space (1948–1950)." In *Israel's War of Independence Revisited* (in Hebrew), Alon Kadish, ed. Tel Aviv: Ministry of Defense, 2004.
Golan, Arnon. *Wartime Spatial Changes: Former Arab Territories within the State of Israel, 1948–1950* (in Hebrew). Sede Boqer Campus: Ben-Gurion Research Center, 2001.
Goren, Tamir. *The Fall of Arab Haifa in 1948* (in Hebrew). Sede Boqer Campus: The Ben-Gurion Research Institute for the Study of Israel and Zionism, Ben-Gurion University of the Negev, 2006.
Ha-Boker (Hebrew-language newspaper), September 14, 1948.

Ha-Yoman (Hebrew-language newspaper), September 15, 1948.
Herut (Hebrew-language newspaper), June 10, 1949.
Jerusalem People's Guard Collection (in Hebrew), 1964.
Kidron, Anat. "The Committee of the Jewish Community in Haifa and its Role in the Struggle to Shape Haifa's Civilian Character." In *Civilians at War: Studies on the Civilian Society During the Israeli War of Independence* (in Hebrew), Mordechai Bar-On and Meir Chazan, eds. Jerusalem and Tel Aviv: Ben-Zvi Institute, 2010.
Levy, Itzhak. *Nine Shares: Jerusalem in the Battles of the War of Independence* (in Hebrew). Tel Aviv: Ministry of Defense Publishing House, 1986.
Ma'ariv (Hebrew-language newspaper), June 2, 1948.
Mathbor, Golam M. "Enhancement of Community Preparedness for Natural Disasters." *International Social Work* 50, no. 3 (2007): 362.
Morris, Benny. *1948: A History of the First Arab-Israeli War*. New Haven, CT: Yale University Press, 2008.
Naor, Moshe. "Post-War Relief and Rehabilitation: The Ministry for War Casualties, 1948–1951" (in Hebrew). *Cathedra* 138 (2011): 139–64.
Patterson, Olivia, Frederick Weil, and Kavita Patel, "The Role of Community in Disaster Response: Conceptual Models." *Population Research and Policy Review* 29 (2010): 127–141.
Radai, Itamar. *A Tale of Two Cities: The Palestinian Arabs in Jerusalem and Jaffa, 1947–1948*. Tel Aviv: The Moshe Dayan Center for Middle Eastern and African Studies, Tel Aviv University, 2015.
Steiner, Puah. *From the Midst of the Turmoil: Between the Walls of Jerusalem in the 1948 War* (in Hebrew). Jerusalem: Tzviya, 1983.
Ulitsky, Yosef. *From Troubles to War: Episodes in the History of the Defense of Tel Aviv* (in Hebrew). Tel Aviv: Hagana Headquarters Publishing House, 1951.

Chapter 5

Al Hamishmar (Hebrew-language newspaper), September 9, 1948.
Alyagon, Ofra. "Herman Hollander's Forty Days." Ofra Alyagon Complete Writings. Accessed February 4, 2020 (quotation from August 30, 2013), http://www.ofra-alyagon.co.il.
Approval of Governance and Jurisprudence Ordinance, 5708–1908. Official Gazette no. 2 (in Hebrew), May 21, 1948.
Davar (Hebrew-language newspaper).
Emergency Regulations (Repair of Houses Damaged by War), amendment to the Law and Administration Ordinance, 1949. *Official News Paper* 46: 143–6.
Golani, Motti. "Jerusalem's Hope Lies Only in Partition: Israeli Policy on the Jerusalem Question, 1948–1967." *International Journal of Middle Eastern Studies* 31, no. 4 (1999): 577–604.
Gross, Nachum T. *Not by Spirit Alone: Studies in the Economic History of Modern Palestine and Israel*. Jerusalem: Magnes and Yad Izhak Ben-Zvi, 1999.
Hatzofe (Hebrew-language newspaper), September 9, 1948, September 17, 1948, September 29, 1948, April 10, 1949.
Herut (Hebrew-language newspaper), May 13, 1949.
Kabalo, Paula. "Occupational Identity in Wartime—The Chambers of Commerce." In *Economy at War: Studies on Civilian Society During the Israeli War of Independence* (in Hebrew), Mordechai Bar-On, Itzhak Greenberg, and Meir Chazan, eds. Jerusalem: Yad Izhak Ben-Zvi, 2017: 166–199.

Ma'ariv (Hebrew-language newspaper), May 6, 1948, May 30, 1948, June 3, 1948, June 22, 1948, June 23, 1948, June 30, 1948, September 29, 1948, October 10, 1948.

Naor, Moshe. "From Economic Globalization to the Austerity Front: Rationing and Price-Control Policy During the War." In *Civilians at War: Studies on the Civilian Society During the Israeli War of Independence* (in Hebrew), Mordechai Bar-On and Meir Chazan, eds. Jerusalem and Tel Aviv: Ben-Zvi Institute, 2006.

Naor, Moshe. *On the Home Front: Tel Aviv and Mobilization of the Yishuv in the War of Independence.* Jerusalem: Ben-Zvi Institute, 2009.

Rozin, Orit. *Duty and Love: Individualism and Collectivism in 1950s Israel* (in Hebrew). Tel Aviv: Am Oved, 2008.

Shetreet, Shimon. "Emergency Legislation in Israel in Light of Basic Law: Legislation" (in Hebrew). *Law and Government* 1 (1993): 433.

Tovy, Jacob. *On Its Own Threshold: The Formulation of Israel's Policy on the Palestinian Refugee Issue, 1948–1956* (in Hebrew). Sede Boqer Campus: The Ben-Gurion Research Institute for the Study of Israel and Zionism, Ben-Gurion University of the Negev, 2008.

Chapter 6

Al Hamishmar (Hebrew-language newspaper), August 1, 1948.

Almog-Bar, Michal, and Ester Zychlinski, "It Was Supposed to Be a Partnership—Interrelations between Philanthropic Funds and Government in the Niv Venture" (in Hebrew). *Social Security* 83 (June 2010).

Bryson, John M., Barbara C. Crosby, and Melissa Middleton Stone. "The Design and Implementation of Cross-Sector Collaborations: Propositions from the Literature." *Public Administration Review* 66 (2006): 44–55.

Davar (Hebrew-language newspaper), August 6, 1948, March 14, 1949.

Gazley, Beth, and Jeffrey L. Brudney. "The Purpose (and Perils) of Government-Nonprofit Partnership." *Nonprofit and Voluntary Sector Quarterly* 36 (2007): 389–415.

Ilan, Amitzur. *The Origin of the Arab-Israeli Arms Race: Arms, Embargo, Military Power and Decision in the 1948 Palestine War.* New York: New York University Press, 1996.

Ma'ariv (Hebrew-language newspaper), May 10, 1948, June 27, 1948, August 8, 1948, September 2, 1948.

Maimon, Ada. *Fifty Years of the Women's Labor Movement, 1904–1954* (in Hebrew). Tel Aviv: Ayanot, 1955.

Markovitzky, Yaakov. "Foreign Recruitment in the War of Independence." In *Israel's War of Independence Revisited, Vol. 1*, Alon Kadish, ed. Tel Aviv: Ministry of Defense, 2004.

Ostfeld, Zehava. *An Army Is Born: Main Stages in the Construction of the Israel Defense Forces and the Ministry of Defense under David Ben-Gurion* (in Hebrew). Tel Aviv: Ministry of Defense, 1994.

Suissa, Esther. "The Politics of Philanthropy: The Creation and the Work of the Israel Education Fund, 1964–1967." MA Thesis in Israel Studies, Ben-Gurion University of the Negev, 2014.

Chapter 7

Al Hamishmar (Hebrew-language newspaper), November 19, 1948, December 22, 1948, December 23, 1948, December 24, 1948, April 5, 1949, April 6, 1949, April 26, 1949, May 13, 1949, May 19, 1949, June 29, 1949, August 5, 1949.

Davar (Hebrew-language newspaper), January 7, 1949, April 17, 1949, May 19, 1949, May 25, 1949, June 12, 1949, June 26, 1949.

Disabled Veterans (Benefits and Rehabilitation) Law, 5709–1949 (second and third discussions). *Divrei ha-Knesset*, Session 79. September 8, 1949, 1633–1636, 1644.

Disabled Veterans Law, 5709–1949 (first discussion). *Divrei ha-Knesset*, Session 76. September 5, 1949, 1572–1573.

Ha-Boker (Hebrew-language newspaper), December 22, 1948.

Hatzofe (Hebrew-language newspaper), March 22, 1949, April 5, 1949, May 19, 1949, May 25, 1949, October 18, 1949.

Herut (Hebrew-language newspaper), March 18, 1949, April 5, 1949, April 15, 1949, April 18, 1949, April 22, 1949, April 27, 1949, May 19, 1949.

Kabalo, Paula. "Constructing Civil Society: Citizen Associations in Israel in the 1950s." *Nonprofit and Voluntary Sector Quarterly* 35, no. 2 (2006): 161–82.

Lautenberg, Yosef (Yoske), and David Green, eds. *Giborei Ha'il, the Full Story, the Organization of Disabled IDF Veterans, 1948–1998* (in Hebrew). Tel Aviv: Green Publications, 2005.

Ma'ariv (Hebrew-language newspaper), April 11, 1949, April 26, 1949, June 2, 1949, June 12, 1949, September 9, 1949.

Markovitzky, Yaakov. "Machal—Overseas Volunteers in Israel's War of Independence." In *Israel's War of Independence Revisited*, Vol. 1, Alon Kadish, ed. Tel Aviv: Ministry of Defense, 2004.

Morris, Benny. *1948: A History of the First Arab-Israeli War*. New Haven, CT: Yale University Press, 2008.

Nadav, Daniel. "The Beginning of Rehabilitation of Casualties in Israel's Wars." *'Alei zayit ve-herev* 4 (2002): 275–299.

Nadav, Daniel. *The Ministry of Defense Rehabilitation Division, 1948–1998: Rehabilitation of IDF and Defense System Disabled Veterans and Survivors, Fundamentals and Changes* (in Hebrew). Tel Aviv: Ministry of Defense Documentation and Historical Research Unit, 1999.

Naor, Moshe. "The 1948 War Veterans and Postwar Reconstruction in Israel." *Journal of Israeli History* 29, no. 1 (2010): 47–59.

Ohry, Avraham, and A. Shaked, eds. *Introduction to Rehabilitation Medicine*. Tel Aviv: Israel Ministry of Defense, 1990.

Paran, Geula. "The Spirit Entered Them and They Came to Life. They Stood Upon their Feet: The Development of the Rehabilitation Medicine in Israel as a Reflection for Changes in Israeli Society, 1948–1974." PhD Dissertation, Bar-Ilan University, 2014.

Conclusion

Aldrich, Daniel P. *Building Resilience: Social Capital in Post-Disaster Recovery*. Chicago: University of Chicago Press, 2012.

Bernstein, Deborah. *Women on the Margins: Gender and Nationalism in Mandate Tel Aviv* (in Hebrew). Jerusalem: Yad Izhak Ben-Zvi, 2008.

Cohen, Joshua, and Joel Rogers. "Associations and Democracy." *Social Philosophy and Policy* 10, no. 2 (1993): 289.

Ehrenwald, Moshe. "Civilians in the Northern Neighborhoods of Jerusalem." In *Civilians at War: Studies on the Civilian Society During the Israeli War of Independence* (in

Hebrew), Mordechai Bar-On and Meir Chazan, eds. Jerusalem and Tel Aviv: Ben-Zvi Institute, 2010.
Ehrenwald, Moshe. *Siege within Siege: The Jewish Quarter in the Old City of Jerusalem During the War of Independence*. Sede Boqer Campus: Ben-Gurion Research Institute, 2004.
Fischer, Henry W. *Response to Disaster: Fact Versus Fiction and Its Perpetuation*. Lanham, MD: University Press of America, 1998.
Fleischmann, Ellen L. *The Nation and Its "New" Women: The Palestinian Women's Movement, 1920–1948*. Berkeley: University of California Press, 2003.
Fung, Archong. "Associations and Democracy: Between Theories, Hopes and Realities." *Annual Review of Sociology* 29 (2003): 520.
Haffner, Sebastian. *Defying Hitler: A Memoir (Geschichte eines Deutschen)*. Oliver Pretzel, trans. New York: Picador, 2002.
Mathbor, Golam M. "Enhancement of Community Preparedness for Natural Disasters: The Role of Social Work in Building Social Capital Sustainable Disaster Relief and Management." *International Social Work* 50, no. 3 (2007): 357–69.
Naor, Moshe. *Social Mobilization in the Arab-Israeli War of 1948: On the Israeli Home Front*. London and New York: Routledge, 2013.
Ozawa, Connie P. "Planning Resilient Communities: Insights from Experiences with Risky Technologies." In *Collaborative Resilience: Moving through a Crisis to Opportunity*, Bruce E. Goldstein. ed. Cambridge, MA: MIT Press, 2012.
Putnam, Robert. *Bowling Alone: The Collapse and Revival of American Community*. New York: Simon and Schuster, 2001.
Razi, Tammy. *Forsaken Children: The Backyard of Mandate Tel Aviv* (in Hebrew). Tel Aviv: Am Oved, 2009.
Rozin, Orit. *A Home for All Jews: Citizenship, Rights and National Identity in the New Israeli State*. Waltham, MA: Brandeis University Press, 2016.
Warren, Mark E. *Democracy and Association*. Princeton, NJ: Princeton University Press, 2001.

LIST OF ARCHIVES

Abba Khoushy Archives
Ben-Gurion Archive
Central Zionist Archives
Haifa Municipal Archives
Israel Defense Forces Archives
Israel State Archives
Jerusalem Municipal Archives
Lavon Labor Archive
Tel Aviv Chamber of Commerce Archives
Tel Aviv Municipal Archives

INDEX

Page numbers in italics denote photos.

Adger, W. Meil, 176
Administration of Enemy Property, 190, 259
Agudath Israel (political party), 16, 170–71, 173, 296
Ahdut ha-'Avoda (political party), 112, 230, 246n49, 258, 285n87
Aldrich, Daniel P., 291–93
Al Hamishmar (newspaper), 189, 209n33, 231, 247n74, 253–54, 260, 270, 282n13, 282n15, 282nn17–18, 284n58, 284n67, 284nn70–71, 284nn75–76, 285n79, 286n123, 288n180
Alperin, Haim, 12, 27, 35, 42, 44, 52–54, 58n80, 60n117, 60n120, 60n126, 60nn128–129, 61n153, 62n166, 62nn174–176, 60n180, 63nn187–188, 160, 163–64, 178n44, 181nn96–98
Alsheich, Yehuda, 173–74, 183n153, 183n160, 183n165
Altalena (arms vessel), 276, 287n156
Amadi, Baruch, 174
Amdur, Alexander, 168
Artisans Center and the Middle Class Organization, 72
Association of Homeowners in Palestine, 61n135
Association of Importers and Wholesalers in Palestine, 67, 70, 72, 74–75, 102n20, 103n54, 104nn66–67, 187,189, 193, 196, 210n53, 210n59
Avniel, Binyamin, 123, 125–26, 133n83, 133n94, 133n103

Baratz, Yosef, 118, 214
Bar Rav Hai, David, 36
Barda, Pini, 169–70, 182n129, 182n134
Barkai, Haim, 73, 103n39
Bavli, Yitzhak, 72, 75–76, 102n32, 103n60

Begin, Menachem, 276
Ben-Ami, Moshe, 167, 179
Ben-Dor, Rafael, 173–74, 182n149, 182n151, 183n154, 183n157
Ben-Eliezer, Arieh, 276
Ben-Gurion, David, 14, 71, 76, 87, 112–20, 125–26, 165, 215, 234–35, 252–53, 257–60, 263–66, 268–70
Ben-Nissan, Emanuel, 159–60, 180nn74–75, 180n81, 180n84, 180n90
Bentov, Mordechai, 234
Ben-Zvi, Izhak, 77, 104n72
Bergman, Abraham, 171, 182n141, 182n143, 203, 212n111
Bernstein, Peretz, 68, 71, 74–75, 102n20, 103n42, 103nn51–52, 103n54, 109n192, 186–87
Better Business Association, 99, 108n186
Bidlowski, Moshe, 97
B'nai B'rith Order in Palestine, 99
Brandwein, Zusha, 174, 183n162
British Army, 30, 53, 111, 129n3, 222, 268, 270, 282n14
British Mandate, 1, 4, 8–10, 13, 23, 29, 64–66, 67, 69–70, 73, 75, 80–81, 89–90, 111, 115, 129n3, 175, 180n85, 186, 194, 203, 216, 275
Brutzkus, Eliezer, 161–62, 180n88
Burg, Joseph, 258, 269

Carmel (Zelicki), Moshe, 12
Central Committee for Soldiers' Families, 241, 243, 249nn125–26, 249n128, 249n136, 249n138, 249n141
Chamber of Commerce, 11, 46, 50, 61n159, 67–68, 69–75, 78–79, 88, 92, 102nn17–18, 102n22, 102n30, 103n37, 103n44, 103nn49–51, 103n55, 103nn57–59, 104nn65–67, 104n71, 107n148, 109n192,

313

Chamber of Commerce (*Cont*)
185–89, 192–97, 207, 208n7, 208nn9–10, 208nn12–18, 209n19, 209nn21–23, 209nn25–26, 209n31, 209nn33–34, 209n37, 209n39, 209n44, 210nn50–53, 210nn58–62, 210n64; Advisory Committee, 61n132, 68–69, 71, 73–75, 102n9, 102n14, 187. *See also* Haifa and Jerusalem, Chambers of Commerce
Chelouche, Moshe, 92
Citizens Union, 80, 83
Cohen, Abraham Zusman (A. Z.), 189
Cohen-Kagan, Rachel, 33
Cohen-Levinovsky, Nurit, 24, 29
Cohen, Meir, 203
Cohen, Menahem, 35, 43–44
Cohen, Rahel, 131n34, 222
Cohen, Wili, 279
Committee for Care of Soldiers' and Guards' Families, 111, 120
Committee of Disabled at Tel Hashomer, 265
Committee of General Labor Exchanges, 128
Committee of Women's Organizations for Refugee Affairs, 58n67
Council of Women's Organizations (CWO), 33, 121–22, 127, 132n65, 133nn106–107, 213
Crohn, David, 257–58, 283n43

Davar (newspaper), 38, 40, 49, 55n14, 56n23, 56n32, 57nn48–49, 57n61, 58n69, 59n89, 59nn95–96, 59n106, 59n108, 60n115, 61nn146–147, 61n152, 61n156, 62n179, 63n186, 92, 120–21, 130n20, 132n56, 132n63, 132n68, 166–67, 179n68, 180n91, 181nn113–114, 181n116, 196, 208n8, 210n57, 210n63, 210n70, 247n93, 249n137, 283n42, 284n73, 285n80, 286nn111–115, 286n119
Deir Yassin massacre, 146
Demobilized Officers Housing Association, 280, 289n186
Demobilized Soldiers (Return to Work) Bill (1948–49), 259, 262, 269–70, 272
Demobilized Soldiers Housing Committee, 280, 289n187
Diamant, Rivka, 219, 245n21, 248n97

Disabled Veterans Law (1949), 264, 266, 285n86
Dror, Shalom, 31, 57n52

Economic Bureau for Palestine, 106n131
Economic Self-Defense Committee, 188
Economic Subcommittee (Subcommittee A), 72, 102nn26–27, 107n145
Eliachar, Menache Hai, 78, 80–82, 89–90, 104nn74–75, 104n78, 104n84, 105n88, 105n92, 105n101, 105n109, 190–92
Emergency Economic Council, 66, 71–72
Etkes, Jacob, 152, 211n91
Etzion (Gruenwald), Moshe, 271–74, 279
Eve's Task Force, 121
Experts Committee, 73

Farmers Association, 104nn66–67, 106n124, 117, 186
Feldman, Michal, 125, 133n97
Fishman-Maimon, Yehuda, 201, 288n164
Foeder, Herbert, 185–86
Friedland, Uriel, 151, 153, 178nn31–32, 178n40, 199
Friedman, Mordechai, 92, 107n143

Gadna (youth troops), 13
Gal (assistance to disabled veterans of the War of Independence in Jerusalem), 275
Galili, Israel, ix, 111, 113, 117–18, 130n9, 130n17, 131nn38–39, 133n93
Gelblum, Arieh, 116, 131n32
General Council of Frontier Refugees, 35, 42
General Federation of the Middle Class in Palestine, 94, 107nn157–158, 109n194
General Merchants Association, 11, 47, 94, 104nn66–67, 186, 200, 207
General Service, 11, 19n33, 55n10, 56n29, 294
General Zionists Party, 76
Globman-Guvrin, Akiva, 264, 272, 274, 285n88
Grabovsky, Meyer, 115, 117, 131n26, 240–41, 248n120
Gronich, Haya, 226, 248n97
Grossman, Meir, 193–94, 210n53
Gruenbaum, Yitzhak, 275, 287n152

Gurion, Yosef, 253, 255, 263, 266–67, 269–74, 283n30, 285n95
Gutel Levin, Moshe, 37

Ha'aretz (newspaper), 116, 122, 129nn3–4, 131nn31–32, 132n74
Ha-Boker (newspaper), 169, 182n130, 253–54, 256, 282nn16–17, 282n20
Haboura, Ezra, 44
Hadassah women's organization, 33, 117
Hadera: Committee of Organization for Inductees' Families, 236, 249n133; Organization of Inductees' Wives, 236, 242, 248n98, 248n101
Hadi, Menahem, 60n119, 165, 167, 181n116
Haganah, 10–15, 30–32, 37, 41, 43, 45, 50, 53, 55n13, 57n52, 59n86, 62n167, 77, 85, 88, 110–14, 117–20, 122, 125, 130n10, 130n17, 131nn40–41, 132n48, 132nn50–55, *140*, 163, 300n12
Haifa: Association of Artisans and Petty Industry, 47, 61n138; Central Committee for Soldiers' Families, 249n133; Chamber of Commerce, 87–88, 106nn121–123, 109n192, 197–98, 209n49, 210nn73–74; Committee of Old Commercial Center Residents and Merchants, 198, 200, 210nn79–80, 211n87, 211nn91–92; Community Council, 13–14, 20n50, 28, 36–40, 48, 50, 54, 56nn33–34, 58n81, 59n101, 60n111, 85–87, 106n124, 149–52, 175–76, 200, 295, 300n12; Community Council committees: Emergency Housing Committee, 28; Executive Committee, 177n20; Situation Committee, 98, 56n34, 60nn110–111; Field Corps, 13; Grocery Merchants Federation in Haifa and the Vicinity, 97, 108n178, 108n185; Hadar Hacarmel Committee, 178n31; Hebrew Scouts Association, 49; Homeowners Association, 204, 212nn115–118; Housing Committee, 149; Housing Department, 151–52, 199–200; Mount Carmel Refugee Camp Committee, 60n110; Neighborhood committees, 88, 106n127, 153; Organization of Hoteliers, Restaurateurs, and Café Owners, 59n104; Organization of Inductees' Families, 249n132; Organization of Inductees' Wives, 220–21, 222–23, 238, 245n29, 245n38, 246nn46–47, 248n105, 248n107, 293; Parents committee of Yavne Reali School and Haifa Religious High School, 61n144; Public Office for Consultation and Maintenance of Economic Life in the City of Haifa, 86, 106n114, 106n118; Refugees Bureau, 37, 52, 56n34, 56n38, 57n62, 57n65, 58n81, 58n84, 59n103, 61n143, 62nn171–173, 150, 178nn21–22; Refugees Committee, 36–37, 39–40, 52, 59n87, 153; Sephardi Community Committee, 62n169; Situation Committee, 13–14, 28, 35–37, 40, 49, 52, 56nn33–35, 56n38, 56nn39–41, 59n85, 59nn90–94, 59n104, 60nn109–111, 60n113, 61n138, 61n155, 86–88, 103n34, 106nn111–112, 106n114, 106nn116–118, 106n121, 106nn127–129, 108n178, 108nn184–185, 151–153, 178n27, 178n29, 178n31, 197–202, 204, 208n6, 210n49, 210nn72–73, 210nn77–80, 211nn82–91, 211n94, 211n96, 211nn99–101, 212nn115–118, 295; Situation Committee: Economic Department, 190; Executive Board, 62n168, 62n170, 177nn18–19, 178n35; Subcommittee for Lower Haifa Affairs, 106n126; Transport Committee, 199–200, 211n88; United Committee of Haifa Refugees, 59n97, 59n101, 60n111, 60n114
Halva'a ve-Hisakhon Bank, 83
Hamashbir Hamerkazi (supplier cooperative), 68, 71, 191
Ha-Mivrak (newspaper), 163–64, 181n99
Hammock, John, 34, 129
Hapoel Hamizrachi (religious Zionist organization), 48, 60n118, 61n149, 180n73, 224, 258
Hashahar (association), 33, 57n64
Ha-Yoman (newspaper), 170, 182n131
Hazan, Yitzhak, 174
Herut (movement), 104, 181, 271, 275, 283
Herut (newspaper), 180n92, 210n68, 260, 283nn44–45, 283n48, 284n57, 284n60, 284n63, 284n65, 284n69, 284n71, 285n78

Histadrut, 66, 71–72, 120, 122, 130n17, 132n71, 191, 193–94, 207, 222, 224–27, 278; Committee for Inductees, 225; Executive Committee, 186, 222, 232, 237, 248nn99–100; Women's Labor Council, 122

Hoffman, Nehama, 58n70, 121, 132n68

Hollander, Hermann, 188–90, 192, 195, 209n24, 209n46

Homeowners Association, 99, 203–4, 212n113, 212nn115–117. *See also* Haifa and Jerusalem Homeowners Association

Housing Department, 56n28, 150, 199–200. *See also* Haifa, Jerusalem, and Tel Aviv Housing Departments

Hurricane Katrina, 5

al-Husseini, Abdel Khadr, 84

Idelson, Beba, 33, 121–22, 222–45, 232, 236–40, 245n38, 245n40, 246n44, 246n47, 248nn99–100

Idud, Ltd. (financial-services company), 83

Importers and Wholesalers Company in Palestine, Ltd., 70

Initiating Committee of Demobilized Soldiers, 269

Internally Displaced Persons (IDP), 12, 23–29, 32–49, 51–54, 92, 101, 110, 145–46, 148–50, 153–54, 156–59, 163–76, 177n12, 178n21, 181n104, 294, 297–99

International Chamber of Commerce, 187, 208n14

Israel Defense Forces (IDF), 9, 11, 154, 180n83, 204, 206, 213, 215, 252, 277–78; Carmeli Brigade, 13; Culture Service, 218; Etzioni Brigade, 14, 57n52, 256; Finance Division, 239; Givati Brigade, 11; Kiriati Brigade, 11; Manpower Division, 213; Medical Service, 252–55, 257–58, 283n31; overseas volunteers (*see* Mahal); Personnel Branch, 218, 248n96

Israel Emergency Damage Mutual Insurance Fund, Ltd., 150

Israel Police, 277, 288nn170–171, 289n186

Israel's War of Independence (1948), xi, xiii, 1–2, 4, 6, 8, 10, 17, 23–24, 65–66, 180n85, 255, 262, 275–77, 279–80, 285n89, 290–91, 293–95, 298–99

IZL (National Military Organization), 11, 53, 62n177, 180n70, 276–77, 287n156, 289n188

Jaffa, 9, 11, 23, 25, 30, 41, 44, 46, 51, 53–54, 62n178, 62n183, 62n185, 68, 90, 107n157, 135f1, 146, 148, 154–59, 161, 163, 180n85, 185, 188, 193–94, 196, 204, 208n13, 208n15, 209n20, 209nn25–26, 210n68, 255–60, 262–63, 283n44, 296; Committee of Mahane Yosef and Other Neighborhoods, 157, 179n62, 179n64; Joint Committee for the annexation of Jaffa's Jewish neighborhoods, 155–56, 179n50; Rehabilitation Center, 251–56, 260–61, 263, 283n49, 285n96; United Committee of Jewish Neighborhoods, 154–57, 179n45

Jerusalem: Bakers Union, 91, 107nn138–40, 107n151, 107n153, 107n156; Ben-Yehuda Street Casualties Committee, 85, 105n110, 202, 293; Casualties Care Committee, 79, 105n98; Chamber of Commerce, 67, 89, 105n89, 106n121, 109n192, 190, 192, 209n46; Committee for Civilian Affairs and the Jewish Quarter, 183n159; Committee for Inductees and Their Families, 245n22; Committee for the Reconstruction of the Commercial Center, 77–78, 81–83, 104n86; Community Council, 15–16, 28–29, 46, 48, 54, 56n42, 57n51, 57n63, 61n133, 77, 79, 84–85, 90–91, 95, 98, 105n102, 105n109, 106n136, 108n176, 169, 171–72, 175, 295, 300n12; Community Council Committees: Emergency Supplies Committee, 89, 100; Housing Committee, 82, 107n145, 182n123; Situation Committee, 15, 29–32, 56n42, 84, 91, 97, 104n83, 104n165, 295; Supply Committee, 89, 92, 94–95, 97, 100, 106n130, 107n141, 108nn174–175, 108n177, 109n189, 192; Council of the Military Government, 151, 172, 192, 205 (*see also* Jerusalem Committee); Crafts and Manufacturing Affairs Committee, 211n107; Department for Care of Old City Refugees in Katamon, 172, 174, 182n147, 182n150, 183n155; Development Commission, 169; Emergency Committee, 92–93, 95–96, 104n85, 107n151, 107nn153–156,

108n168; Emergency Committee: Supply Subcommittee, 108n170, 108n172, 109n191; Emergency Committee of Merchants and Residents on Princess Mary Street, Julian's Way, Storrs Avenue, and Central Building, 82, 105n94, 105n96; Fund for Casualties of the Events in Jerusalem, 203, 212n108; Grocers' Situation Committee, 99, 108n170, 108n172, 108nn174–177, 109n189, 109n191; Hebrew Neighborhoods Bloc, 57n71; Homeowners Association, 46, 61n133, 202–3, 211n102, 212n111; Housing Department, 171; Institutions Committee, 31, 91; Investigative Committee on Bread Prices, 107n144; Jerusalem Association of Crafts and Petty Manufacturing, 203, 211n107; Jerusalem Committee, 15–16, 123, 126, 149, 151, 172, 190–92, 205–6, 212n120, 219, 284n70 (*see also* Council of the Military Government); Jerusalem Council, 177nn14–15, 178n23, 182n147, 182n150, 183n155; Katamon Jewish Committee in the Holy City of Jerusalem, 175, 183n161, 183nn163–164; Katamon Old City Refugees Committee, 172, 174–75, 183n152, 183n165; Labor Council, 78, 245n26; Merchants Organization, 101, 190; Military Governor, 15–16, 133n97, 149, 167, 169–71, 174–75, 177n15, 182nn139–141, 182n143, 183n157, 183nn160–161, 183nn164–165, 192, 202–4, 209nn44–45, 212n124, 275–76, 287n151; Military Governor committee: Social Affairs Committee, 133n97; Mobilization and Salvage Fundraising Committee, 105n98; Municipal Council, 104n68, 107n143, 169; National Institutions and Chamber of Commerce Committee for Care of Casualties of the Events in Jerusalem, 79, 81, 85, 104n73, 104n76, 104n82, 105n90, 105nn92–93, 105n100; Old City Evacuees Committee, 174, 183n160; Organization of Cafés, Restaurants, and Hotels, 205–6, 108n165, 212n120, 212n124, 212n126; Organization of Wholesalers, 192; People's Guard, 13–16, 29, 123, 149, 167–171, 175–76, 181nn119–120, 181n122, 182nn123–124, 182n127, 294, 300n14; People's Guard department: Population Care Department, 182n129; Reconstruction Committee, 104n83; Security Committee, 105n96; Talpiot and North Talpiot Situation Committee, 57n54, 57n57; Talpiot Bloc Committee, 31; United Bakeries, Berman, Angel Keter, Ltd., 106n136; War Casualties Department, 178n23

Jewish Agency, 16, 61n135, 68, 70, 74, 83, 91, 105n101, 107n138, 132n60, 164, 169; Department of Trade and Industry, 67–68, 102n9, 102n14; Economic Department, 193–94; Import-Export Department, 73; Jewish Agency Executive, 67, 73, 76, 130n17, 185, 242, 252; Political Department, 35
Jewish Community Council, 105n92, 105n102, 106n136, 108n176
Jewish National Fund, 36
Journalists Association, 89

Kahane, Avraham, 69, 193–94
Kaplan, Eliezer, 70–71, 189, 195, 209nn29–30, 209n32, 233, 235
Kaplan, Elisheva, 226, 232–33, 238, 242–43, 248n121, 249nn132–133, 248n141
Katz, Shmuel, 276
Kesari, Uri, 217, 245n15, 260, 284n60
Knesset, 58, 167, 181n110, 194, 212n112, 243, 246n59, 248n115, 258–59, 262, 264, 267, 269–70, 277–78, 283n46, 283nn48–49, 284n54, 284nn75–77, 285nn78–79, 288n180; Labor Committee, 243, 267, 271–72, 283n30, 285n95, 285n102, 285n106, 285n109, 287n137, 287nn141–142
Kobashi, Saadia, 222
Kofer Hayishuv (special fund to cover the Yishuv's security needs), 112
Kotzer, Rafi, 265, 268, 273
Kroch, Arieh, 49, 61n155

Labor Movement, 68, 94, 108n171, 120, 191, 247n69
Lamdan, Hannah, 264, 267, 274, 285n87
Landau, Chaim, 276
Laskow, Tsipora, 226, 232
Lautze, Sue, 34, 129

Lehi (Jewish Freedom Fighters), 11, 163, 180n70, 277–78, 288n168
Lev-Ari, Shulamit, 124
Levi, Meir Moshe, 77
Levin-Epstein, Eliezer, 252, 255–56, 283n31
Levine, Yitzhak Meir, 173
Lifschitz, Shaul, 70, 75, 103nn51–52, 106n117, 188, 195–97
Lipson, Eliezer, 117–18, 131n41
Loewenstein, Fritz, 124, 133n89, 133n98, 133nn100–101, 133n104
Lubianker (Lavon), Pinhas, 262
Lubianker, Zvi, 98
Lubinski (Lotan), Georg (Giora), 120, 131n40, 132n60, 132n67, 132n73, 133n93, 134n108, 220, 236, 241, 243, 245n25, 247n95
Luria, Arthur, 252, 282n10
Lurie, Zvi, 95, 108nn162–63

Maccabi Neighborhood Cooperative Association, 156
Maccabi World Union, 117
Mahal (volunteer enlistees from abroad), 270, 275, 278–81, 288n175
Maki (Israel Communist Party), 262, 271
Manufacturers Association, 11, 72, 75–76, 99, 186, 207
Mapai (political party), 58n79, 71, 107n143, 115, 178n31, 181n110, 239, 245n33, 246n59, 248n121, 264, 273, 285n87
Mapam (political party), 230–31, 234, 246n49, 247nn74–75, 260, 264, 267–68, 273, 285n97; Mapam Central Committee, 249nn125–126
Markovitzki, Yaakov, 279–80
Mathbor, Golam M., 176, 292
Meir, Golda, 104n64, 115, 131n27
Merchants Association, 11, 94, 186, 200
Meridor, Ya'akov, 276
Merlin, Shmuel, 276
Middle Class Organization, 72, 104nn66–67, 186
Milk Producers Union, 89
Min-Hahar, Shlomo, 174, 183nn159–160
Ministry of Defense, 218, 236, 243, 247n95, 248n96, 249n135, 253, 258, 265–66, 270, 278–79, 288n172, 288n175; Division for Soldiers' Families, 236, 243, 247n95, 248n96; Inspection Division, 256; Public Relations Division, 263; Rehabilitation Division, 265, 267
Ministry of Finance, 189, 195–96, 228, 233, 234
Ministry of Housing, 170
Ministry of Industry and Trade, 186, 188, 195
Ministry of the Interior, 156, 159, 180n77, 202, 275–76, 278, 280, 287n151, 287nn153–155, 288n159, 288n166, 288nn171–172, 288n175, 289n184, 289n187
Ministry of Labor and Construction, 227, 246n43, 246n51
Ministry of Minorities and Police, 180n74
Ministry of Religious Affairs, 159, 180n77, 201
Ministry of Supply and Rationing, 195–96
Ministry of Welfare, 159, 172, 180n77, 180n84
Mizrahi, Avraham Yosef, 174
Mollek, Eliezer, 152
Müller, A., 188, 209

Nadivi, Yehuda, 30, 60n118, 177n12, 180nn78–80, 180n83, 181n107
Naor, Moshe, 47, 71
Naqibli, Gabriel, 36, 58n81, 59n86
Nathan, Hans, 124, 133n89
National Command Center, 130n11
National Committee, 16, 35, 61n134, 79, 83, 95, 99, 107n149, 108n179, 108n186, 111, 115, 118, 130, 131n26, 185, 222, 242, 246n59, 248n123; Economics Department, 68, 102n18, 102n27; Social Work Department, 33, 116, 131n40
National Committee for the Jewish Soldier, 118, 131n40
National Committee of Disabled Veterans of the Current War, Rehabilitation Center No. 1, 254, 260–61, 282n24, 283n40, 284nn68–69
National Council, 69, 99
National Institutions, 3, 6, 9–10, 13, 15–16, 64–84, 86, 89–90, 92, 99, 111, 114, 117, 120, 131n37, 169, 177n14, 185, 197, 199, 223, 290, 295–96, 300n12; Committee for Jerusalem Affairs, 31, 91; Emergency Committee for Jerusalem, 92
National Service Census Board, 120, 123, 125

National Union of Sephardim and Mizrahim, 167
Nir (Rafalkes), Nahum, 231, 258
Nissan, Meir, 41, 60n110, 60n113

Office of the Controller of Imports and Stocks, 186
Olshan, Yitzhak, 92, 107n143
Oren, Baruch, 260–61, 284n61, 284nn63–65
Organization of Demobilized Soldiers and Disabled and Wounded Veterans of the War of Independence, 262. *See also* Gal
Organization of Disabled Veterans, 265, 267–68, 271, 285n97. *See also* Committee of Disabled at Tel Hashomer; Disabled Veterans Law
Organization of Inductees' Wives, x, 221, 224–25, 227–28, 233, 236, 238–39, 241–42, 297. *See also* Hadera and Haifa Organization of Inductees' Wives
Organization of Small Public Car Drivers, 89
Organization of Soldiers' Families, 229, 232–33, 242, 247n76, 247n85, 248n101, 249n132. *See also* Central Committee for Soldiers' Families; Ministry of Defense Division for Soldiers' Families
Organization of Working Mothers (OWM), 28, 120–22, 132n61, 220, 222, 225–27, 233, 245n17, 245n27, 246n48
Ottoman Law of Societies, 275–76, 280, 287n155
Ovadia, Yehuda, 174, 183nn159–160
Owners in Internal Service, 89
Ozawa, Connie P., 292

Padeh, Baruch, 266
Palestine Pharmacists Federation, 89
Palestine Union, Ltd., 203, 212n108
Palestinian Nakba, 2, 8, 296
People's Administration, 154
Perlson, Eliezer, 30, 35, 44, 57n46, 58n80, 60nn125–126, 61n149, 94, 98, 103n36, 107n157, 108n186, 131n40, 133n93, 185–86, 210n74
Persons with Disabilities Law, 277
Petah Tikva Organization of Inductees' Wives, 222
Pinkas, David-Zvi, 238–39, 241, 248

Pitchon, Menachem, 98, 165–67, 243
Provisional Government, 72, 76, 102n12, 154, 187, 199, 227, 232–35, 242, 246n43, 247n86, 249n128, 300n12
Provisional State Council, 222, 228, 232, 234–35, 238–39, 245n34, 246n58, 246n60, 246n65, 247n89
Public Organization for the Soldier's Family, 230, 235, 238

Rabinov, Baruch, 120, 239
Refugees, x, 2, 8, 15, 24–25, 27–30, 33–43, 46–47, 49–54, 56n22, 56nn27–28, 56nn31–32, 56n34, 57n61, 58n67, 58n70, 58nn77–78, 59n89, 59nn95–96, 59n106, 61n152, 61n156, 62n165, 62n169, 63n186, 132n68, 149, 157, 159, 164–65, 167–70, 177n16, 179n63, 181n99, 181n104, 181n120, 182n131, 296. *See also* Committee of Tel Aviv Frontier Refugees in Salameh Village; General Council of Frontier Refugees; Haifa Refugees Bureau; Jerusalem Department for Care of Old City Refugees in Katamon; Katamon Old City Refugee Committee; Manshiya and Hassan Bek Refugees Committee; Mount Carmel Refugee Camp Committee; United Committee of Haifa Refugees
Rehovot Labor Council, 245n27
Reifen, David, 251, 282n5, 283n32
Remez, David, 35, 58n81, 115, 118, 127, 131n34, 131n43
Repetur, Berl, 112, 130n14, 230–32, 234–35, 239, 247n69, 247n74, 260, 284n58
Revisionist Movement, 193
Rishon Lezion Labor Council, 237, 248nn99–100
Robert, Jean-Louis, 100
Rokach, Israel, 29, 42, 50, 57nn46–47, 58n78, 60n117, 60n119, 60n127, 61n139, 61n159, 62nn161–164, 62n166, 100, 107n158, 108n186, 109n194, 155–56, 161, 166, 177n11, 178nn41–44, 178n44, 179nn48–49, 179nn51–53, 179nn55–56, 179n58, 179nn61–62, 179n64, 180nn75–76, 180nn81–82, 180nn86–88, 180n90, 181n96, 181n106, 181nn109–110
Rosen, Dov, 170, 181n119, 182n133, 182n136

Rosetti, Moshe, 269
Rozin, Orit, 3, 294
Rubin, Hanan, 267
Rwanda, genocide, 5

Sakharov, Israel, 194
Salomon, Haim, 77, 104n71, 105n92, 105n105, 108n176, 177n15, 182n147, 182n150, 183n155
Salomon, Nehemia, 92, 107n143
Scheiber (Sheba), Chaim, 252, 266, 283n31
Scheinsohn, Benjamin, 194
Schneider, Nahum, 165
Second Lebanon War (2006), xi
Serri, Naomi, 173
Shafrir, Dov, 257, 283n42
Shaltiel, David, 256–57, 283n34
Shatner, Mordechai, 68–69, 73, 98, 102n18, 103n36, 106n135, 107n145, 108n162, 108nn179–180, 228–29, 231, 241, 243, 246n59, 249n128, 249nn134–135, 249n141
Sheetrit, Bechor, 159–60, 179n45, 179n47, 180n76
Shenkar, Arieh, 76, 104n64
Shkolnik (Eshkol), Levi, 112, 117, 130n10, 133n84
Shoshan, Yehuda, 174
Shoshani, Nuriel, 174
Shoshani, Sa'adia, 50, 61n135, 203–4, 212n113
Shoshani, Yehezkel, 30, 57n47
Shotet, B., 164, 181nn99–104
Slutsky, Yehuda, 12
Social Relief Bureau, 58n67
Society for the Rehabilitation of Freedom Fighters, 276, 287n158
Soldier's Welfare Committee, 117–18, 127, 248n98
Solel Boneh (construction company), 71, 82
Special Sale Committee, 188
Supplies Committee, 96
Suzajev, Zalman, 102n20, 103n49, 196
Svirsky, Moshe, 111–12, 129n2
Swiss-Palestine Chamber of Commerce, 99

Tabachnik, Riva, 226–27
Taneh, David, 59n90, 151, 153, 178nn33–34
Tel Aviv: Association of Home and Property Owners, 47, 50, 62n160, 154; Association of Importers, 109n192, 186; Blobstein Orphanage, 58n73; Builders Association, 47, 61n139; Central Parents Committee, 48; Civil Guard, 11–12, 27, 30, 164; Committee of Tel Aviv Frontier Refugees in Salameh Village, 166–67, 181n110; Committee of Tel Aviv Workers Quarters G, 62n164; Committee of Workers Quarters E–F, 62n164; Eliyahu Hanavi Synagogue Committee, 61n153; Emergency Internal Executive Committee, 106n133; Field Corps, 10–11; Frontier Refugees Secretariat, 60n119; General Committee of New Immigrants, Salameh Neighborhood, 81nn106–107; General Council for Frontier Refugees, 43, 58n78, 60n119, 165; General Federation of Merchants, 107n157; Hebrew Medical Association, 46, 51, 61n136, 62n163; Jamusin Village Committee, 43–44, 60n125, 60nn128–129; Joint Committee. See Jaffa Joint Committee; Kerem Hatemanim Committee, 60n127, 180n86; Lahmeinu Cooperative Bakery of Consumers Unions in Tel Aviv and the Vicinity, Ltd., 106n135; Maccabi Barracks Neighborhood Cooperative Association, 29, 57n46, 156, 179nn55–56; Maccabi Neighborhood Committee, 57n46; Manshiya and Hassan Bek Refugees Committee, 180nn74–75, 180n82, 180n84; Municipality: Economic Department, 90, 92, 106n133; Health Department, 131n42; Housing Department, 56n28, 61n136; Hygiene Committee, 51, 62n163; Inspection Department, 45, 53, 149, 160, 166, 177n11; Municipal Council, 98, 155, 161–62, 165–67; Neighborhoods Department, 58n79; Property Damage Department, 179n54; Sanitation Department, 12, 154; Social Work Department, 12, 34, 58nn72–73, 154, 178n43; Supply Committee, 94; New Shapira Neighborhood Committee, 179; Organization of Cafés, Restaurants, and Sausage Stands, 107n158; Salameh Village Committee, 181n109; Shivat Tziyon National Religious Association, 61n153; Situation Committee for Control of the Sale of Flour and Bread, 92; Tel Amal Neighborhood Com-

mittee, 30, 57n49, 106n127; Town Council, 49–51, 63n186, 92, 156; United Committee of Jewish Neighborhoods, 154–55, 179n45, 179n52
Tepper, Eliyahu, 165
Third sector, x, 3, 207, 214
Tnuva, 71, 82, 186
Trade and Industry Club, 195

Union of Commissioners, 187
Union of Demobilized Soldiers, 262, 268–69, 270–75, 279, 281, 286n110, 286n120, 286nn123–125, 286n129, 287n150
Union of Margarine Manufacturers, 89
Union of Oil Manufacturers, 89
United Nations, 18n10, 252; Department of Humanitarian Affairs, 18n10, 58n75, 134n111; General Assembly, 8, 10, 25, 67; Resolution 181 (United Nations Partition Plan for Palestine), 8, 10–11, 16, 25, 67, 85, 145

Vogel, David, 41, 59n101
Voice of Israel (VOI; radio station), 38

War Casualties Ministry, 150, 156, 159, 168, 173–74, 178nn23–24, 180n77, 180n84, 201, 204, 212n113, 261, 275–77, 287n152, 287n154, 288n164; Property Damage Department, 156, 175n54, 180n84
Warhaftig, Zerach, 77
Warren, Mark E., 6–7, 293
Weizmann, Chaim, 165
Werfel, Yitzhak, 105n101, 178n23, 277, 288n164
Wilner, Meir, 262
WIZO (Women's International Zionist Organization), 28, 33, 58n67, 58n74, 94, 222, 224
Women Workers Council, 218
Women's Labor Council, 33, 117, 120, 122, 218–19, 221–27, 232, 237, 239, 245n18, 245n20, 245n28, 245n36, 246nn42–43,
246n46, 246n48, 246nn50–51, 248n103, 249n130, 249n133, 249n136
World War I (1914–1918), x, 24, 66, 100, 244, 270–71
World War II (1939–1945), 13, 65, 95, 111–12, 117–18, 214, 218, 221–22, 226, 228, 244, 251, 268, 270, 282n14, 284n71

Yedioth Ma'ariv (newspaper), 51
Yemenite Association Party, 222
Yeshaya, S. B., 276, 287n151, 287n153, 288nn170–171
Yishuv Casualties Committee, 84
Yishuv Committee for Casualties of the Events, 104n75, 104n78
Yishuv Defense Committee, 111–17, 119, 123, 128, 129n2, 130nn9–12, 130n17, 131n39, 131n41, 131n43, 131n45, 132n50, 132nn59–60, 133n83, 133n92, 238–39, 241, 248n108, 248nn111–116, 248nn120–122
Yishuv Inductee and Family Committee, 114, 119–20, 122, 124–25, 127–28, 129n3, 132n60, 132n70, 133n92, 133nn97–102, 133nn104–105, 134n108, 213–14, 216, 218, 220, 225, 236, 245nn23–24, 247n95, 248n98. *See also* Jerusalem Committee for Inductees and Their Families
Yishuv Rescue and Mobilization Fund, 83, 112, 115, 122, 245n22
Yishuv Supply Committee, 72–73, 75, 92, 103n35, 107n141. *See also* Jerusalem and Tel Aviv Supply Committees
Yizre'eli, Yosef, 117
Yosef, Dov, 16, 20n67, 31–32, 57n54, 57n57, 91, 95, 149, 169–70, 173–74, 177nn14–15, 182n133, 182n138, 182n142, 182n149, 182n151, 183n152, 183n154, 190–92, 195–97, 205, 209n39, 209n44
Yosha, Meir, 77

Zabrasky, Abraham, 133n93, 239–40
Zionist General Council, 16

PAULA KABALO is an Associate Professor at Ben-Gurion University of the Negev (BGU), Israel. She is currently the director of the Ben-Gurion Research Institute for the Study of Israel and Zionism at BGU, and the head of BGU's Azrieli Center for Israel Studies. She is author of *Shurat Hamitnadvim: The Story of a Civic Association* (in Hebrew).